THE HARLEM HELLFIGHTERS

ALSO BY MAX BROOKS

The Zombie Survival Guide:
Complete Protection from the Living Dead

World War Z:
An Oral History of the Zombie War

The Zombie Survival Guide: Recorded Attacks

THE HARLEM HELLFIGHTERS

MAX BROOKS

ILLUSTRATED BY

CAANAN WHITE

B \ D \ W \ Y

BROADWAY BOOKS
NEW YORK

Copyright © 2014 by Max Brooks

Published in the United States by Broadway Books,
an imprint of the Crown Publishing Group,
a division of Random House LLC,
a Penguin Random House Company, New York.
www.crownpublishing.com

Broadway Books and its logo,
B \ D \ W \ Y, are trademarks of Random House LLC.

Library of Congress Cataloging-in-Publication Data
Brooks, Max.
The Harlem Hellfighters / Max Brooks ; illustrated by Caanan White.
Summary: "This is a graphic novel about the first African American regiment
to fight in World War One"—Provided by publisher.
1. United States. Army. Infantry Regiment, 369th—Comic books, strips, etc. 2. United
States. Army. Infantry Regiment, 369th—Juvenile literature. 3. World War, 1914–1918—
Participation, African American—Comic books, strips, etc. 4. World War, 1914–1918—
Participation, African American—Juvenile literature. 5. United States. Army—African
American troops—History—20th century—Comic books, strips, etc. 6. United States.
Army—African American troops—History—20th century—Juvenile literature. 7. African
American soldiers—History—20th century—Comic books, strips, etc. 8. African Ameri-
can soldiers—History—20th century—Juvenile literature. 9. Graphic novels.
I. White, Caanan, illustrator. II. Title.
D570.33369th .B76 2014
940.54'03—dc23
2013039522

ISBN 978-0-307-46497-2
eBook ISBN 978-0-8041-4033-1

PRINTED IN THE UNITED STATES OF AMERICA

Book design by Jaclyn Reyes
Cover and interior illustrations by Caanan White
Cover design by Cardon Webb
Inker: Keith Williams
Cover color: Digikore Studios
Lettering: Kurt Hathaway
Production: Mark Seifert
Editor: William Christensen

3 5 7 9 10 8 6 4 2

First Edition

To Those who served with the 369th,
in the War to End All Wars

The story that follows is a fictionalized account of the 369th Infantry Regiment in World War I.

"Once let the black man get upon his person the brass letters, U.S., let him get an eagle on his button, and a musket on his shoulder, and bullets in his pocket; and there is no power on earth, or under the earth, which can deny that he has earned the right to citizenship in the United States."
                                        –Frederick Douglass

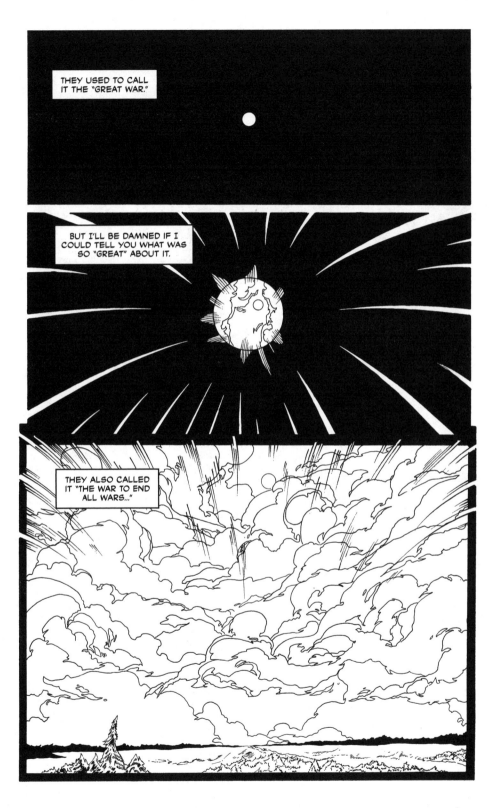

THEY USED TO CALL IT THE "GREAT WAR."

BUT I'LL BE DAMNED IF I COULD TELL YOU WHAT WAS SO "GREAT" ABOUT IT.

THEY ALSO CALLED IT "THE WAR TO END ALL WARS..."

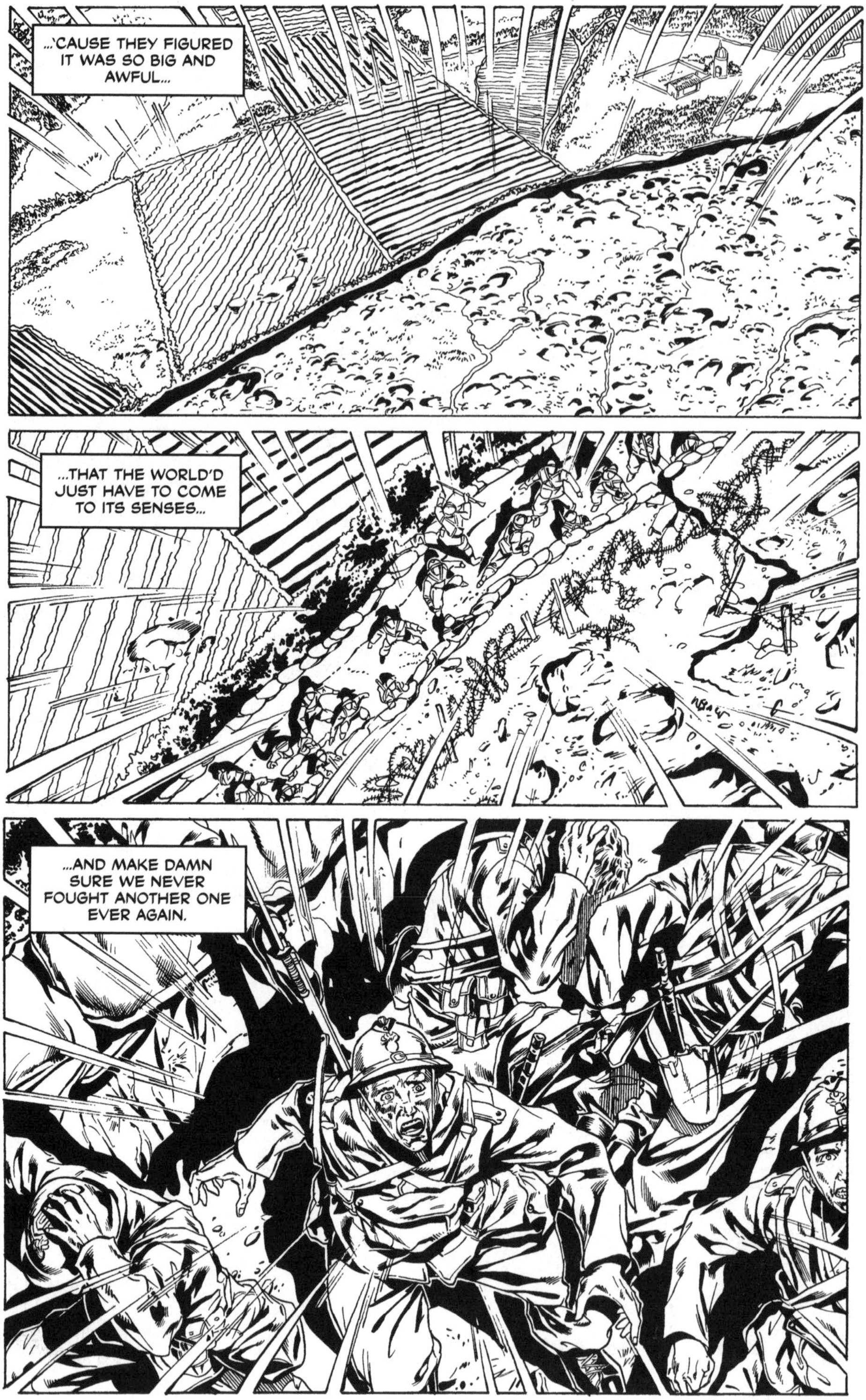
...'CAUSE THEY FIGURED IT WAS SO BIG AND AWFUL...
...THAT THE WORLD'D JUST HAVE TO COME TO ITS SENSES...
...AND MAKE DAMN SURE WE NEVER FOUGHT ANOTHER ONE EVER AGAIN.

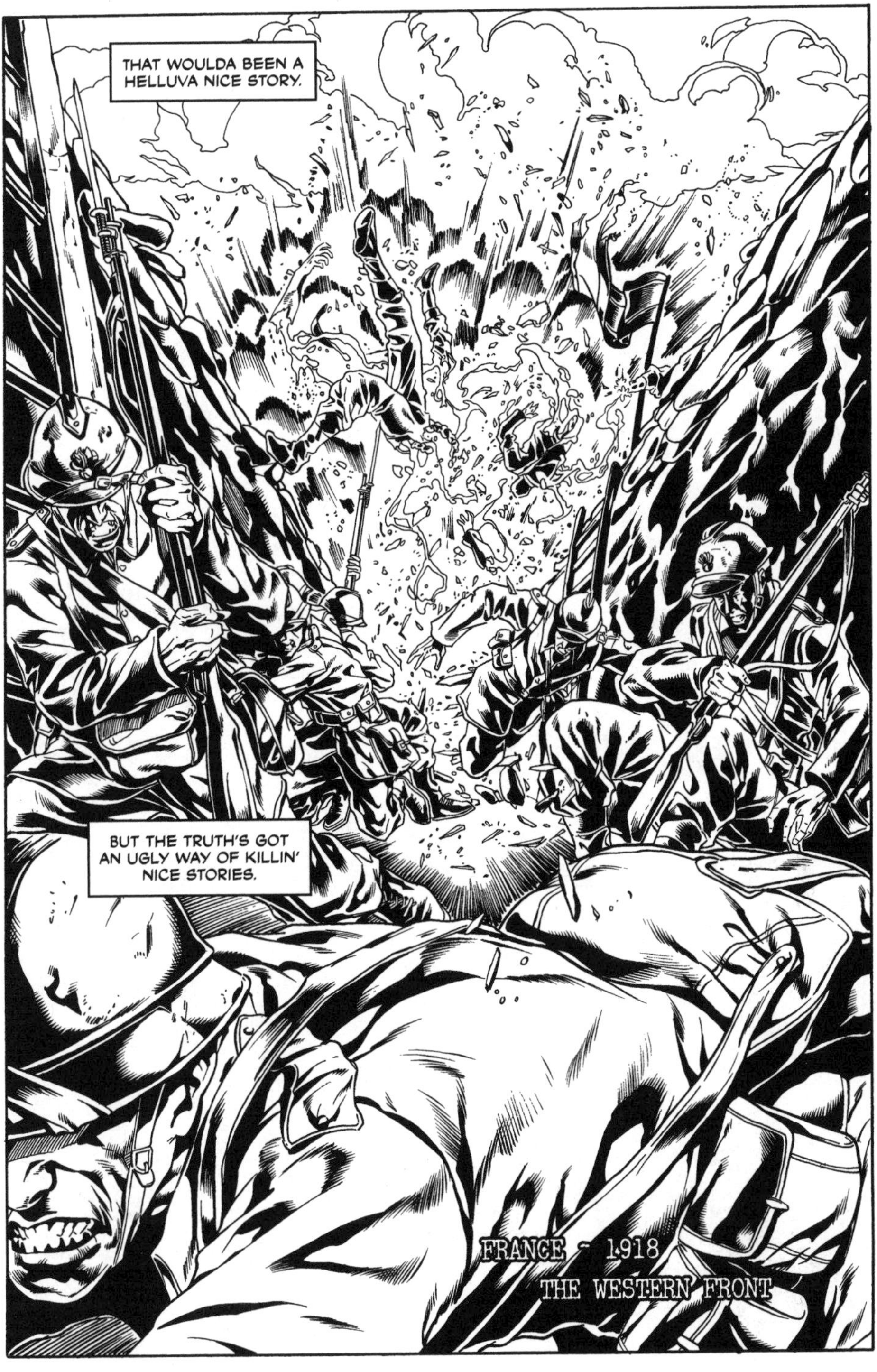
THAT WOULDA BEEN A HELLUVA NICE STORY.
BUT THE TRUTH'S GOT AN UGLY WAY OF KILLIN' NICE STORIES.
FRANCE - 1918
THE WESTERN FRONT

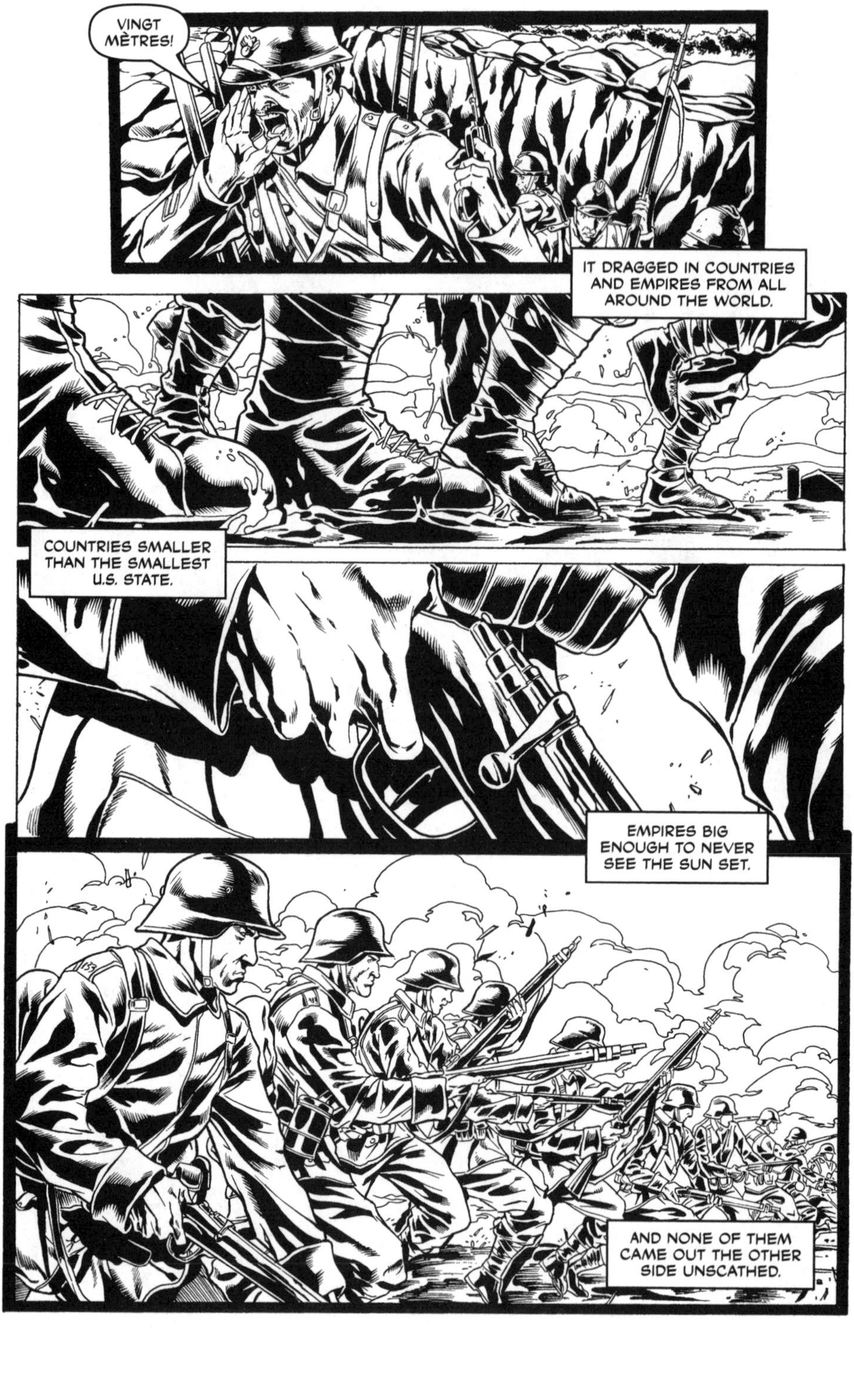
VINGT MÈTRES!
IT DRAGGED IN COUNTRIES AND EMPIRES FROM ALL AROUND THE WORLD.
COUNTRIES SMALLER THAN THE SMALLEST U.S. STATE.
EMPIRES BIG ENOUGH TO NEVER SEE THE SUN SET.
AND NONE OF THEM CAME OUT THE OTHER SIDE UNSCATHED.

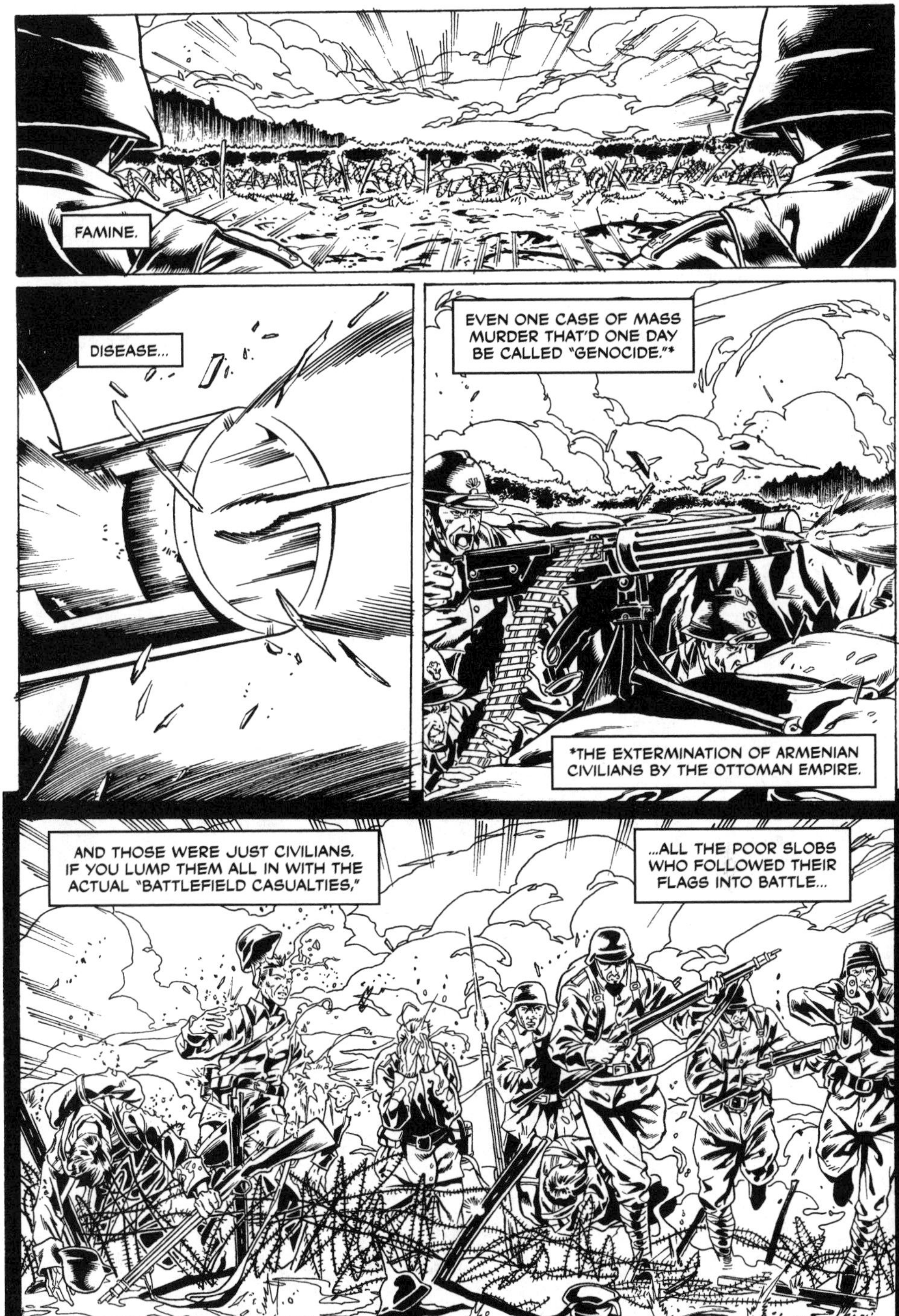
FAMINE.
DISEASE...
EVEN ONE CASE OF MASS MURDER THAT'D ONE DAY BE CALLED "GENOCIDE."*
*THE EXTERMINATION OF ARMENIAN CIVILIANS BY THE OTTOMAN EMPIRE.
AND THOSE WERE JUST CIVILIANS. IF YOU LUMP THEM ALL IN WITH THE ACTUAL "BATTLEFIELD CASUALTIES,"
...ALL THE POOR SLOBS WHO FOLLOWED THEIR FLAGS INTO BATTLE...

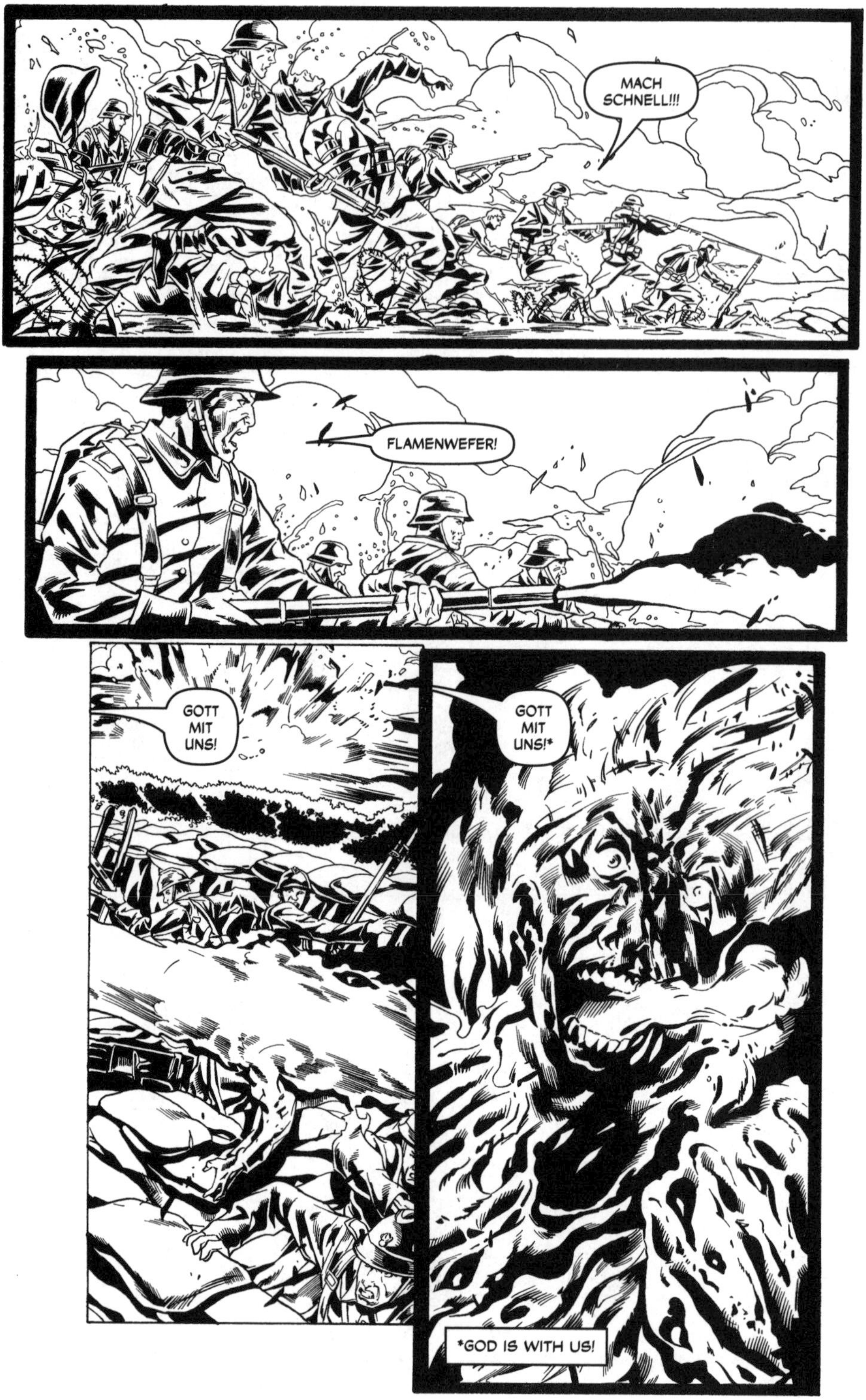
MACH SCHNELL!!!
FLAMENWEFER!
GOTT MIT UNS!
GOTT MIT UNS!*
*GOD IS WITH US!

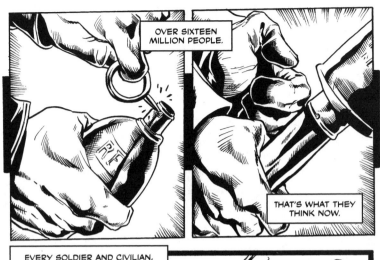

OVER SIXTEEN MILLION PEOPLE.

THAT'S WHAT THEY THINK NOW.

EVERY SOLDIER AND CIVILIAN, EVERY CAUSE AND COUNTRY. THAT'S WHAT THEY *THINK*, BUT NO ONE'LL EVER KNOW FOR SURE.

OVER SIXTEEN *MILLION!*

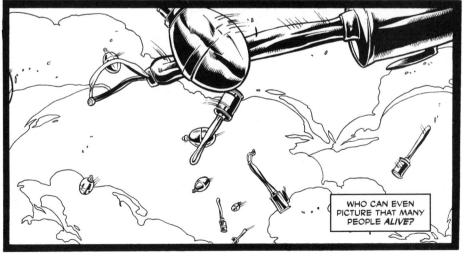

WHO CAN EVEN PICTURE THAT MANY PEOPLE *ALIVE?*

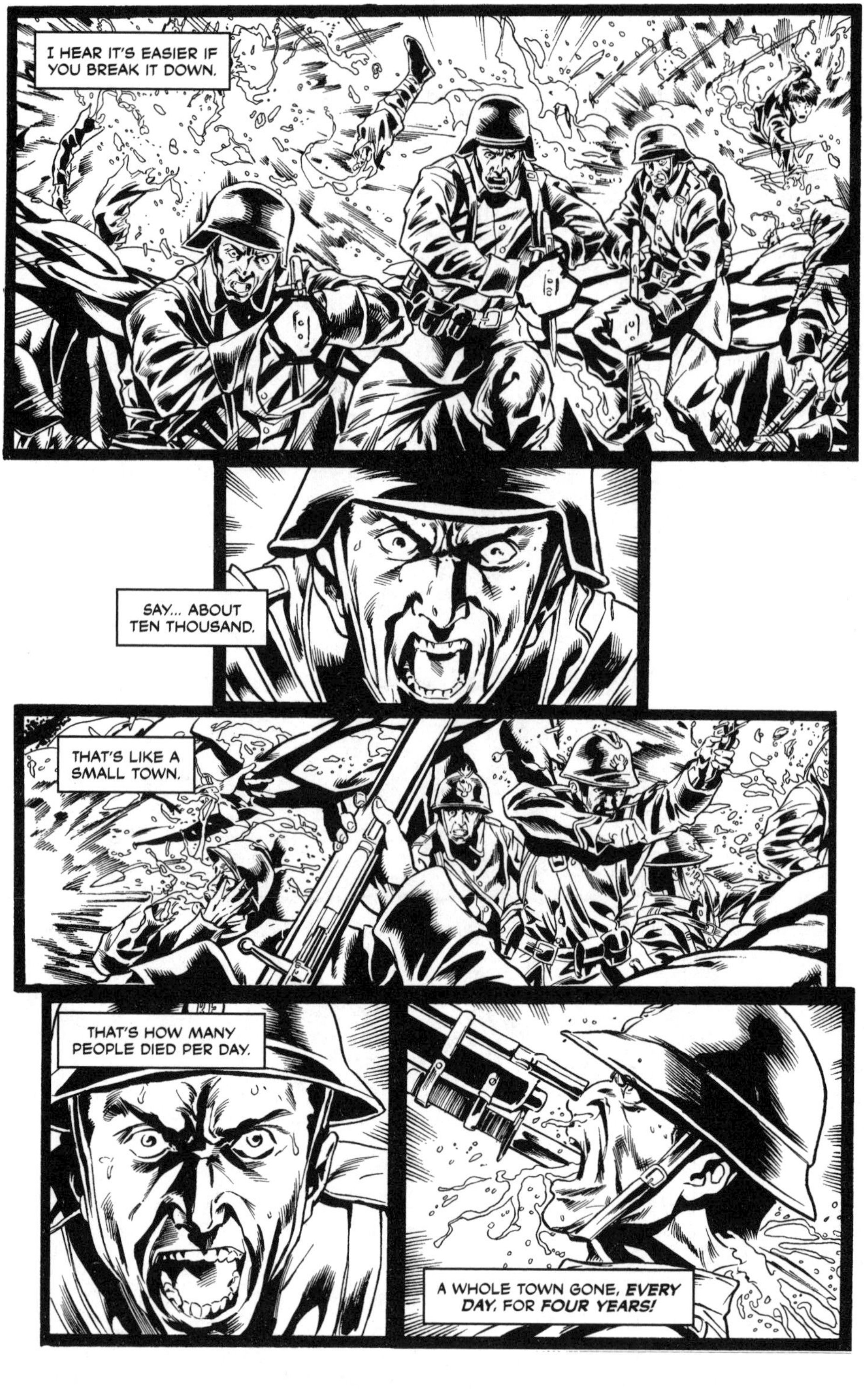
I HEAR IT'S EASIER IF YOU BREAK IT DOWN.
SAY... ABOUT TEN THOUSAND.
THAT'S LIKE A SMALL TOWN.
THAT'S HOW MANY PEOPLE DIED PER DAY.
A WHOLE TOWN GONE, **EVERY DAY**, FOR **FOUR YEARS!**

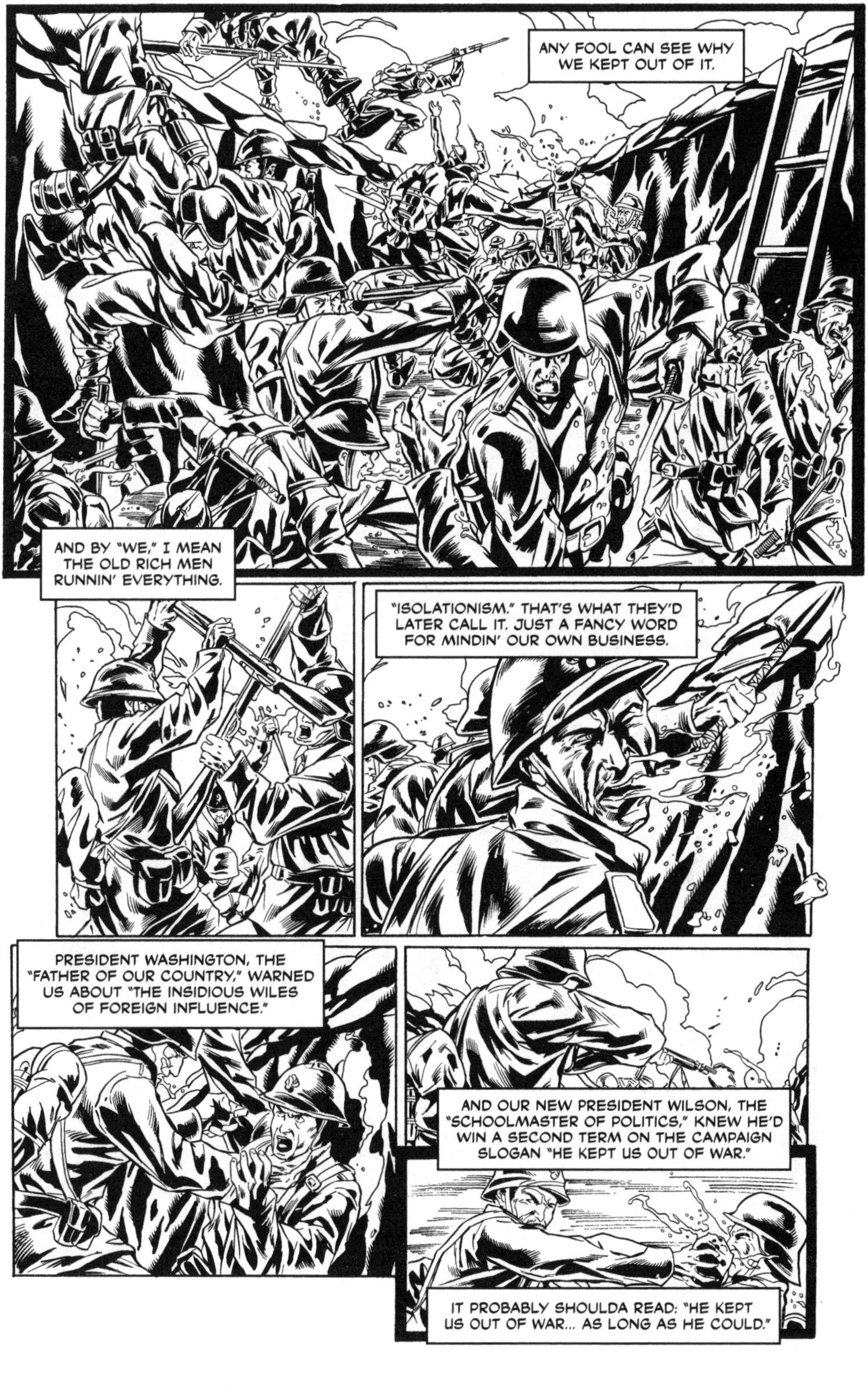
ANY FOOL CAN SEE WHY WE KEPT OUT OF IT.
AND BY "WE," I MEAN THE OLD RICH MEN RUNNIN' EVERYTHING.
"ISOLATIONISM." THAT'S WHAT THEY'D LATER CALL IT. JUST A FANCY WORD FOR MINDIN' OUR OWN BUSINESS.
PRESIDENT WASHINGTON, THE "FATHER OF OUR COUNTRY," WARNED US ABOUT "THE INSIDIOUS WILES OF FOREIGN INFLUENCE."
AND OUR NEW PRESIDENT WILSON, THE "SCHOOLMASTER OF POLITICS," KNEW HE'D WIN A SECOND TERM ON THE CAMPAIGN SLOGAN "HE KEPT US OUT OF WAR."
IT PROBABLY SHOULDA READ: "HE KEPT US OUT OF WAR... AS LONG AS HE COULD."

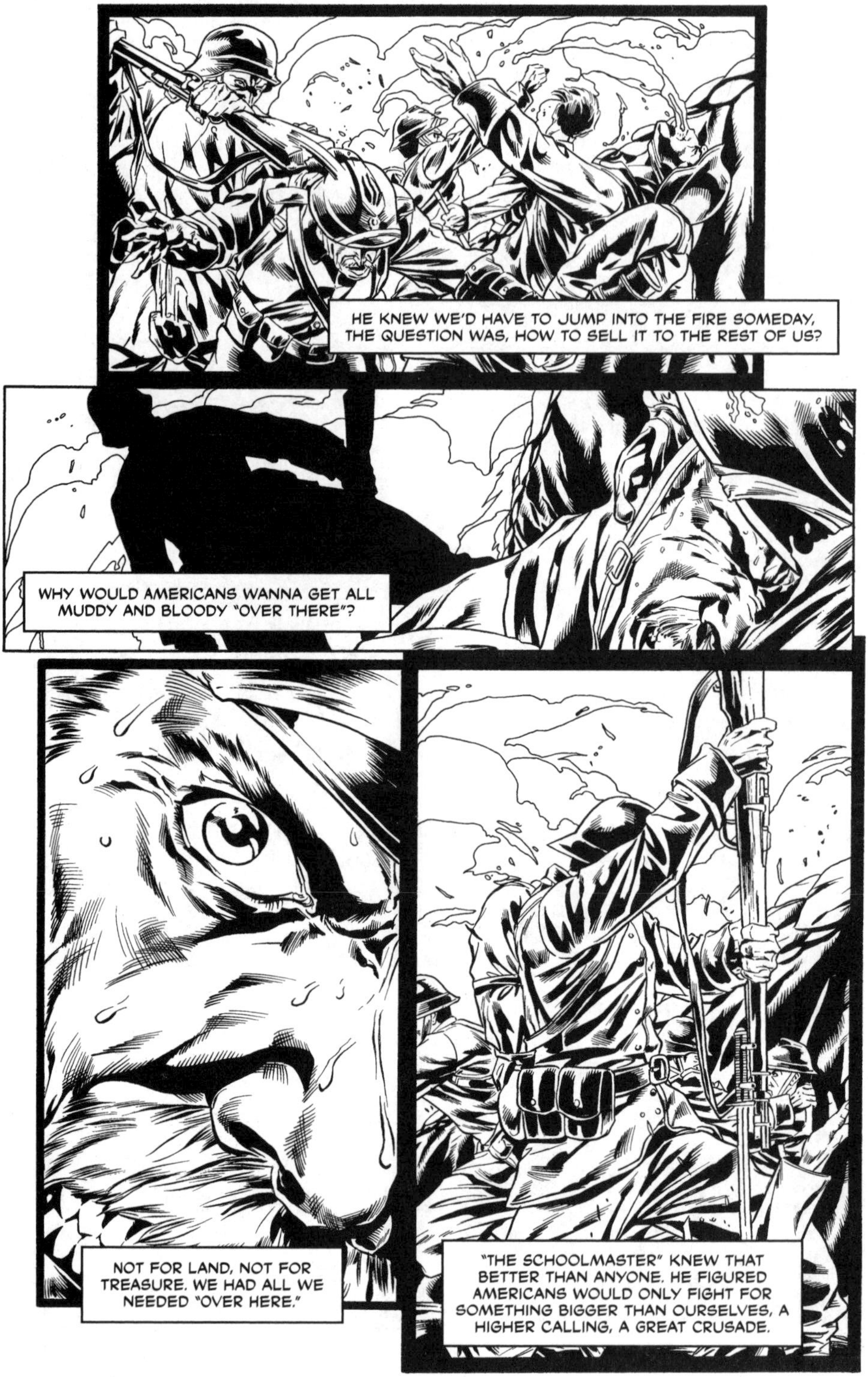
HE KNEW WE'D HAVE TO JUMP INTO THE FIRE SOMEDAY. THE QUESTION WAS, HOW TO SELL IT TO THE REST OF US?
WHY WOULD AMERICANS WANNA GET ALL MUDDY AND BLOODY "OVER THERE"?
NOT FOR LAND, NOT FOR TREASURE. WE HAD ALL WE NEEDED "OVER HERE."
"THE SCHOOLMASTER" KNEW THAT BETTER THAN ANYONE. HE FIGURED AMERICANS WOULD ONLY FIGHT FOR SOMETHING BIGGER THAN OURSELVES, A HIGHER CALLING, A GREAT CRUSADE.

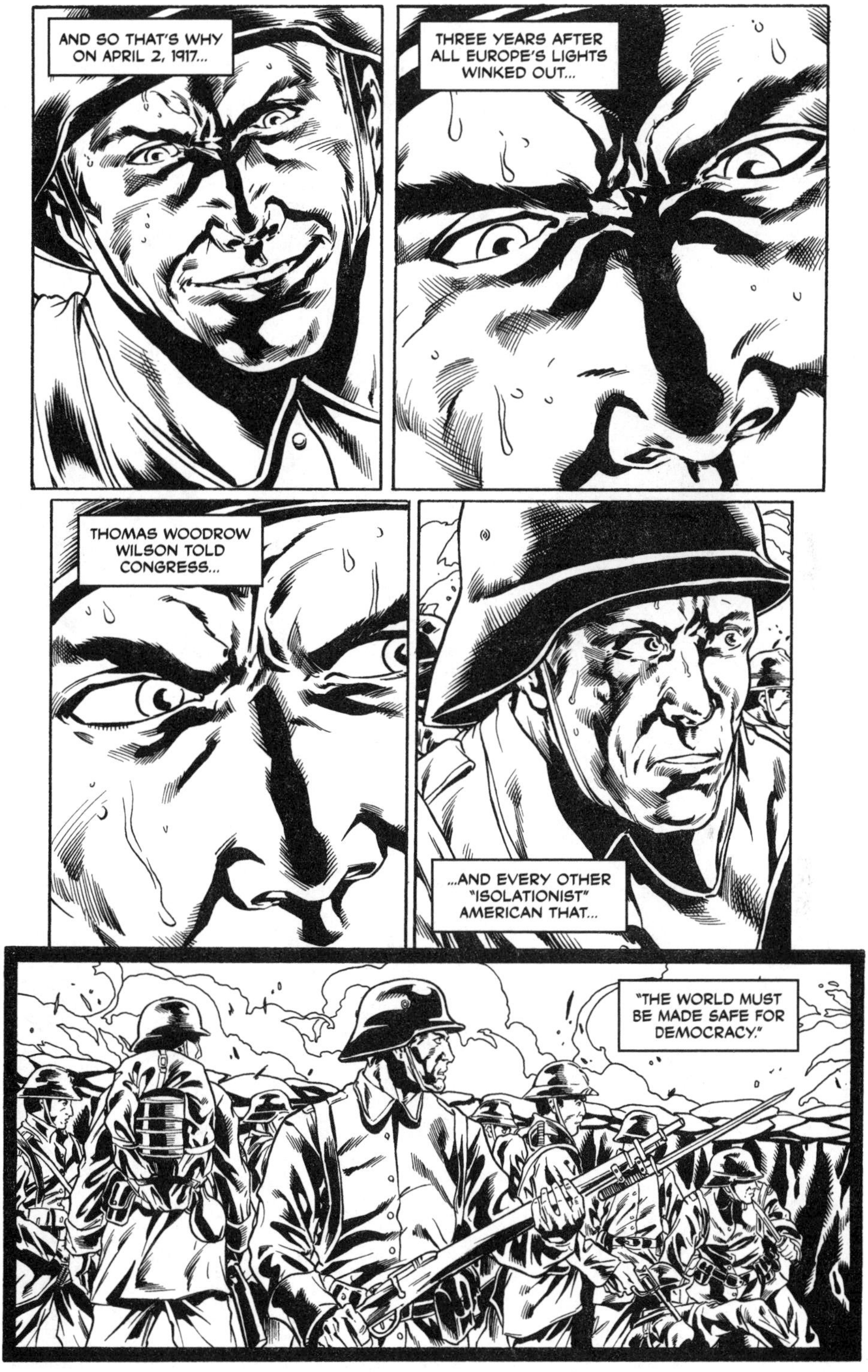
AND SO THAT'S WHY ON APRIL 2, 1917...
THREE YEARS AFTER ALL EUROPE'S LIGHTS WINKED OUT...
THOMAS WOODROW WILSON TOLD CONGRESS...
...AND EVERY OTHER "ISOLATIONIST" AMERICAN THAT...
"THE WORLD MUST BE MADE SAFE FOR DEMOCRACY."

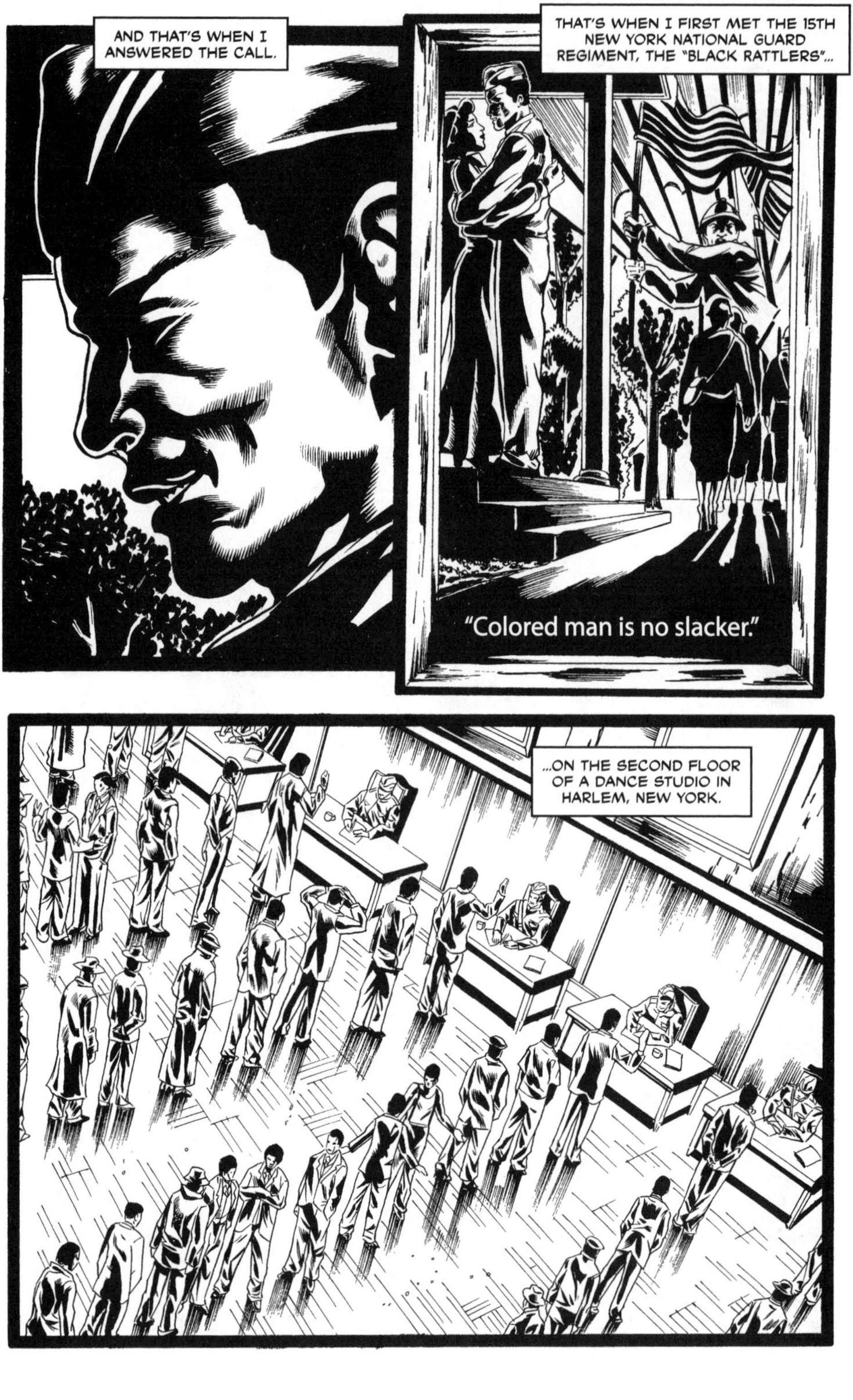
AND THAT'S WHEN I ANSWERED THE CALL.
THAT'S WHEN I FIRST MET THE 15TH NEW YORK NATIONAL GUARD REGIMENT, THE "BLACK RATTLERS"...
"Colored man is no slacker."
...ON THE SECOND FLOOR OF A DANCE STUDIO IN HARLEM, NEW YORK.

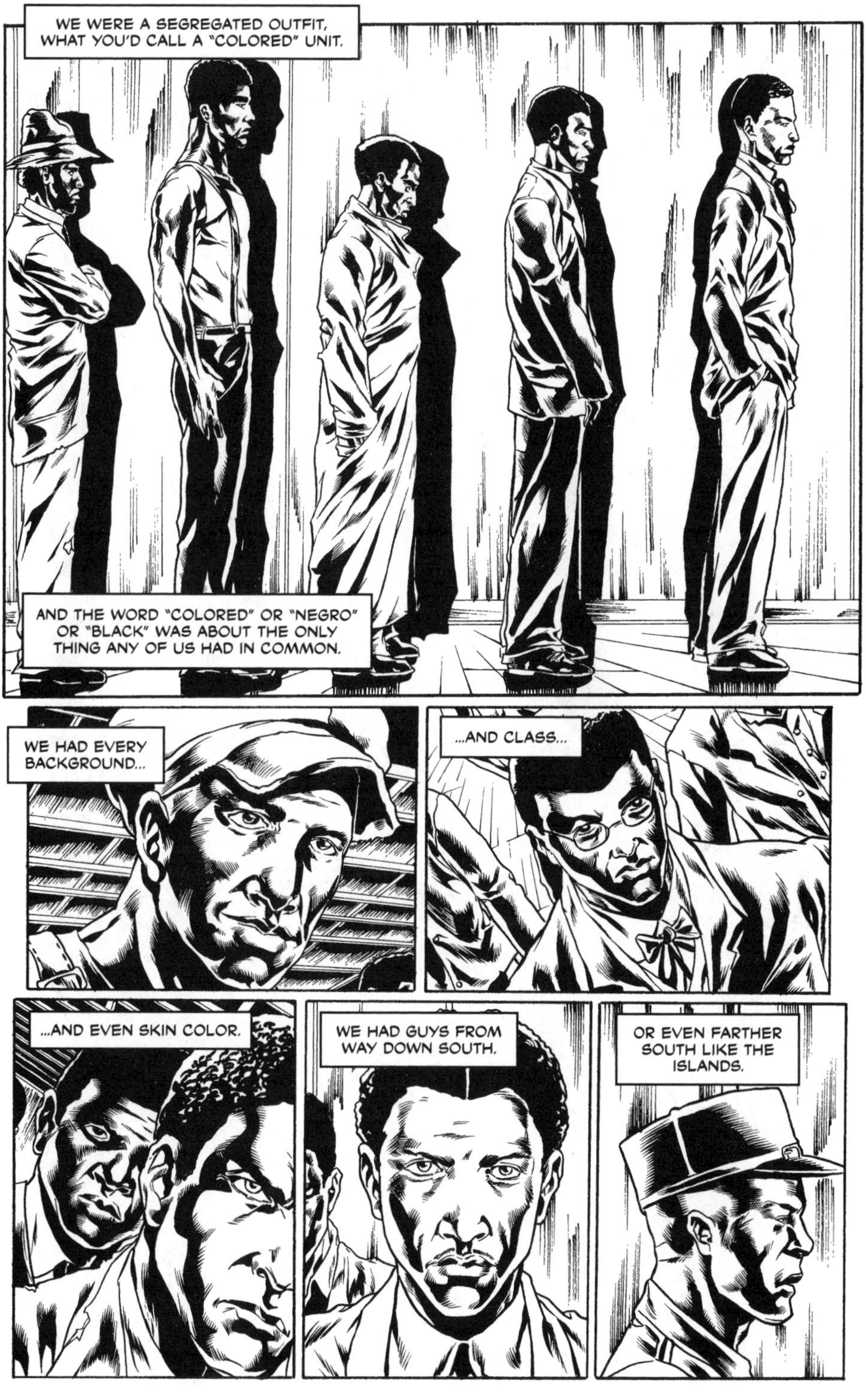
WE WERE A SEGREGATED OUTFIT, WHAT YOU'D CALL A "COLORED" UNIT.
AND THE WORD "COLORED" OR "NEGRO" OR "BLACK" WAS ABOUT THE ONLY THING ANY OF US HAD IN COMMON.
WE HAD EVERY BACKGROUND...
...AND CLASS...
...AND EVEN SKIN COLOR.
WE HAD GUYS FROM WAY DOWN SOUTH.
OR EVEN FARTHER SOUTH LIKE THE ISLANDS.

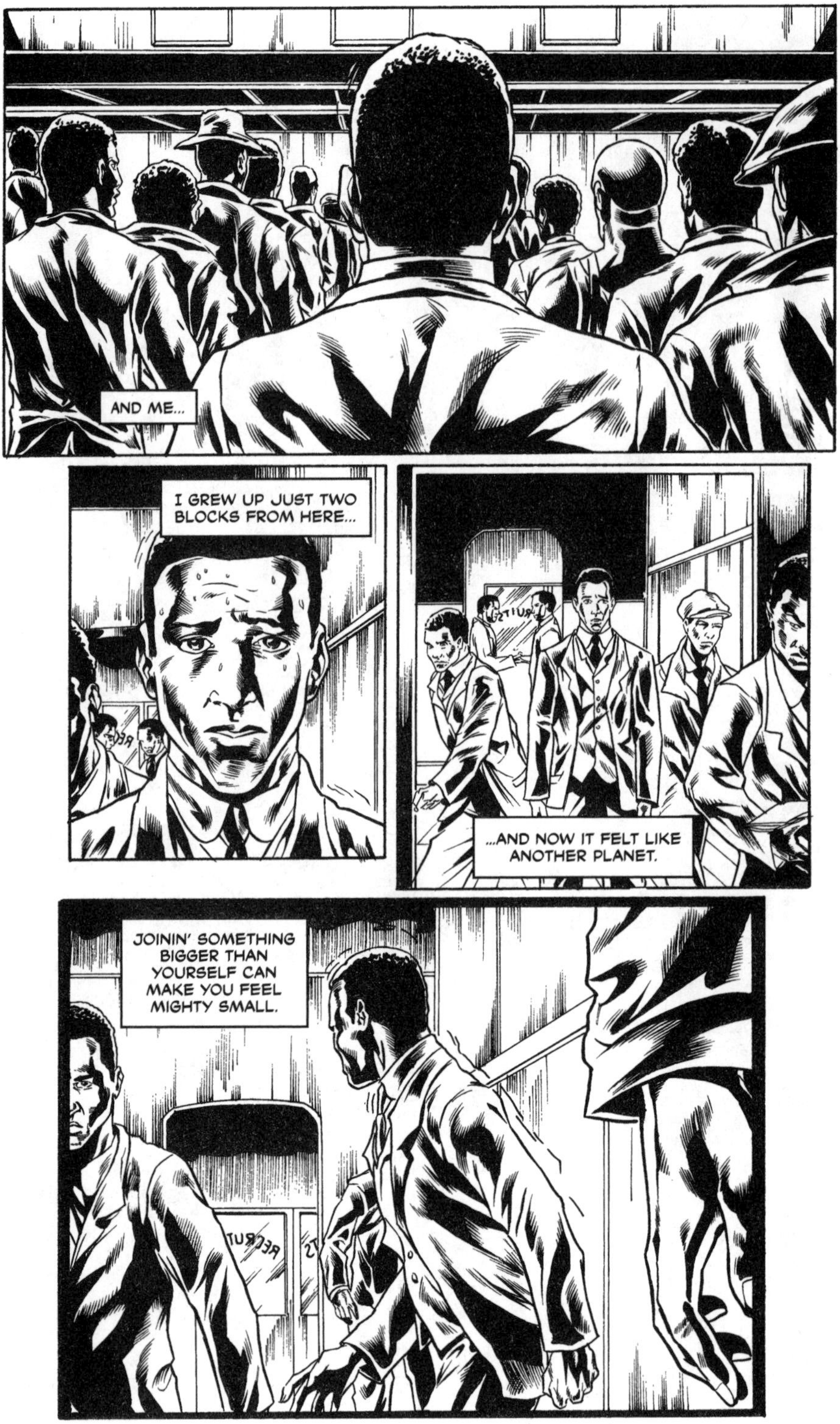
AND ME...
I GREW UP JUST TWO BLOCKS FROM HERE...
...AND NOW IT FELT LIKE ANOTHER PLANET.
JOININ' SOMETHING BIGGER THAN YOURSELF CAN MAKE YOU FEEL MIGHTY SMALL.

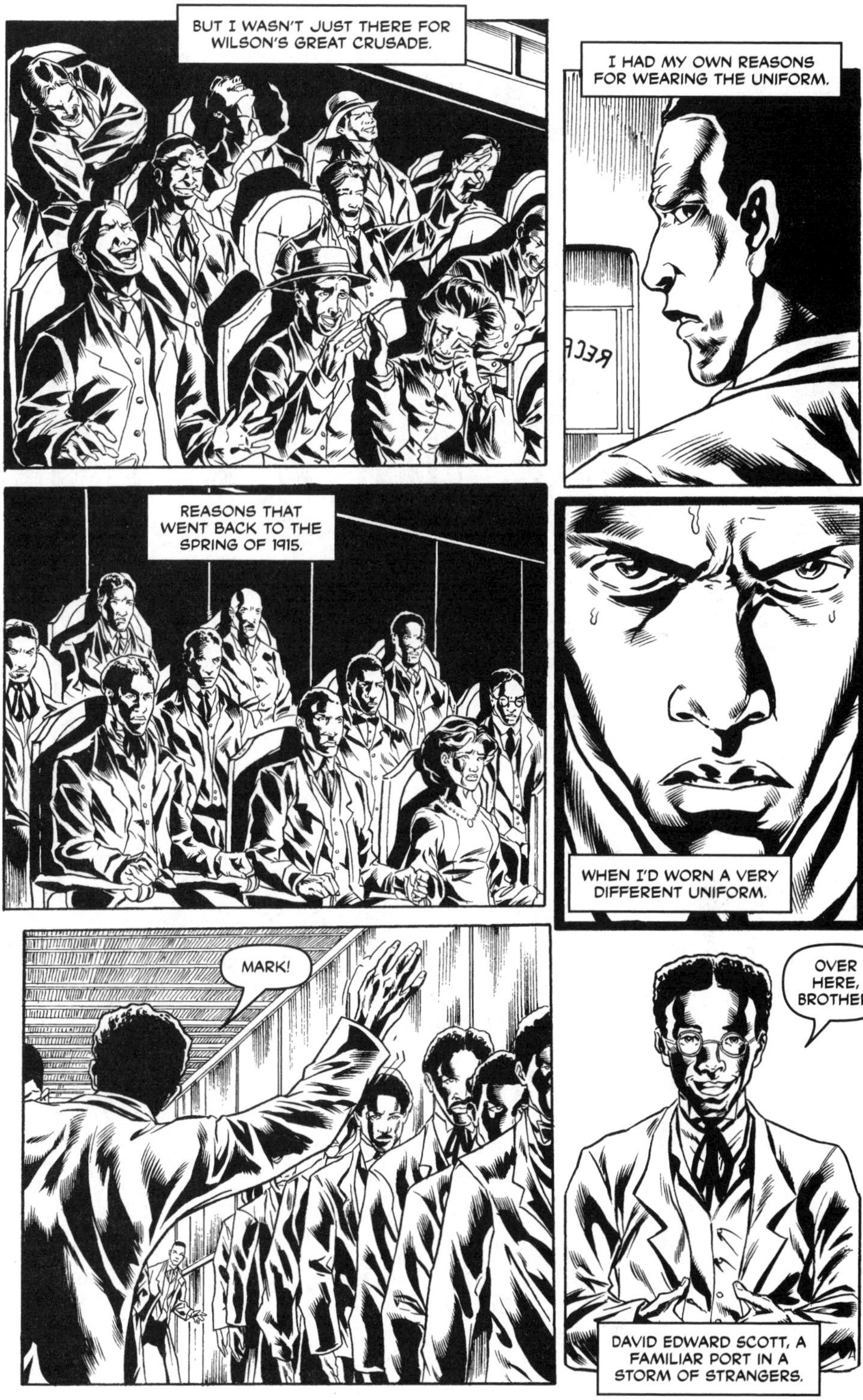
BUT I WASN'T JUST THERE FOR WILSON'S GREAT CRUSADE.
I HAD MY OWN REASONS FOR WEARING THE UNIFORM.
REASONS THAT WENT BACK TO THE SPRING OF 1915.
WHEN I'D WORN A VERY DIFFERENT UNIFORM.
MARK!
OVER HERE, BROTHER!
DAVID EDWARD SCOTT, A FAMILIAR PORT IN A STORM OF STRANGERS.

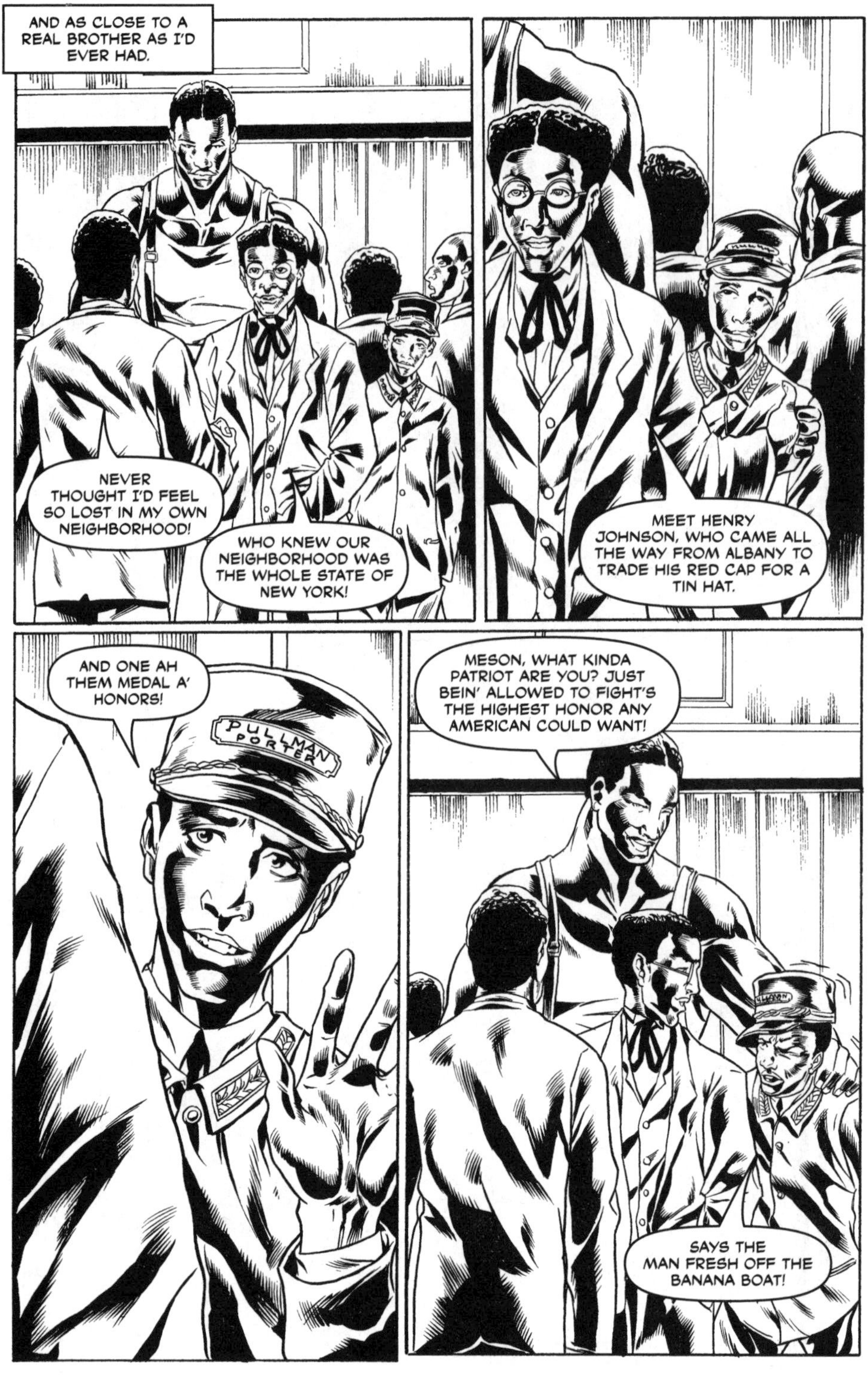
AND AS CLOSE TO A REAL BROTHER AS I'D EVER HAD.
NEVER THOUGHT I'D FEEL SO LOST IN MY OWN NEIGHBORHOOD!
WHO KNEW OUR NEIGHBORHOOD WAS THE WHOLE STATE OF NEW YORK!
MEET HENRY JOHNSON, WHO CAME ALL THE WAY FROM ALBANY TO TRADE HIS RED CAP FOR A TIN HAT.
AND ONE AH THEM MEDAL A' HONORS!
PULLMAN PORTER
MESON, WHAT KINDA PATRIOT ARE YOU? JUST BEIN' ALLOWED TO FIGHT'S THE HIGHEST HONOR ANY AMERICAN COULD WANT!
SAYS THE MAN FRESH OFF THE BANANA BOAT!

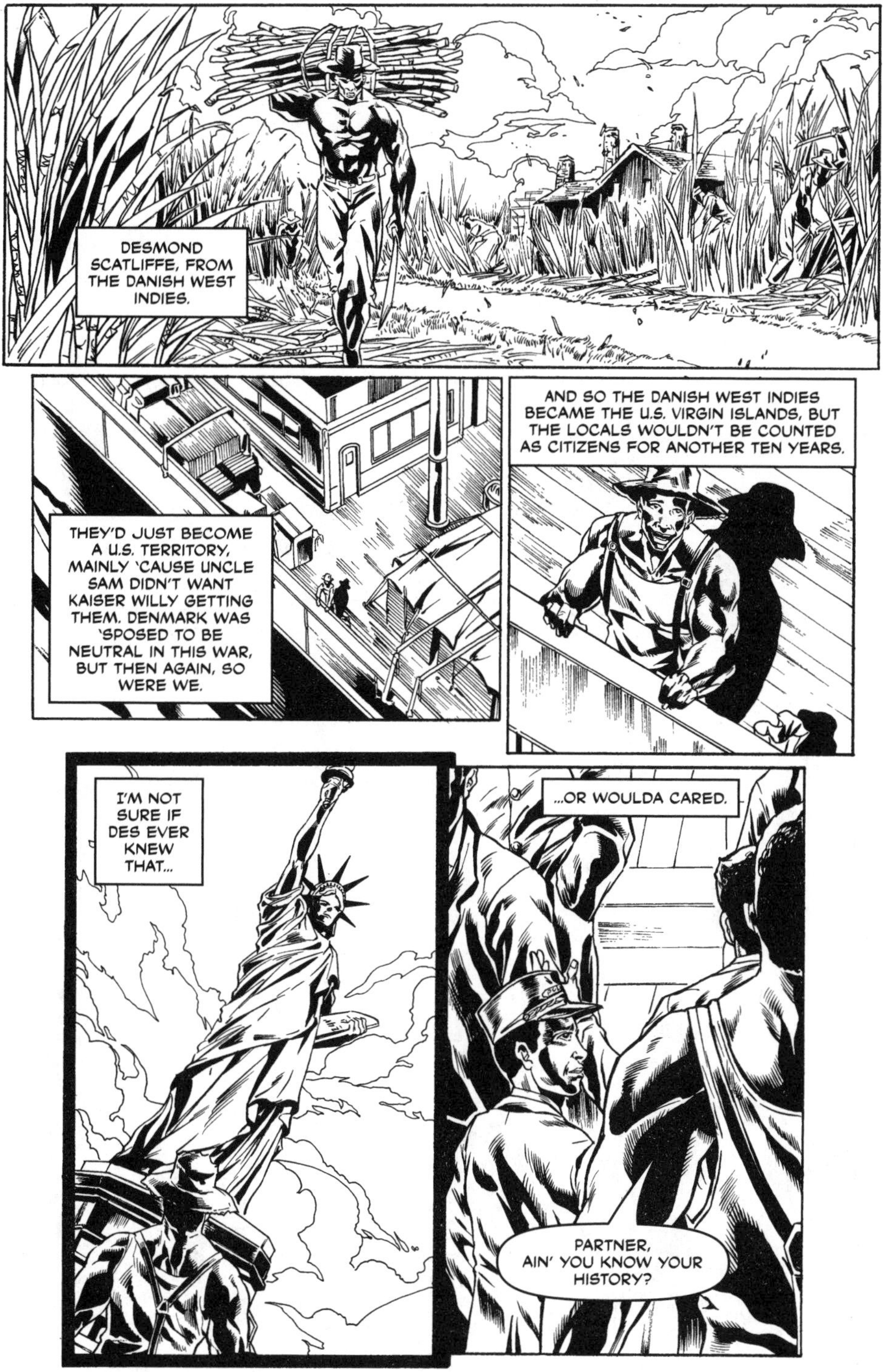
DESMOND SCATLIFFE, FROM THE DANISH WEST INDIES.
THEY'D JUST BECOME A U.S. TERRITORY, MAINLY 'CAUSE UNCLE SAM DIDN'T WANT KAISER WILLY GETTING THEM. DENMARK WAS 'SPOSED TO BE NEUTRAL IN THIS WAR, BUT THEN AGAIN, SO WERE WE.
AND SO THE DANISH WEST INDIES BECAME THE U.S. VIRGIN ISLANDS, BUT THE LOCALS WOULDN'T BE COUNTED AS CITIZENS FOR ANOTHER TEN YEARS.
I'M NOT SURE IF DES EVER KNEW THAT...
...OR WOULDA CARED.
PARTNER, AIN' YOU KNOW YOUR HISTORY?

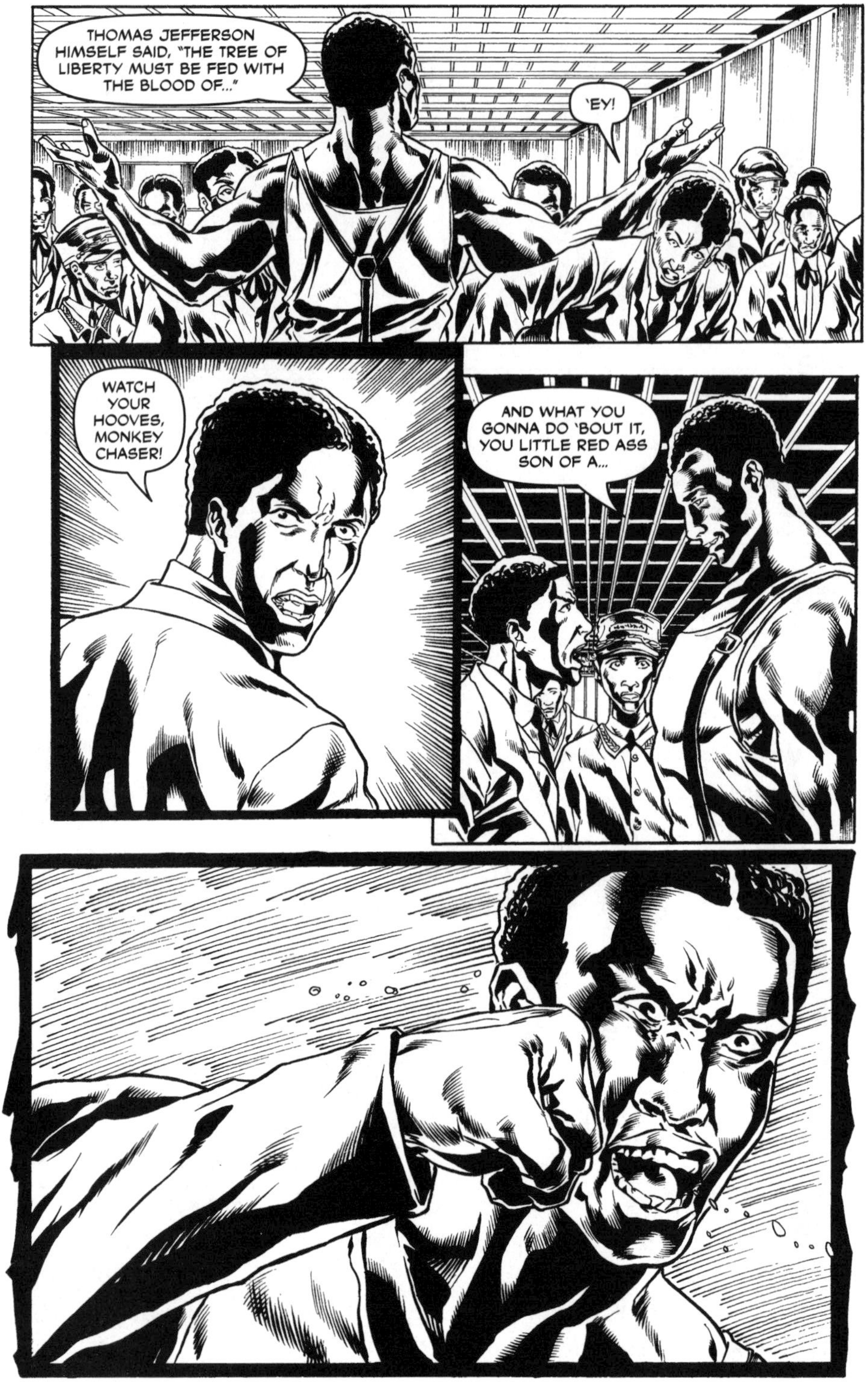
THOMAS JEFFERSON HIMSELF SAID, "THE TREE OF LIBERTY MUST BE FED WITH THE BLOOD OF..."
'EY!
WATCH YOUR HOOVES, MONKEY CHASER!
AND WHAT YOU GONNA DO 'BOUT IT, YOU LITTLE RED ASS SON OF A...

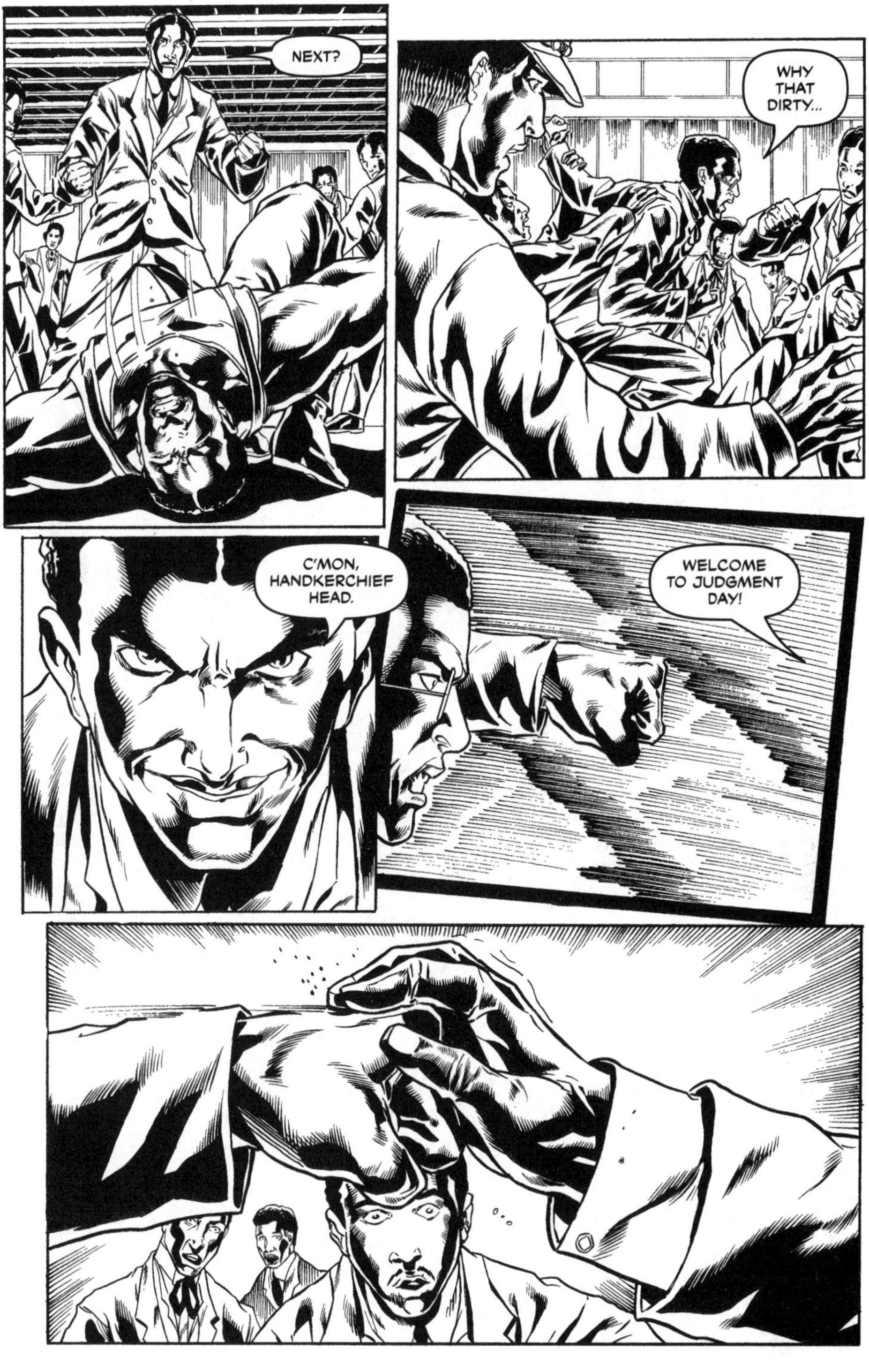
NEXT?
WHY THAT DIRTY...
C'MON, HANDKERCHIEF HEAD.
WELCOME TO JUDGMENT DAY!

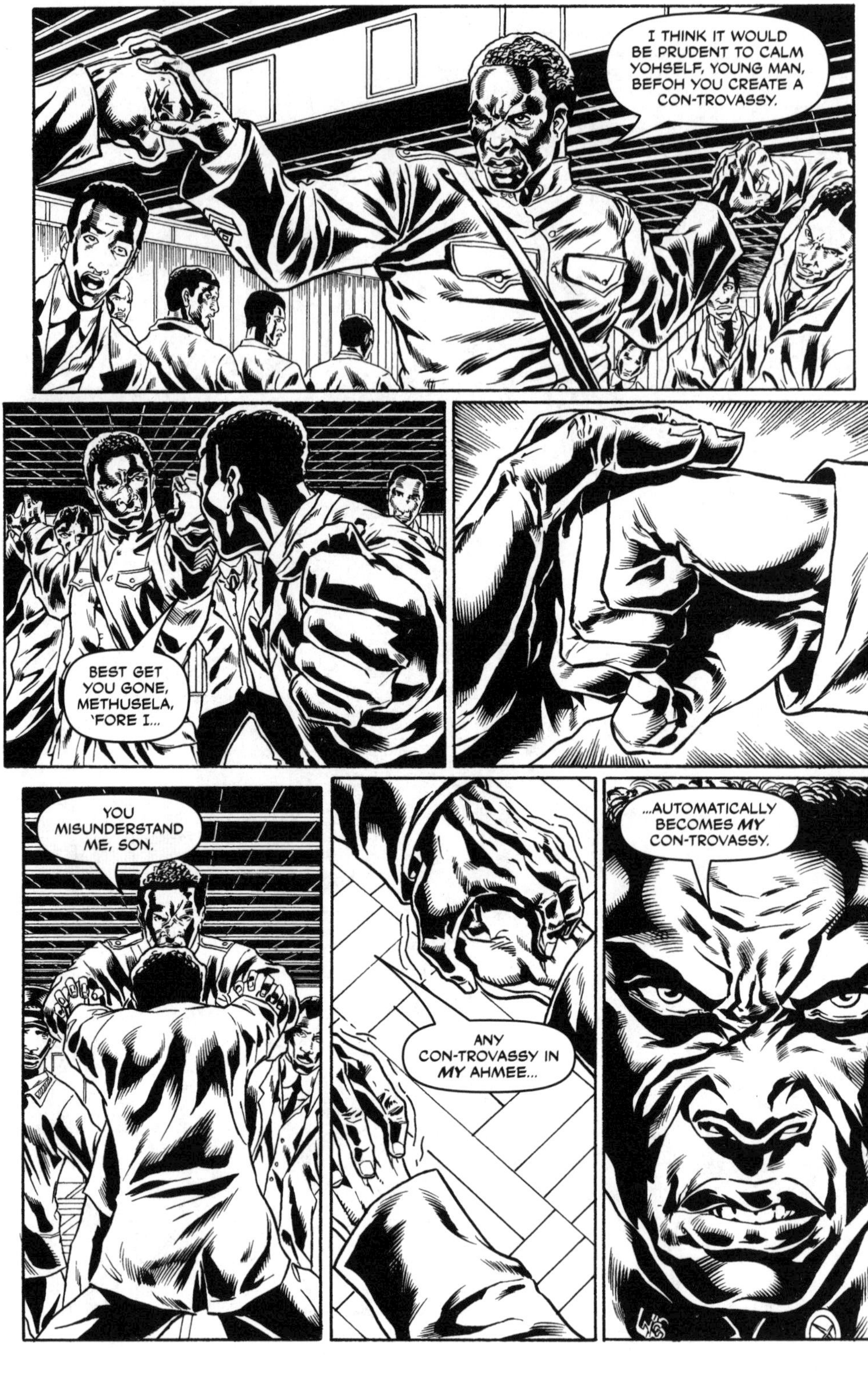
I THINK IT WOULD BE PRUDENT TO CALM YOHSELF, YOUNG MAN, BEFOH YOU CREATE A CON-TROVASSY.
BEST GET YOU GONE, METHUSELA, 'FORE I...
YOU MISUNDERSTAND ME, SON.
ANY CON-TROVASSY IN *MY* AHMEE...
...AUTOMATICALLY BECOMES *MY* CON-TROVASSY.

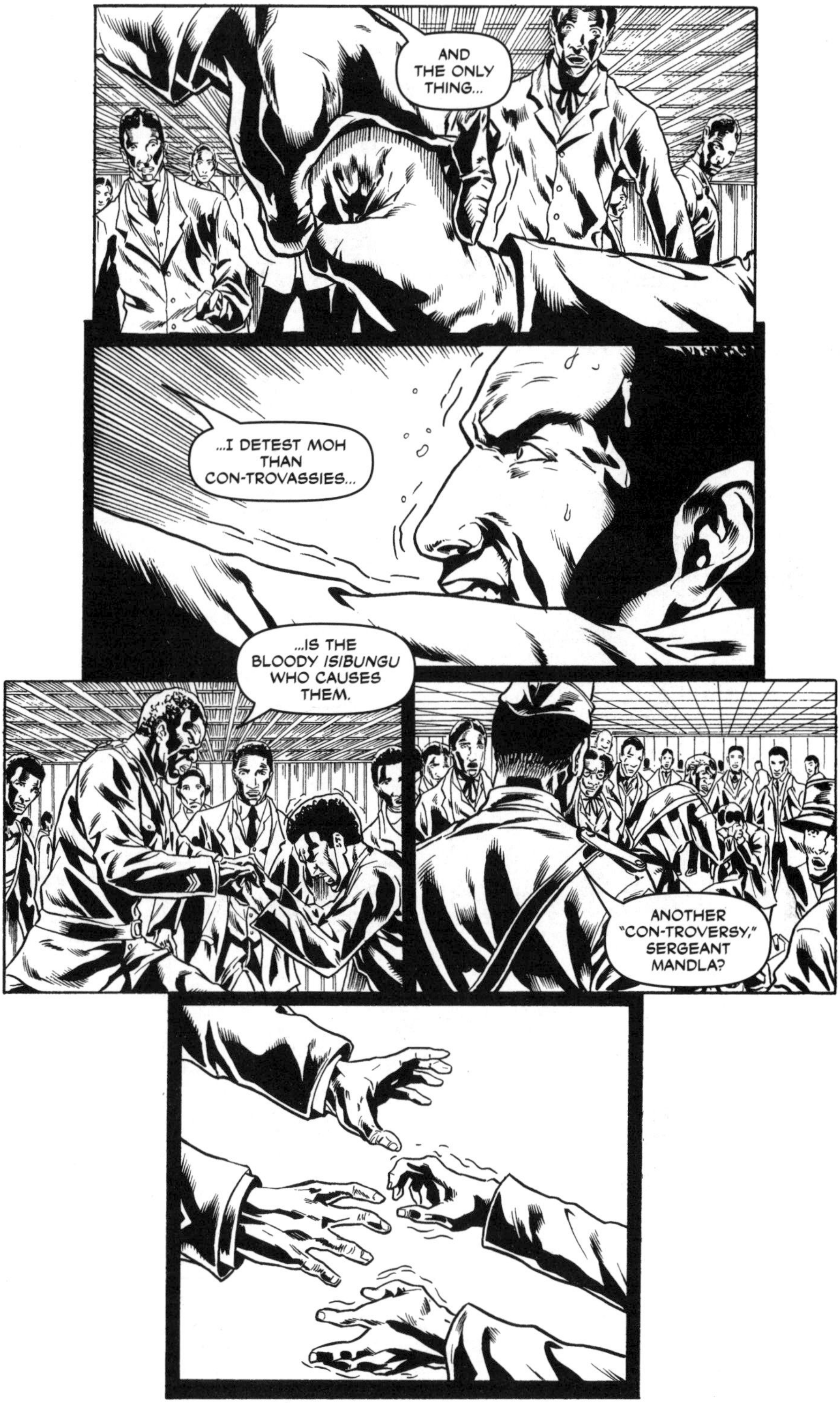
AND THE ONLY THING...
...I DETEST MOH THAN CON-TROVASSIES...
...IS THE BLOODY *ISIBUNGU* WHO CAUSES THEM.
ANOTHER "CON-TROVERSY," SERGEANT MANDLA?

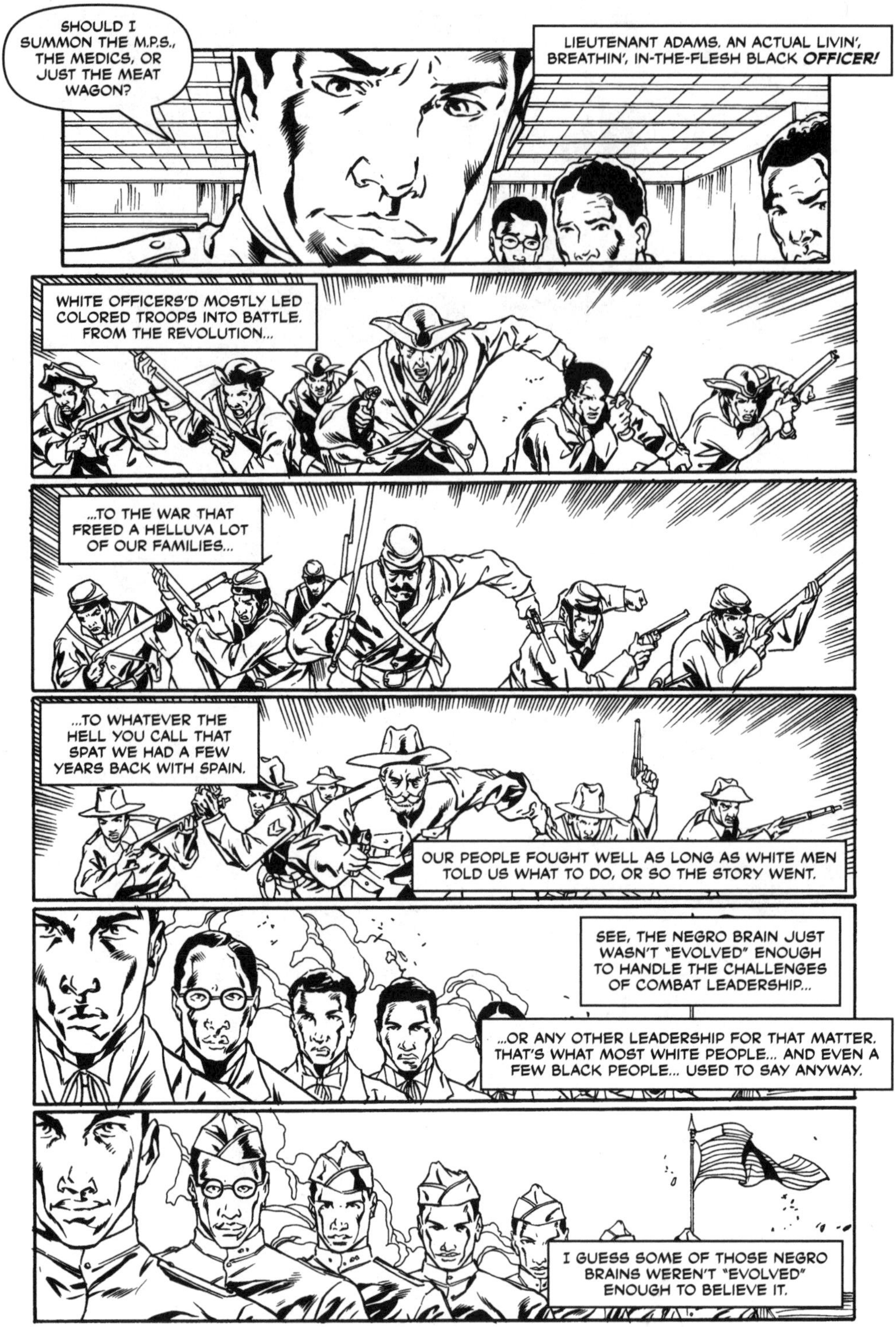
SHOULD I SUMMON THE M.P.S., THE MEDICS, OR JUST THE MEAT WAGON?
LIEUTENANT ADAMS. AN ACTUAL LIVIN', BREATHIN', IN-THE-FLESH BLACK *OFFICER!*
WHITE OFFICERS'D MOSTLY LED COLORED TROOPS INTO BATTLE. FROM THE REVOLUTION...
...TO THE WAR THAT FREED A HELLUVA LOT OF OUR FAMILIES...
...TO WHATEVER THE HELL YOU CALL THAT SPAT WE HAD A FEW YEARS BACK WITH SPAIN.
OUR PEOPLE FOUGHT WELL AS LONG AS WHITE MEN TOLD US WHAT TO DO, OR SO THE STORY WENT.
SEE, THE NEGRO BRAIN JUST WASN'T "EVOLVED" ENOUGH TO HANDLE THE CHALLENGES OF COMBAT LEADERSHIP...
...OR ANY OTHER LEADERSHIP FOR THAT MATTER. THAT'S WHAT MOST WHITE PEOPLE... AND EVEN A FEW BLACK PEOPLE... USED TO SAY ANYWAY.
I GUESS SOME OF THOSE NEGRO BRAINS WEREN'T "EVOLVED" ENOUGH TO BELIEVE IT.

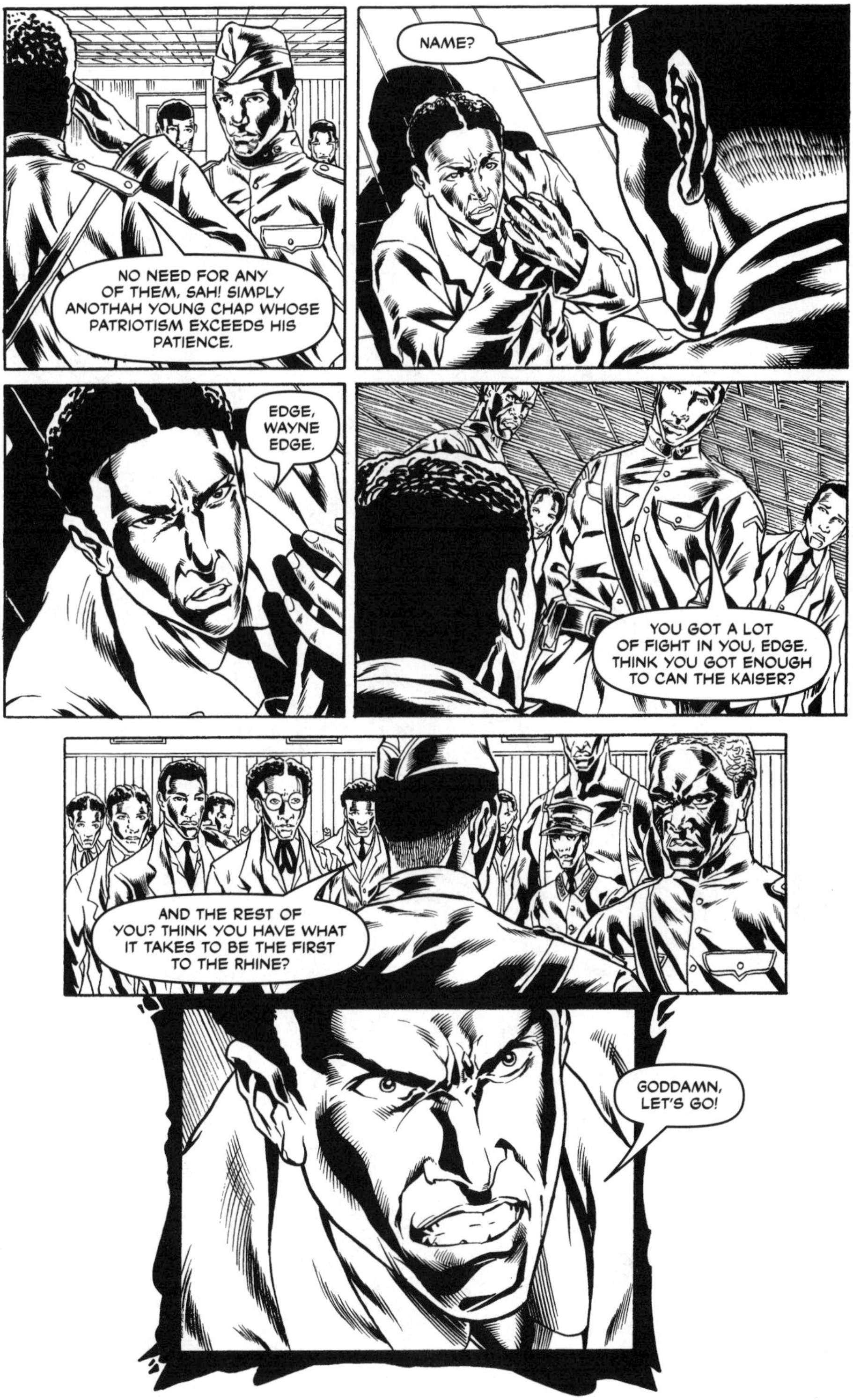
NO NEED FOR ANY OF THEM, SAH! SIMPLY ANOTHAH YOUNG CHAP WHOSE PATRIOTISM EXCEEDS HIS PATIENCE.
NAME?
EDGE, WAYNE EDGE.
YOU GOT A LOT OF FIGHT IN YOU, EDGE. THINK YOU GOT ENOUGH TO CAN THE KAISER?
AND THE REST OF YOU? THINK YOU HAVE WHAT IT TAKES TO BE THE FIRST TO THE RHINE?
GODDAMN, LET'S GO!

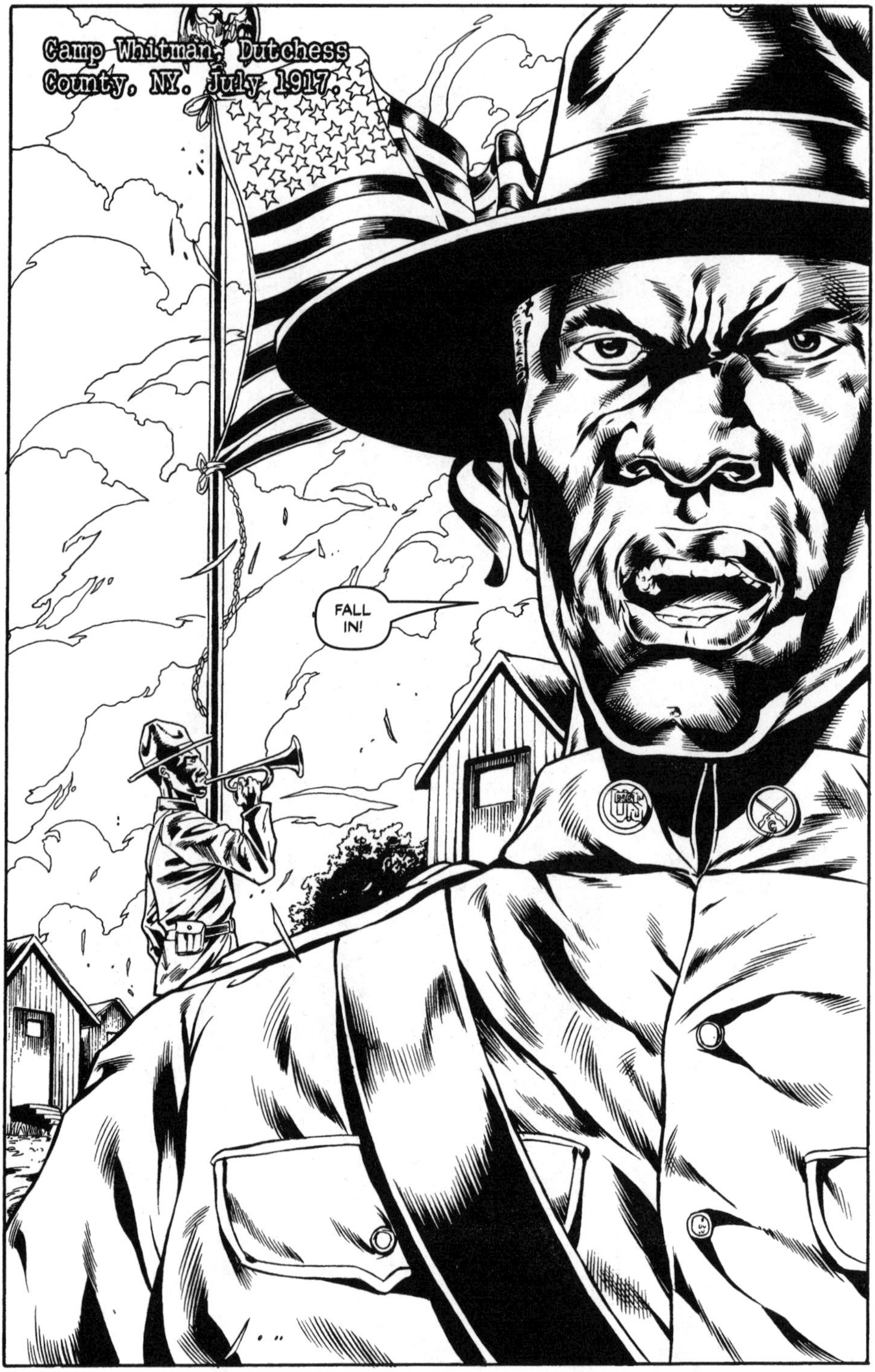
Camp Whitman, Dutchess County, NY. July 1917.
FALL IN!

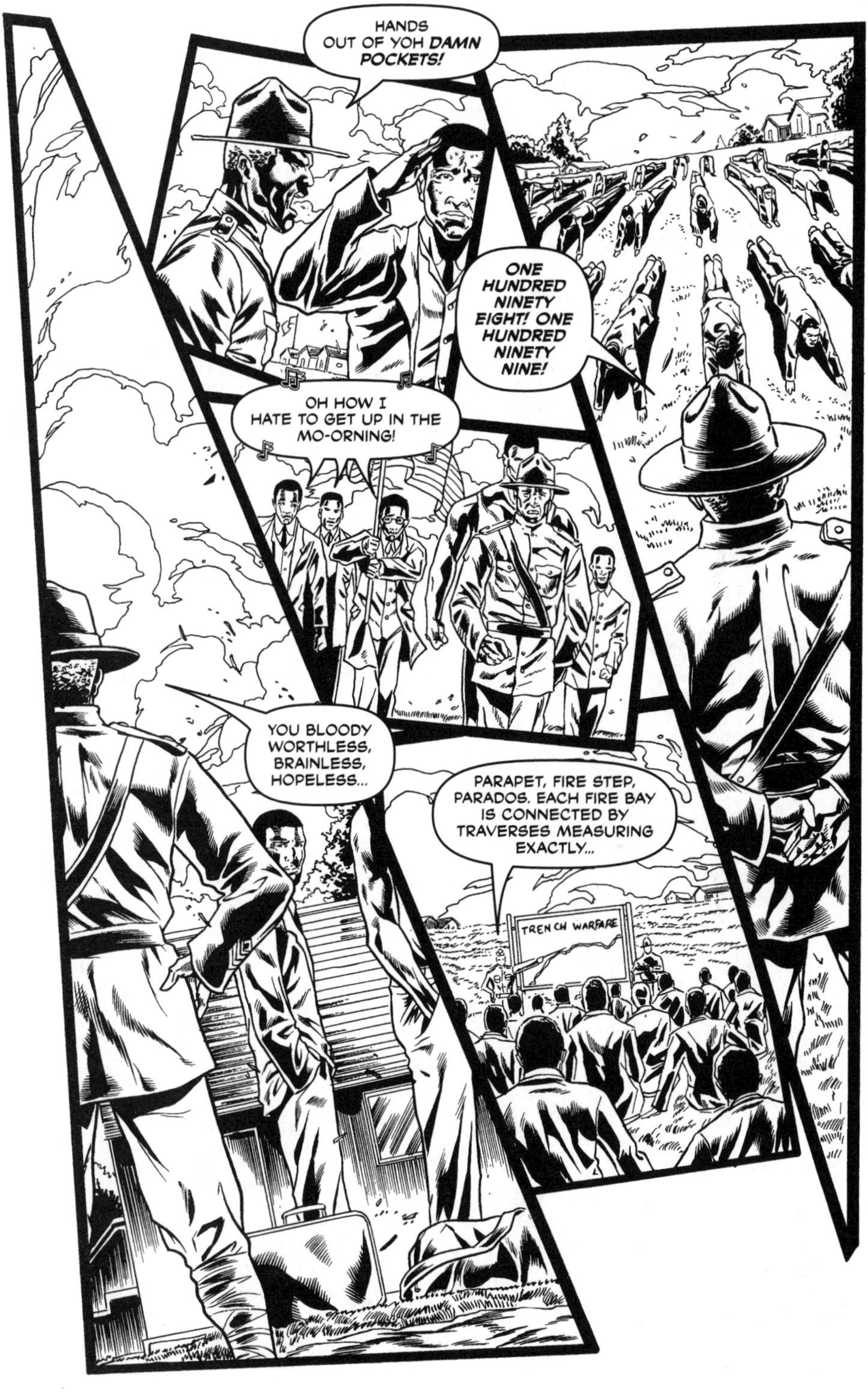
HANDS OUT OF YOH DAMN POCKETS!
ONE HUNDRED NINETY EIGHT! ONE HUNDRED NINETY NINE!
OH HOW I HATE TO GET UP IN THE MO-ORNING!
YOU BLOODY WORTHLESS, BRAINLESS, HOPELESS...
PARAPET, FIRE STEP, PARADOS. EACH FIRE BAY IS CONNECTED BY TRAVERSES MEASURING EXACTLY...
TRENCH WARFARE

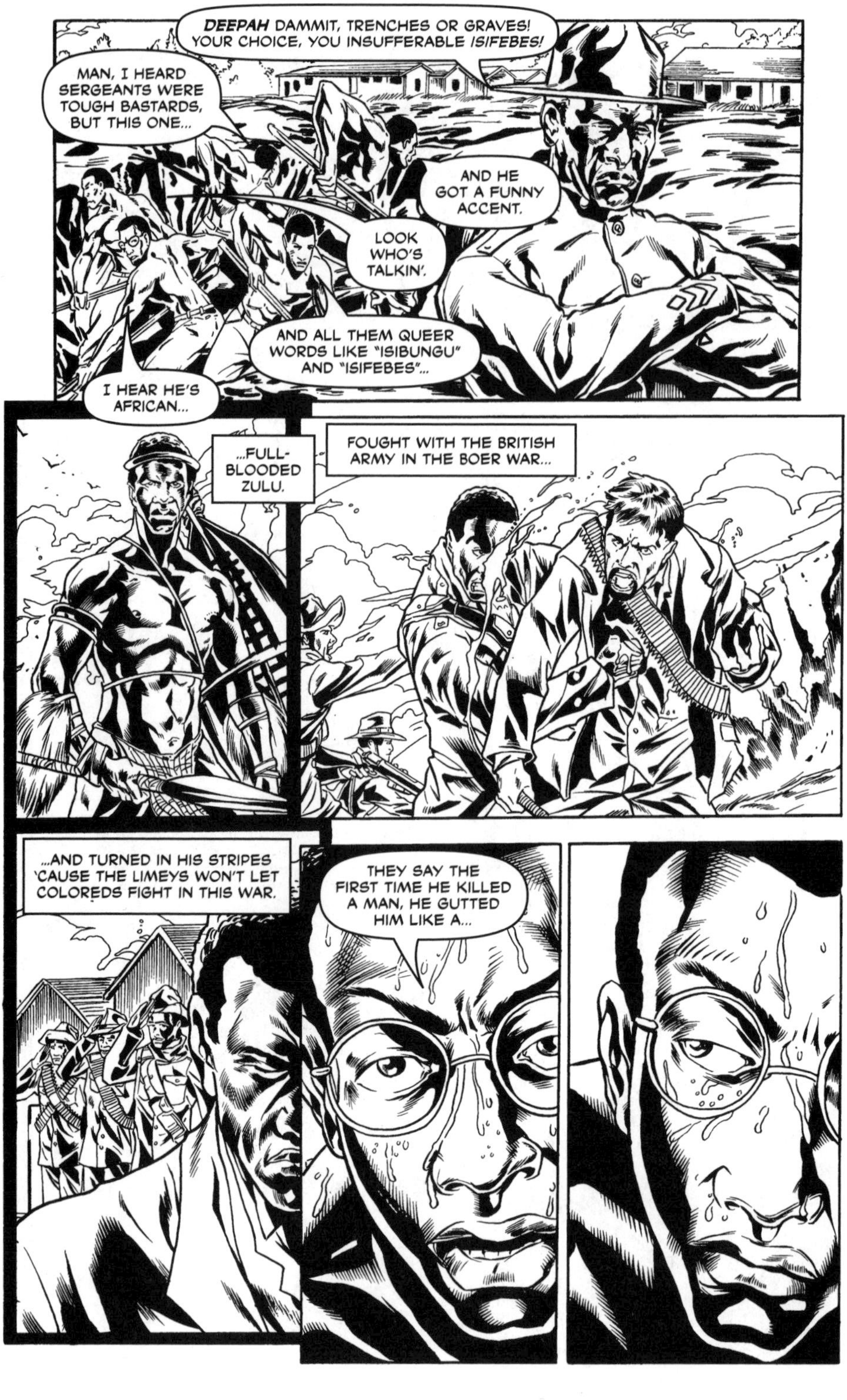

DEEPAH DAMMIT, TRENCHES OR GRAVES! YOUR CHOICE, YOU INSUFFERABLE *ISIFEBES!*
MAN, I HEARD SERGEANTS WERE TOUGH BASTARDS, BUT THIS ONE...
AND HE GOT A FUNNY ACCENT.
LOOK WHO'S TALKIN'.
AND ALL THEM QUEER WORDS LIKE "ISIBUNGU" AND "ISIFEBES"...
I HEAR HE'S AFRICAN...
...FULL-BLOODED ZULU.
FOUGHT WITH THE BRITISH ARMY IN THE BOER WAR...
...AND TURNED IN HIS STRIPES 'CAUSE THE LIMEYS WON'T LET COLOREDS FIGHT IN THIS WAR.
THEY SAY THE FIRST TIME HE KILLED A MAN, HE GUTTED HIM LIKE A...

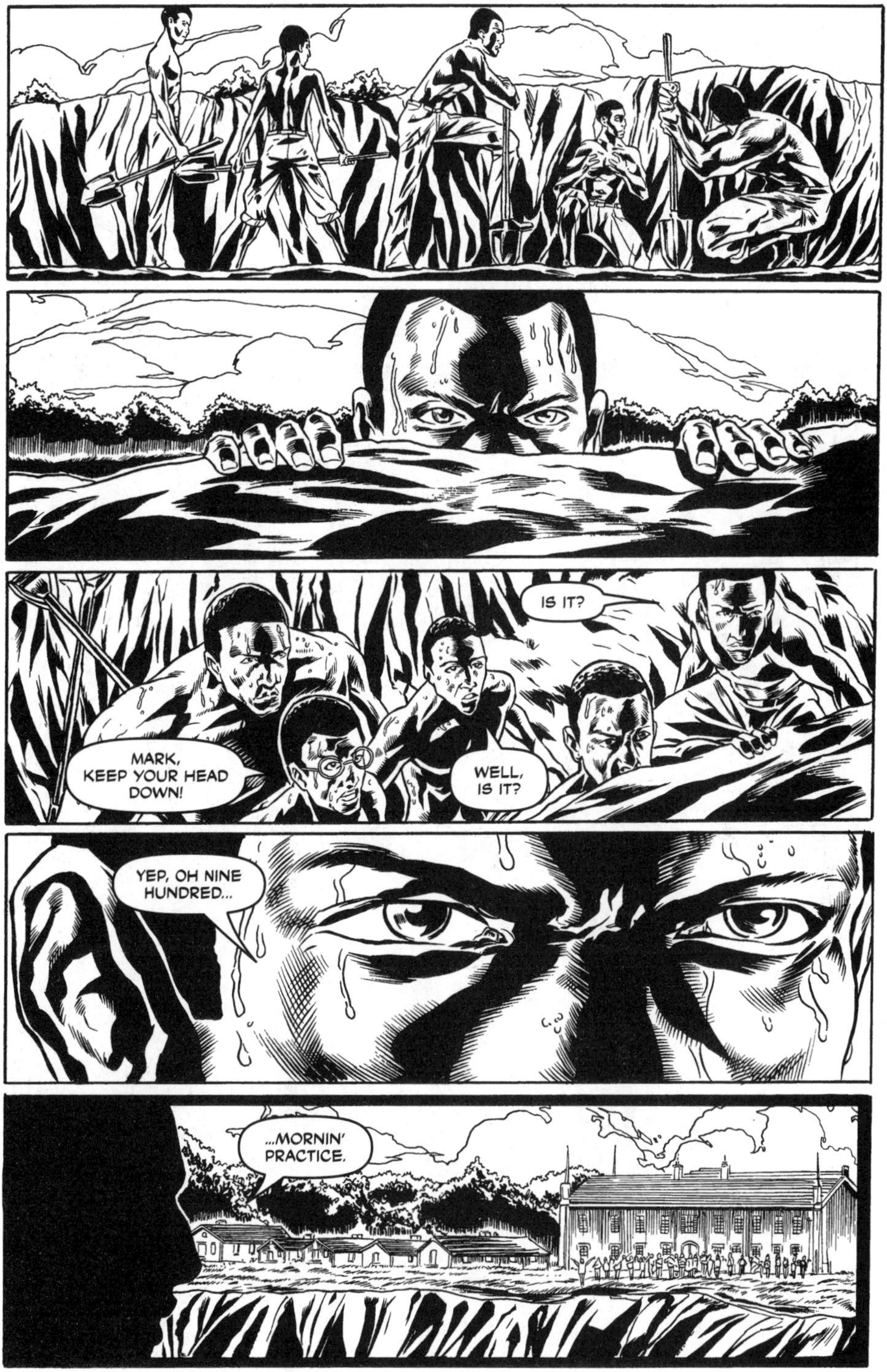
MARK, KEEP YOUR HEAD DOWN!
WELL, IS IT?
IS IT?
YEP, OH NINE HUNDRED...
...MORNIN' PRACTICE.

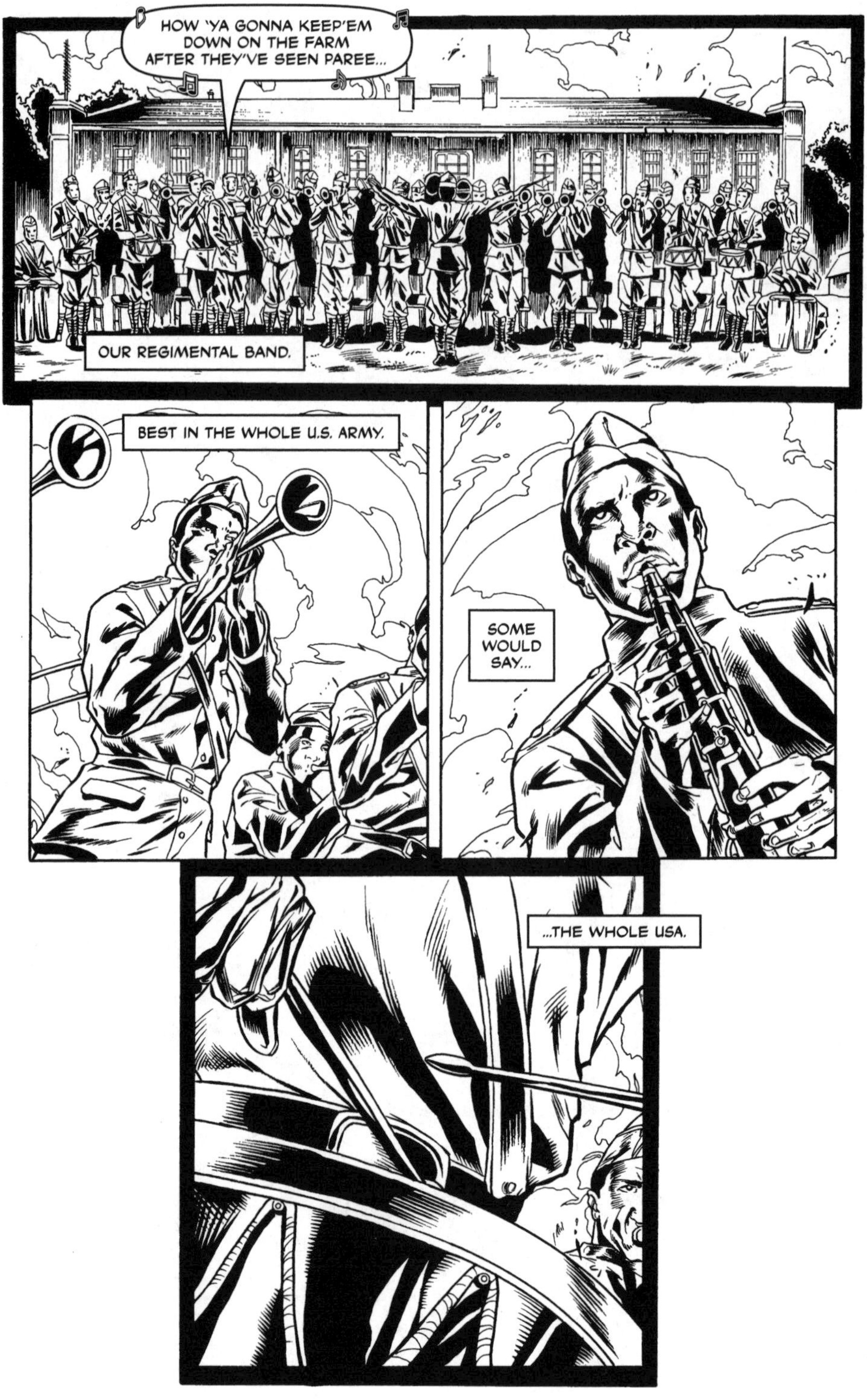
HOW 'YA GONNA KEEP'EM DOWN ON THE FARM AFTER THEY'VE SEEN PAREE...
OUR REGIMENTAL BAND.
BEST IN THE WHOLE U.S. ARMY.
SOME WOULD SAY...
...THE WHOLE USA.

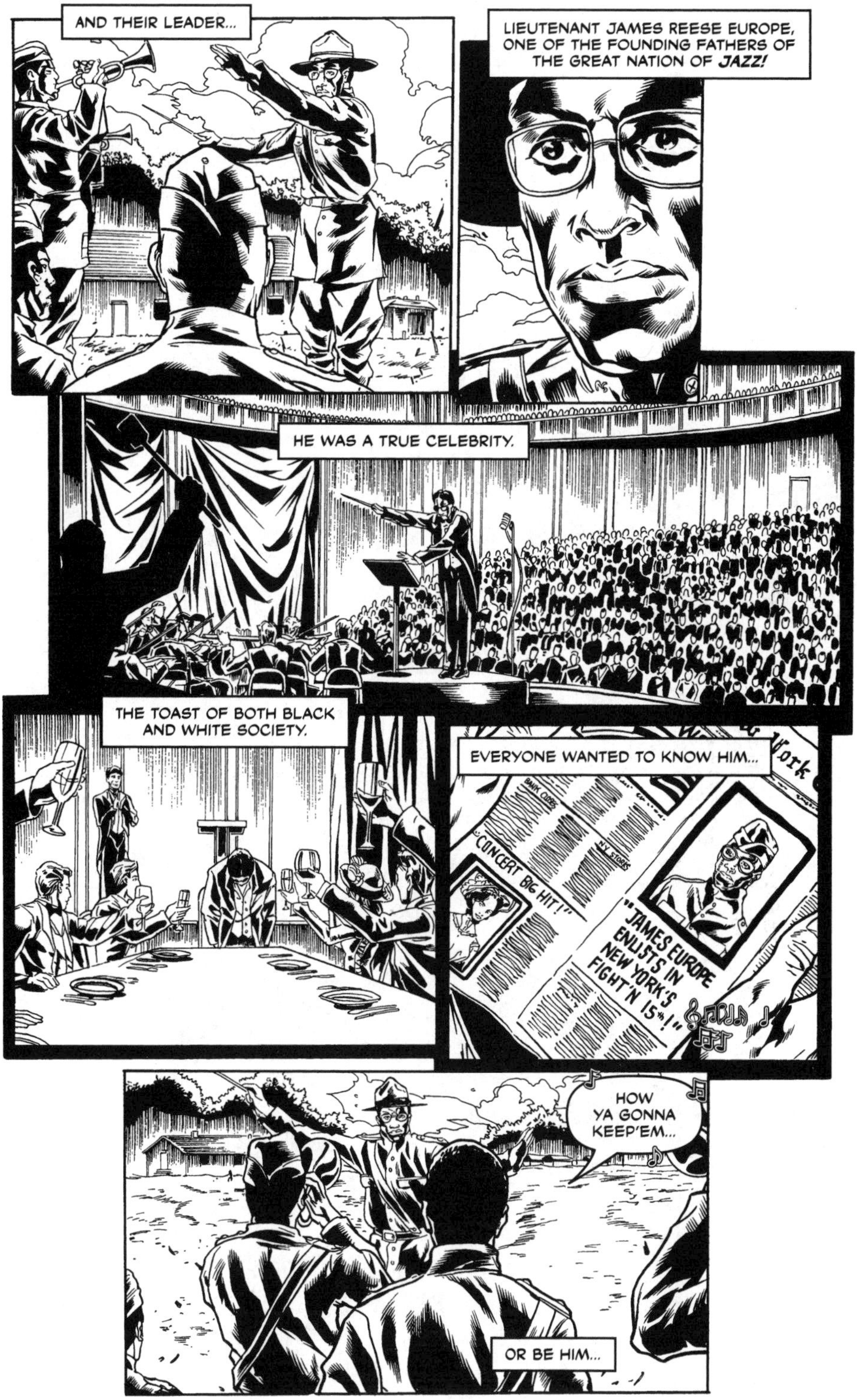
AND THEIR LEADER...
LIEUTENANT JAMES REESE EUROPE, ONE OF THE FOUNDING FATHERS OF THE GREAT NATION OF *JAZZ!*
HE WAS A TRUE CELEBRITY.
THE TOAST OF BOTH BLACK AND WHITE SOCIETY.
EVERYONE WANTED TO KNOW HIM...
"CONCERT BIG HIT!"
"JAMES EUROPE ENLISTS IN NEW YORK'S FIGHT'N 15th!"
HOW YA GONNA KEEP'EM...
OR BE HIM...

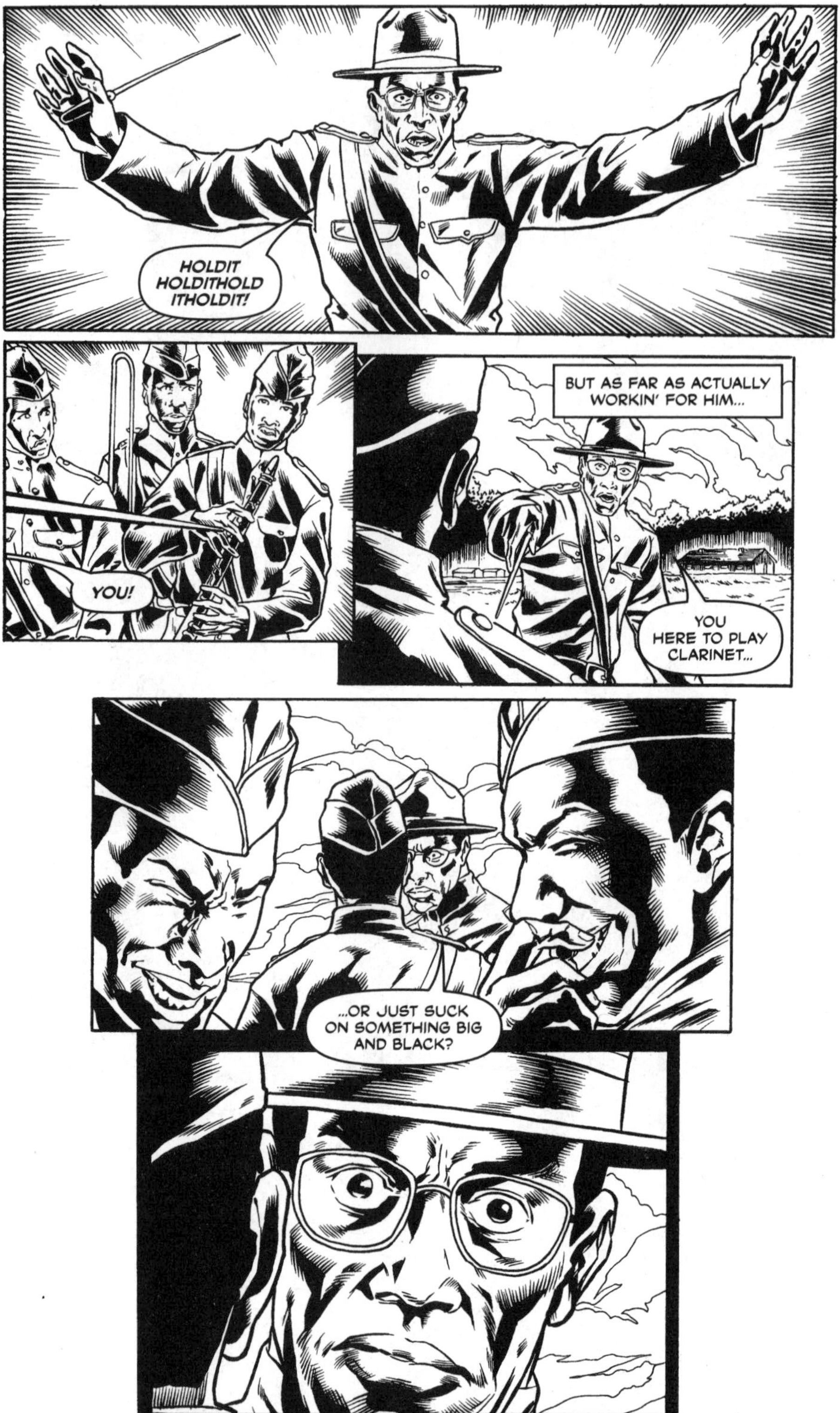
HOLDIT HOLDITHOLD ITHOLDIT!
YOU!
BUT AS FAR AS ACTUALLY WORKIN' FOR HIM...
YOU HERE TO PLAY CLARINET...
...OR JUST SUCK ON SOMETHING BIG AND BLACK?

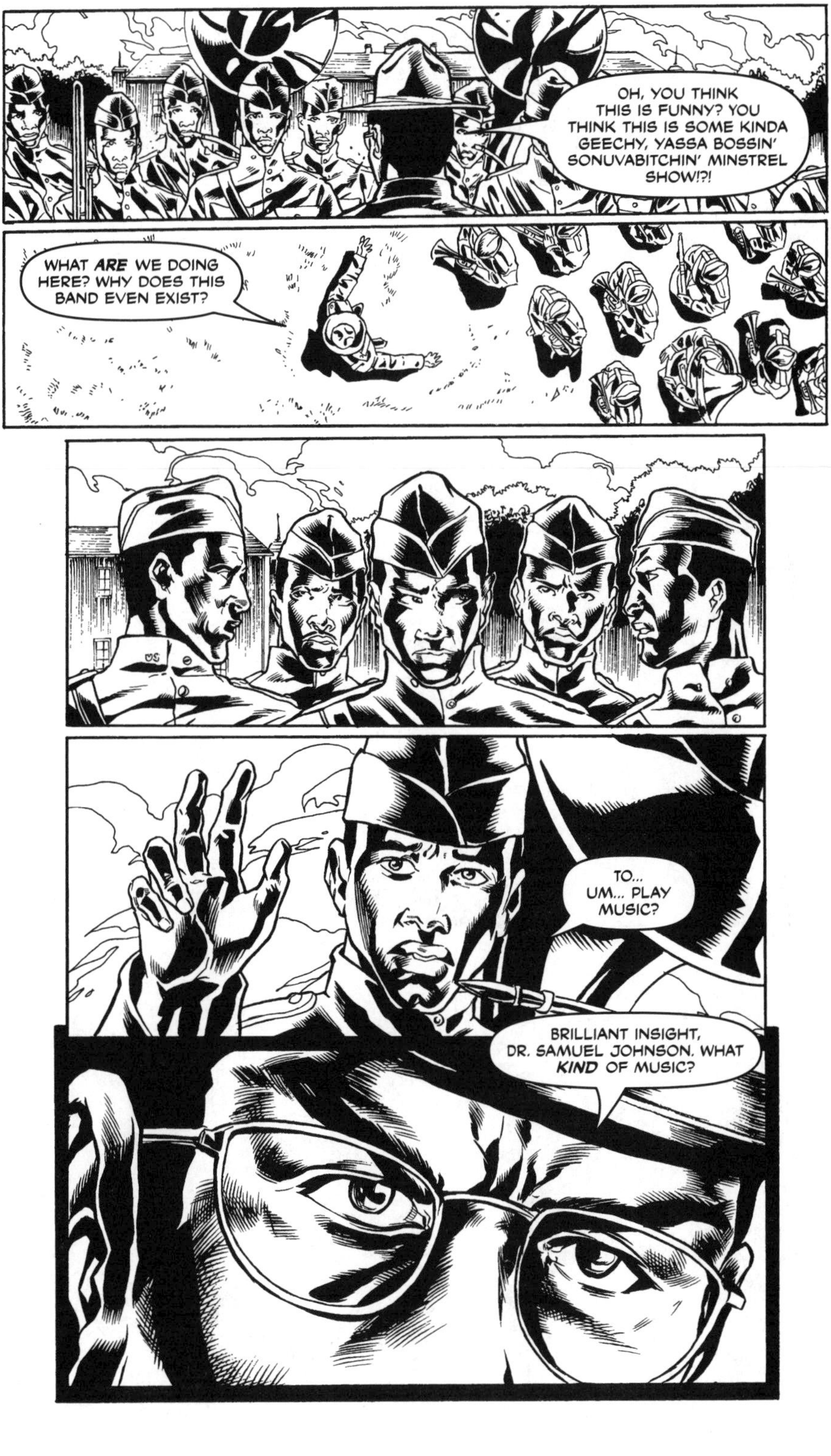
OH, YOU THINK THIS IS FUNNY? YOU THINK THIS IS SOME KINDA GEECHY, YASSA BOSSIN' SONUVABITCHIN' MINSTREL SHOW!?!
WHAT ARE WE DOING HERE? WHY DOES THIS BAND EVEN EXIST?
TO... UM... PLAY MUSIC?
BRILLIANT INSIGHT, DR. SAMUEL JOHNSON. WHAT KIND OF MUSIC?

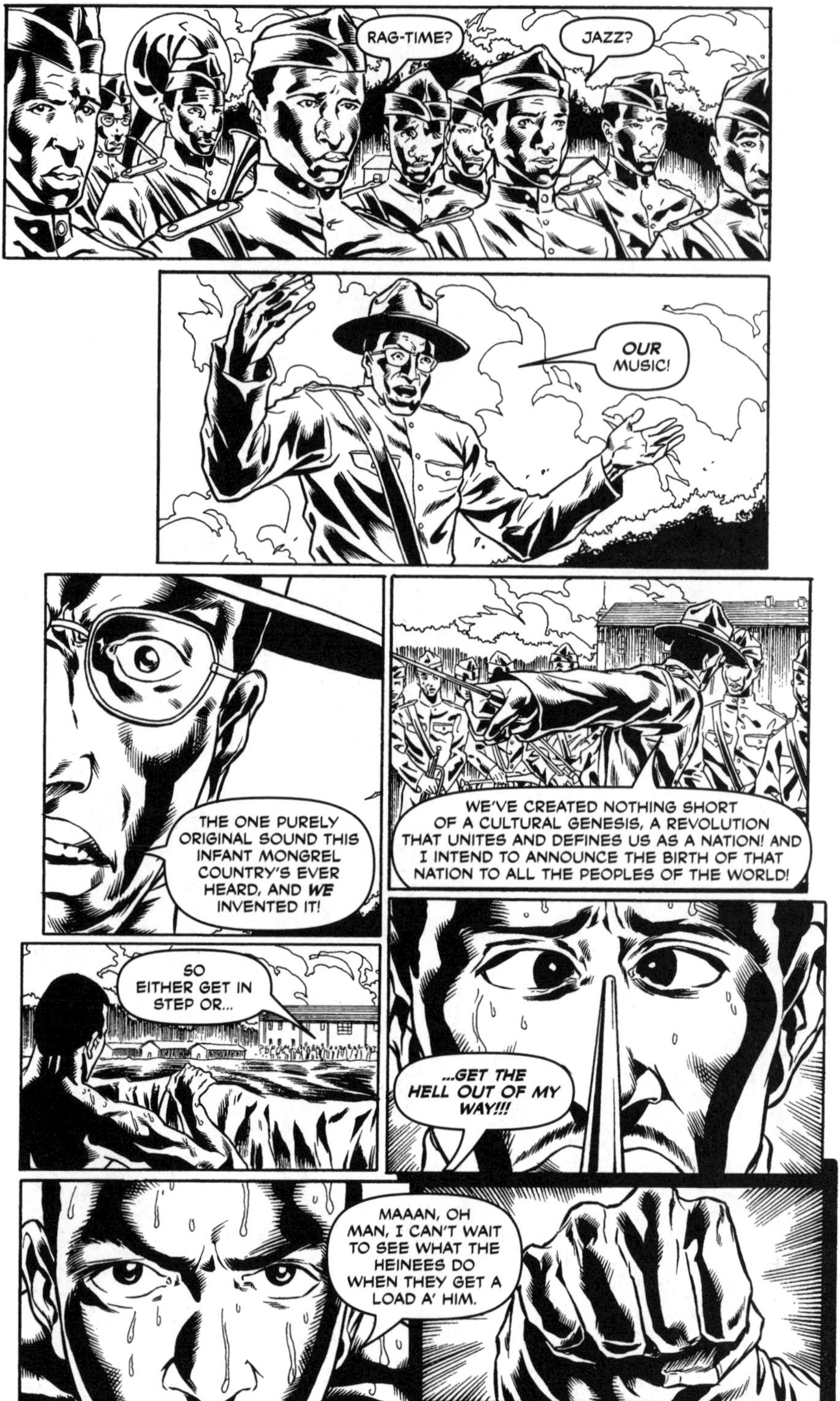
RAG-TIME?
JAZZ?
OUR MUSIC!
THE ONE PURELY ORIGINAL SOUND THIS INFANT MONGREL COUNTRY'S EVER HEARD, AND WE INVENTED IT!
WE'VE CREATED NOTHING SHORT OF A CULTURAL GENESIS, A REVOLUTION THAT UNITES AND DEFINES US AS A NATION! AND I INTEND TO ANNOUNCE THE BIRTH OF THAT NATION TO ALL THE PEOPLES OF THE WORLD!
SO EITHER GET IN STEP OR...
...GET THE HELL OUT OF MY WAY!!!
MAAAN, OH MAN, I CAN'T WAIT TO SEE WHAT THE HEINEES DO WHEN THEY GET A LOAD A' HIM.

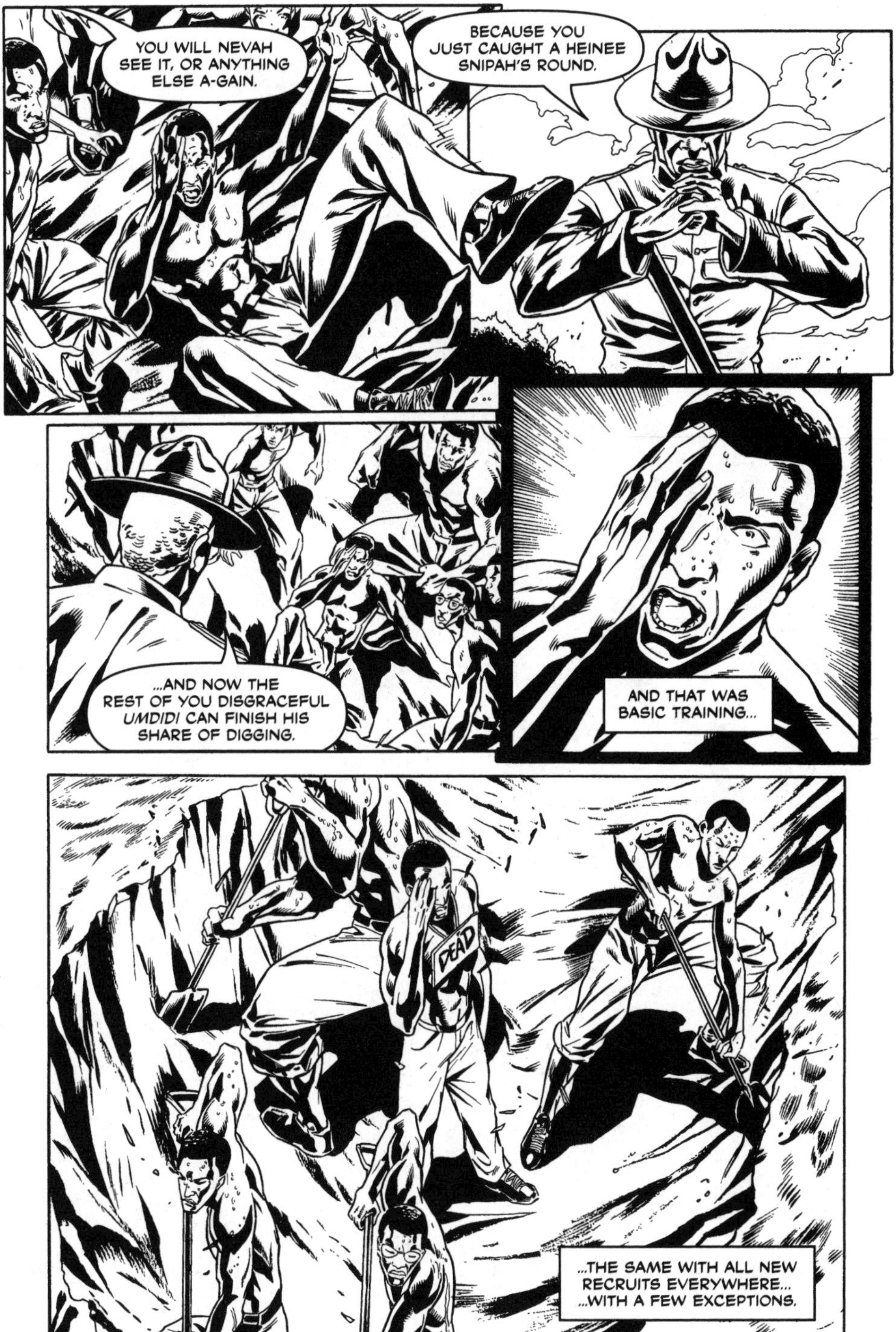
YOU WILL NEVAH SEE IT, OR ANYTHING ELSE A-GAIN.
BECAUSE YOU JUST CAUGHT A HEINEE SNIPAH'S ROUND.
...AND NOW THE REST OF YOU DISGRACEFUL *UMDIDI* CAN FINISH HIS SHARE OF DIGGING.
AND THAT WAS BASIC TRAINING...
DEAD
...THE SAME WITH ALL NEW RECRUITS EVERYWHERE... ...WITH A FEW EXCEPTIONS.

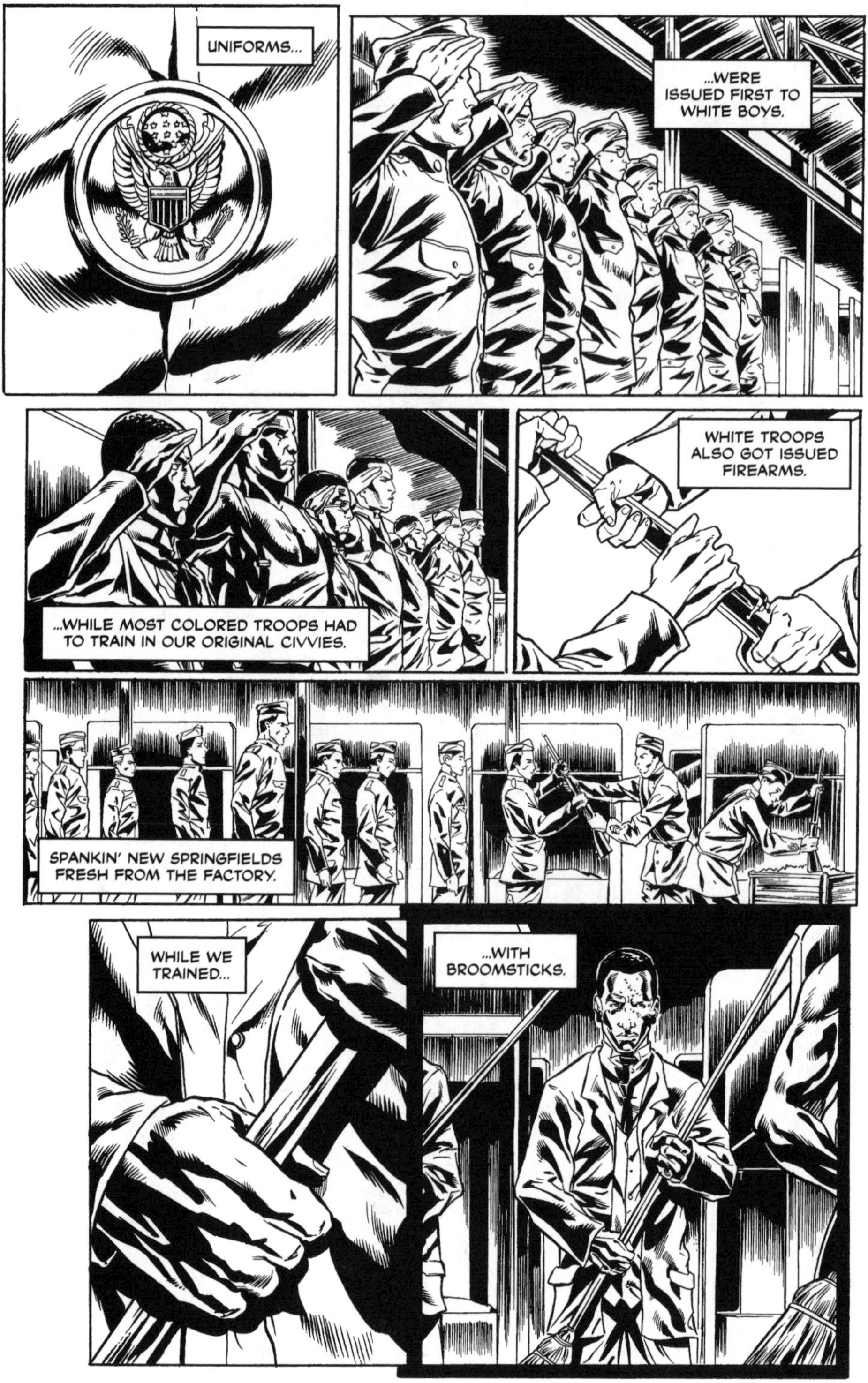
UNIFORMS...
...WERE ISSUED FIRST TO WHITE BOYS.
...WHILE MOST COLORED TROOPS HAD TO TRAIN IN OUR ORIGINAL CIVVIES.
WHITE TROOPS ALSO GOT ISSUED FIREARMS.
SPANKIN' NEW SPRINGFIELDS FRESH FROM THE FACTORY.
WHILE WE TRAINED...
...WITH BROOMSTICKS.

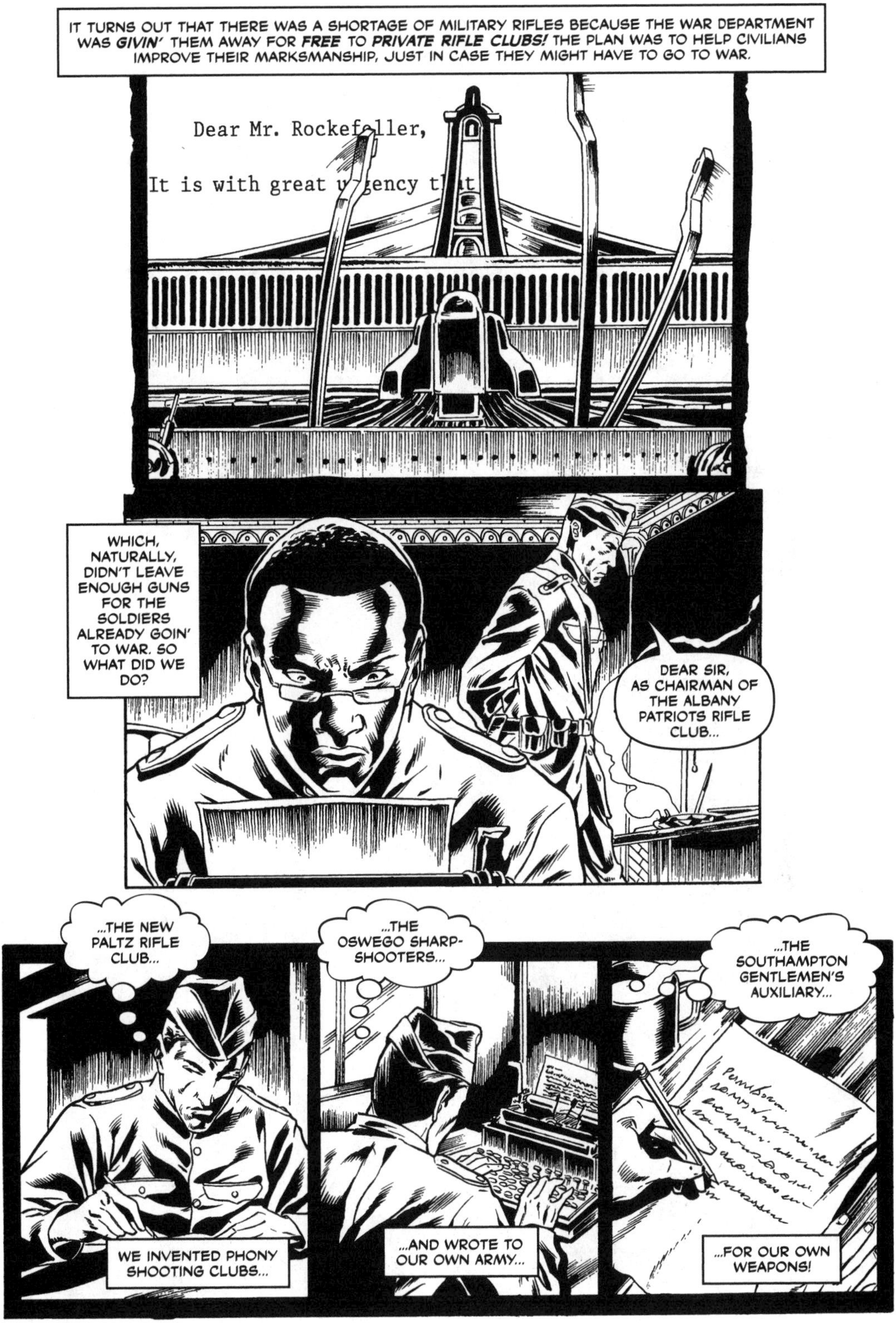
IT TURNS OUT THAT THERE WAS A SHORTAGE OF MILITARY RIFLES BECAUSE THE WAR DEPARTMENT WAS *GIVIN'* THEM AWAY FOR ***FREE*** TO ***PRIVATE RIFLE CLUBS!*** THE PLAN WAS TO HELP CIVILIANS IMPROVE THEIR MARKSMANSHIP, JUST IN CASE THEY MIGHT HAVE TO GO TO WAR.
Dear Mr. Rockefeller,
It is with great
WHICH, NATURALLY, DIDN'T LEAVE ENOUGH GUNS FOR THE SOLDIERS ALREADY GOIN' TO WAR. SO WHAT DID WE DO?
DEAR SIR, AS CHAIRMAN OF THE ALBANY PATRIOTS RIFLE CLUB...
...THE NEW PALTZ RIFLE CLUB...
WE INVENTED PHONY SHOOTING CLUBS...
...THE OSWEGO SHARP-SHOOTERS...
...AND WROTE TO OUR OWN ARMY...
...THE SOUTHAMPTON GENTLEMEN'S AUXILIARY...
...FOR OUR OWN WEAPONS!

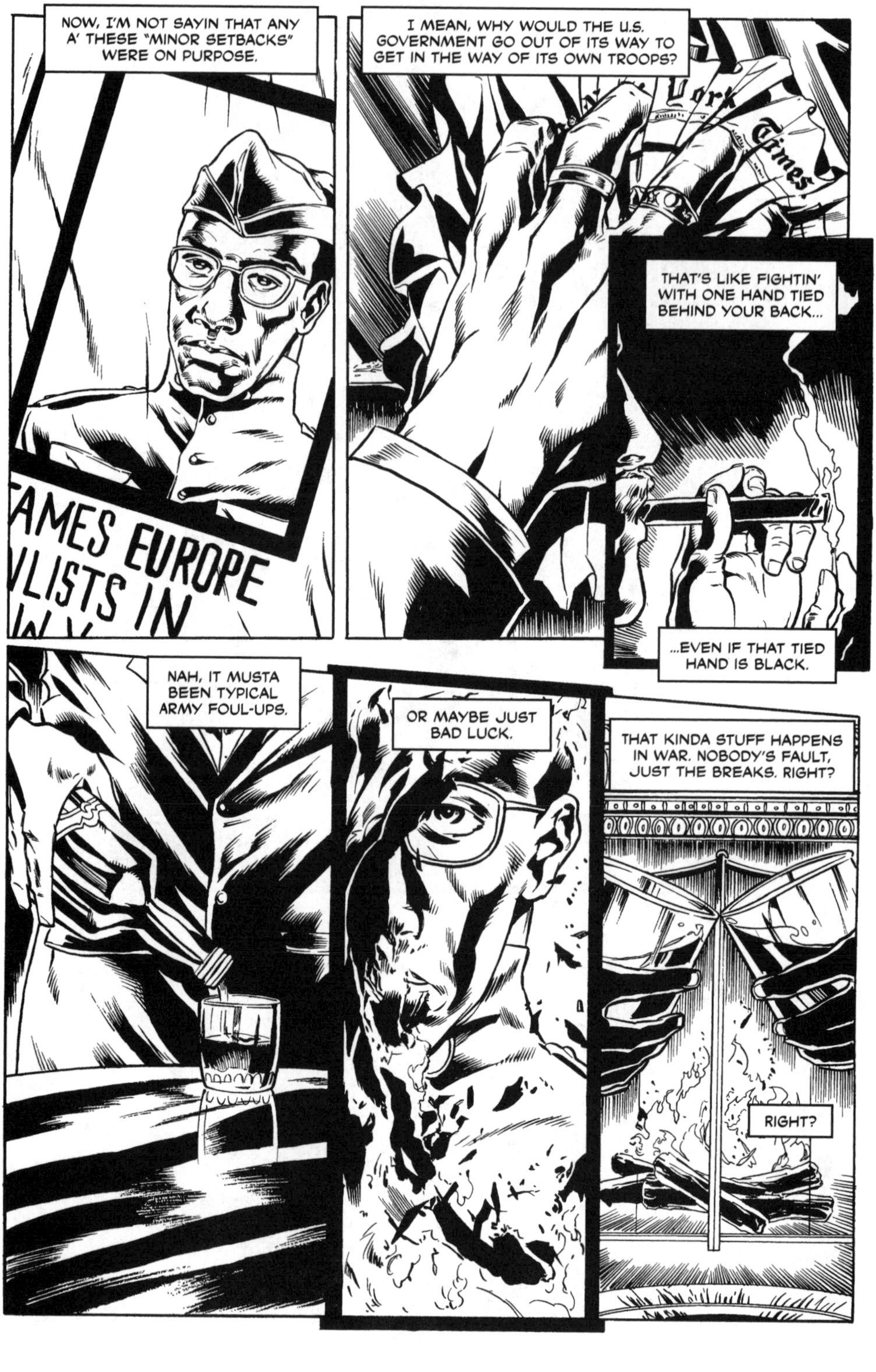
NOW, I'M NOT SAYIN THAT ANY A' THESE "MINOR SETBACKS" WERE ON PURPOSE.
AMES EUROPE
LISTS IN
I MEAN, WHY WOULD THE U.S. GOVERNMENT GO OUT OF ITS WAY TO GET IN THE WAY OF ITS OWN TROOPS?
THAT'S LIKE FIGHTIN' WITH ONE HAND TIED BEHIND YOUR BACK...
...EVEN IF THAT TIED HAND IS BLACK.
NAH, IT MUSTA BEEN TYPICAL ARMY FOUL-UPS.
OR MAYBE JUST BAD LUCK.
THAT KINDA STUFF HAPPENS IN WAR. NOBODY'S FAULT, JUST THE BREAKS. RIGHT?
RIGHT?

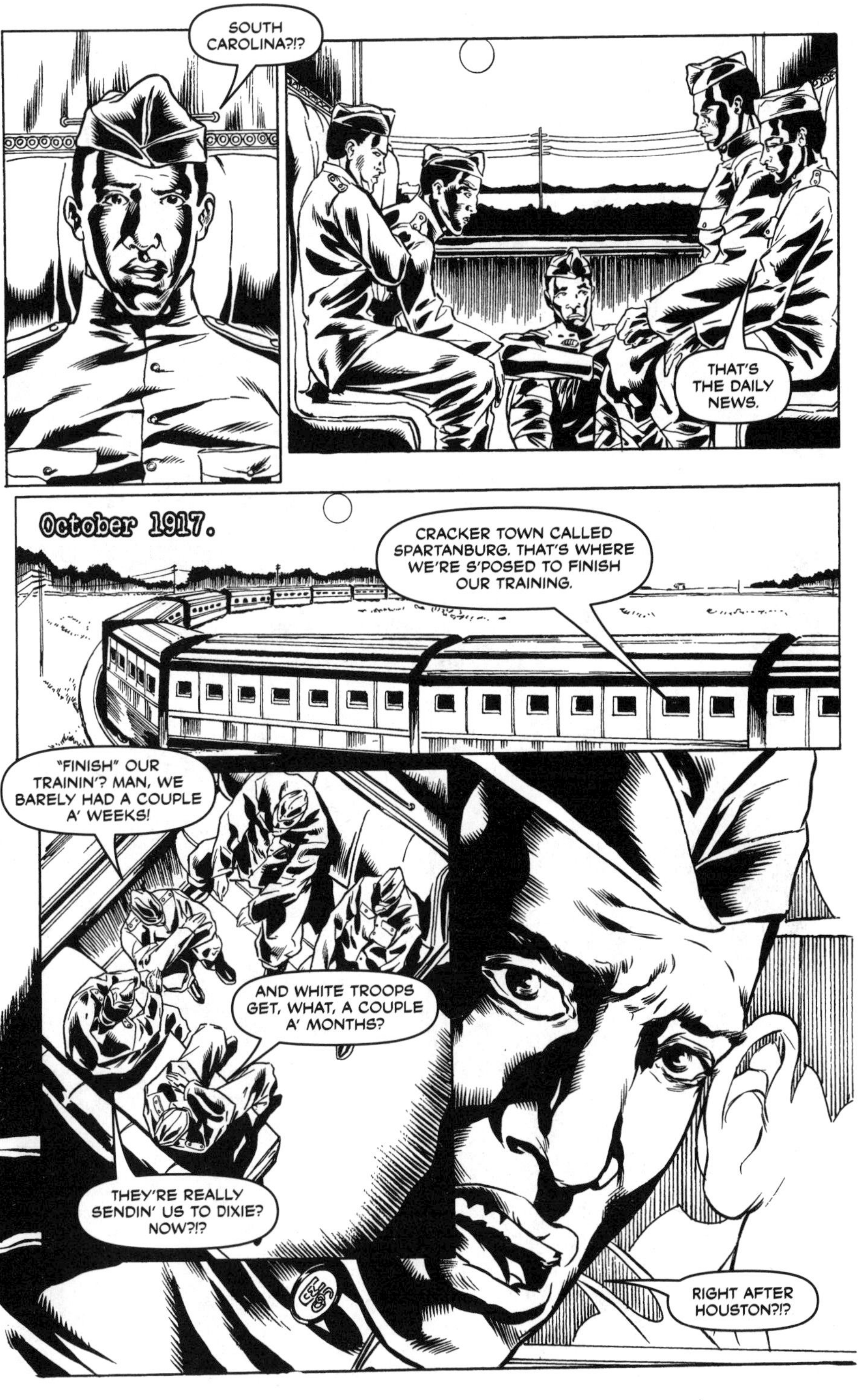
SOUTH CAROLINA?!?
THAT'S THE DAILY NEWS.
October 1917.
CRACKER TOWN CALLED SPARTANBURG. THAT'S WHERE WE'RE S'POSED TO FINISH OUR TRAINING.
"FINISH" OUR TRAININ'? MAN, WE BARELY HAD A COUPLE A' WEEKS!
AND WHITE TROOPS GET, WHAT, A COUPLE A' MONTHS?
THEY'RE REALLY SENDIN' US TO DIXIE? NOW?!?
RIGHT AFTER HOUSTON?!?

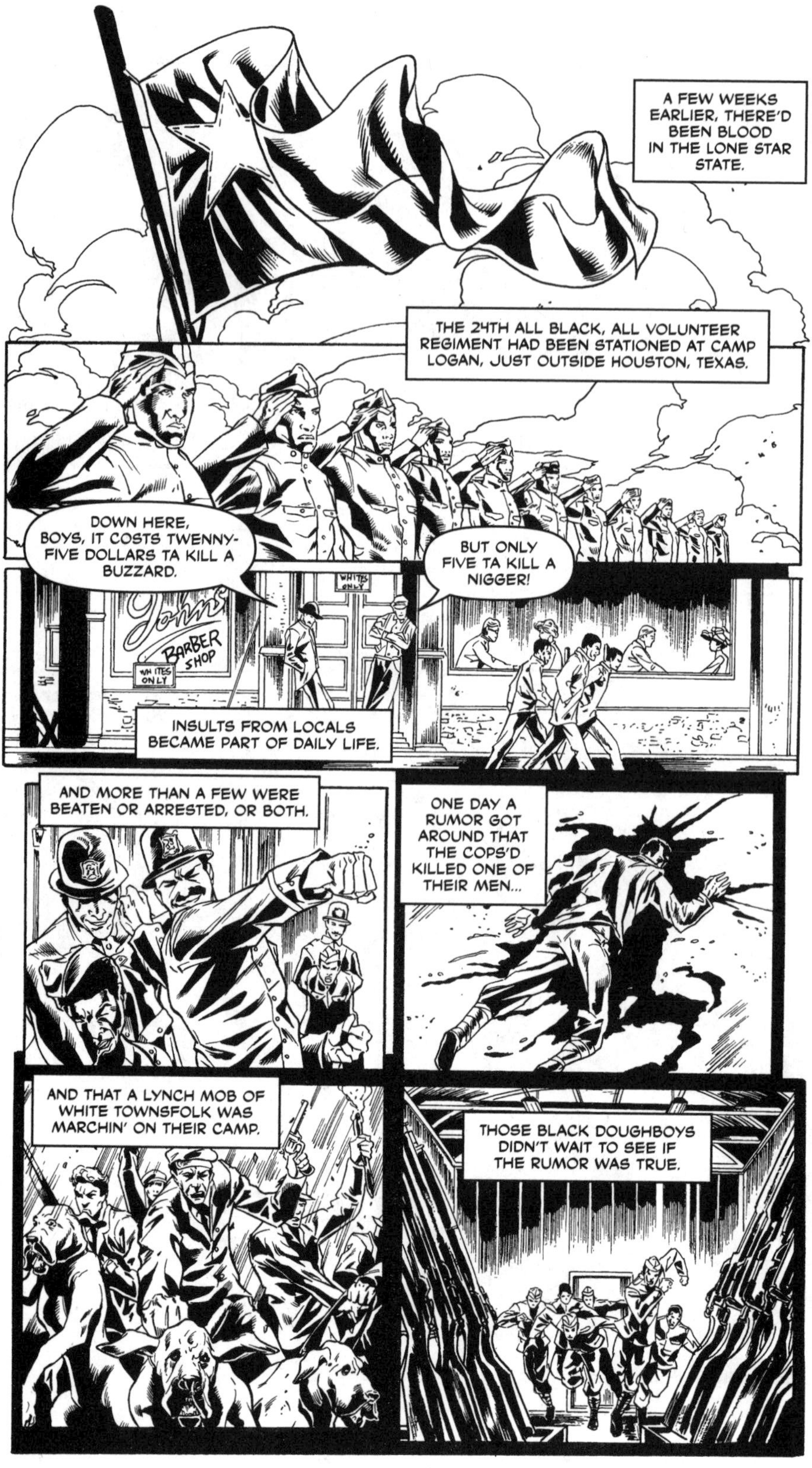
A FEW WEEKS EARLIER, THERE'D BEEN BLOOD IN THE LONE STAR STATE.
THE 24TH ALL BLACK, ALL VOLUNTEER REGIMENT HAD BEEN STATIONED AT CAMP LOGAN, JUST OUTSIDE HOUSTON, TEXAS.
DOWN HERE, BOYS, IT COSTS TWENNY-FIVE DOLLARS TA KILL A BUZZARD.
BUT ONLY FIVE TA KILL A NIGGER!
WHITES ONLY
John's
BARBER SHOP
WHITES ONLY
INSULTS FROM LOCALS BECAME PART OF DAILY LIFE.
AND MORE THAN A FEW WERE BEATEN OR ARRESTED, OR BOTH.
ONE DAY A RUMOR GOT AROUND THAT THE COPS'D KILLED ONE OF THEIR MEN...
AND THAT A LYNCH MOB OF WHITE TOWNSFOLK WAS MARCHIN' ON THEIR CAMP.
THOSE BLACK DOUGHBOYS DIDN'T WAIT TO SEE IF THE RUMOR WAS TRUE.

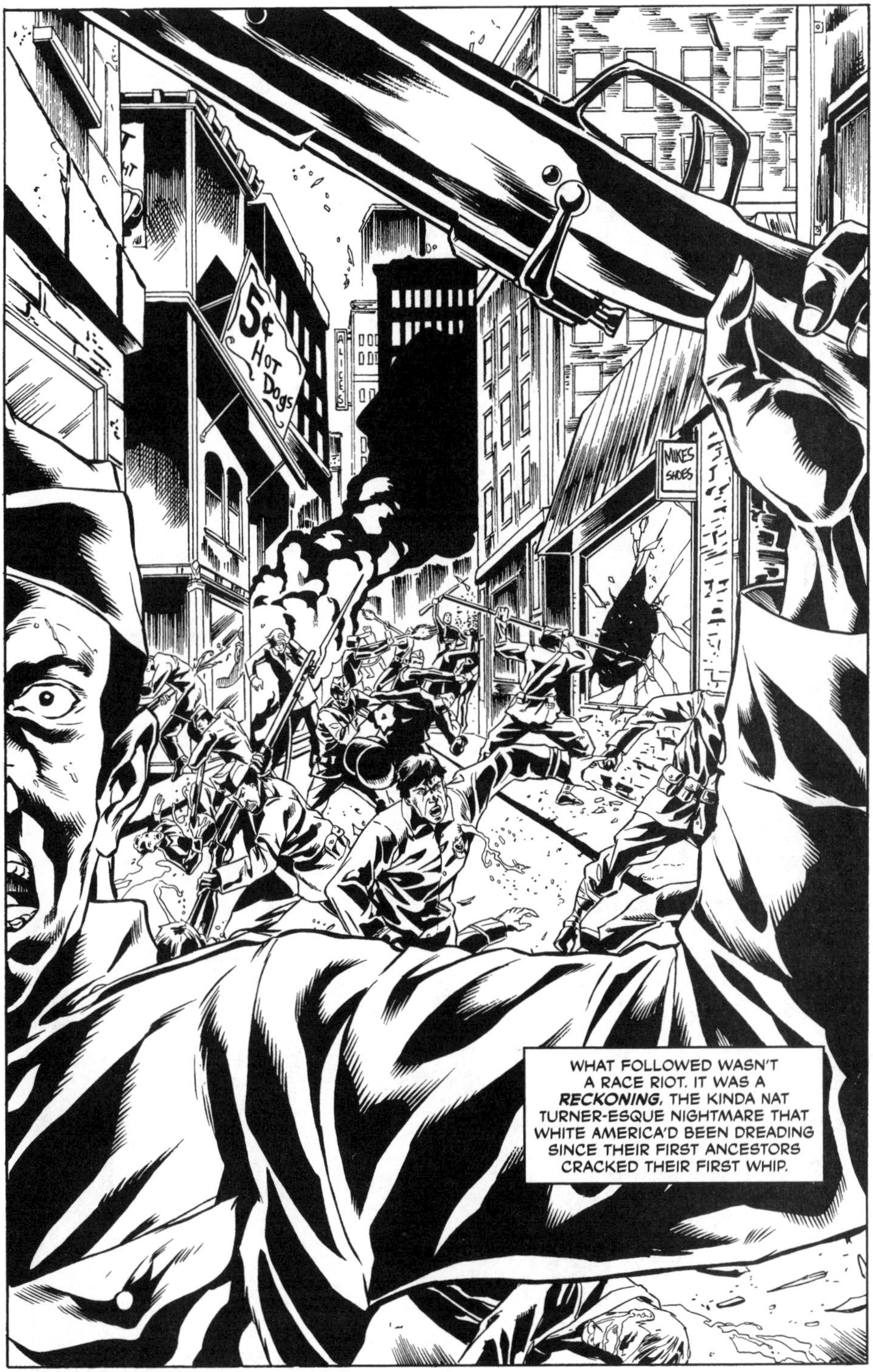
5¢ Hot Dogs
ALICE'S
MIKE'S SHOES
WHAT FOLLOWED WASN'T A RACE RIOT. IT WAS A ***RECKONING,*** THE KINDA NAT TURNER-ESQUE NIGHTMARE THAT WHITE AMERICA'D BEEN DREADING SINCE THEIR FIRST ANCESTORS CRACKED THEIR FIRST WHIP.

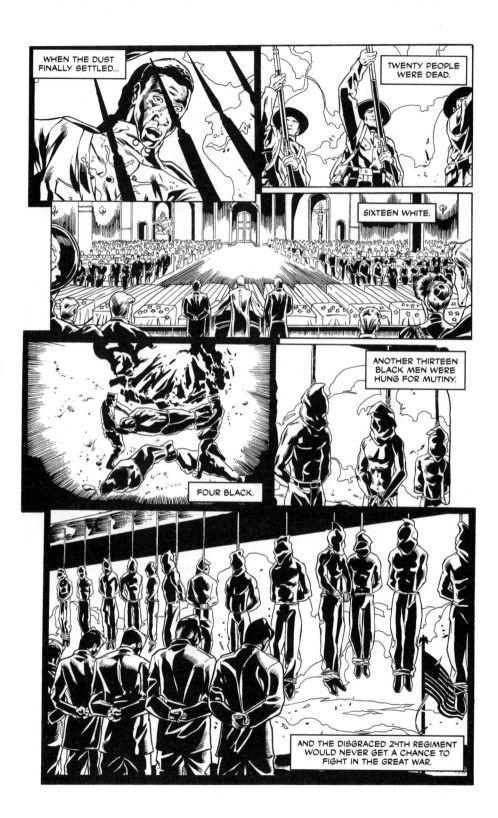

WHEN THE DUST FINALLY SETTLED...

TWENTY PEOPLE WERE DEAD.

SIXTEEN WHITE.

FOUR BLACK.

ANOTHER THIRTEEN BLACK MEN WERE HUNG FOR MUTINY.

AND THE DISGRACED 24TH REGIMENT WOULD NEVER GET A CHANCE TO FIGHT IN THE GREAT WAR.

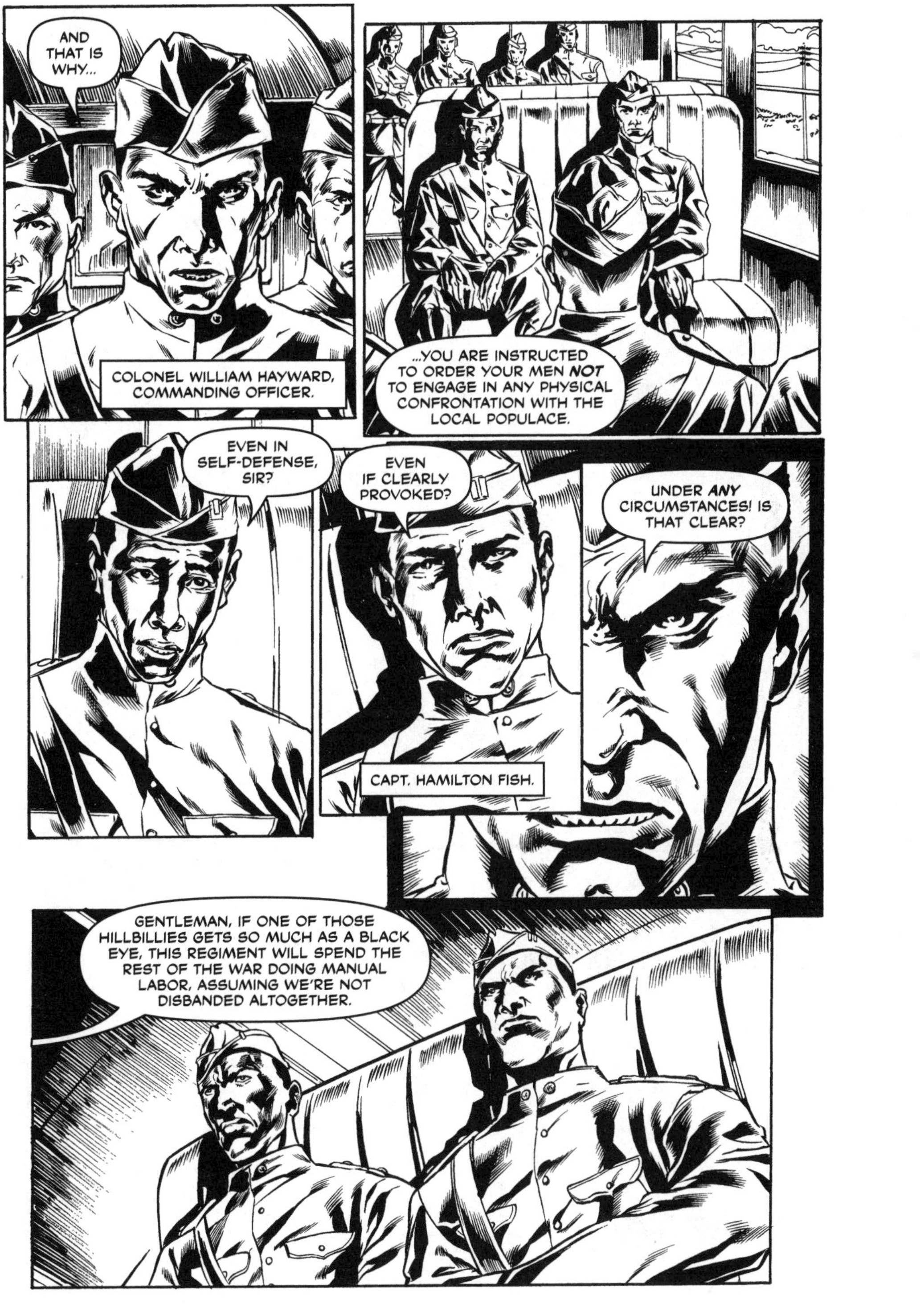
AND THAT IS WHY...
COLONEL WILLIAM HAYWARD, COMMANDING OFFICER.
...YOU ARE INSTRUCTED TO ORDER YOUR MEN NOT TO ENGAGE IN ANY PHYSICAL CONFRONTATION WITH THE LOCAL POPULACE.
EVEN IN SELF-DEFENSE, SIR?
EVEN IF CLEARLY PROVOKED?
CAPT. HAMILTON FISH.
UNDER ANY CIRCUMSTANCES! IS THAT CLEAR?
GENTLEMAN, IF ONE OF THOSE HILLBILLIES GETS SO MUCH AS A BLACK EYE, THIS REGIMENT WILL SPEND THE REST OF THE WAR DOING MANUAL LABOR, ASSUMING WE'RE NOT DISBANDED ALTOGETHER.

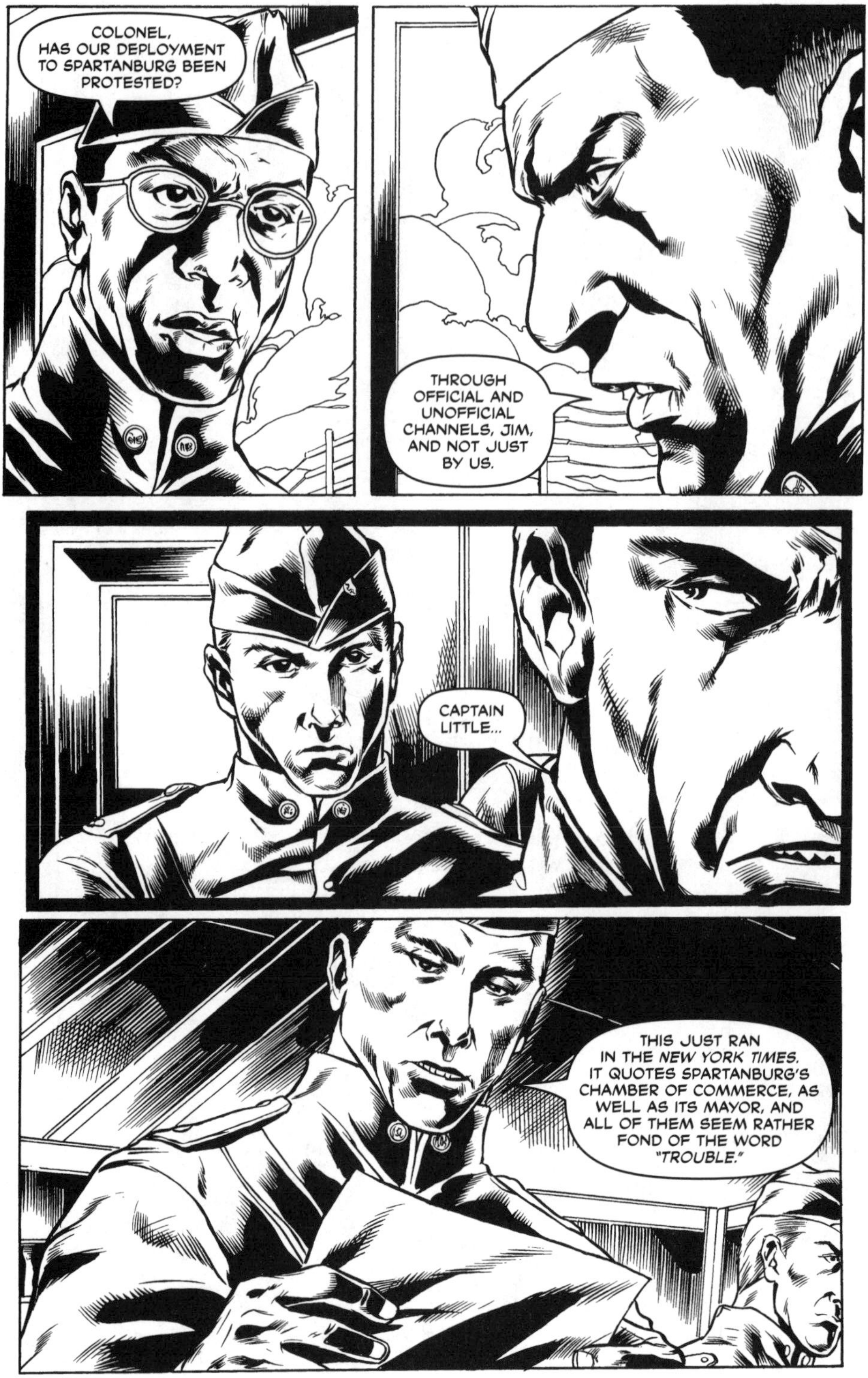
COLONEL, HAS OUR DEPLOYMENT TO SPARTANBURG BEEN PROTESTED?
THROUGH OFFICIAL AND UNOFFICIAL CHANNELS, JIM, AND NOT JUST BY US.
CAPTAIN LITTLE...
THIS JUST RAN IN THE *NEW YORK TIMES.* IT QUOTES SPARTANBURG'S CHAMBER OF COMMERCE, AS WELL AS ITS MAYOR, AND ALL OF THEM SEEM RATHER FOND OF THE WORD *"TROUBLE."*

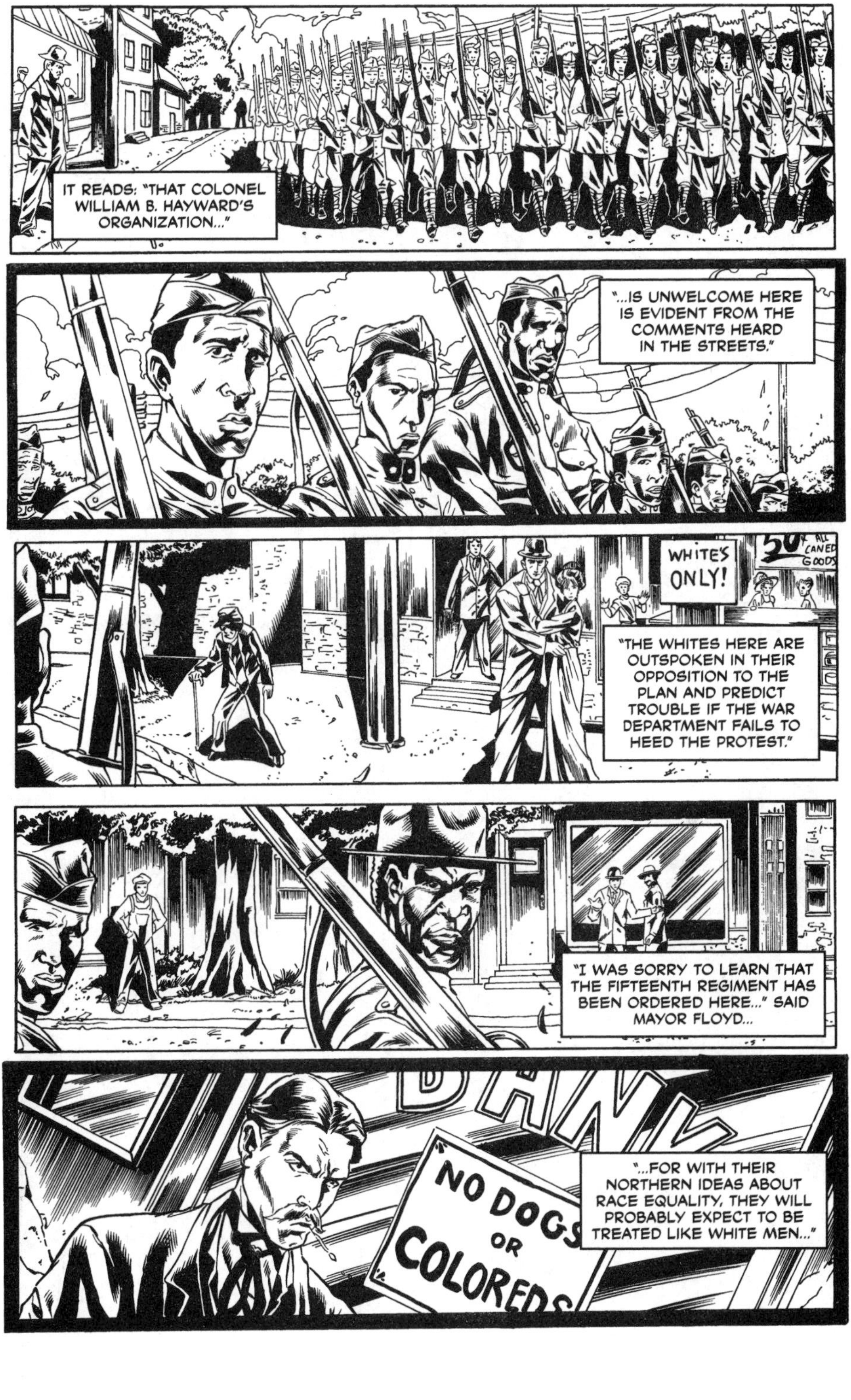
IT READS: "THAT COLONEL WILLIAM B. HAYWARD'S ORGANIZATION..."
"...IS UNWELCOME HERE IS EVIDENT FROM THE COMMENTS HEARD IN THE STREETS."
WHITE'S ONLY!
ALL CANED GOODS
"THE WHITES HERE ARE OUTSPOKEN IN THEIR OPPOSITION TO THE PLAN AND PREDICT TROUBLE IF THE WAR DEPARTMENT FAILS TO HEED THE PROTEST."
"I WAS SORRY TO LEARN THAT THE FIFTEENTH REGIMENT HAS BEEN ORDERED HERE..." SAID MAYOR FLOYD...
NO DOGS OR COLOREDS
"...FOR WITH THEIR NORTHERN IDEAS ABOUT RACE EQUALITY, THEY WILL PROBABLY EXPECT TO BE TREATED LIKE WHITE MEN..."

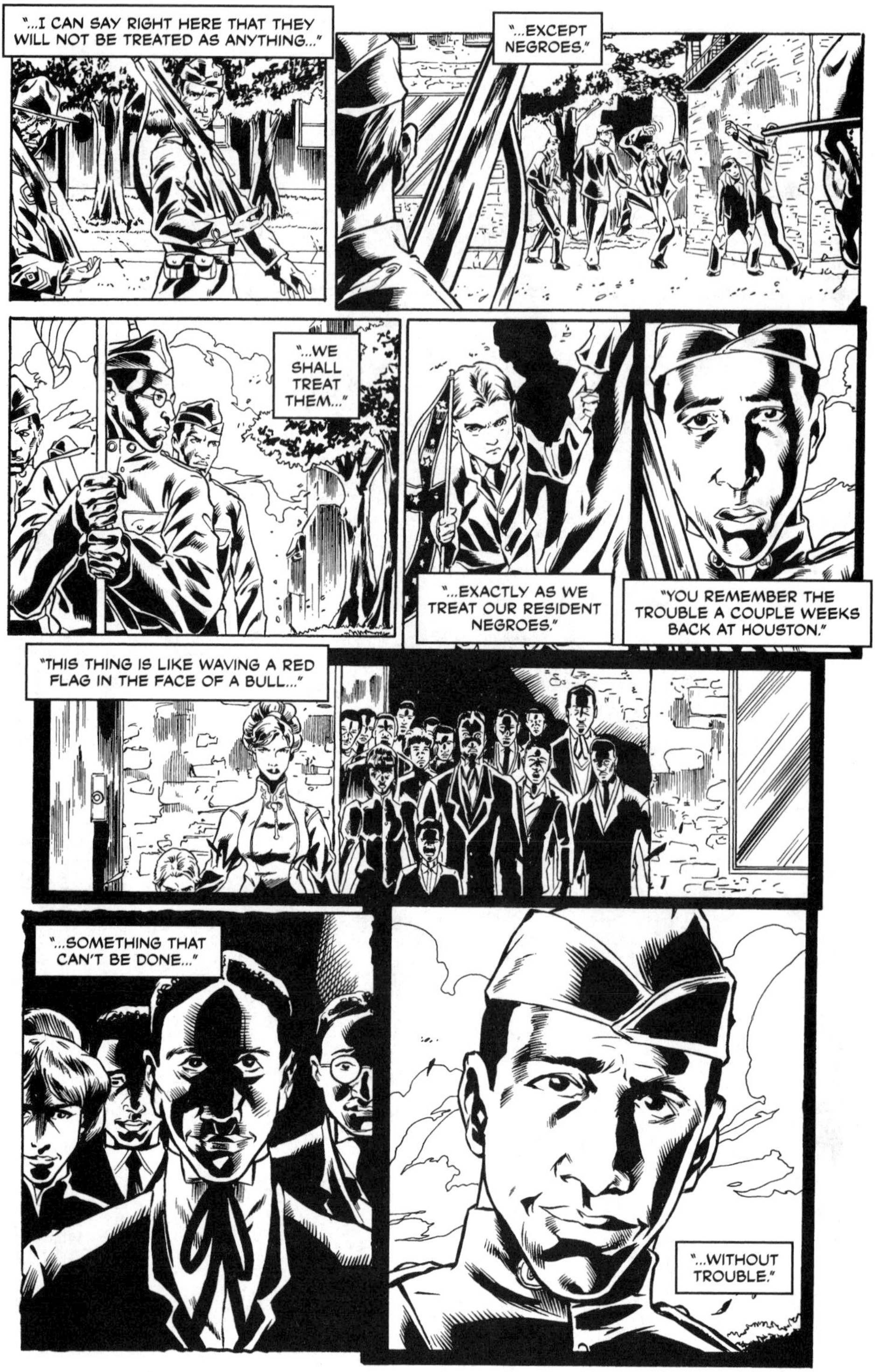
"...I CAN SAY RIGHT HERE THAT THEY WILL NOT BE TREATED AS ANYTHING..."
"...EXCEPT NEGROES."
"...WE SHALL TREAT THEM..."
"...EXACTLY AS WE TREAT OUR RESIDENT NEGROES."
"YOU REMEMBER THE TROUBLE A COUPLE WEEKS BACK AT HOUSTON."
"THIS THING IS LIKE WAVING A RED FLAG IN THE FACE OF A BULL..."
"...SOMETHING THAT CAN'T BE DONE..."
"...WITHOUT TROUBLE."

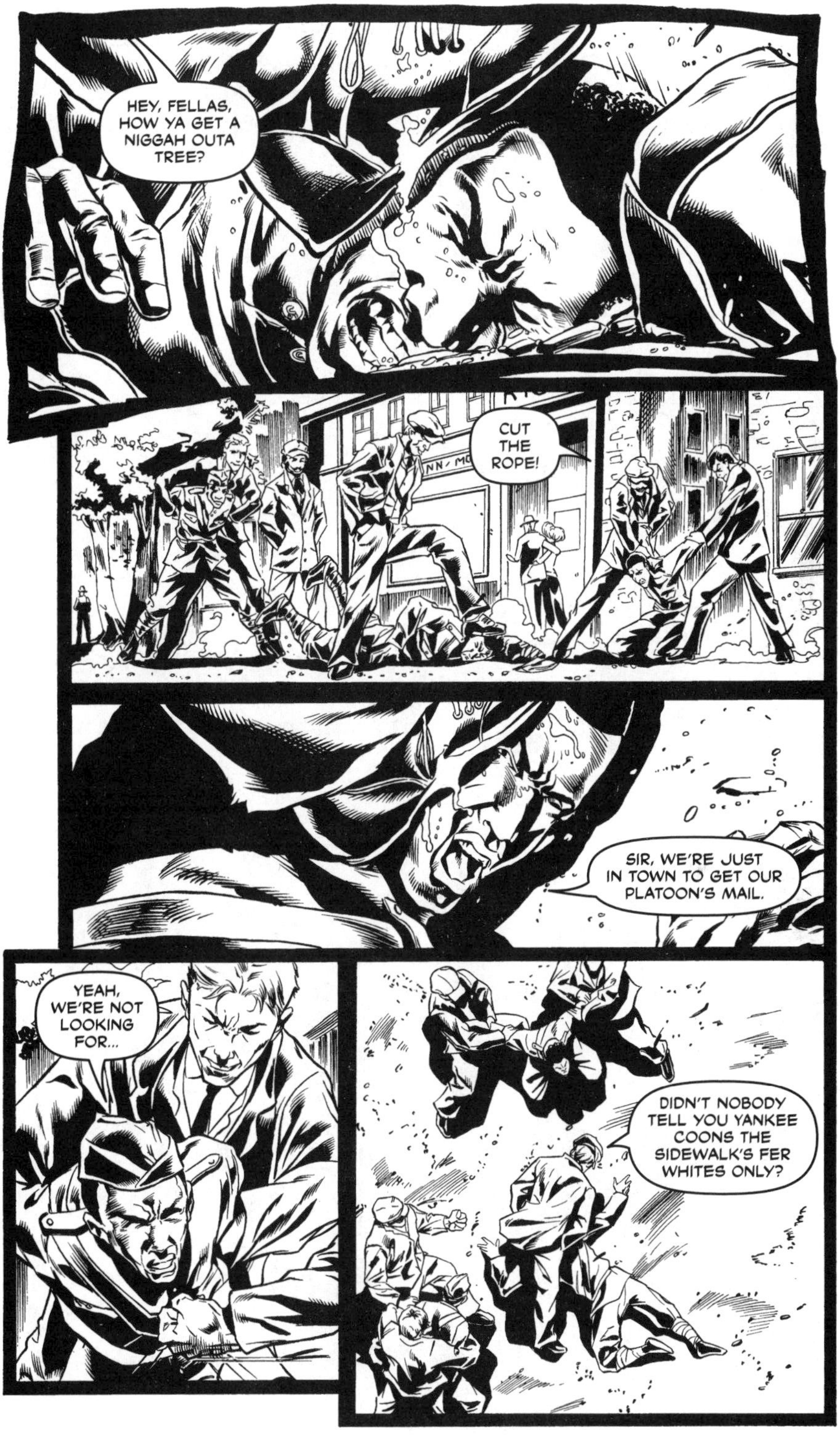
HEY, FELLAS, HOW YA GET A NIGGAH OUTA TREE?
CUT THE ROPE!
SIR, WE'RE JUST IN TOWN TO GET OUR PLATOON'S MAIL.
YEAH, WE'RE NOT LOOKING FOR...
DIDN'T NOBODY TELL YOU YANKEE COONS THE SIDEWALK'S FER WHITES ONLY?

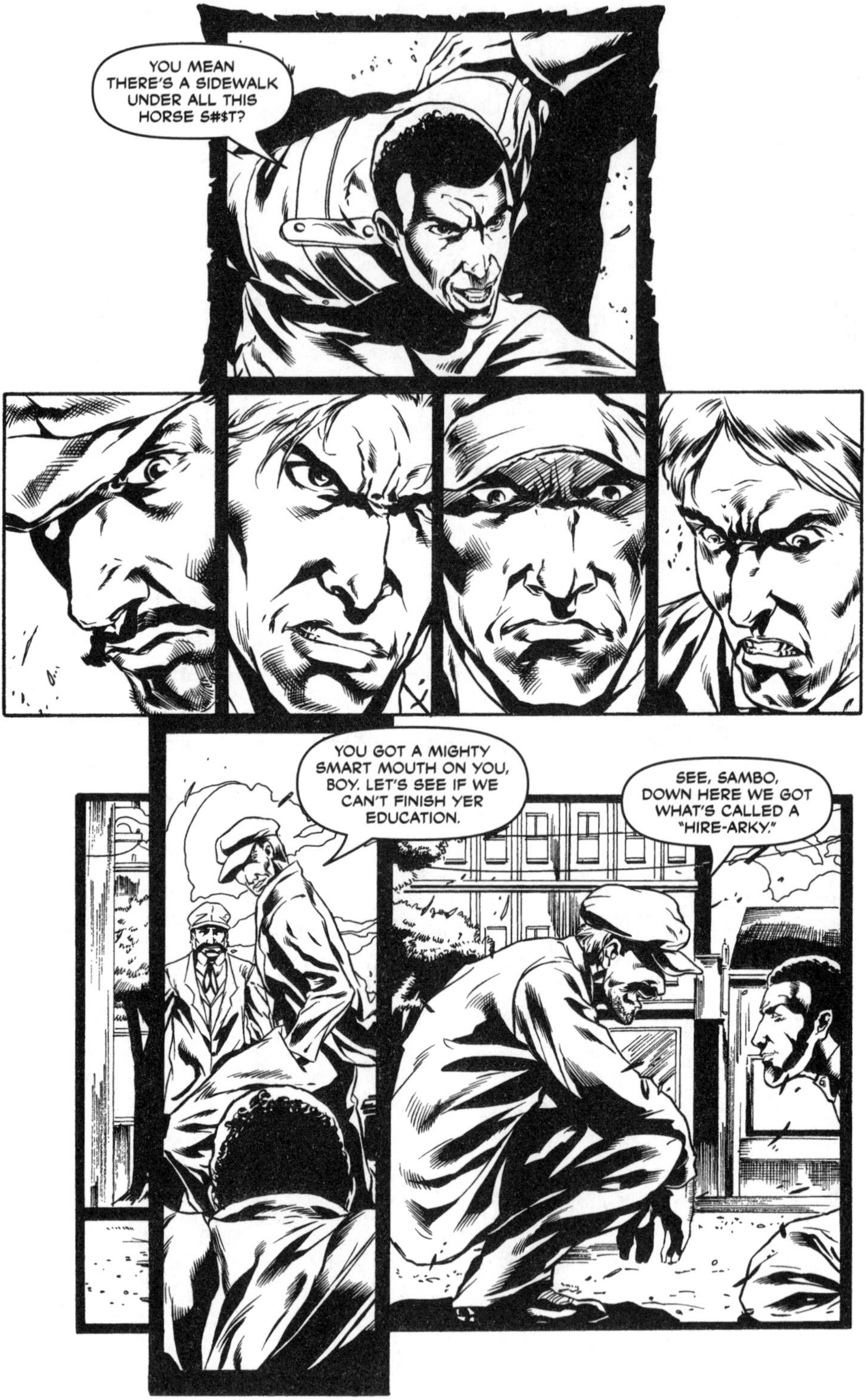
YOU MEAN THERE'S A SIDEWALK UNDER ALL THIS HORSE S#$T?
YOU GOT A MIGHTY SMART MOUTH ON YOU, BOY. LET'S SEE IF WE CAN'T FINISH YER EDUCATION.
SEE, SAMBO, DOWN HERE WE GOT WHAT'S CALLED A "HIRE-ARKY."

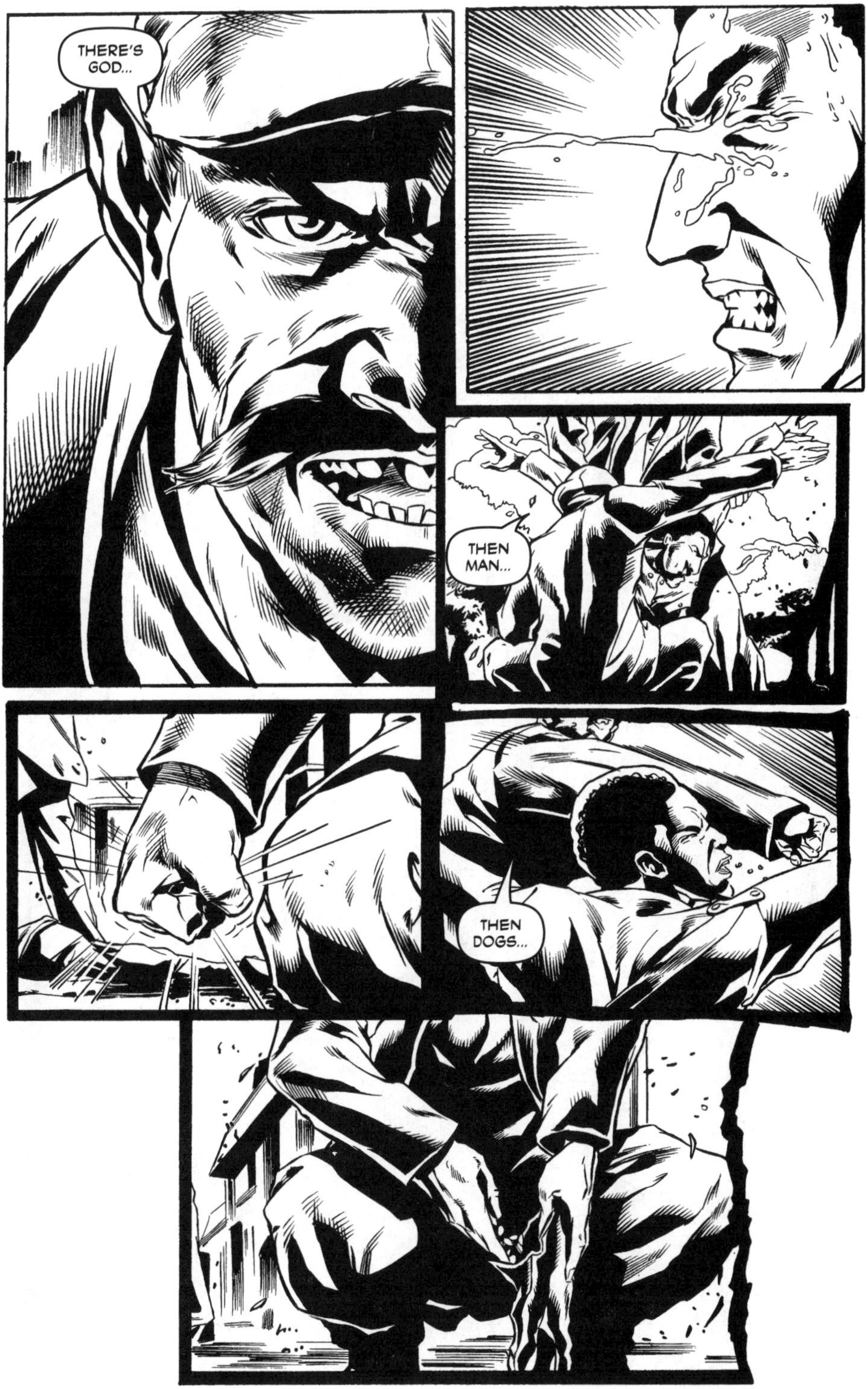

THERE'S GOD...
THEN MAN...
THEN DOGS...

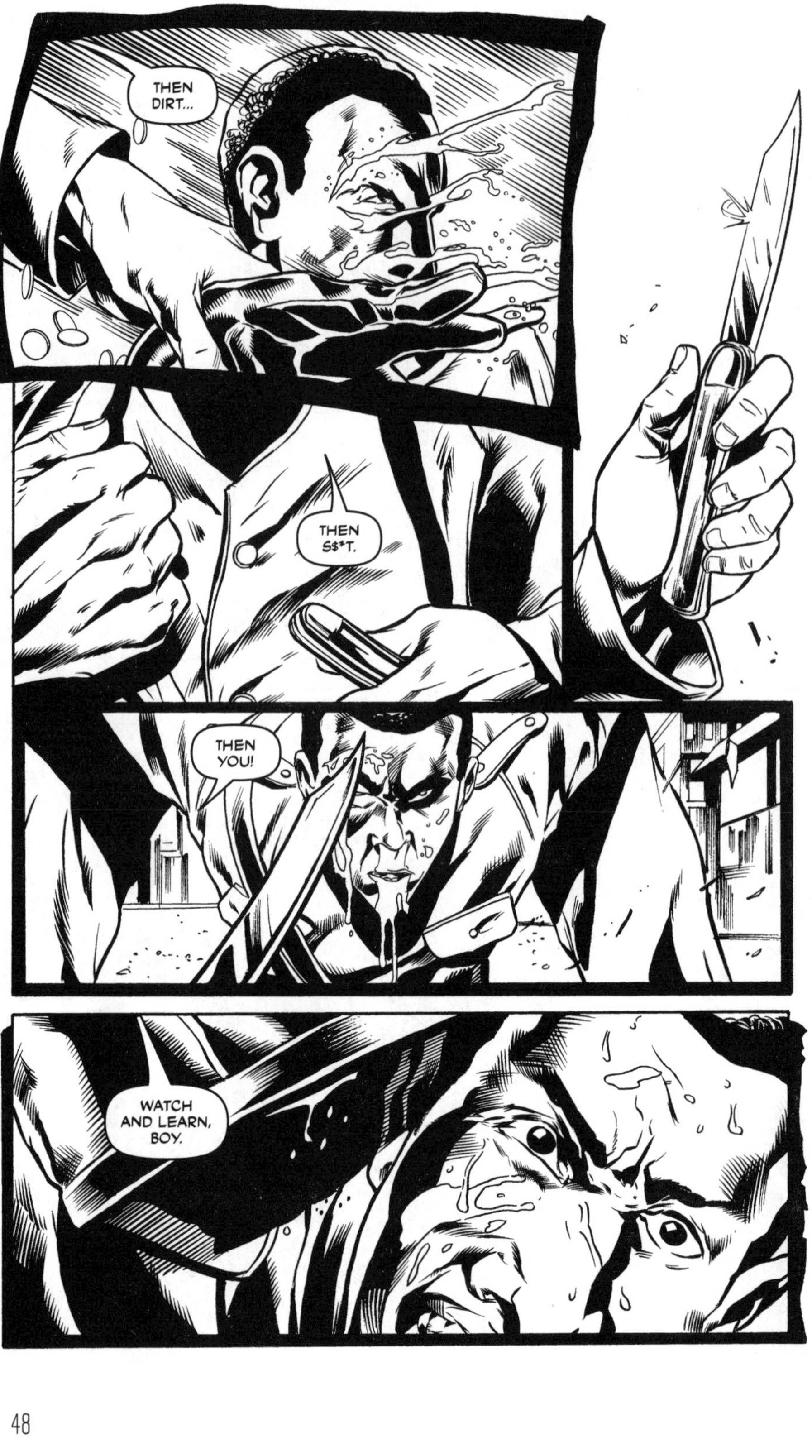
THEN DIRT...
THEN S$*T.
THEN YOU!
WATCH AND LEARN, BOY.

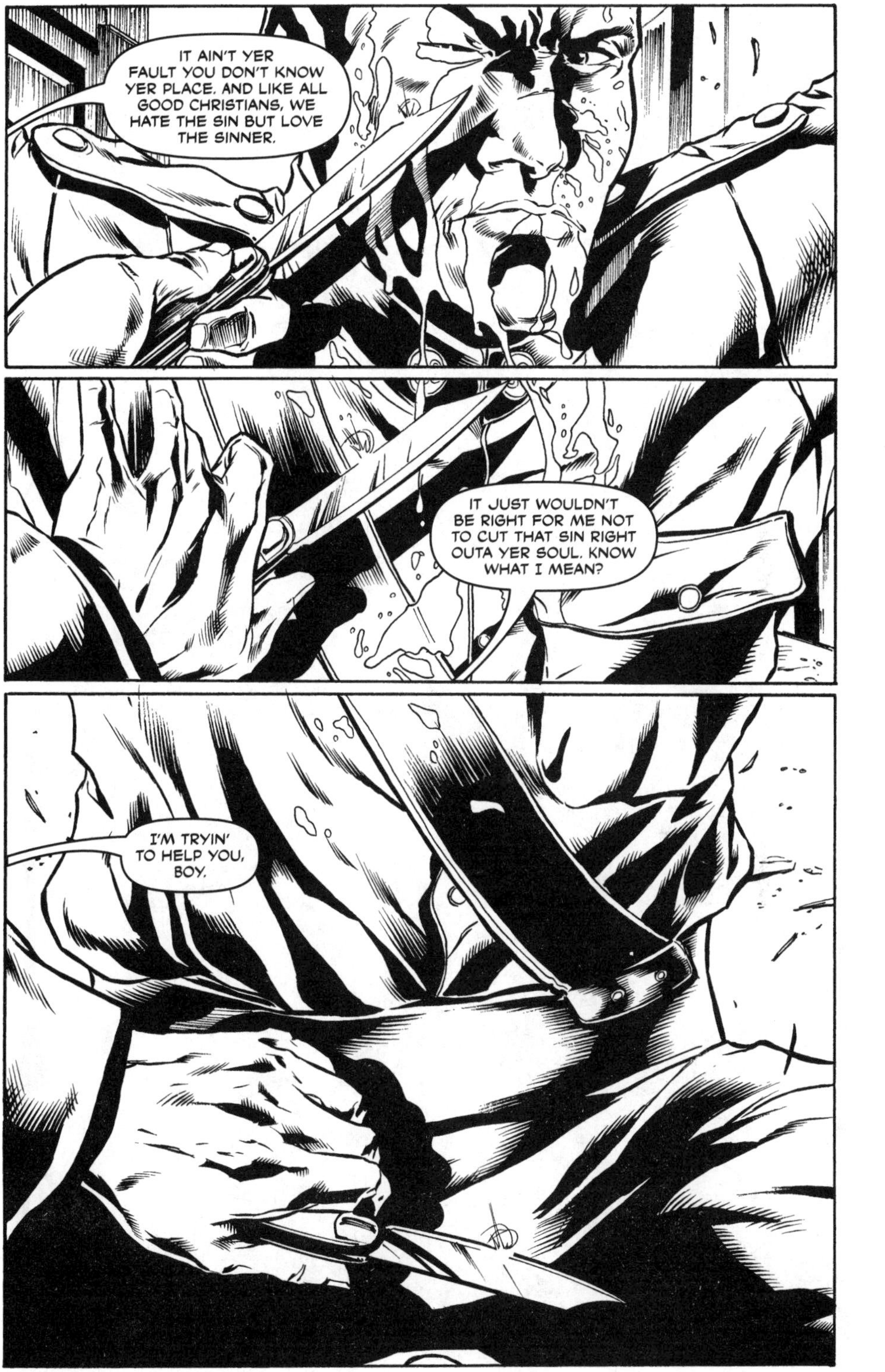
IT AIN'T YER FAULT YOU DON'T KNOW YER PLACE. AND LIKE ALL GOOD CHRISTIANS, WE HATE THE SIN BUT LOVE THE SINNER.
IT JUST WOULDN'T BE RIGHT FOR ME NOT TO CUT THAT SIN RIGHT OUTA YER SOUL. KNOW WHAT I MEAN?
I'M TRYIN' TO HELP YOU, BOY.

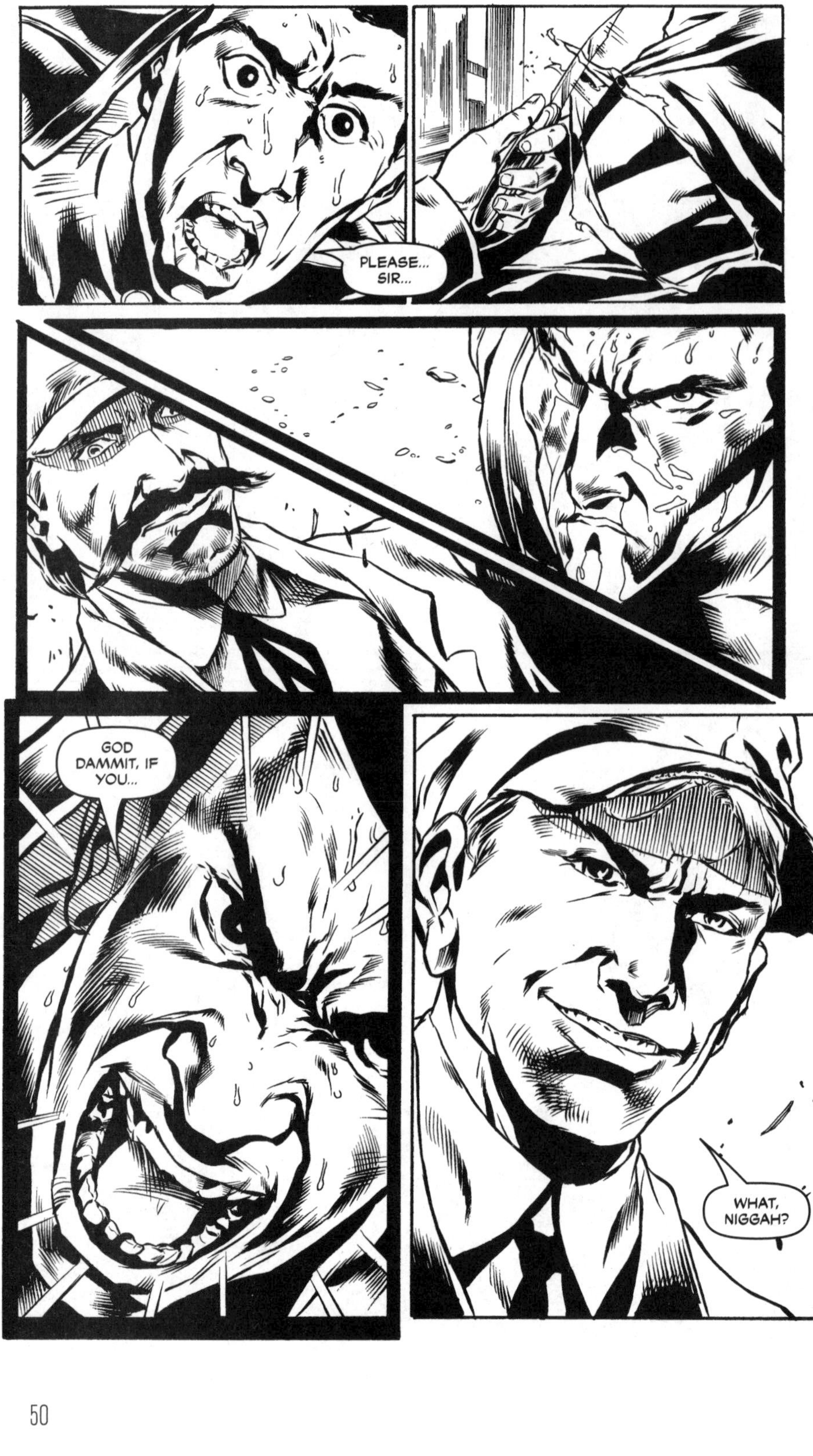
PLEASE... SIR...
GOD DAMMIT, IF YOU...
WHAT, NIGGAH?

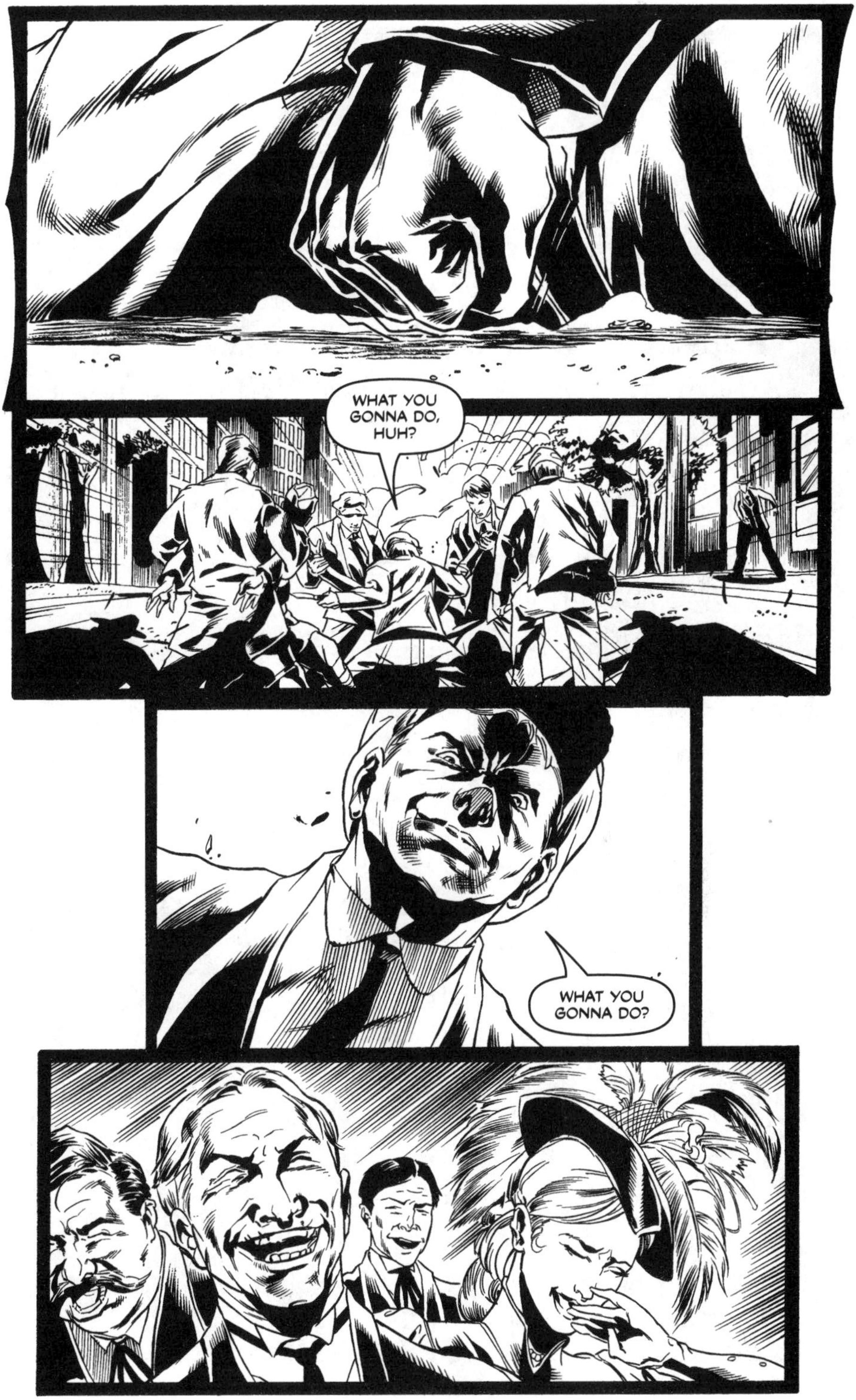
WHAT YOU GONNA DO, HUH?
WHAT YOU GONNA DO?

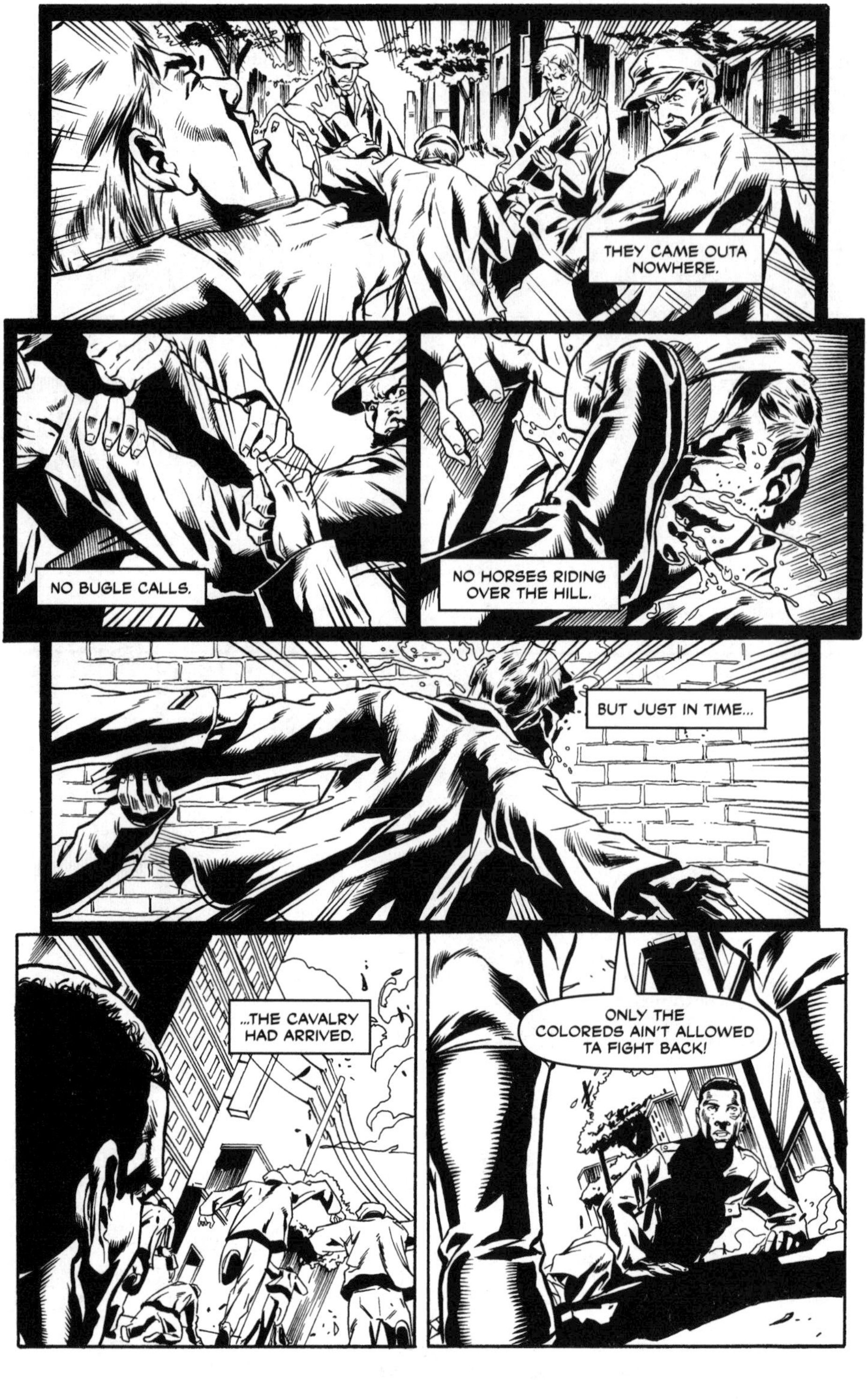
THEY CAME OUTA NOWHERE.
NO BUGLE CALLS.
NO HORSES RIDING OVER THE HILL.
BUT JUST IN TIME...
...THE CAVALRY HAD ARRIVED.
ONLY THE COLOREDS AIN'T ALLOWED TA FIGHT BACK!

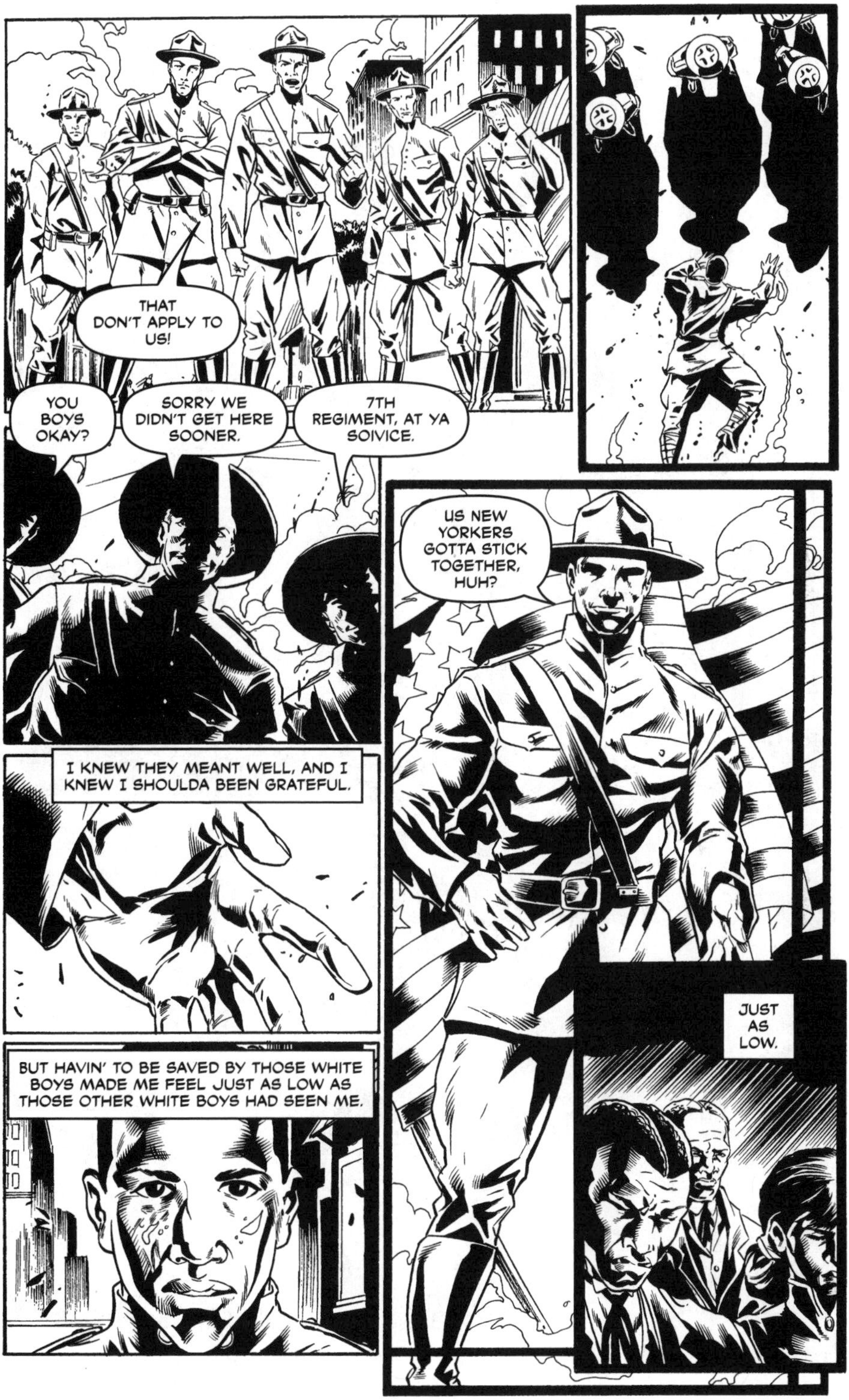
THAT DON'T APPLY TO US!
YOU BOYS OKAY?
SORRY WE DIDN'T GET HERE SOONER.
7TH REGIMENT, AT YA SOIVICE.
US NEW YORKERS GOTTA STICK TOGETHER, HUH?
I KNEW THEY MEANT WELL, AND I KNEW I SHOULDA BEEN GRATEFUL.
BUT HAVIN' TO BE SAVED BY THOSE WHITE BOYS MADE ME FEEL JUST AS LOW AS THOSE OTHER WHITE BOYS HAD SEEN ME.
JUST AS LOW.

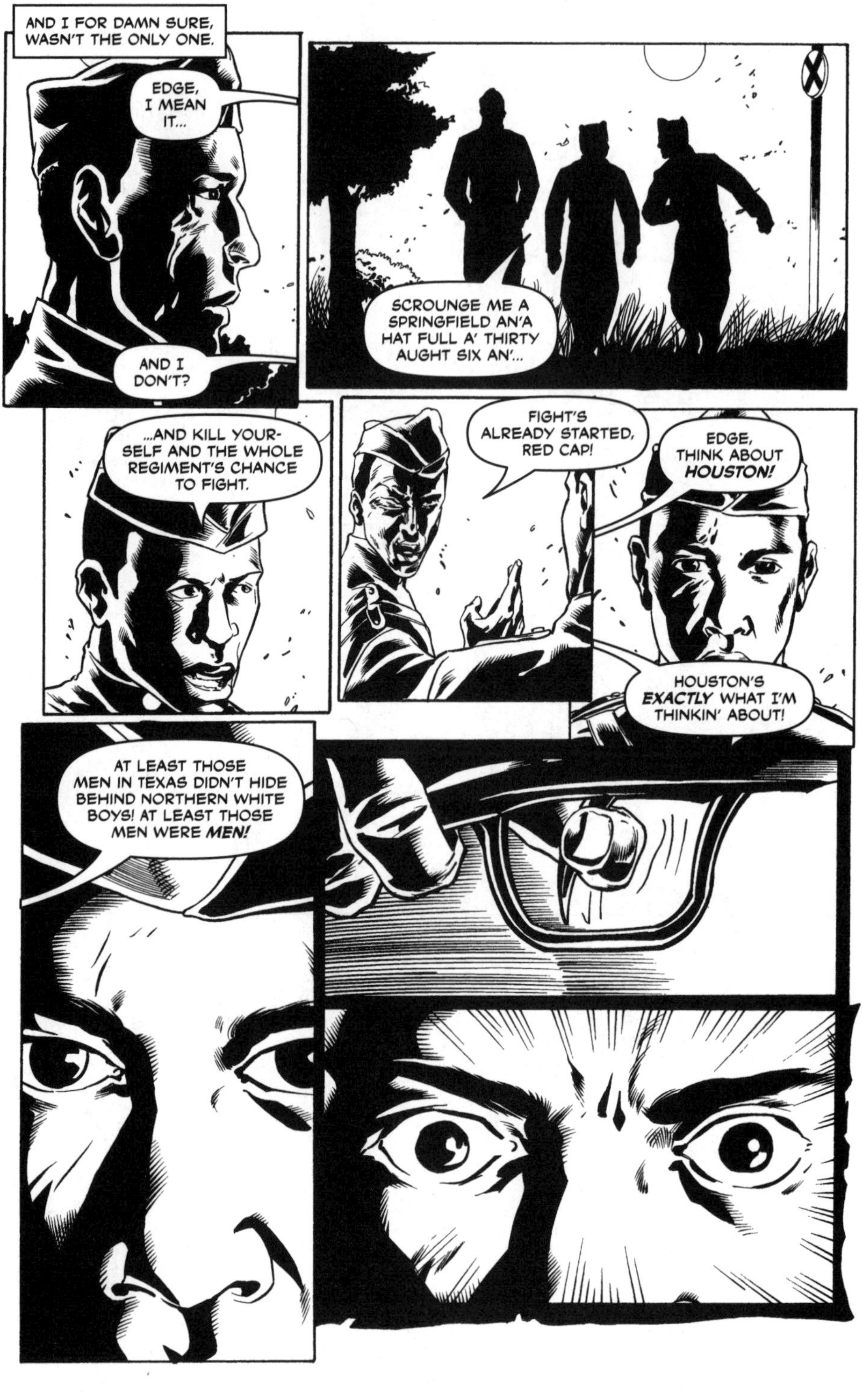
AND I FOR DAMN SURE, WASN'T THE ONLY ONE.
EDGE, I MEAN IT...
AND I DON'T?
SCROUNGE ME A SPRINGFIELD AN'A HAT FULL A' THIRTY AUGHT SIX AN'...
...AND KILL YOURSELF AND THE WHOLE REGIMENT'S CHANCE TO FIGHT.
FIGHT'S ALREADY STARTED, RED CAP!
EDGE, THINK ABOUT HOUSTON!
HOUSTON'S EXACTLY WHAT I'M THINKIN' ABOUT!
AT LEAST THOSE MEN IN TEXAS DIDN'T HIDE BEHIND NORTHERN WHITE BOYS! AT LEAST THOSE MEN WERE MEN!

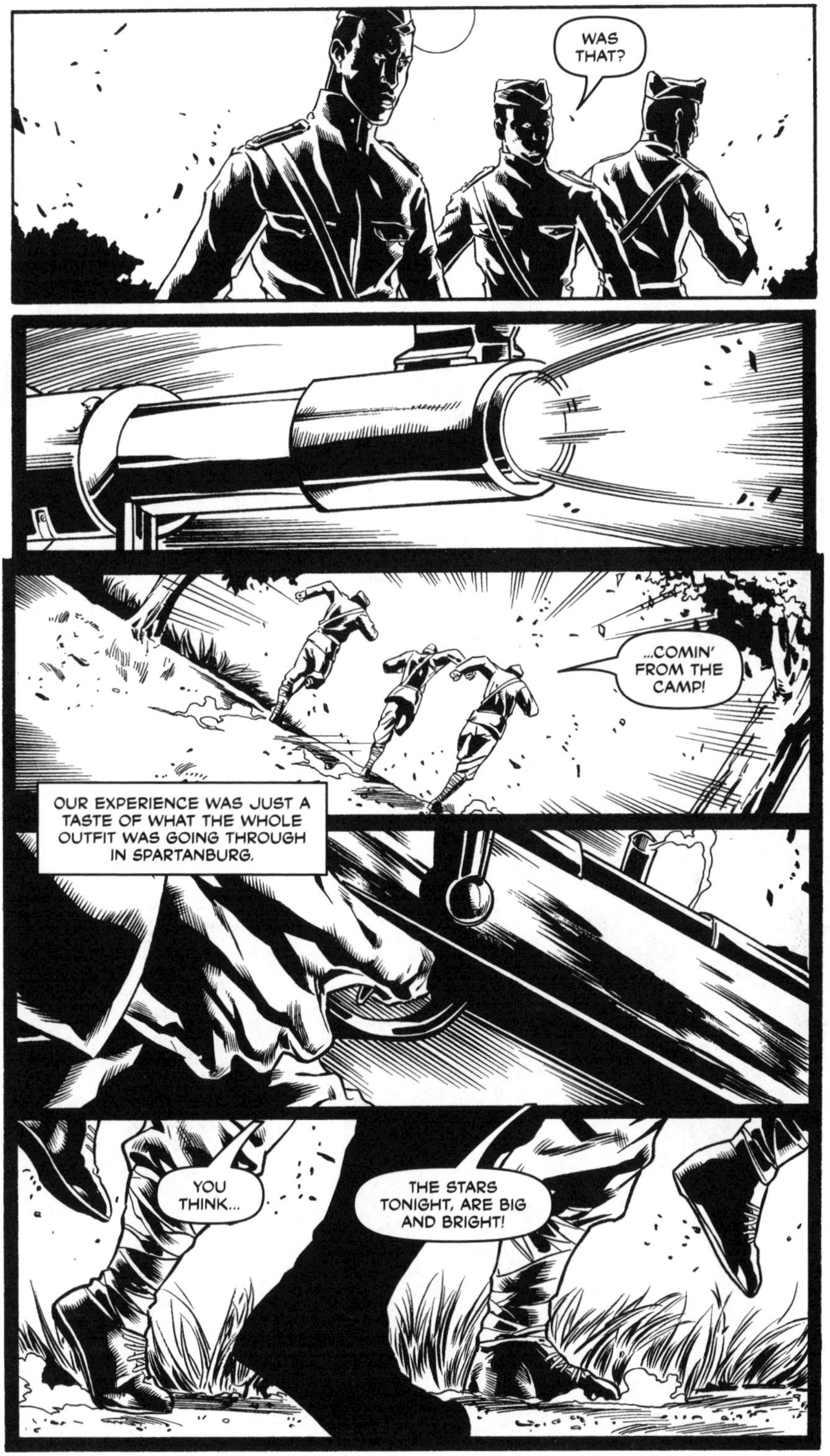
WAS THAT?
...COMIN' FROM THE CAMP!
OUR EXPERIENCE WAS JUST A TASTE OF WHAT THE WHOLE OUTFIT WAS GOING THROUGH IN SPARTANBURG.
YOU THINK...
THE STARS TONIGHT, ARE BIG AND BRIGHT!

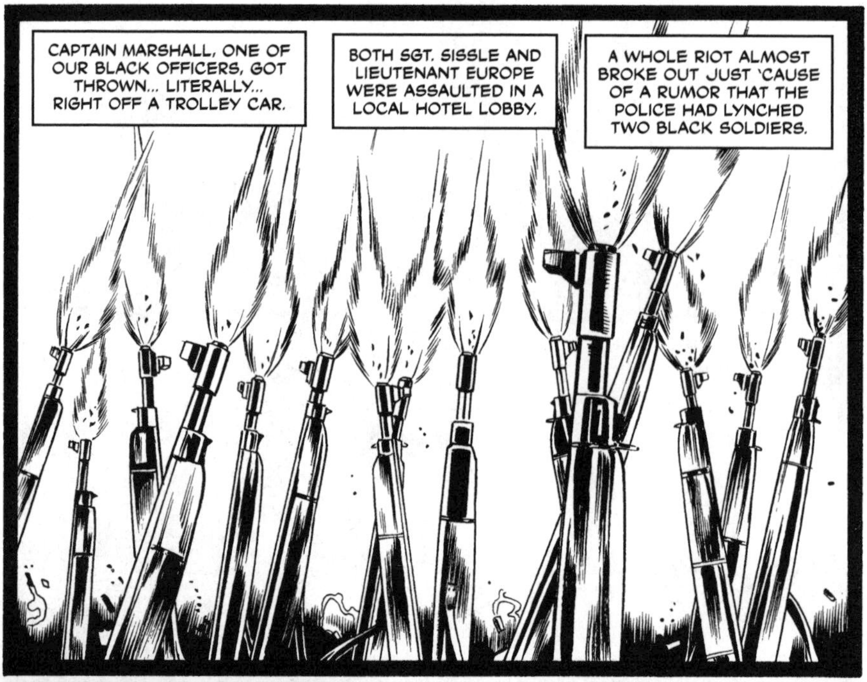
CAPTAIN MARSHALL, ONE OF OUR BLACK OFFICERS, GOT THROWN... LITERALLY... RIGHT OFF A TROLLEY CAR.
BOTH SGT. SISSLE AND LIEUTENANT EUROPE WERE ASSAULTED IN A LOCAL HOTEL LOBBY.
A WHOLE RIOT ALMOST BROKE OUT JUST 'CAUSE OF A RUMOR THAT THE POLICE HAD LYNCHED TWO BLACK SOLDIERS.

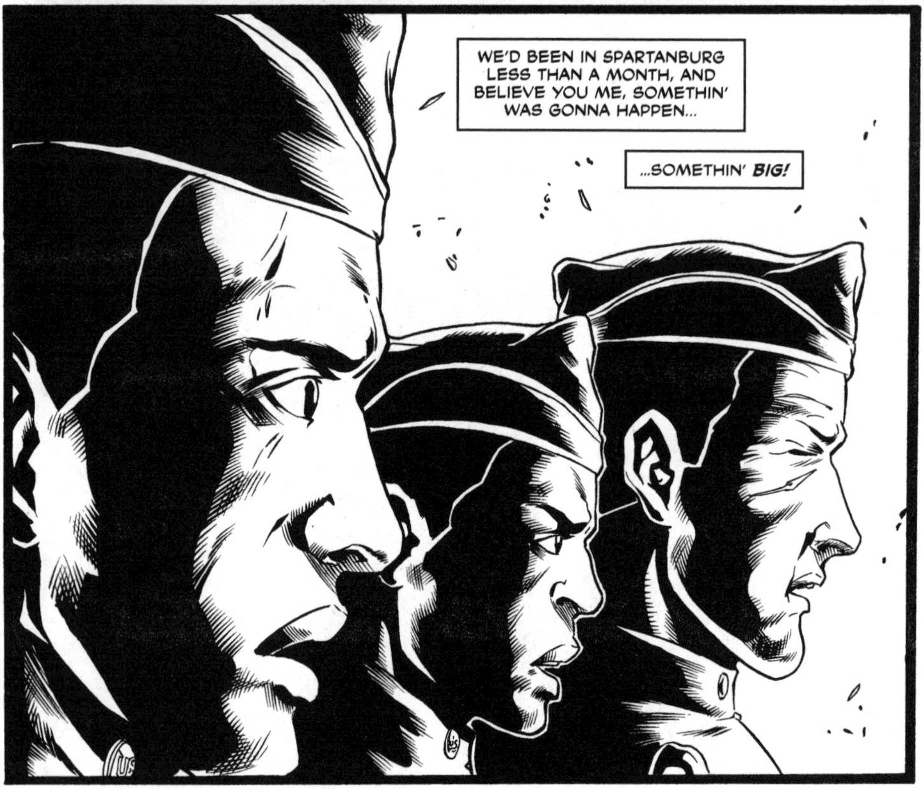
WE'D BEEN IN SPARTANBURG LESS THAN A MONTH, AND BELIEVE YOU ME, SOMETHIN' WAS GONNA HAPPEN...
...SOMETHIN' *BIG!*

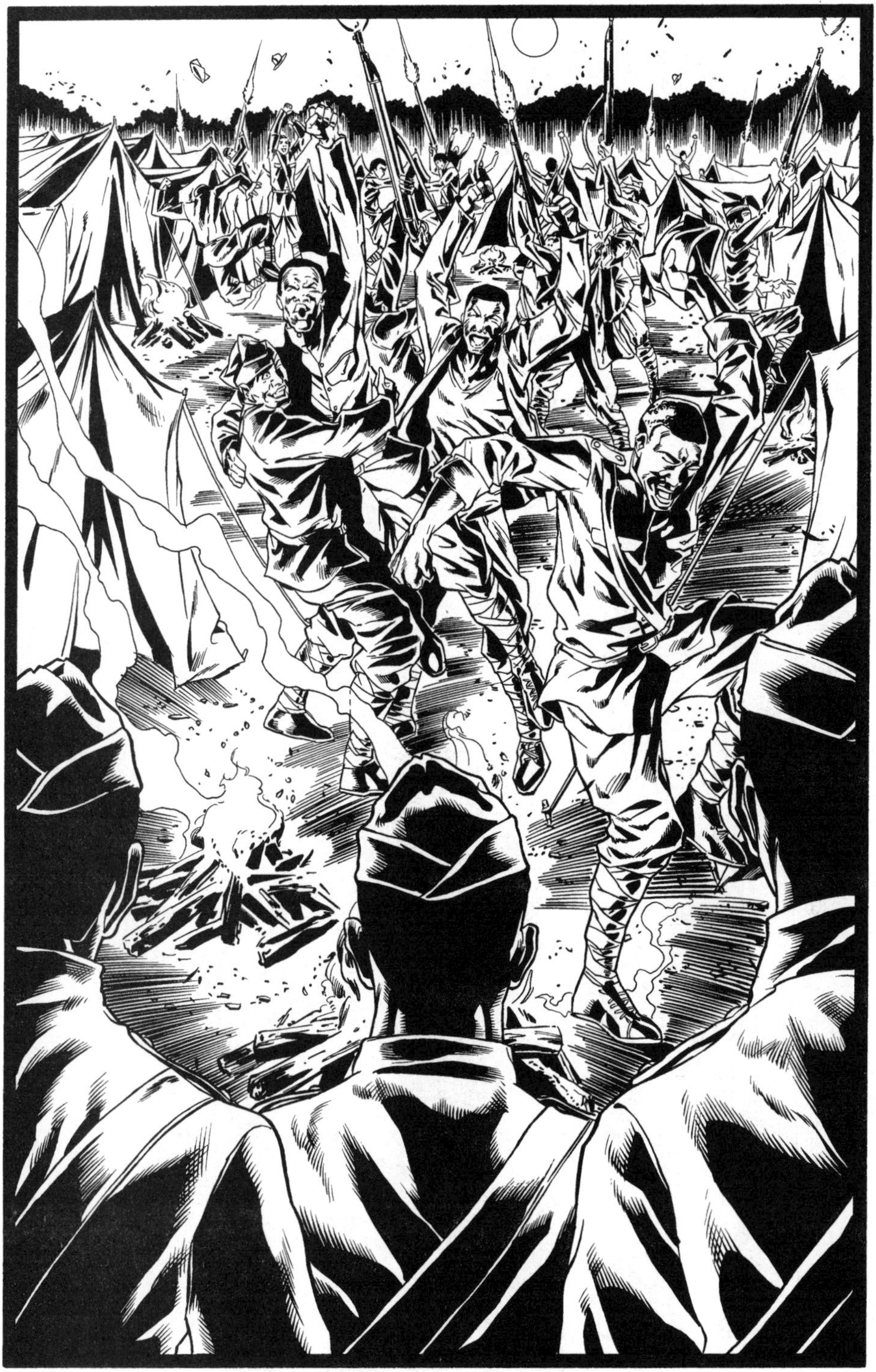

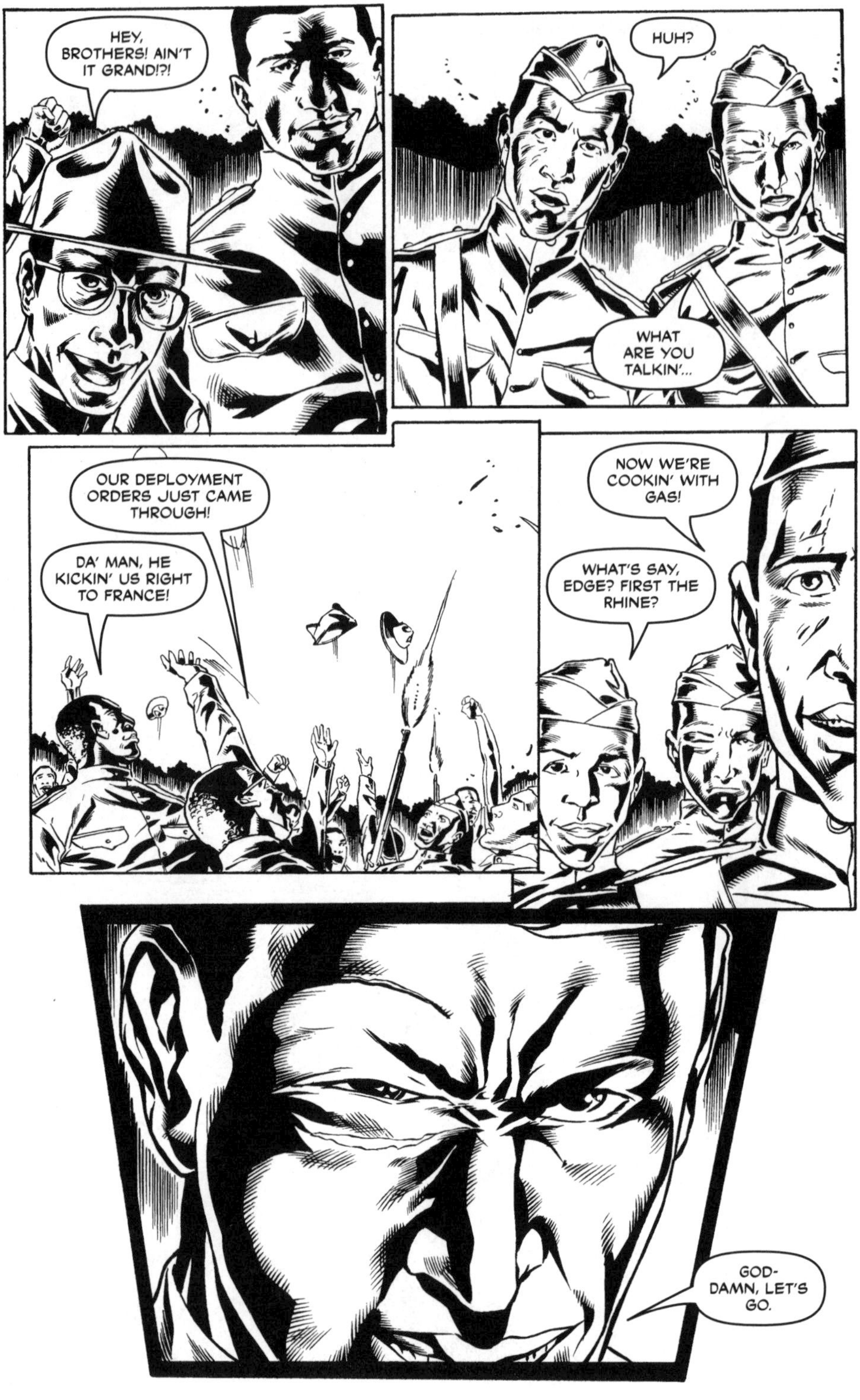
HEY, BROTHERS! AIN'T IT GRAND!?!
HUH?
WHAT ARE YOU TALKIN'...
OUR DEPLOYMENT ORDERS JUST CAME THROUGH!
DA' MAN, HE KICKIN' US RIGHT TO FRANCE!
NOW WE'RE COOKIN' WITH GAS!
WHAT'S SAY, EDGE? FIRST THE RHINE?
GOD-DAMN, LET'S GO.

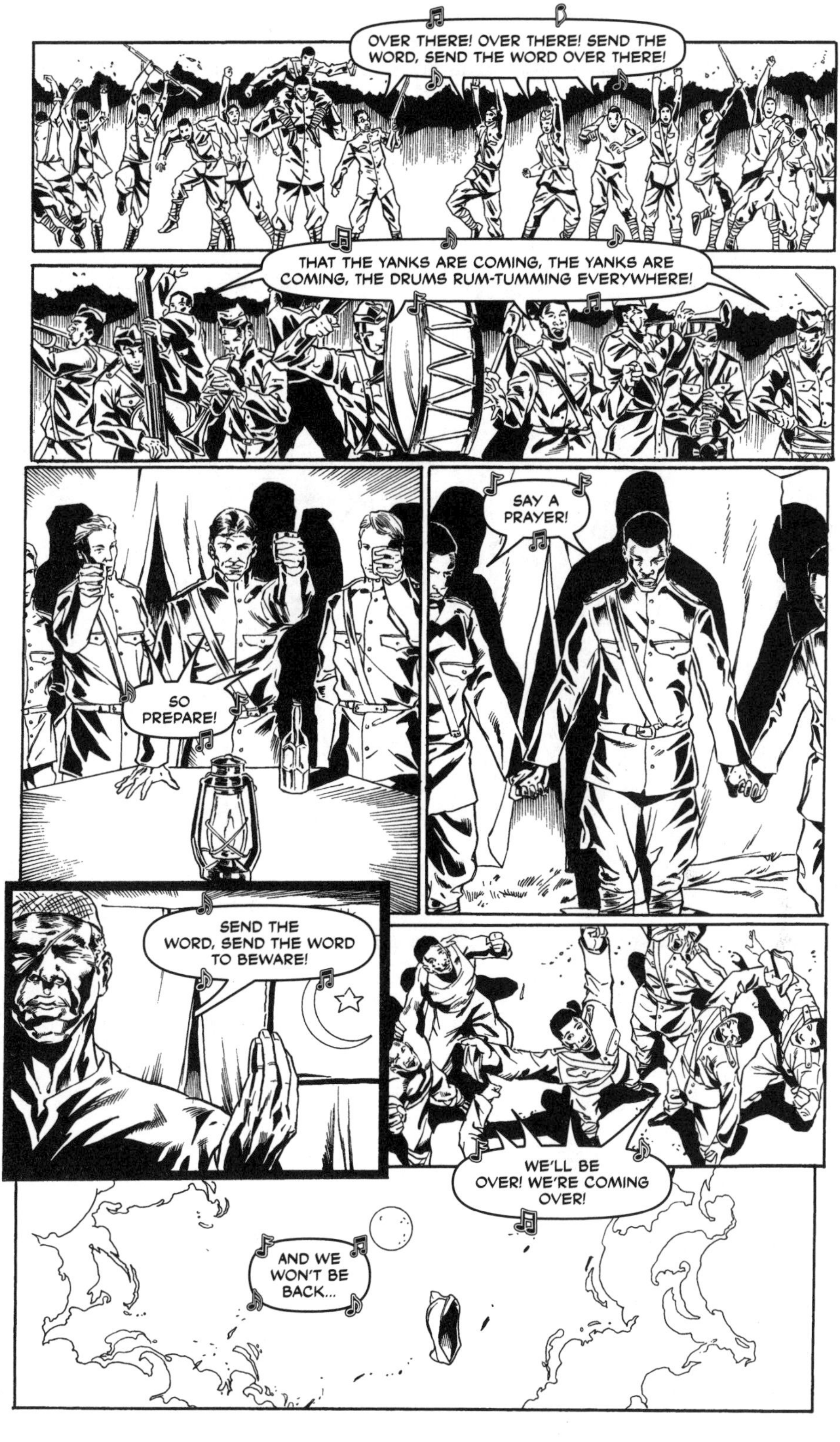
OVER THERE! OVER THERE! SEND THE WORD, SEND THE WORD OVER THERE!
THAT THE YANKS ARE COMING, THE YANKS ARE COMING, THE DRUMS RUM-TUMMING EVERYWHERE!
SO PREPARE!
SAY A PRAYER!
SEND THE WORD, SEND THE WORD TO BEWARE!
WE'LL BE OVER! WE'RE COMING OVER!
AND WE WON'T BE BACK...

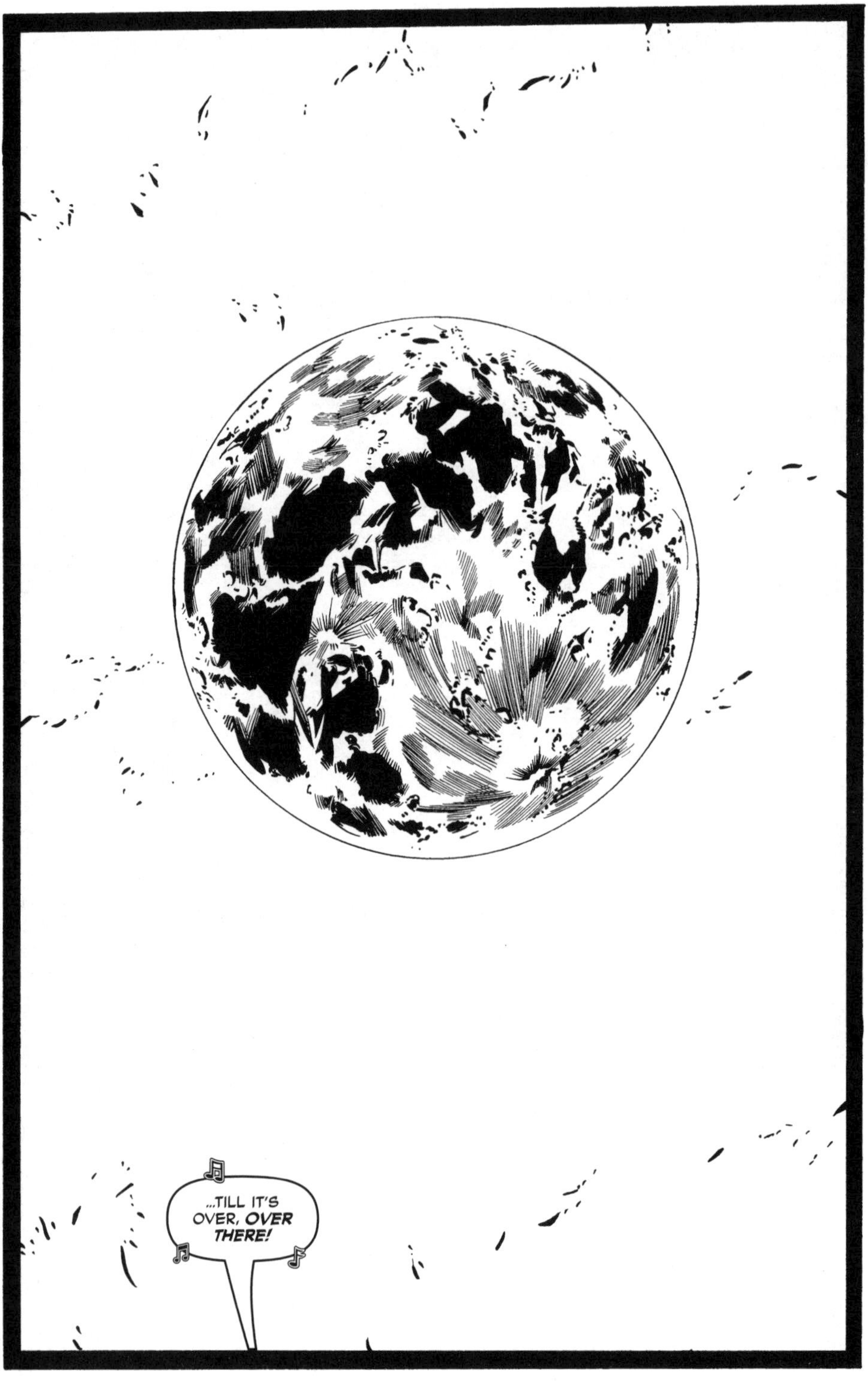
...TILL IT'S OVER, **OVER THERE!**

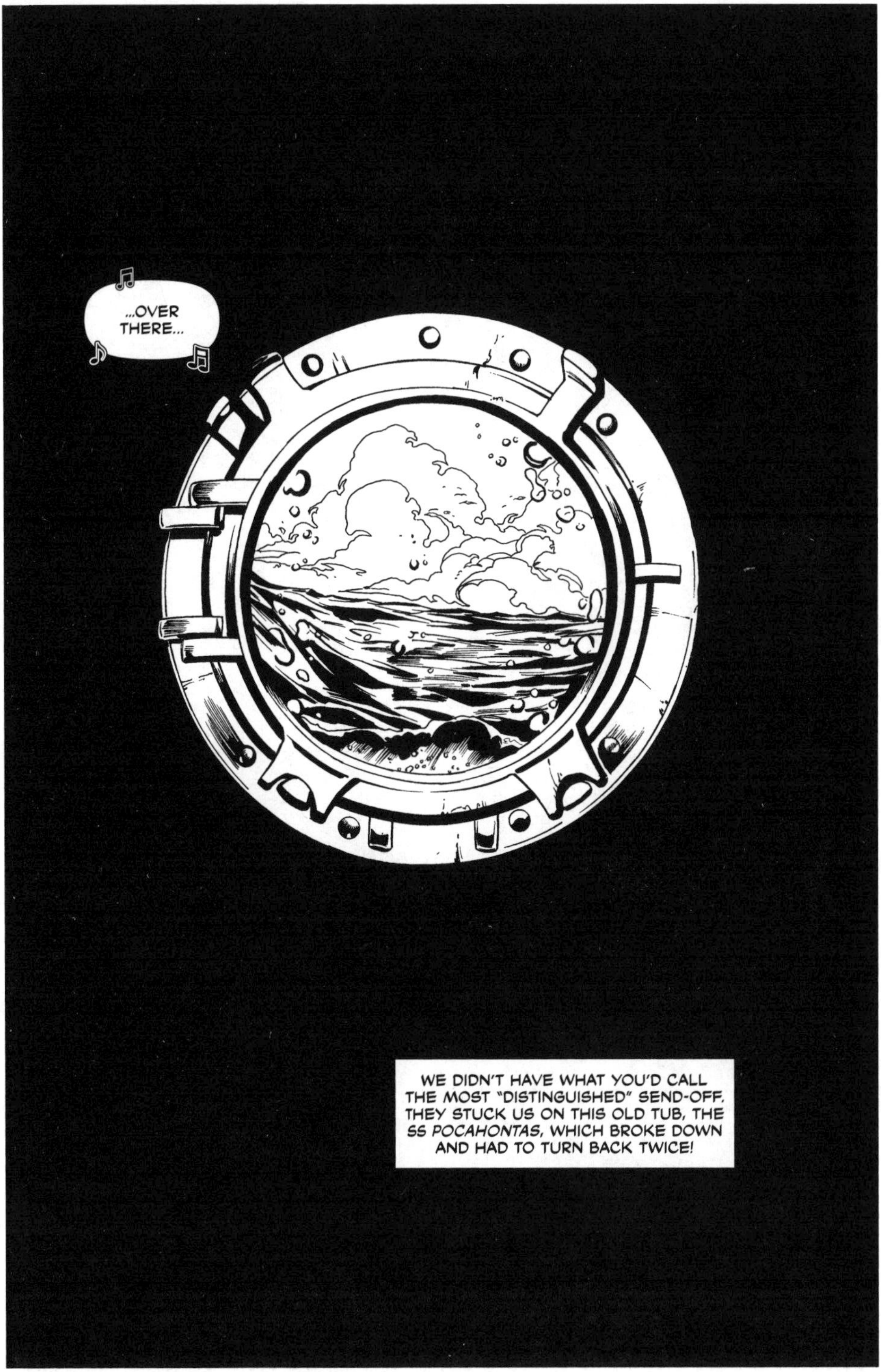
...OVER THERE...
WE DIDN'T HAVE WHAT YOU'D CALL THE MOST "DISTINGUISHED" SEND-OFF. THEY STUCK US ON THIS OLD TUB, THE SS *POCAHONTAS*, WHICH BROKE DOWN AND HAD TO TURN BACK TWICE!

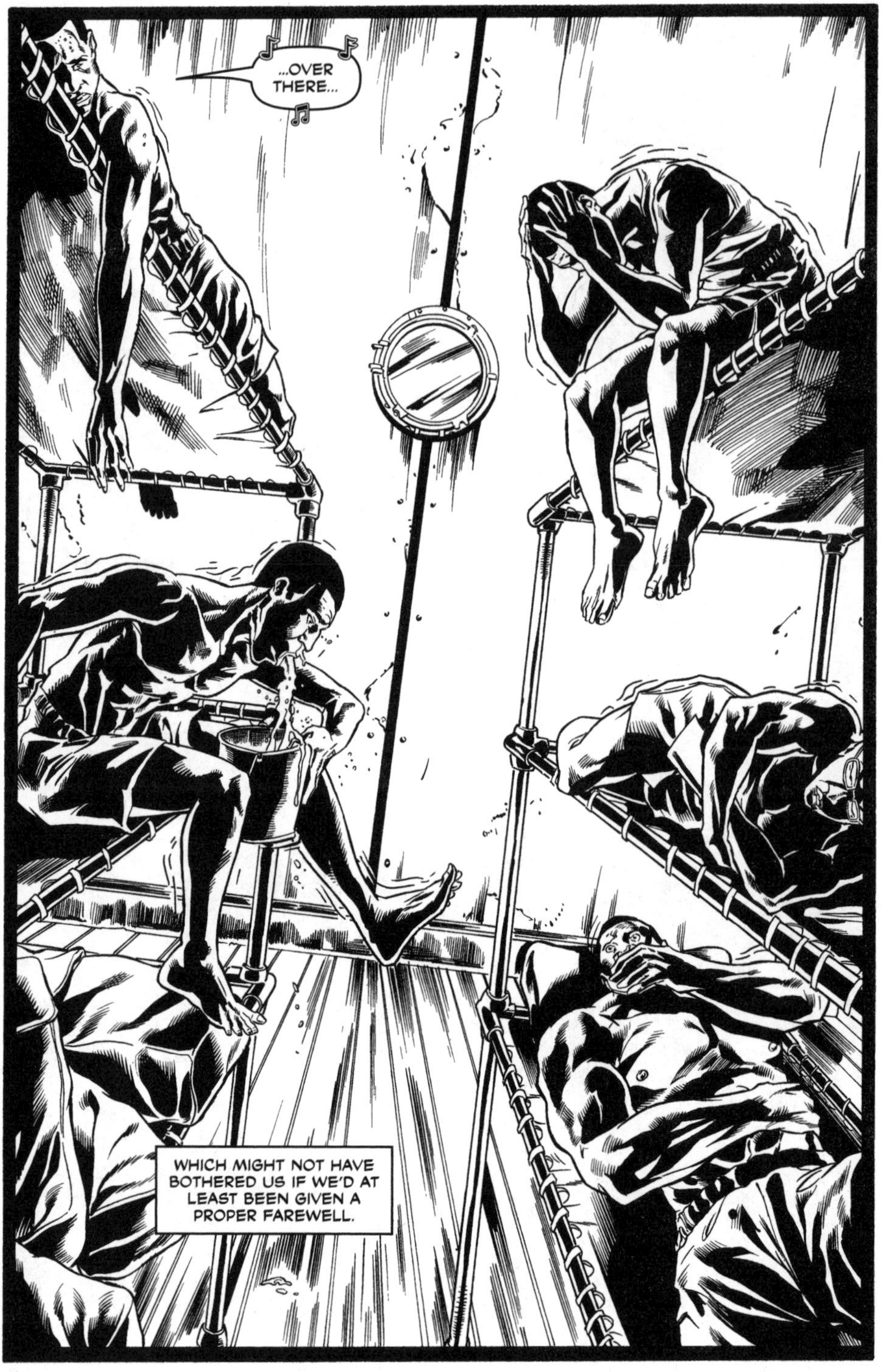
...OVER THERE...
WHICH MIGHT NOT HAVE BOTHERED US IF WE'D AT LEAST BEEN GIVEN A PROPER FAREWELL.

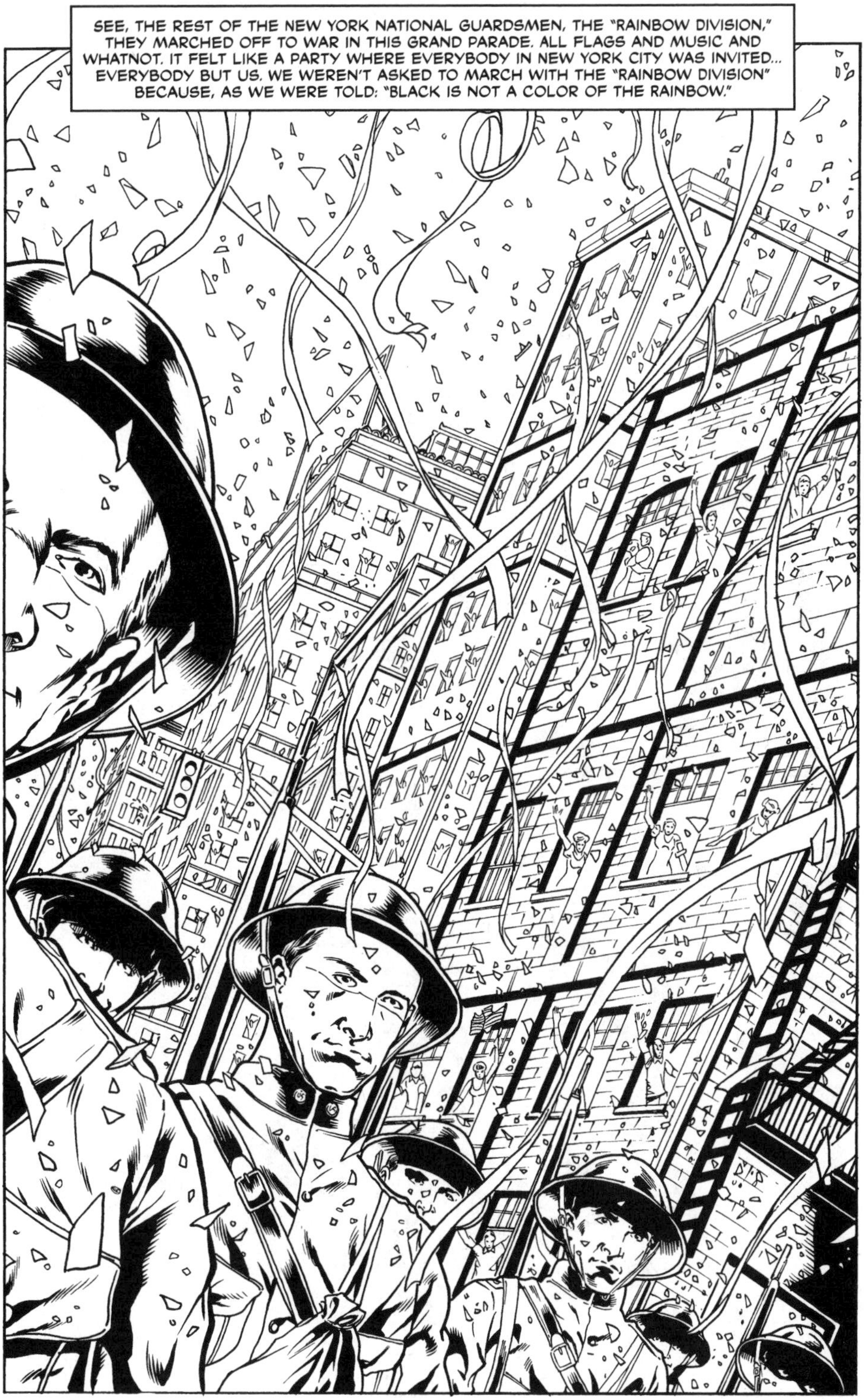
SEE, THE REST OF THE NEW YORK NATIONAL GUARDSMEN, THE "RAINBOW DIVISION," THEY MARCHED OFF TO WAR IN THIS GRAND PARADE. ALL FLAGS AND MUSIC AND WHATNOT. IT FELT LIKE A PARTY WHERE EVERYBODY IN NEW YORK CITY WAS INVITED... EVERYBODY BUT US. WE WEREN'T ASKED TO MARCH WITH THE "RAINBOW DIVISION" BECAUSE, AS WE WERE TOLD: "BLACK IS NOT A COLOR OF THE RAINBOW."

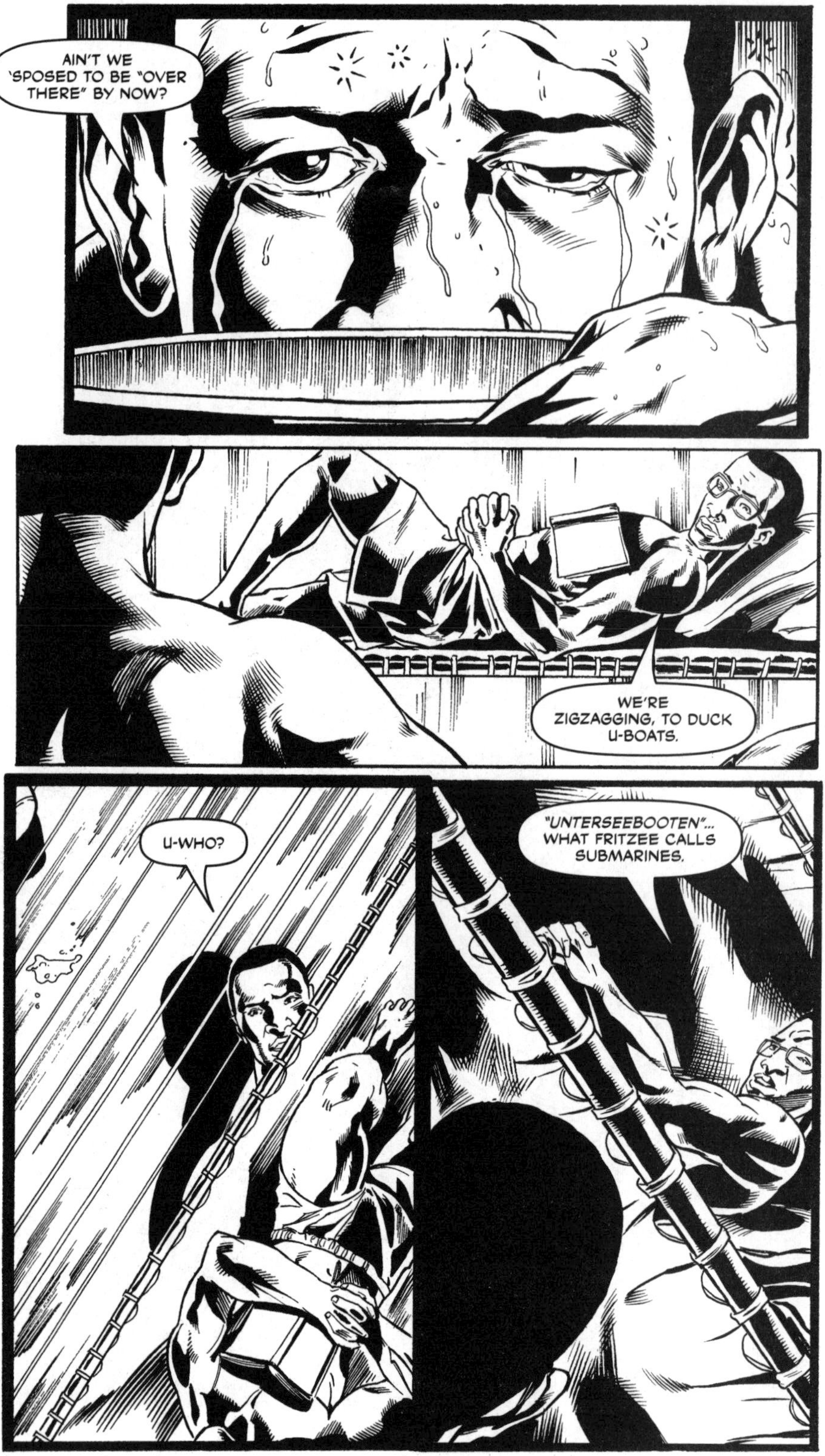
AIN'T WE 'SPOSED TO BE "OVER THERE" BY NOW?
WE'RE ZIGZAGGING, TO DUCK U-BOATS.
U-WHO?
"UNTERSEEBOOTEN"... WHAT FRITZEE CALLS SUBMARINES.

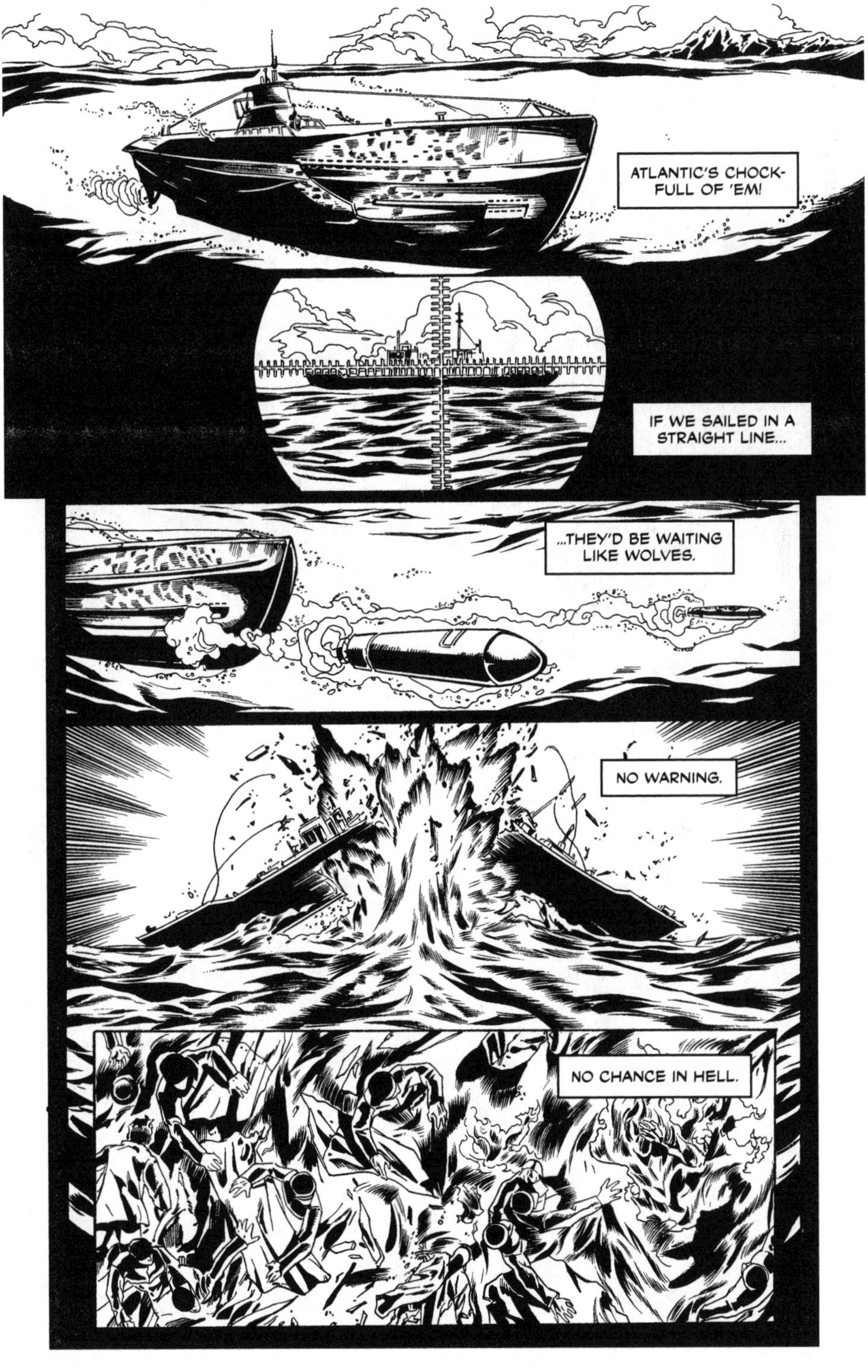
ATLANTIC'S CHOCK-FULL OF 'EM!
IF WE SAILED IN A STRAIGHT LINE...
...THEY'D BE WAITING LIKE WOLVES.
NO WARNING.
NO CHANCE IN HELL.

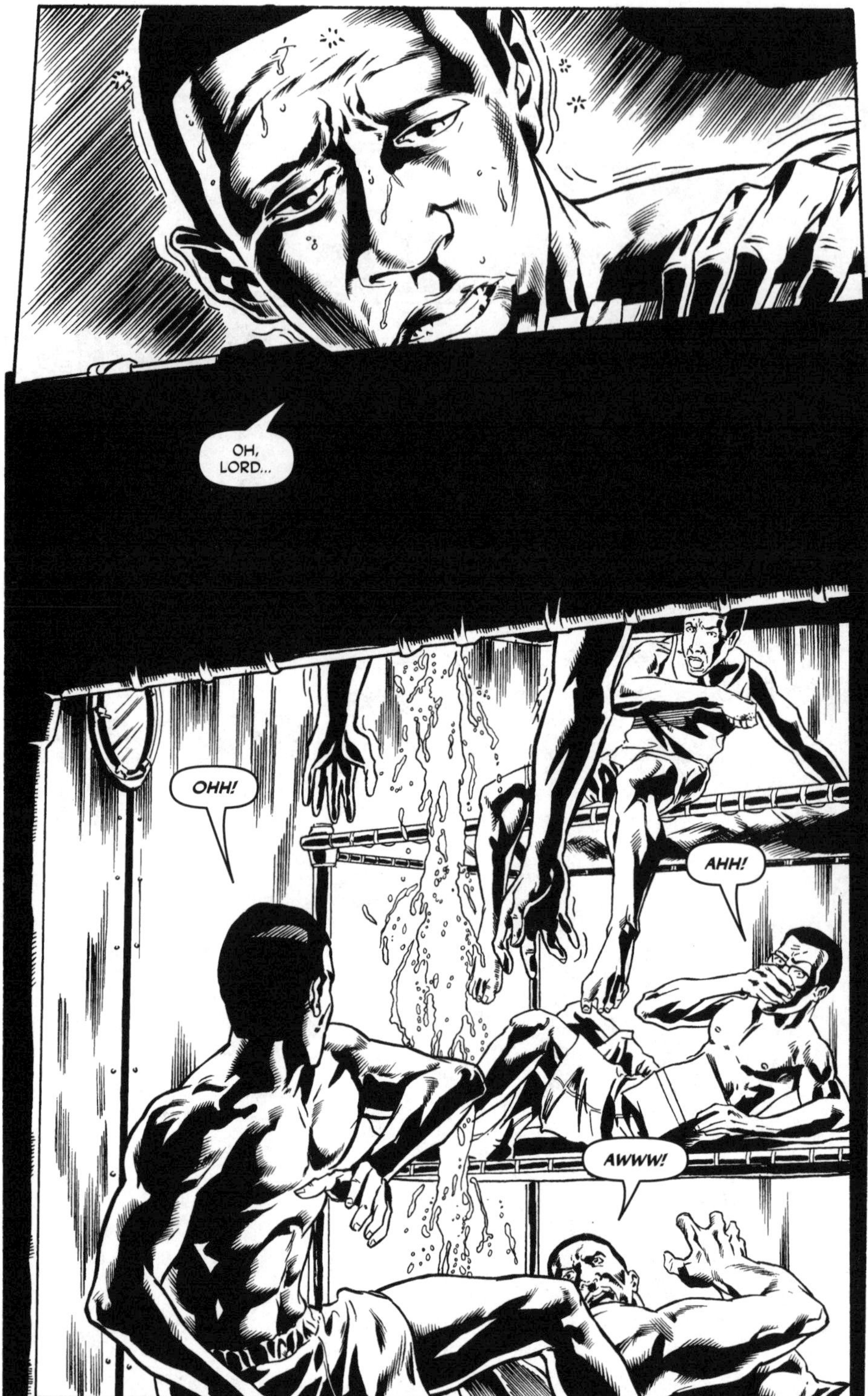
OH, LORD...
OHH!
AHH!
AWWW!

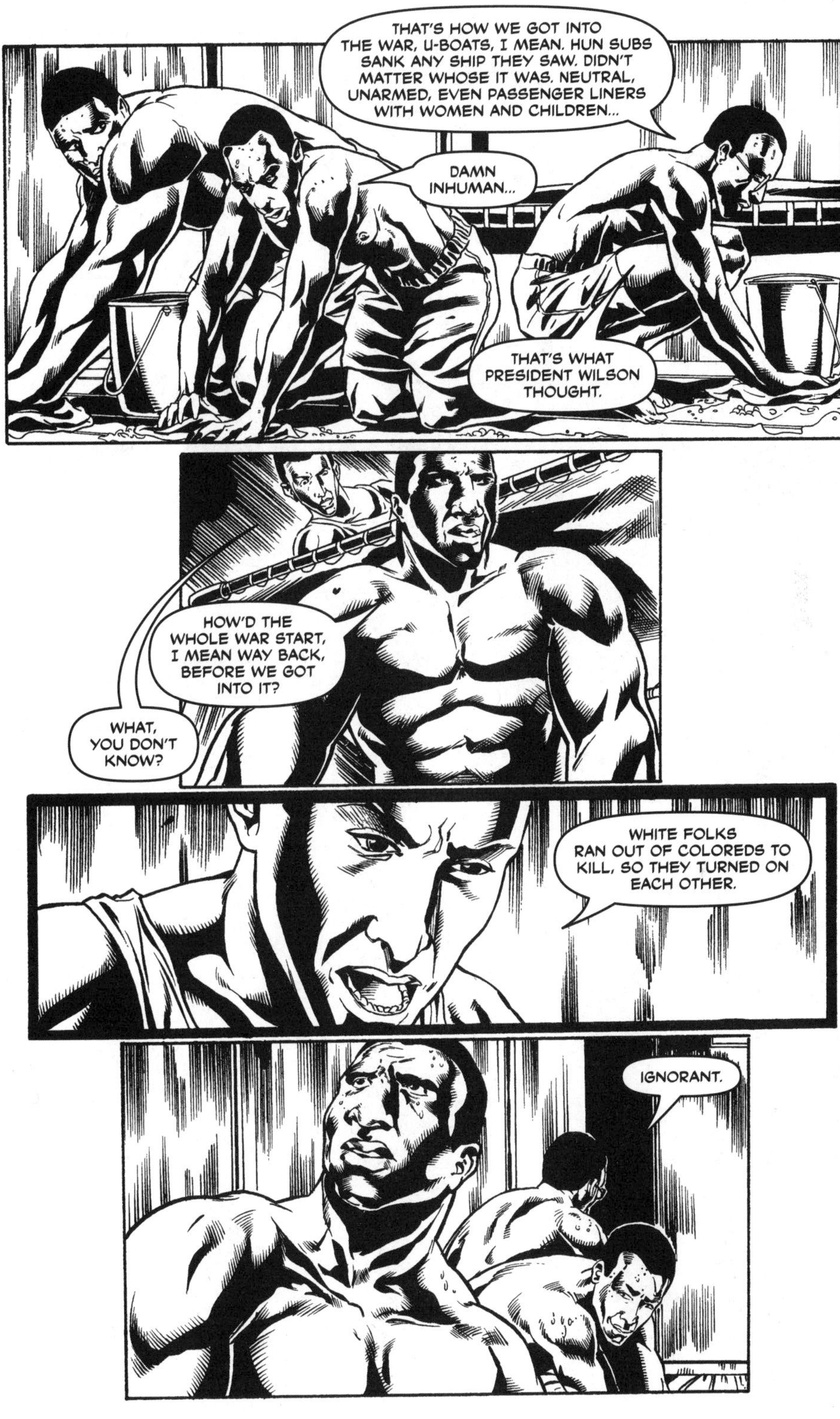
THAT'S HOW WE GOT INTO THE WAR, U-BOATS, I MEAN. HUN SUBS SANK ANY SHIP THEY SAW. DIDN'T MATTER WHOSE IT WAS. NEUTRAL, UNARMED, EVEN PASSENGER LINERS WITH WOMEN AND CHILDREN...
DAMN INHUMAN...
THAT'S WHAT PRESIDENT WILSON THOUGHT.
HOW'D THE WHOLE WAR START, I MEAN WAY BACK, BEFORE WE GOT INTO IT?
WHAT, YOU DON'T KNOW?
WHITE FOLKS RAN OUT OF COLOREDS TO KILL, SO THEY TURNED ON EACH OTHER.
IGNORANT.

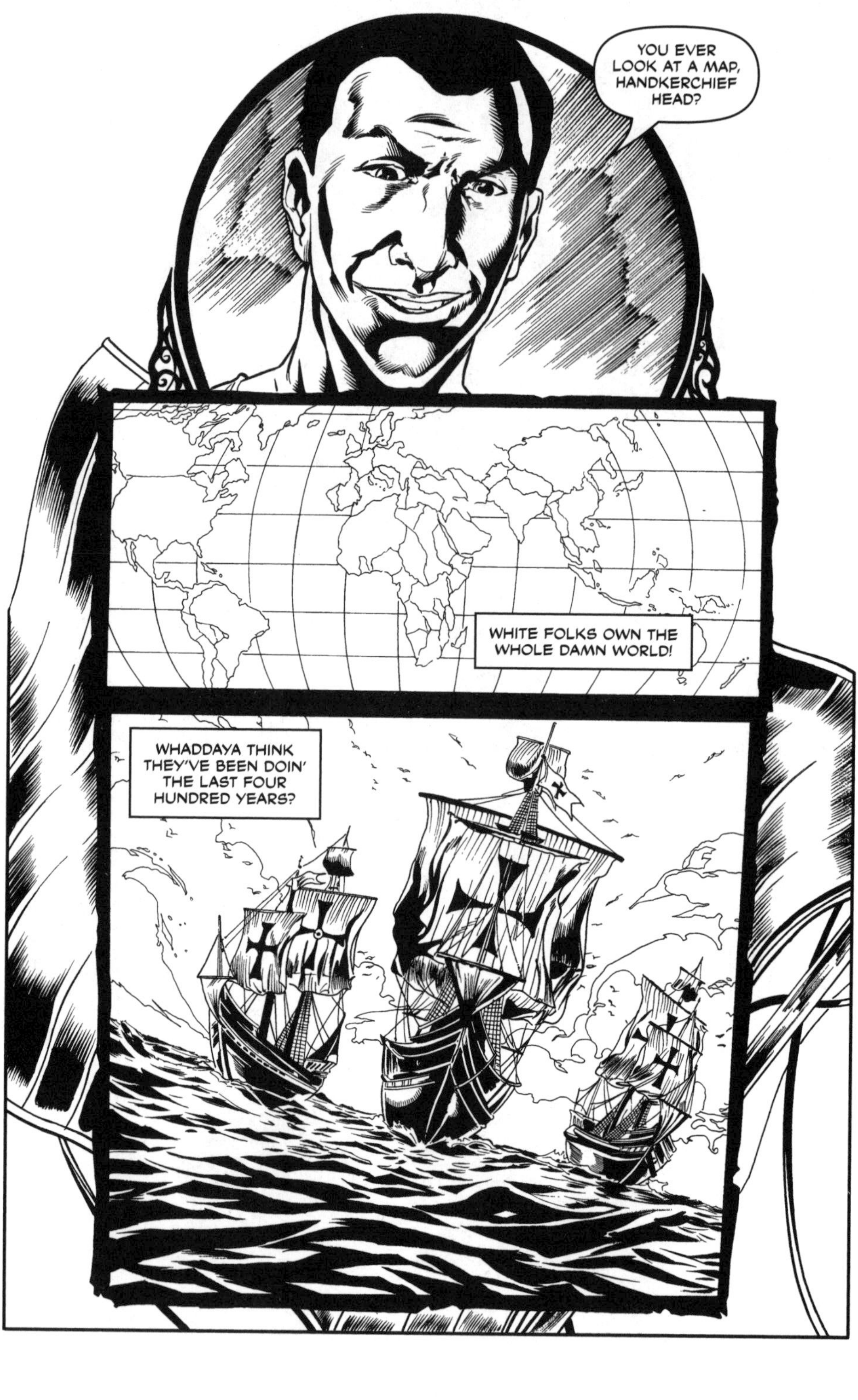

YOU EVER LOOK AT A MAP, HANDKERCHIEF HEAD?
WHITE FOLKS OWN THE WHOLE DAMN WORLD!
WHADDAYA THINK THEY'VE BEEN DOIN' THE LAST FOUR HUNDRED YEARS?

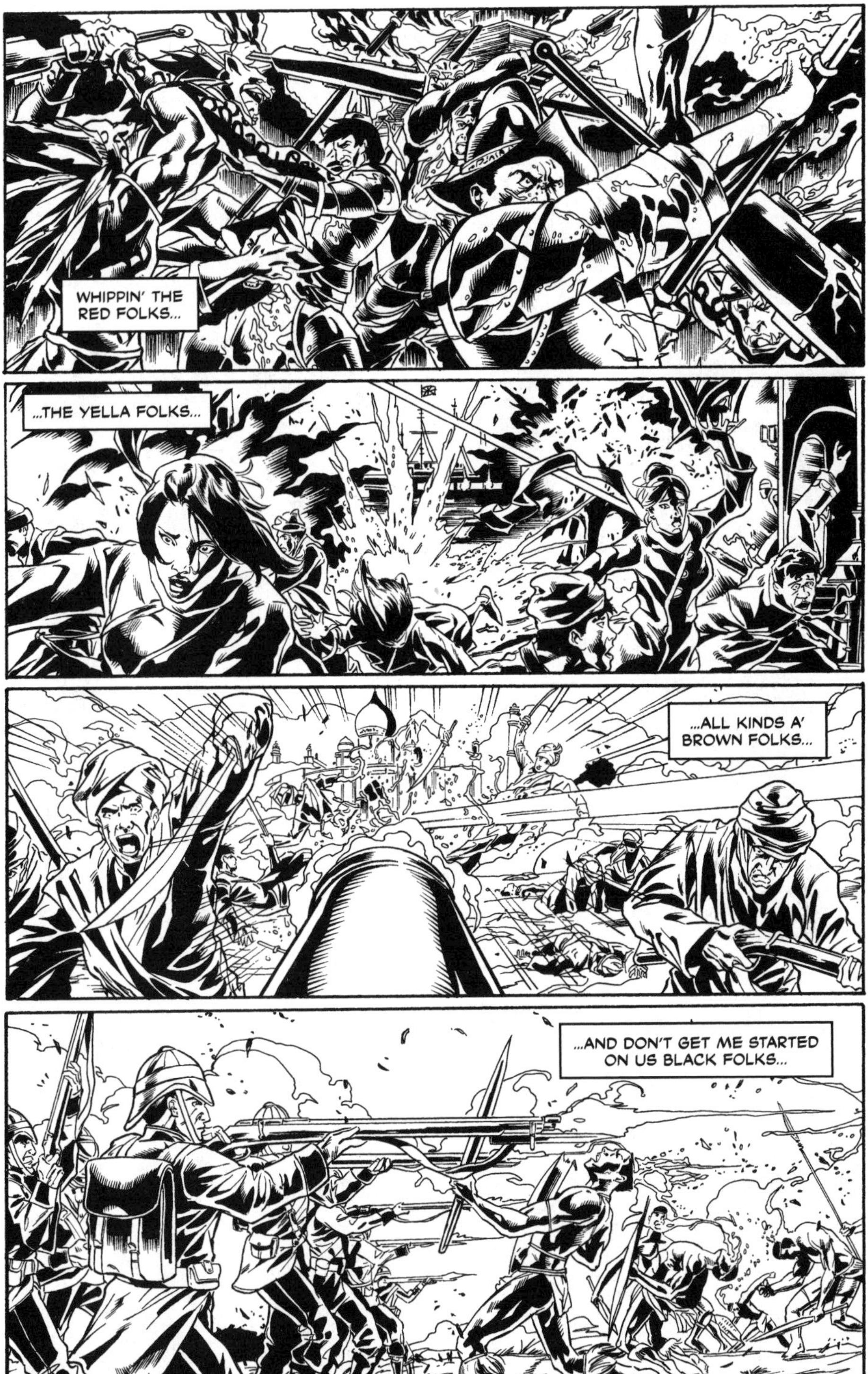
WHIPPIN' THE RED FOLKS...
...THE YELLA FOLKS...
...ALL KINDS A' BROWN FOLKS...
...AND DON'T GET ME STARTED ON US BLACK FOLKS...

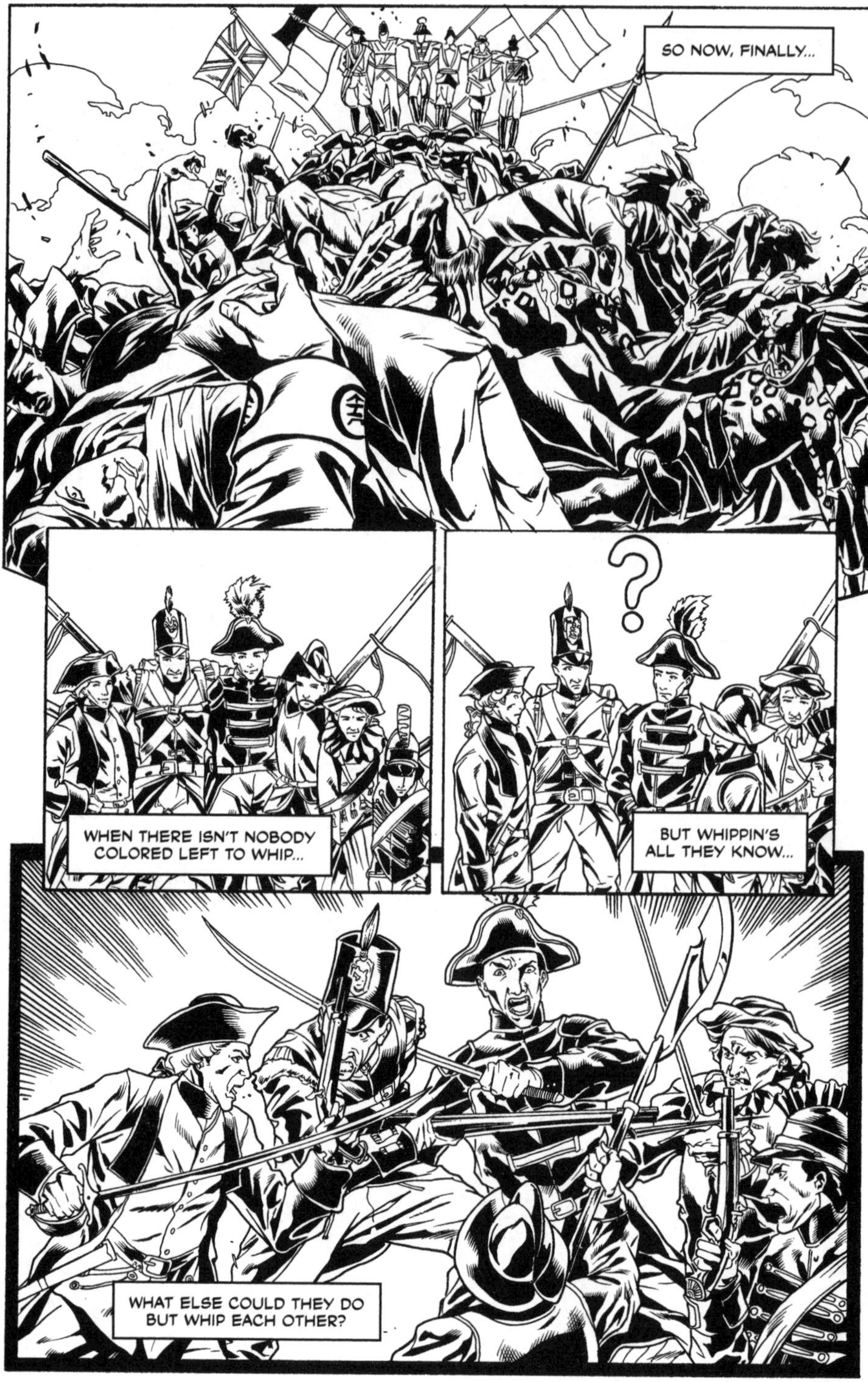
SO NOW, FINALLY...
WHEN THERE ISN'T NOBODY COLORED LEFT TO WHIP...
?
BUT WHIPPIN'S ALL THEY KNOW...
WHAT ELSE COULD THEY DO BUT WHIP EACH OTHER?

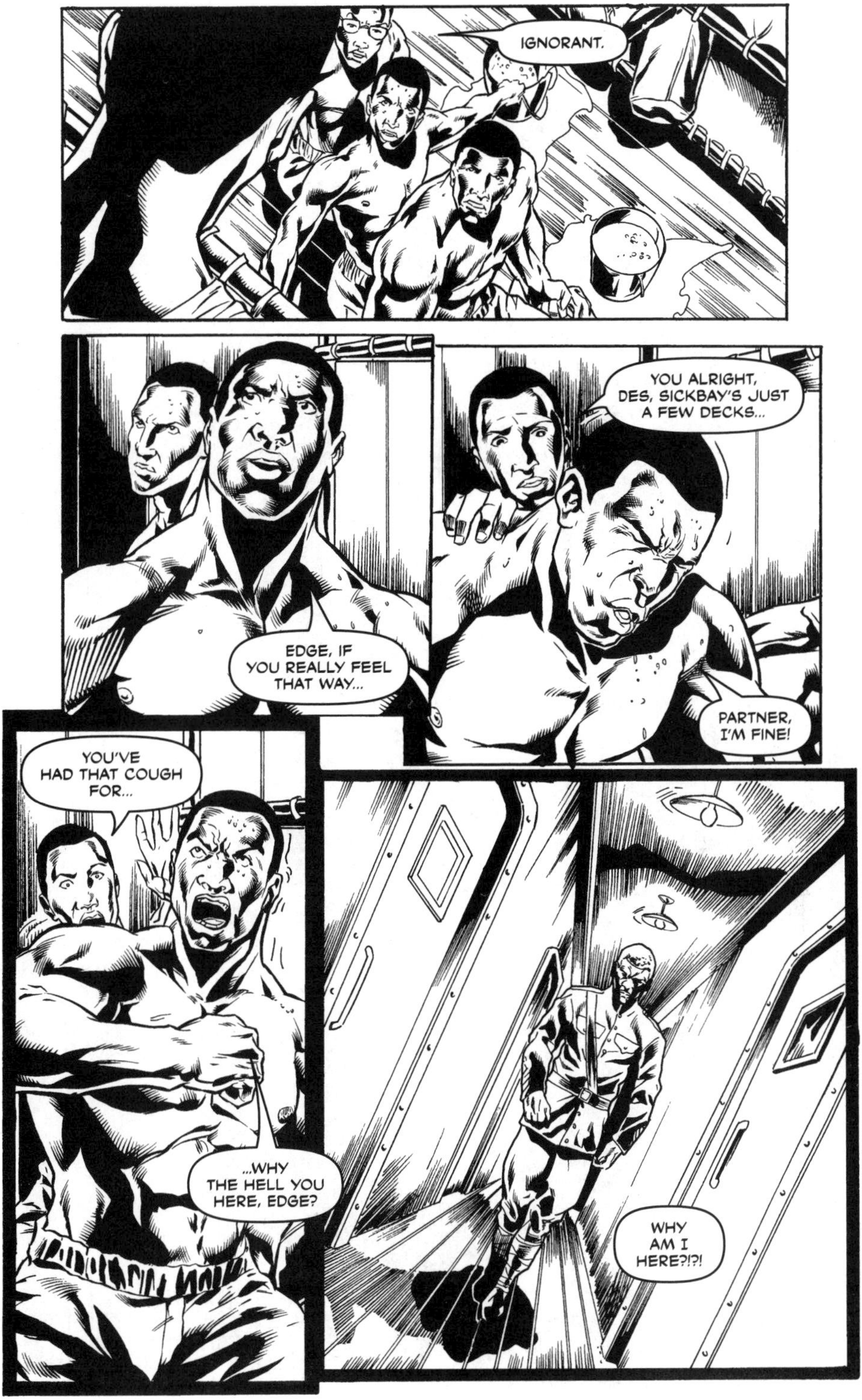
IGNORANT.
EDGE, IF YOU REALLY FEEL THAT WAY...
YOU ALRIGHT, DES, SICKBAY'S JUST A FEW DECKS...
PARTNER, I'M FINE!
YOU'VE HAD THAT COUGH FOR...
...WHY THE HELL YOU HERE, EDGE?
WHY AM I HERE?!?!

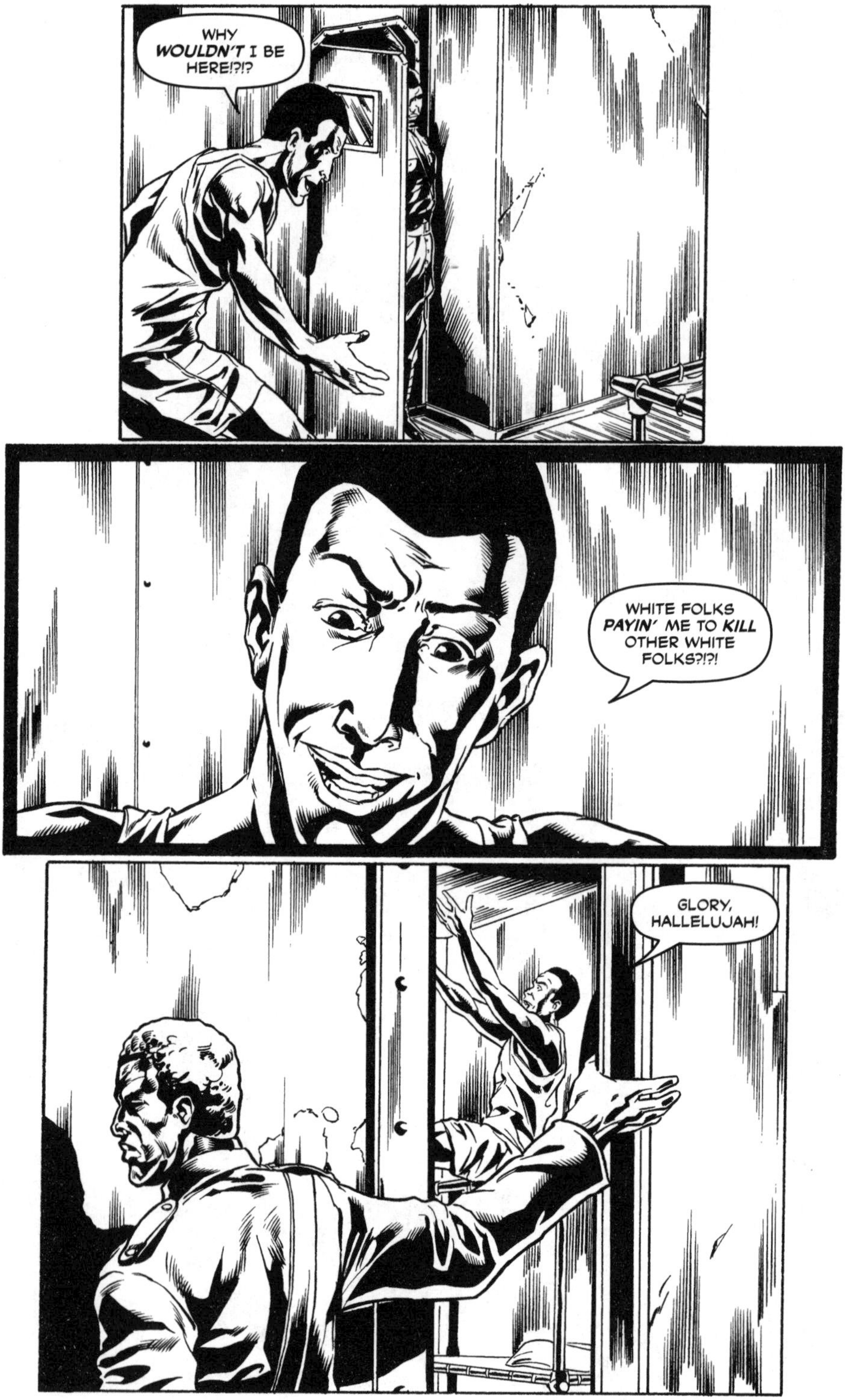
WHY *WOULDN'T* I BE HERE!?!?
WHITE FOLKS *PAYIN'* ME TO *KILL* OTHER WHITE FOLKS?!?!
GLORY, HALLELUJAH!

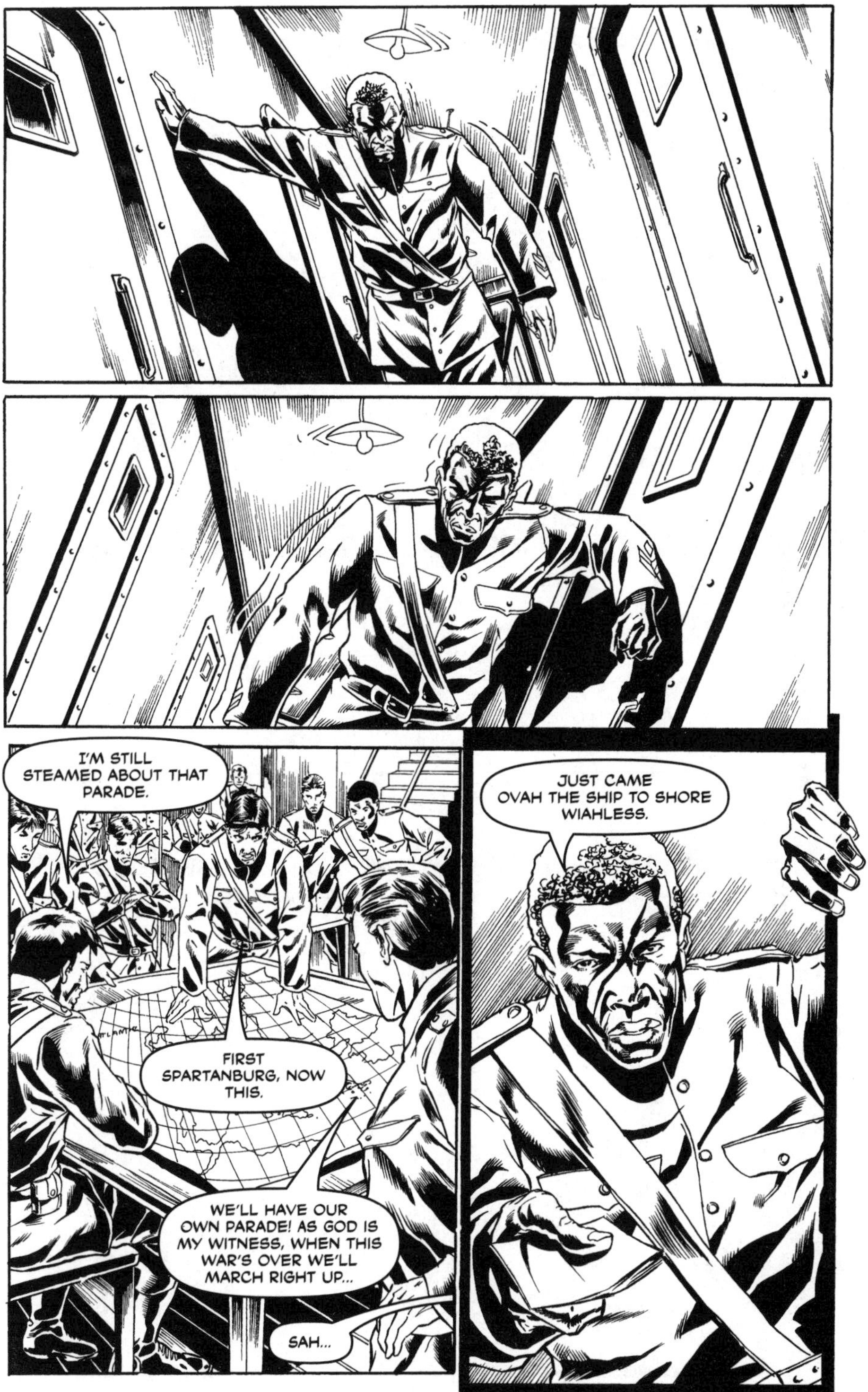
I'M STILL STEAMED ABOUT THAT PARADE.
FIRST SPARTANBURG, NOW THIS.
WE'LL HAVE OUR OWN PARADE! AS GOD IS MY WITNESS, WHEN THIS WAR'S OVER WE'LL MARCH RIGHT UP...
SAH...
JUST CAME OVAH THE SHIP TO SHORE WIAHLESS.

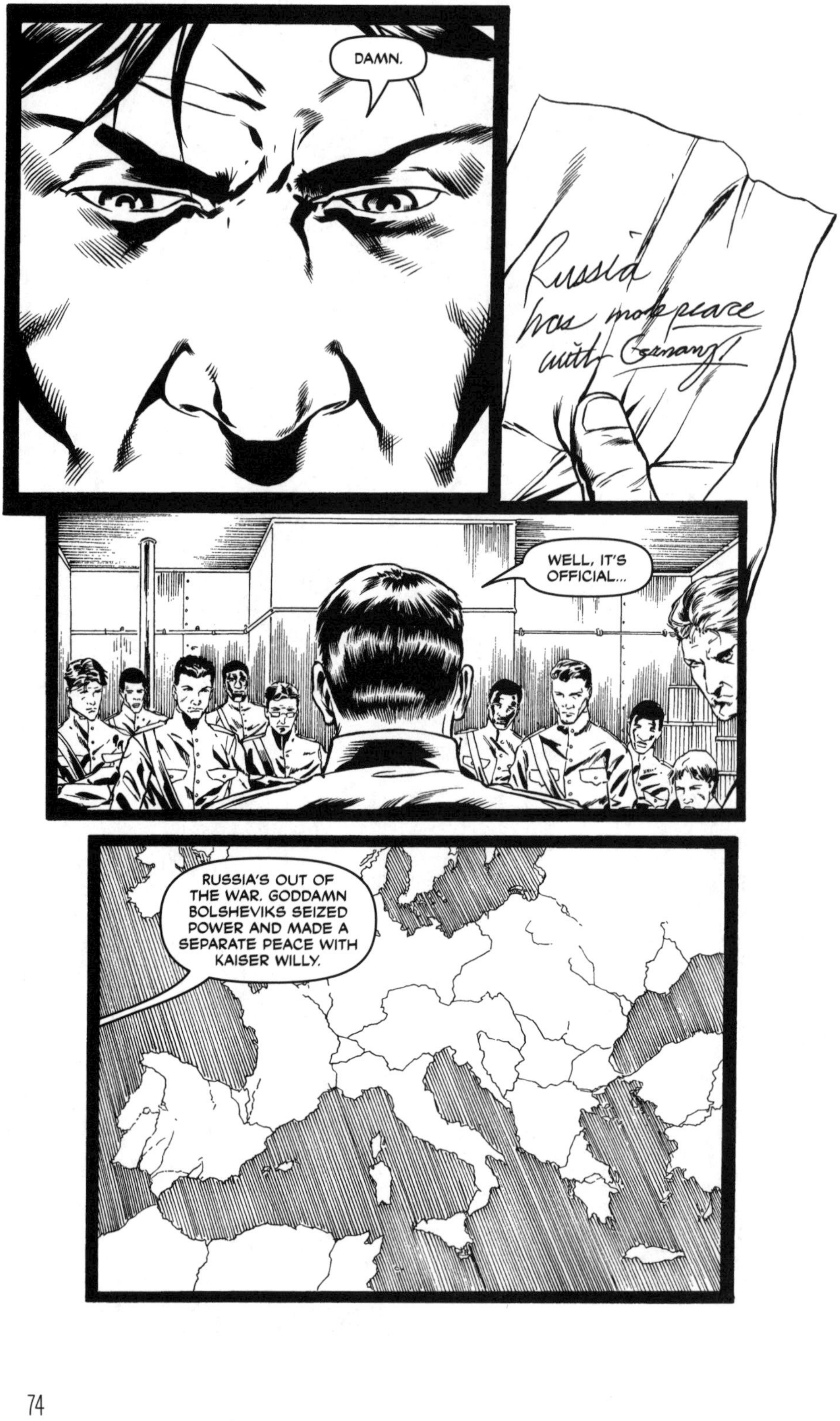
DAMN.
Russia has made peace with Germany!
WELL, IT'S OFFICIAL...
RUSSIA'S OUT OF THE WAR. GODDAMN BOLSHEVIKS SEIZED POWER AND MADE A SEPARATE PEACE WITH KAISER WILLY.

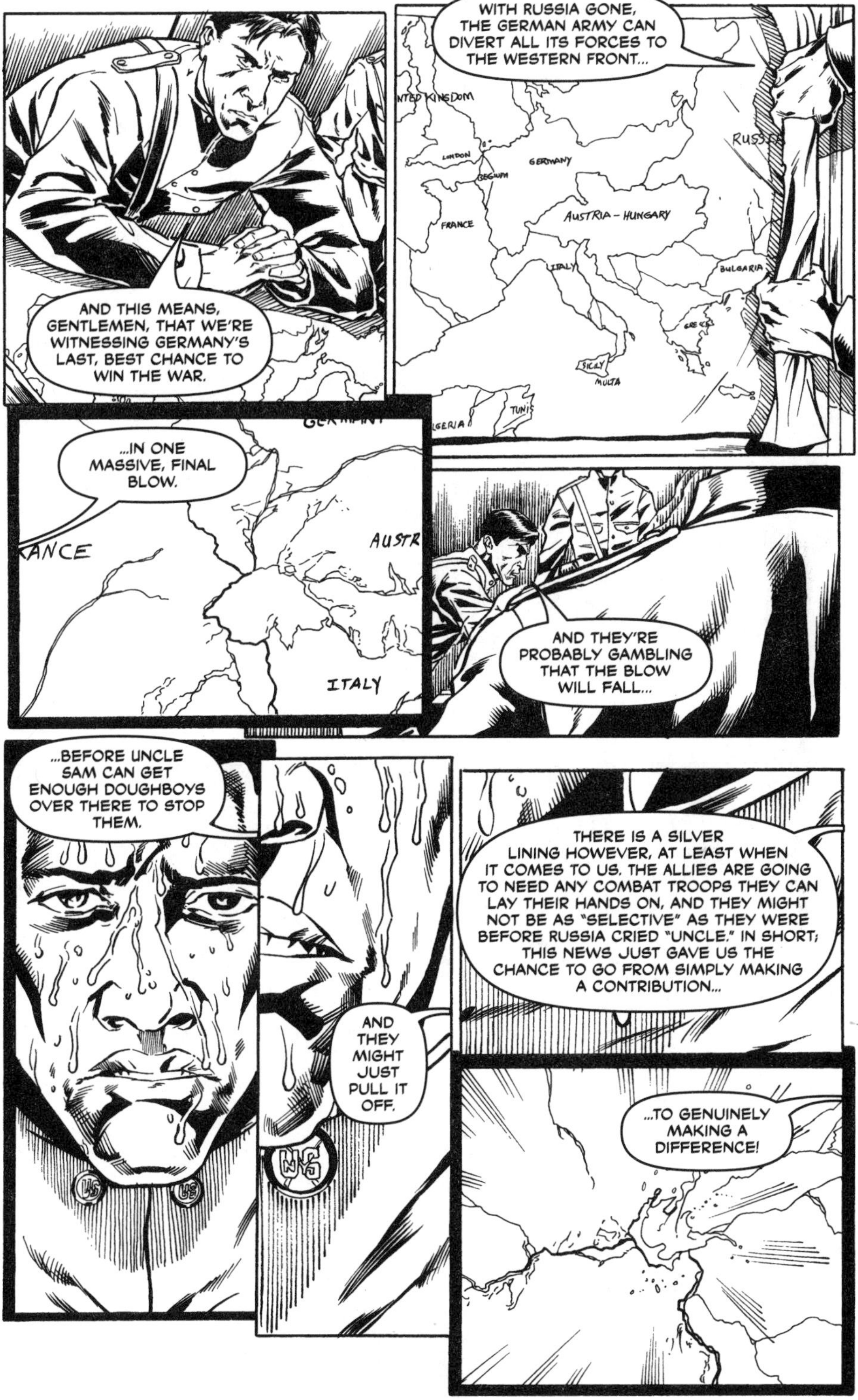
AND THIS MEANS, GENTLEMEN, THAT WE'RE WITNESSING GERMANY'S LAST, BEST CHANCE TO WIN THE WAR.
WITH RUSSIA GONE, THE GERMAN ARMY CAN DIVERT ALL ITS FORCES TO THE WESTERN FRONT...
RUSSIA
GERMANY
FRANCE
AUSTRIA - HUNGARY
ITALY
BULGARIA
SICILY
...IN ONE MASSIVE, FINAL BLOW.
ITALY
AND THEY'RE PROBABLY GAMBLING THAT THE BLOW WILL FALL...
...BEFORE UNCLE SAM CAN GET ENOUGH DOUGHBOYS OVER THERE TO STOP THEM.
AND THEY MIGHT JUST PULL IT OFF.
THERE IS A SILVER LINING HOWEVER, AT LEAST WHEN IT COMES TO US. THE ALLIES ARE GOING TO NEED ANY COMBAT TROOPS THEY CAN LAY THEIR HANDS ON, AND THEY MIGHT NOT BE AS "SELECTIVE" AS THEY WERE BEFORE RUSSIA CRIED "UNCLE." IN SHORT; THIS NEWS JUST GAVE US THE CHANCE TO GO FROM SIMPLY MAKING A CONTRIBUTION...
...TO GENUINELY MAKING A DIFFERENCE!

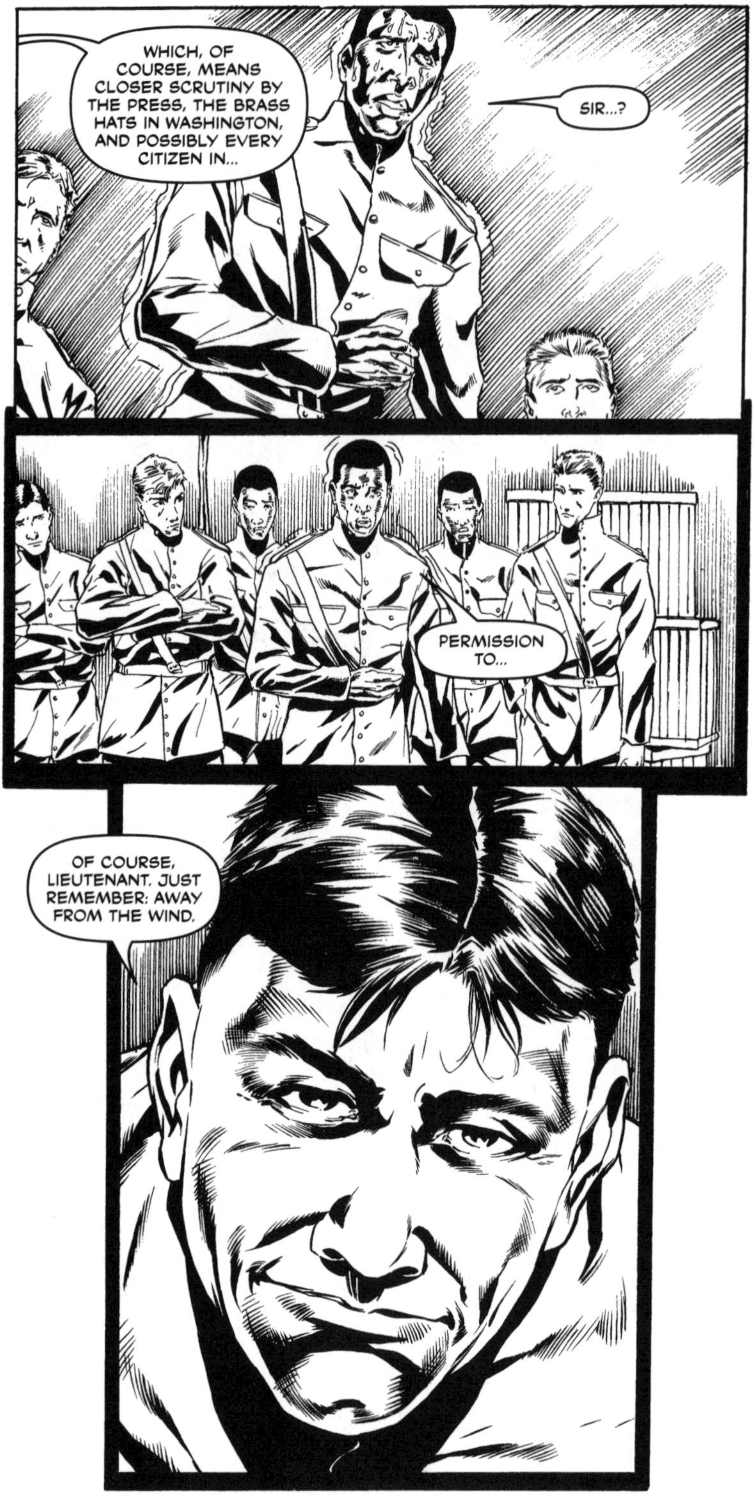
WHICH, OF COURSE, MEANS CLOSER SCRUTINY BY THE PRESS, THE BRASS HATS IN WASHINGTON, AND POSSIBLY EVERY CITIZEN IN...
SIR...?
PERMISSION TO...
OF COURSE, LIEUTENANT. JUST REMEMBER: AWAY FROM THE WIND.

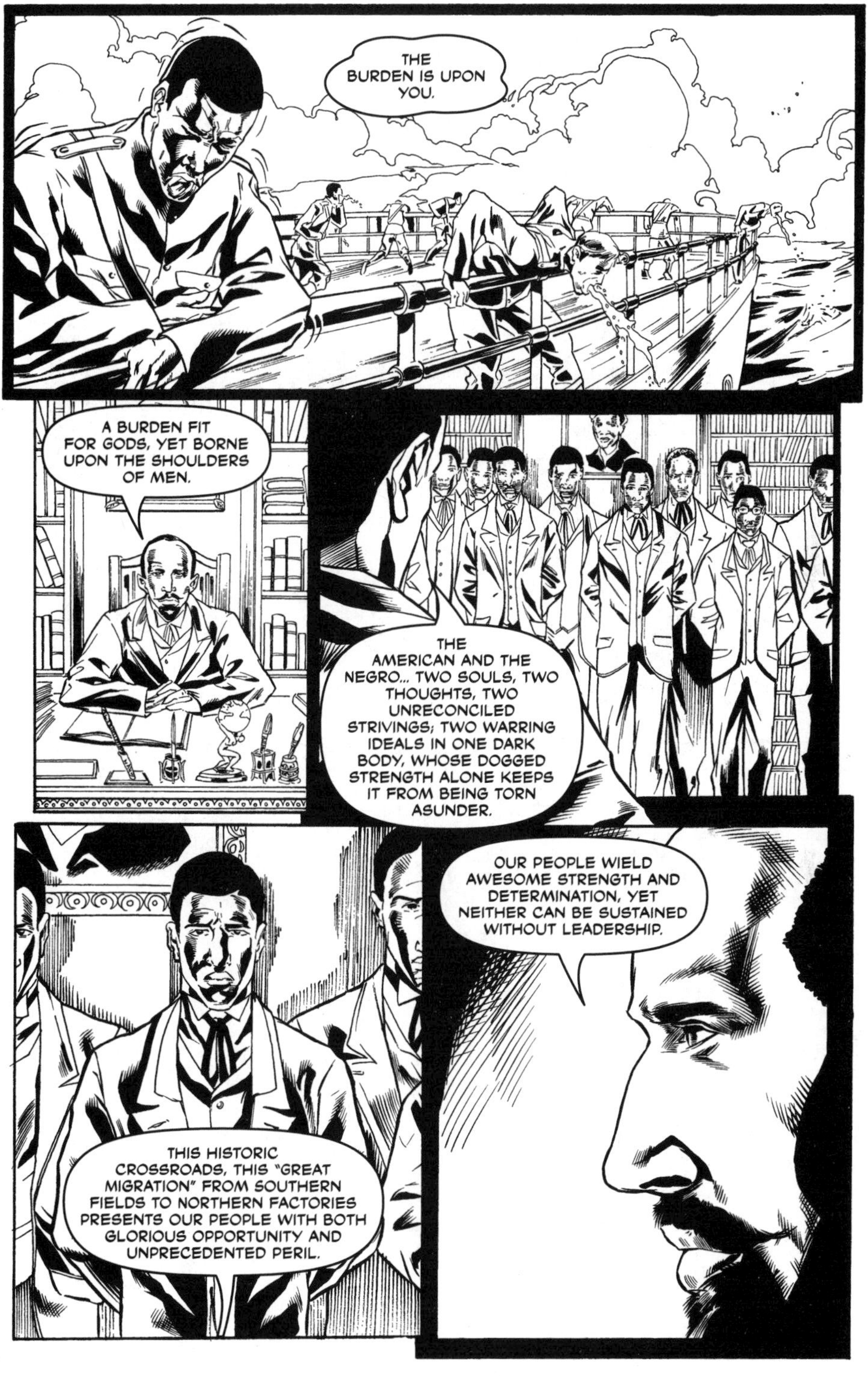
THE BURDEN IS UPON YOU.
A BURDEN FIT FOR GODS, YET BORNE UPON THE SHOULDERS OF MEN.
THE AMERICAN AND THE NEGRO... TWO SOULS, TWO THOUGHTS, TWO UNRECONCILED STRIVINGS; TWO WARRING IDEALS IN ONE DARK BODY, WHOSE DOGGED STRENGTH ALONE KEEPS IT FROM BEING TORN ASUNDER.
THIS HISTORIC CROSSROADS, THIS "GREAT MIGRATION" FROM SOUTHERN FIELDS TO NORTHERN FACTORIES PRESENTS OUR PEOPLE WITH BOTH GLORIOUS OPPORTUNITY AND UNPRECEDENTED PERIL.
OUR PEOPLE WIELD AWESOME STRENGTH AND DETERMINATION, YET NEITHER CAN BE SUSTAINED WITHOUT LEADERSHIP.

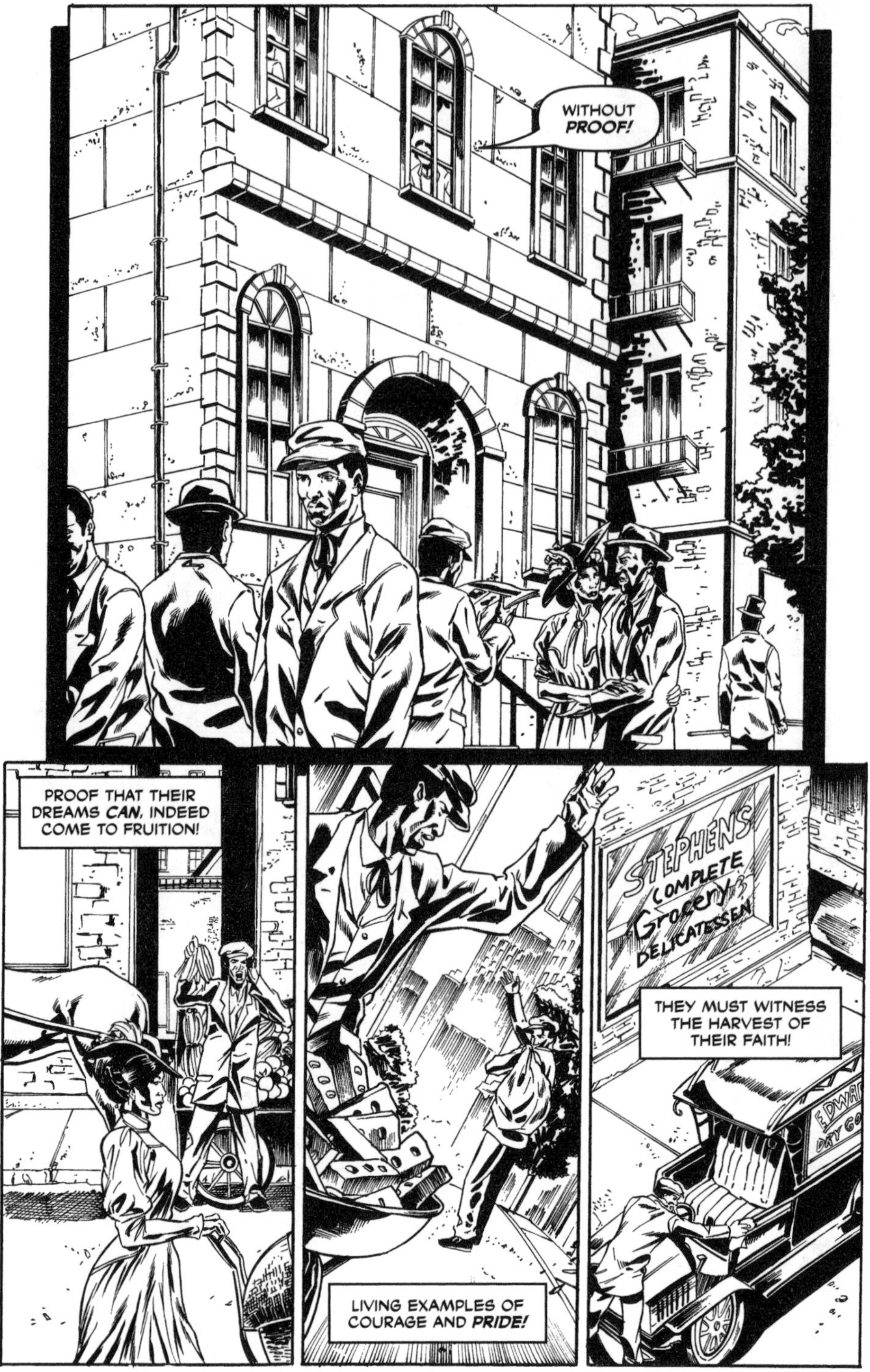
WITHOUT PROOF!
PROOF THAT THEIR DREAMS CAN, INDEED COME TO FRUITION!
LIVING EXAMPLES OF COURAGE AND PRIDE!
STEPHENS
COMPLETE
Grocery
DELICATESSEN
THEY MUST WITNESS THE HARVEST OF THEIR FAITH!

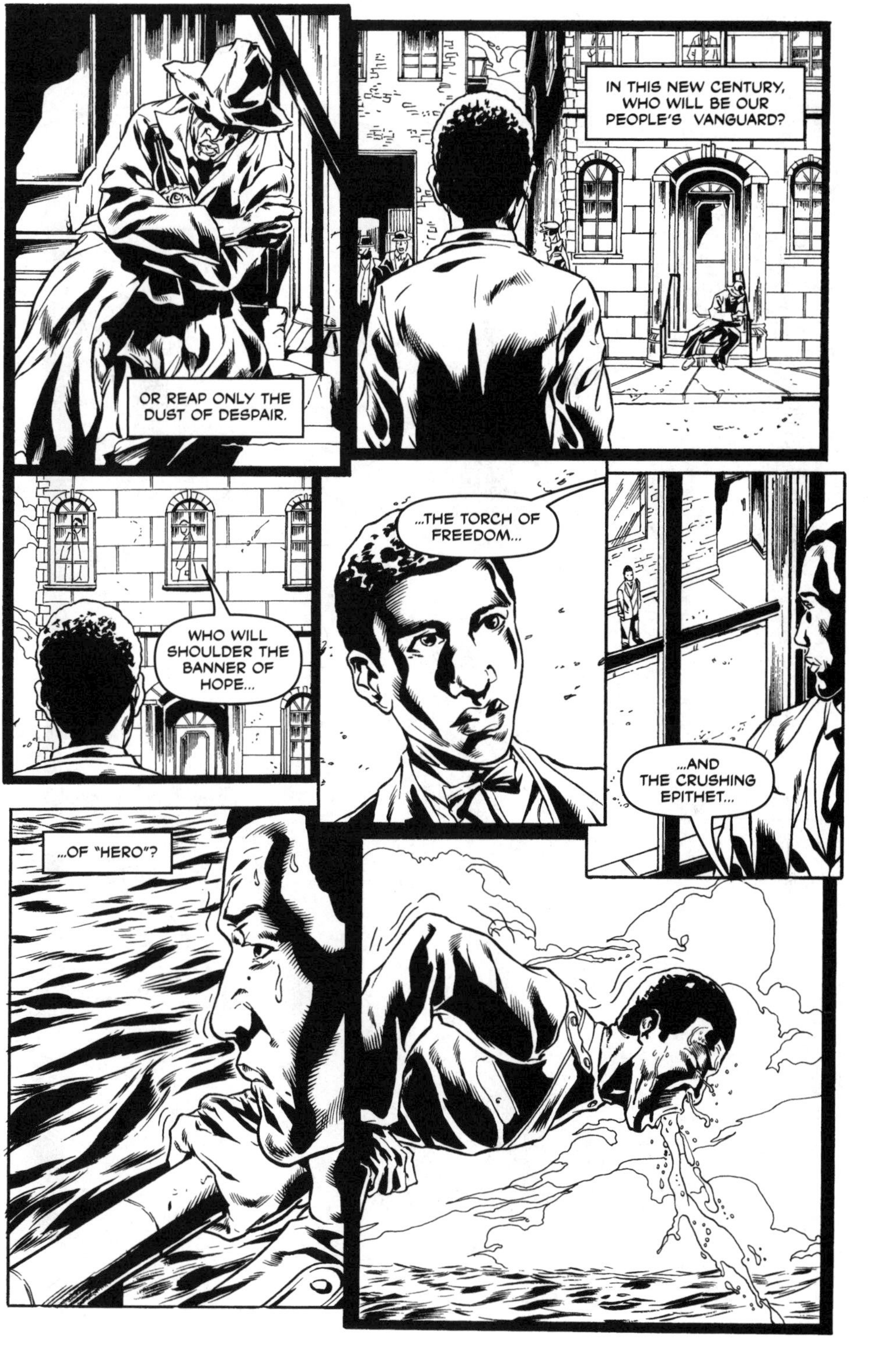
OR REAP ONLY THE DUST OF DESPAIR.
IN THIS NEW CENTURY, WHO WILL BE OUR PEOPLE'S VANGUARD?
WHO WILL SHOULDER THE BANNER OF HOPE...
...THE TORCH OF FREEDOM...
...AND THE CRUSHING EPITHET...
...OF "HERO"?

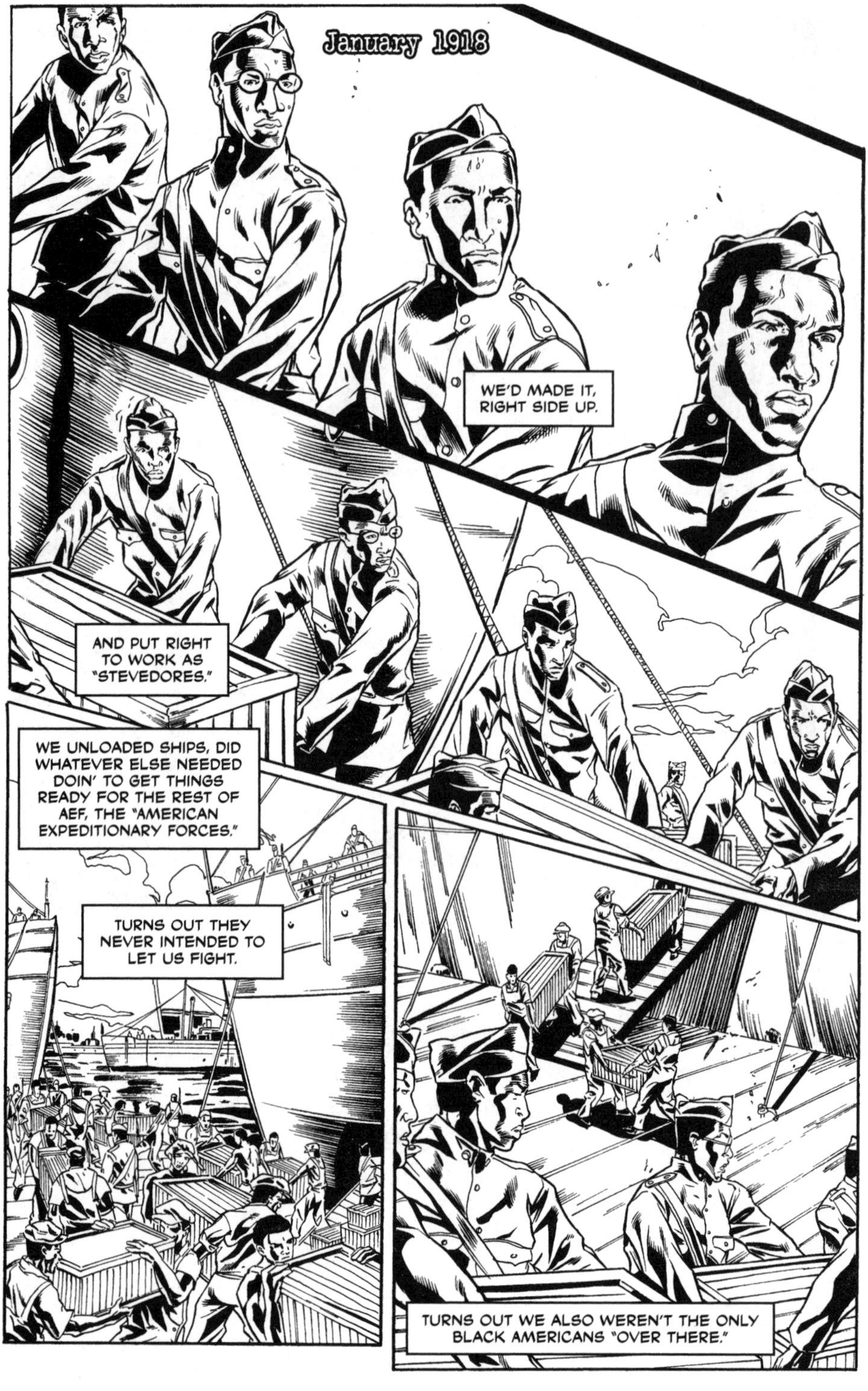
January 1918
WE'D MADE IT, RIGHT SIDE UP.
AND PUT RIGHT TO WORK AS "STEVEDORES."
WE UNLOADED SHIPS, DID WHATEVER ELSE NEEDED DOIN' TO GET THINGS READY FOR THE REST OF AEF, THE "AMERICAN EXPEDITIONARY FORCES."
TURNS OUT THEY NEVER INTENDED TO LET US FIGHT.
TURNS OUT WE ALSO WEREN'T THE ONLY BLACK AMERICANS "OVER THERE."

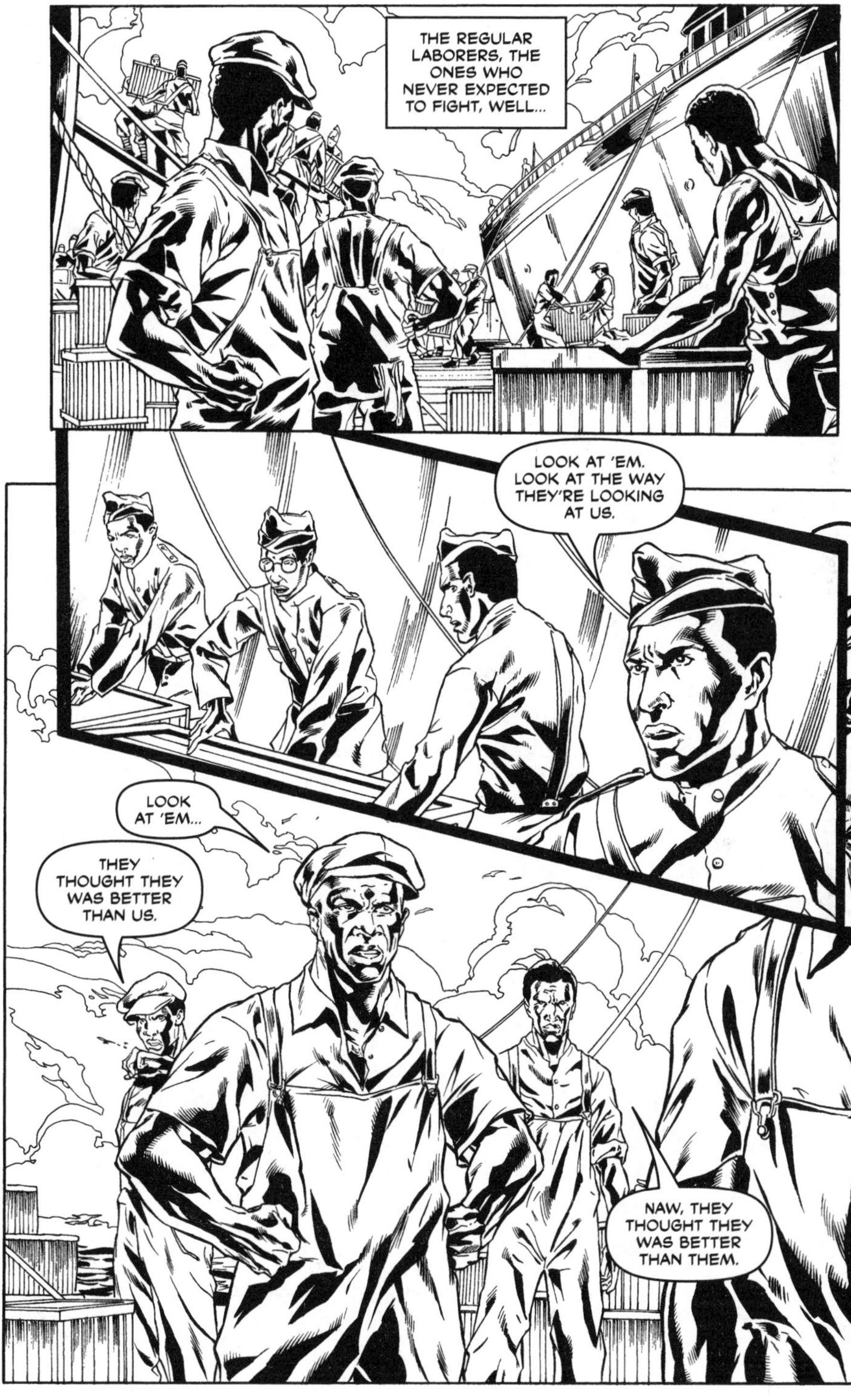
THE REGULAR LABORERS, THE ONES WHO NEVER EXPECTED TO FIGHT, WELL...
LOOK AT 'EM. LOOK AT THE WAY THEY'RE LOOKING AT US.
LOOK AT 'EM...
THEY THOUGHT THEY WAS BETTER THAN US.
NAW, THEY THOUGHT THEY WAS BETTER THAN THEM.

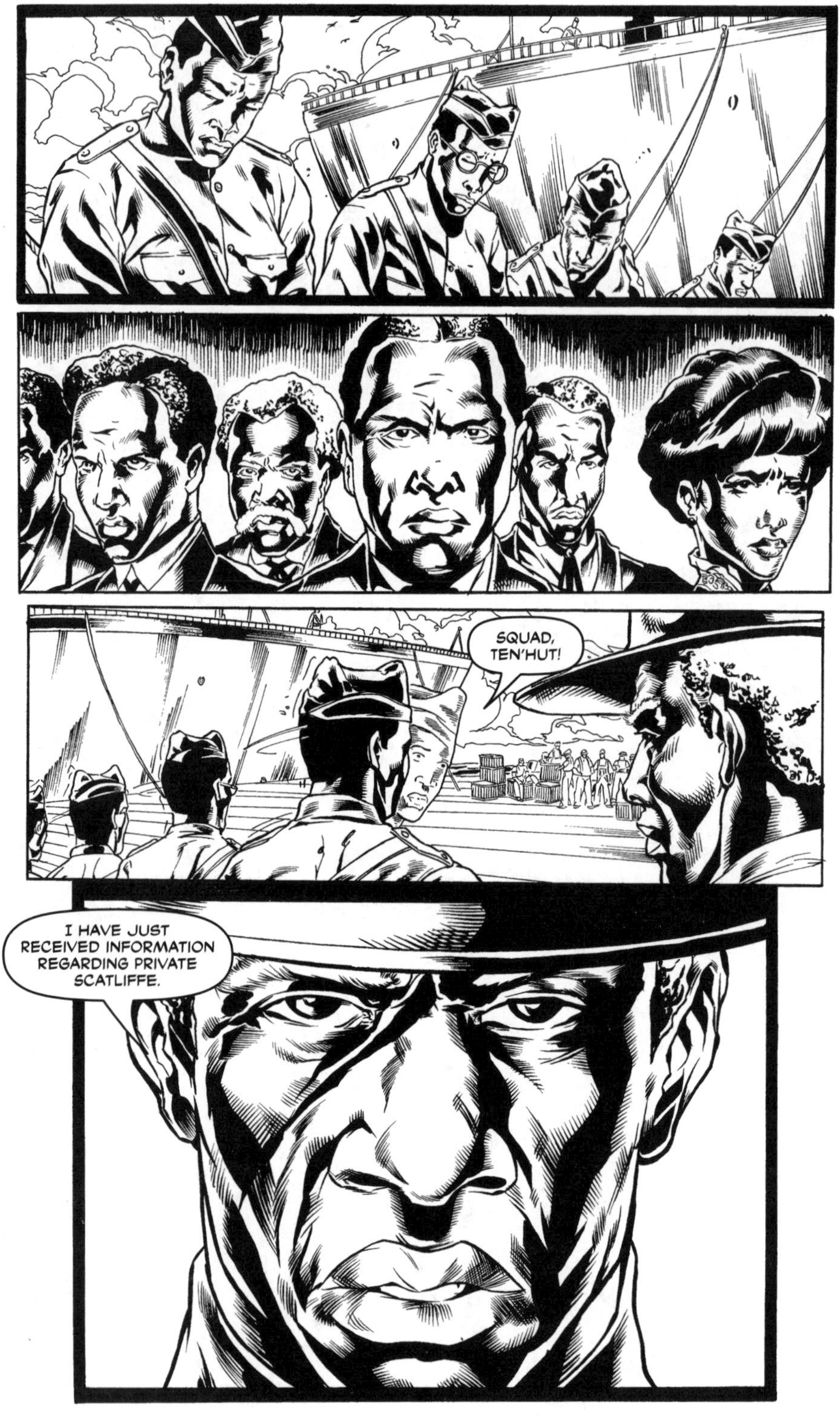
SQUAD, TEN'HUT!
I HAVE JUST RECEIVED INFORMATION REGARDING PRIVATE SCATLIFFE.

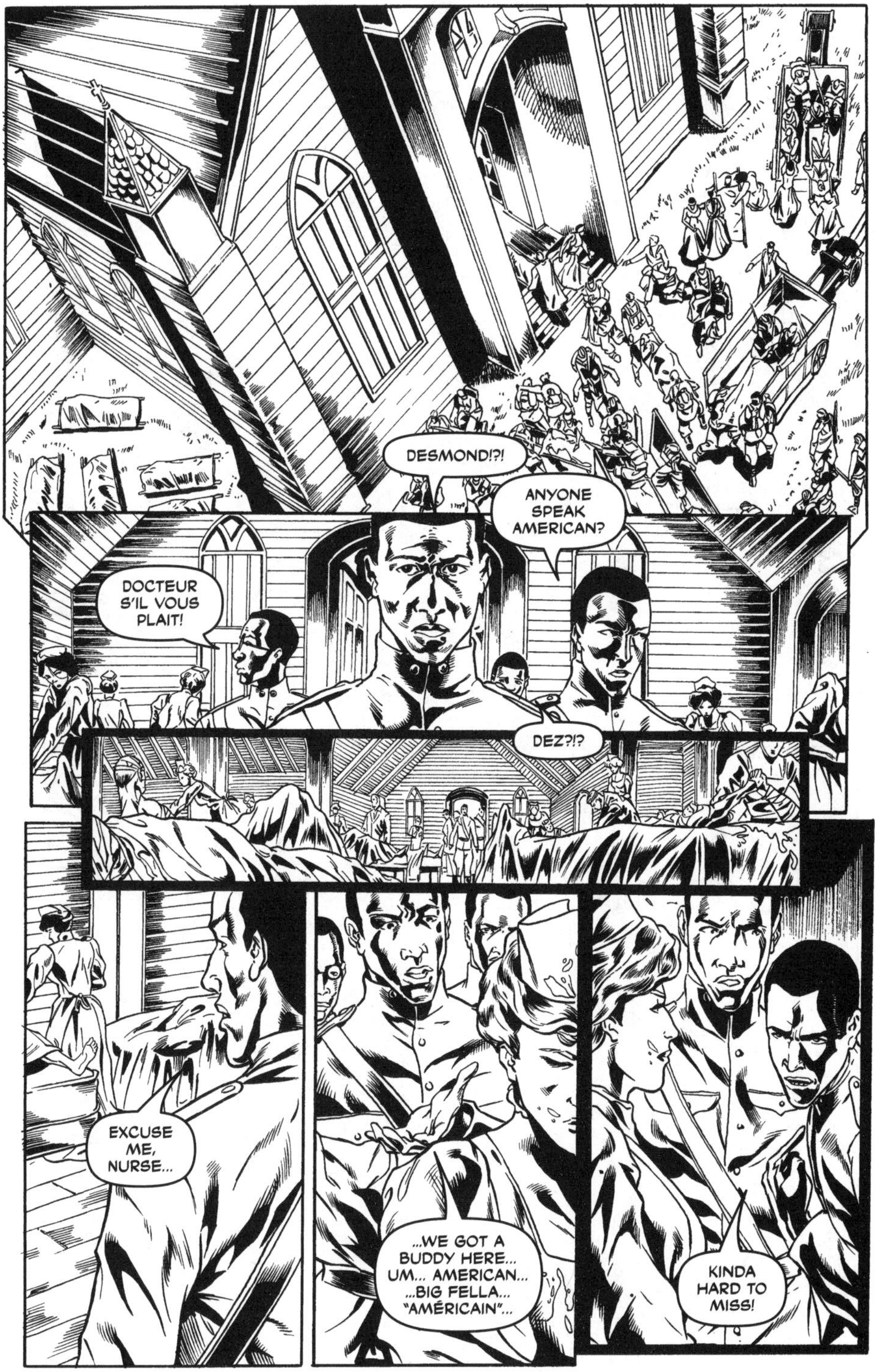
DESMOND!?!
ANYONE SPEAK AMERICAN?
DOCTEUR S'IL VOUS PLAIT!
DEZ?!?
EXCUSE ME, NURSE...
...WE GOT A BUDDY HERE... UM... AMERICAN... ...BIG FELLA... "AMÉRICAIN"...
KINDA HARD TO MISS!

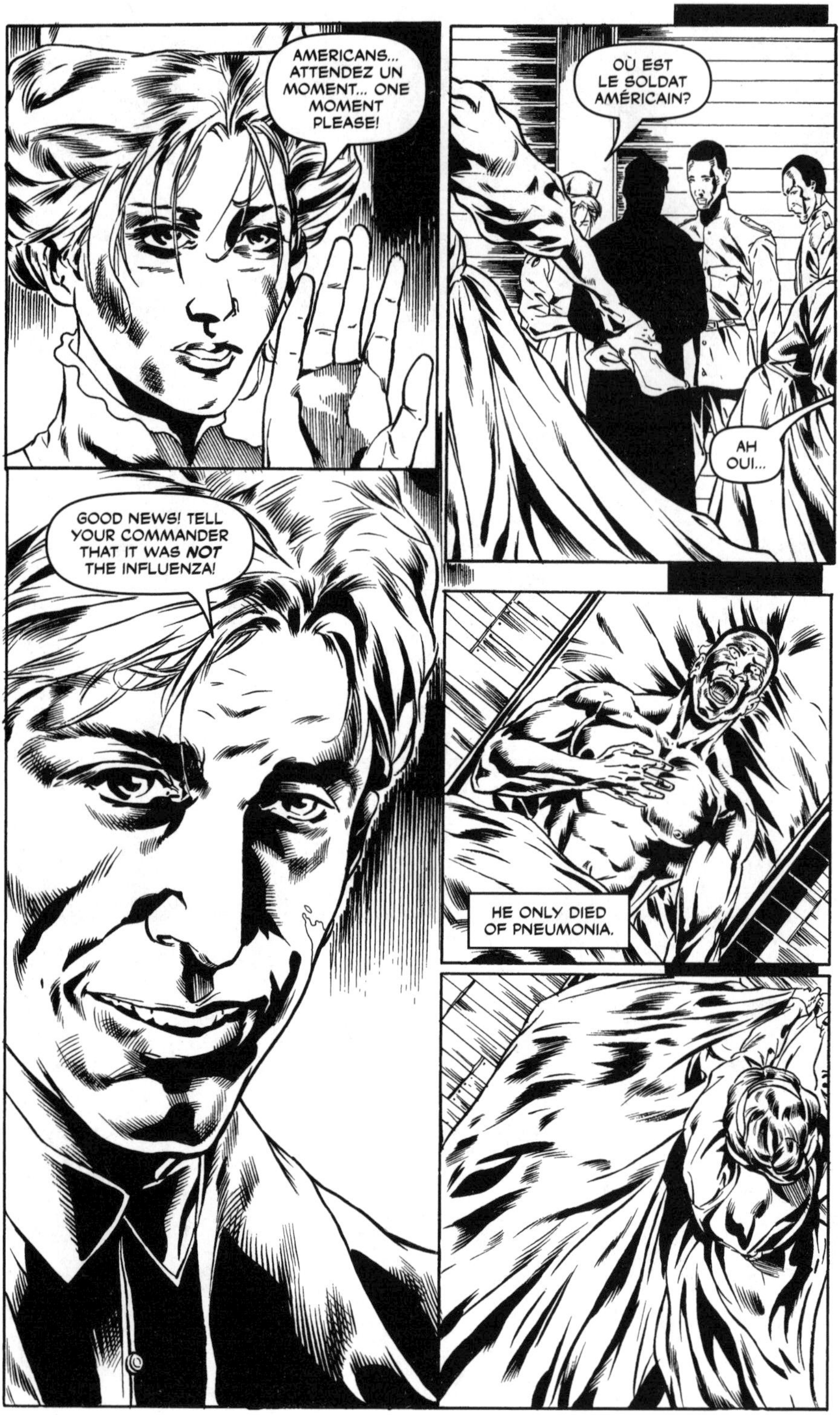
AMERICANS... ATTENDEZ UN MOMENT... ONE MOMENT PLEASE!
OÙ EST LE SOLDAT AMÉRICAIN?
AH OUI...
GOOD NEWS! TELL YOUR COMMANDER THAT IT WAS *NOT* THE INFLUENZA!
HE ONLY DIED OF PNEUMONIA.

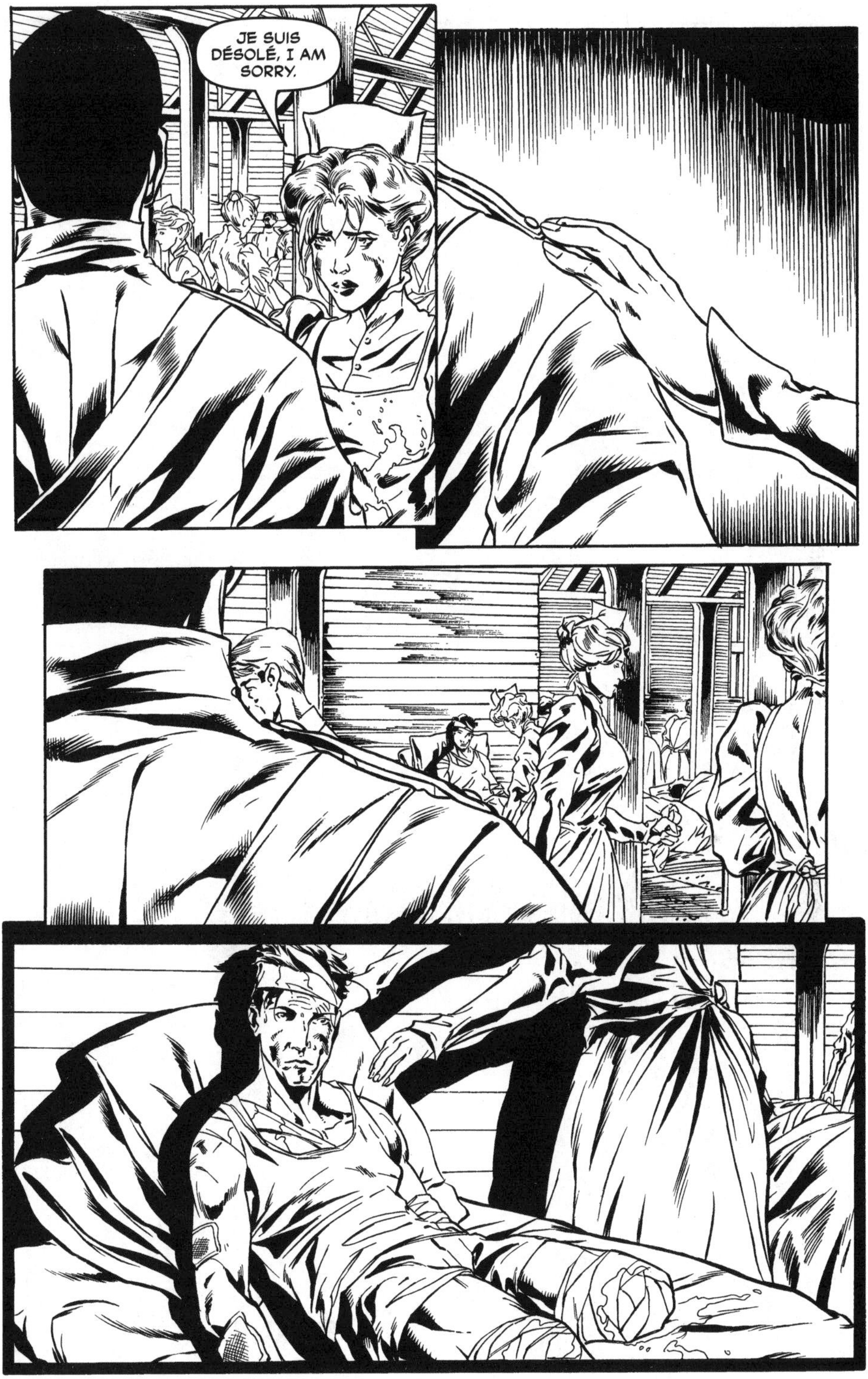
JE SUIS DÉSOLÉ, I AM SORRY.

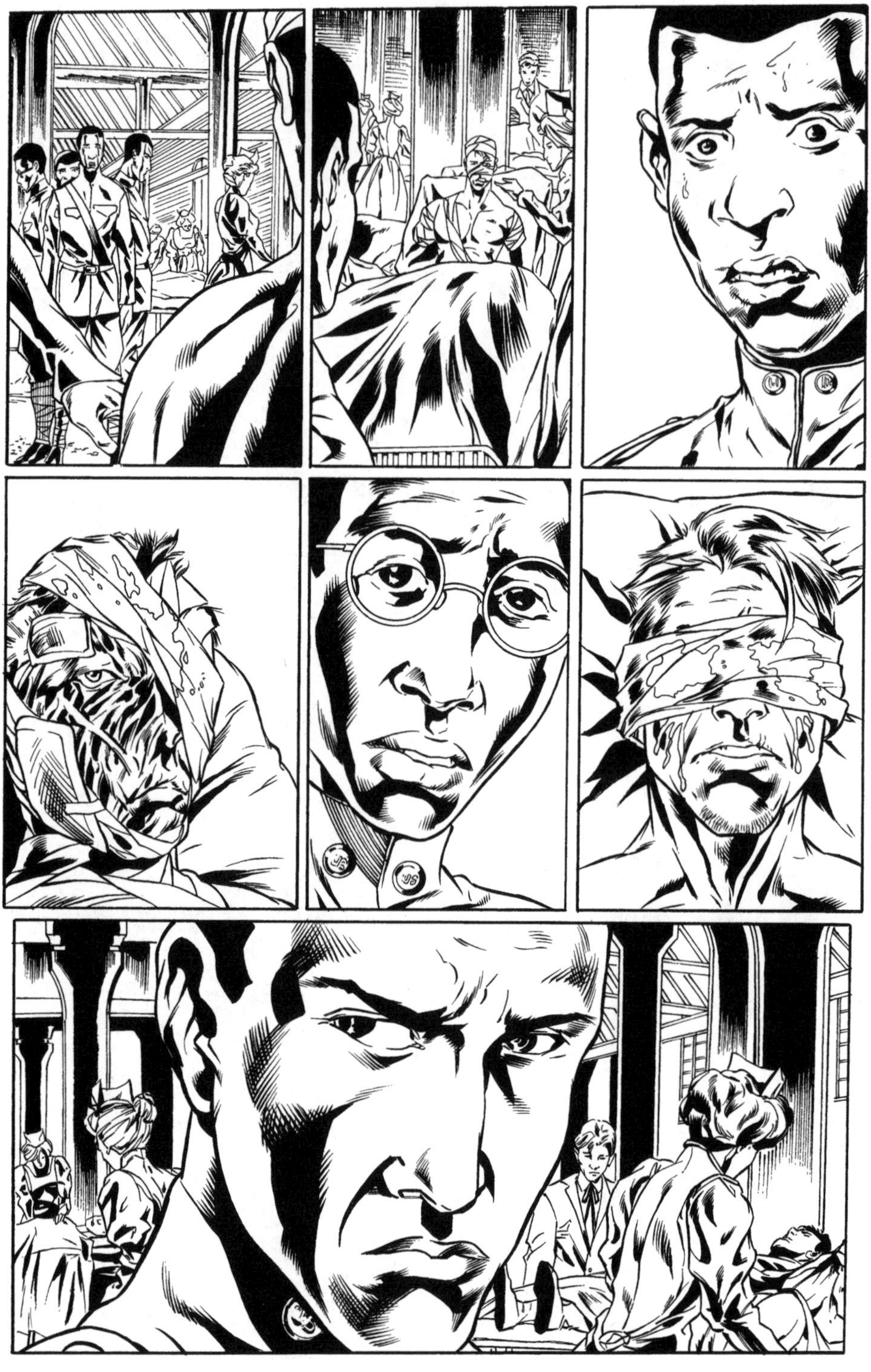

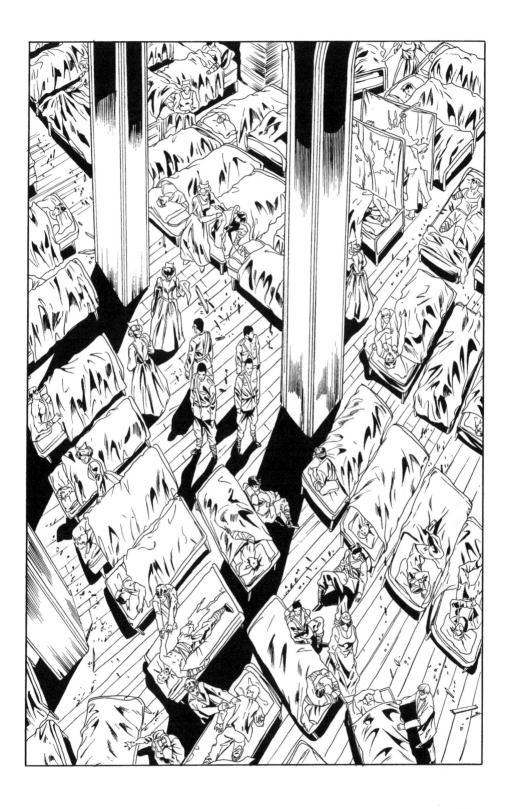

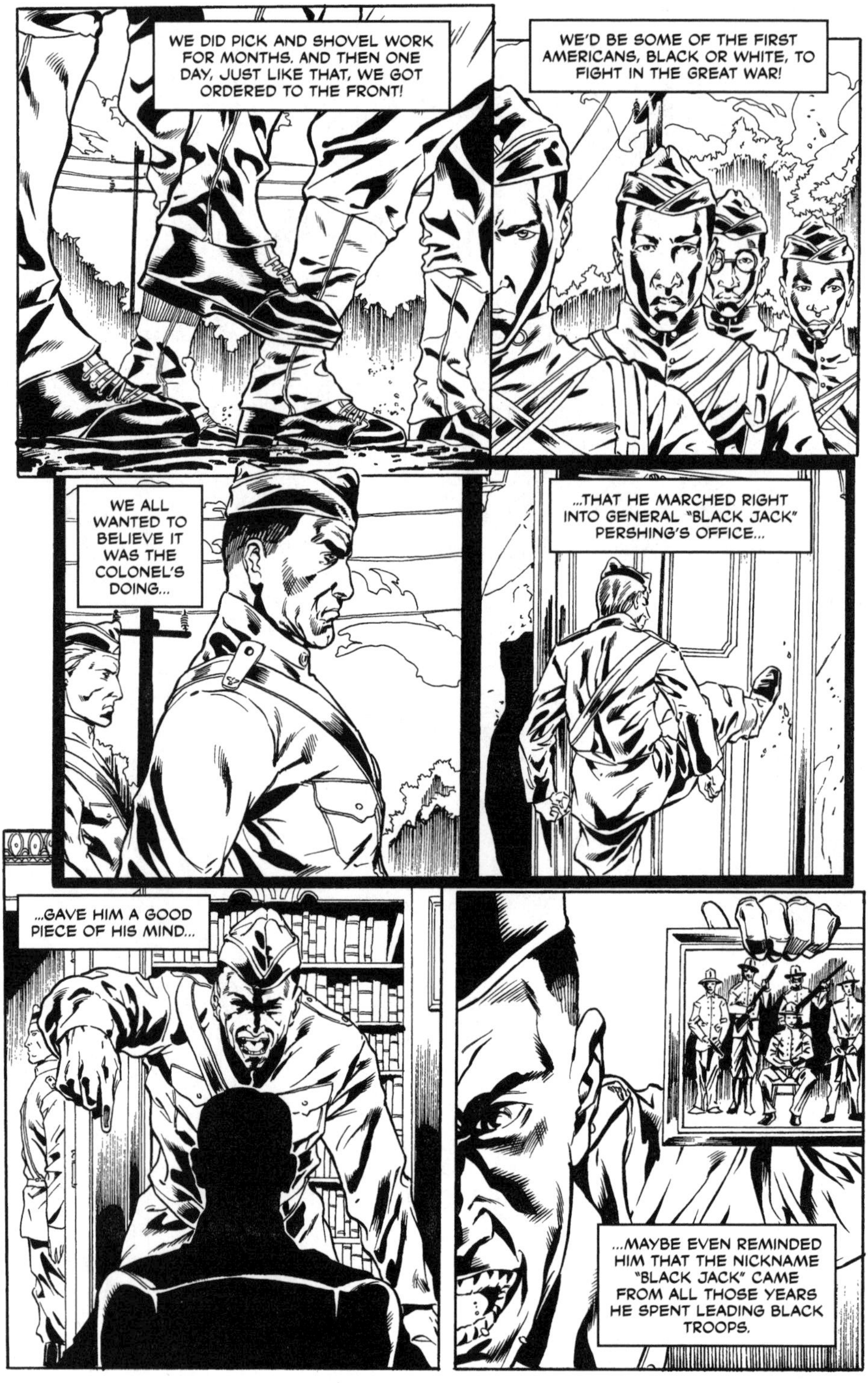
WE DID PICK AND SHOVEL WORK FOR MONTHS. AND THEN ONE DAY, JUST LIKE THAT, WE GOT ORDERED TO THE FRONT!
WE'D BE SOME OF THE FIRST AMERICANS, BLACK OR WHITE, TO FIGHT IN THE GREAT WAR!
WE ALL WANTED TO BELIEVE IT WAS THE COLONEL'S DOING...
...THAT HE MARCHED RIGHT INTO GENERAL "BLACK JACK" PERSHING'S OFFICE...
...GAVE HIM A GOOD PIECE OF HIS MIND...
...MAYBE EVEN REMINDED HIM THAT THE NICKNAME "BLACK JACK" CAME FROM ALL THOSE YEARS HE SPENT LEADING BLACK TROOPS.

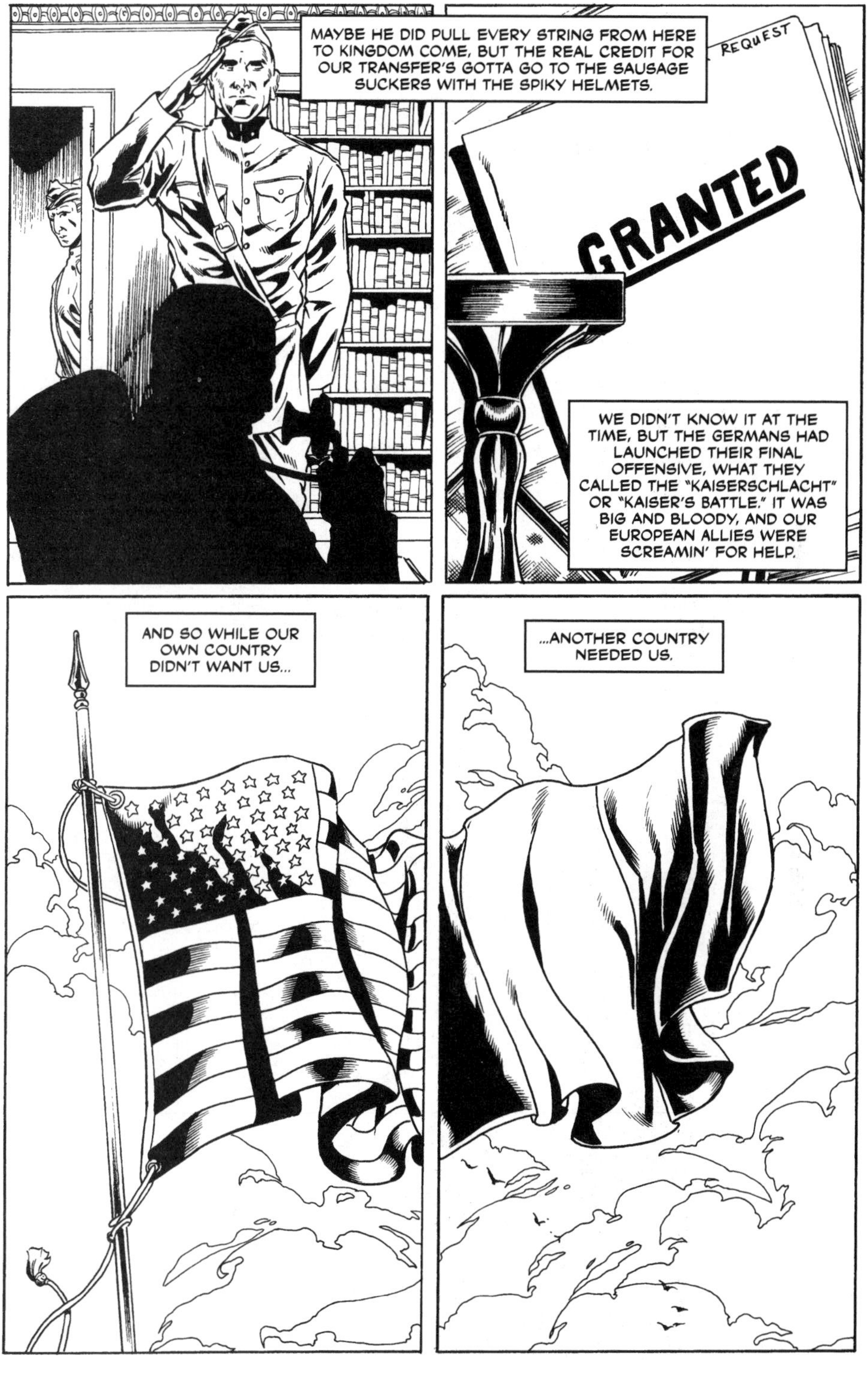
MAYBE HE DID PULL EVERY STRING FROM HERE TO KINGDOM COME, BUT THE REAL CREDIT FOR OUR TRANSFER'S GOTTA GO TO THE SAUSAGE SUCKERS WITH THE SPIKY HELMETS.
REQUEST
GRANTED
WE DIDN'T KNOW IT AT THE TIME, BUT THE GERMANS HAD LAUNCHED THEIR FINAL OFFENSIVE, WHAT THEY CALLED THE "KAISERSCHLACHT" OR "KAISER'S BATTLE." IT WAS BIG AND BLOODY, AND OUR EUROPEAN ALLIES WERE SCREAMIN' FOR HELP.
AND SO WHILE OUR OWN COUNTRY DIDN'T WANT US...
...ANOTHER COUNTRY NEEDED US.

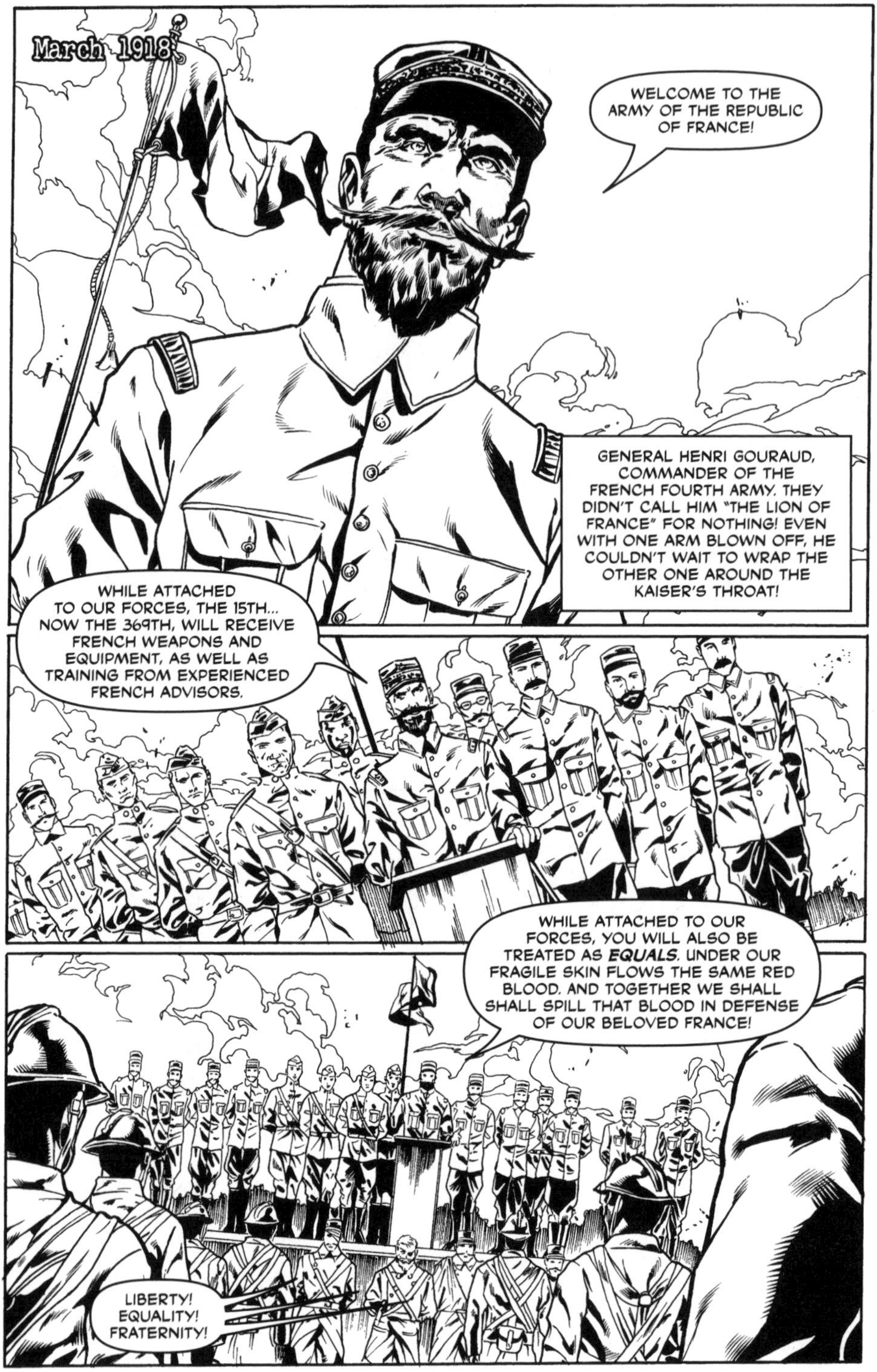
March 1918
WELCOME TO THE ARMY OF THE REPUBLIC OF FRANCE!
GENERAL HENRI GOURAUD, COMMANDER OF THE FRENCH FOURTH ARMY. THEY DIDN'T CALL HIM "THE LION OF FRANCE" FOR NOTHING! EVEN WITH ONE ARM BLOWN OFF, HE COULDN'T WAIT TO WRAP THE OTHER ONE AROUND THE KAISER'S THROAT!
WHILE ATTACHED TO OUR FORCES, THE 15TH... NOW THE 369TH, WILL RECEIVE FRENCH WEAPONS AND EQUIPMENT, AS WELL AS TRAINING FROM EXPERIENCED FRENCH ADVISORS.
WHILE ATTACHED TO OUR FORCES, YOU WILL ALSO BE TREATED AS ***EQUALS***. UNDER OUR FRAGILE SKIN FLOWS THE SAME RED BLOOD. AND TOGETHER WE SHALL SHALL SPILL THAT BLOOD IN DEFENSE OF OUR BELOVED FRANCE!
LIBERTY! EQUALITY! FRATERNITY!

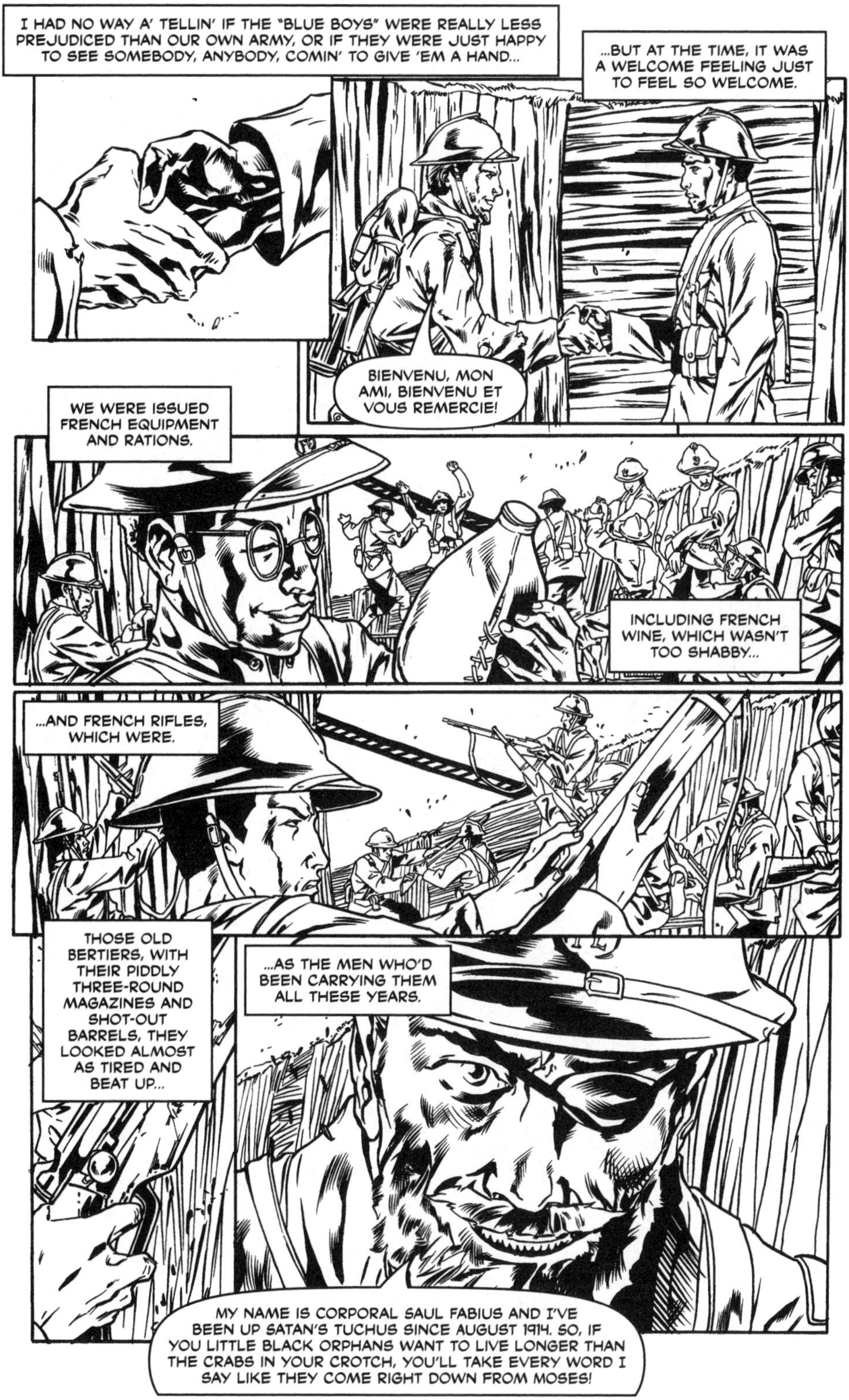
I HAD NO WAY A' TELLIN' IF THE "BLUE BOYS" WERE REALLY LESS PREJUDICED THAN OUR OWN ARMY, OR IF THEY WERE JUST HAPPY TO SEE SOMEBODY, ANYBODY, COMIN' TO GIVE 'EM A HAND...
...BUT AT THE TIME, IT WAS A WELCOME FEELING JUST TO FEEL SO WELCOME.
BIENVENU, MON AMI, BIENVENU ET VOUS REMERCIE!
WE WERE ISSUED FRENCH EQUIPMENT AND RATIONS.
INCLUDING FRENCH WINE, WHICH WASN'T TOO SHABBY...
...AND FRENCH RIFLES, WHICH WERE.
THOSE OLD BERTIERS, WITH THEIR PIDDLY THREE-ROUND MAGAZINES AND SHOT-OUT BARRELS, THEY LOOKED ALMOST AS TIRED AND BEAT UP...
...AS THE MEN WHO'D BEEN CARRYING THEM ALL THESE YEARS.
MY NAME IS CORPORAL SAUL FABIUS AND I'VE BEEN UP SATAN'S TUCHUS SINCE AUGUST 1914. SO, IF YOU LITTLE BLACK ORPHANS WANT TO LIVE LONGER THAN THE CRABS IN YOUR CROTCH, YOU'LL TAKE EVERY WORD I SAY LIKE THEY COME RIGHT DOWN FROM MOSES!

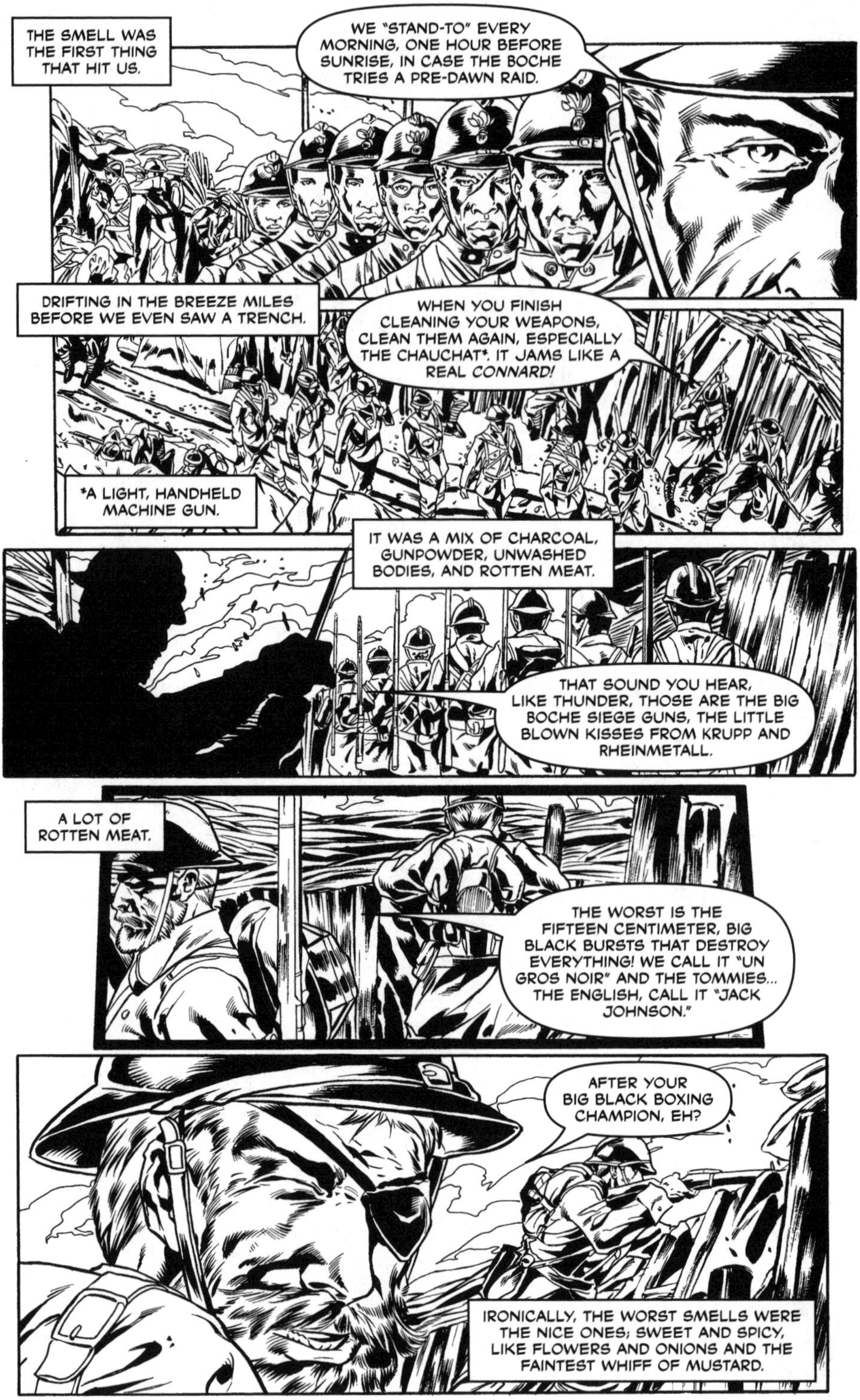

THE SMELL WAS THE FIRST THING THAT HIT US.
WE "STAND-TO" EVERY MORNING, ONE HOUR BEFORE SUNRISE, IN CASE THE BOCHE TRIES A PRE-DAWN RAID.
DRIFTING IN THE BREEZE MILES BEFORE WE EVEN SAW A TRENCH.
WHEN YOU FINISH CLEANING YOUR WEAPONS, CLEAN THEM AGAIN, ESPECIALLY THE CHAUCHAT*. IT JAMS LIKE A REAL *CONNARD!*
*A LIGHT, HANDHELD MACHINE GUN.
IT WAS A MIX OF CHARCOAL, GUNPOWDER, UNWASHED BODIES, AND ROTTEN MEAT.
THAT SOUND YOU HEAR, LIKE THUNDER, THOSE ARE THE BIG BOCHE SIEGE GUNS, THE LITTLE BLOWN KISSES FROM KRUPP AND RHEINMETALL.
A LOT OF ROTTEN MEAT.
THE WORST IS THE FIFTEEN CENTIMETER, BIG BLACK BURSTS THAT DESTROY EVERYTHING! WE CALL IT "UN GROS NOIR" AND THE TOMMIES... THE ENGLISH, CALL IT "JACK JOHNSON."
AFTER YOUR BIG BLACK BOXING CHAMPION, EH?
IRONICALLY, THE WORST SMELLS WERE THE NICE ONES; SWEET AND SPICY, LIKE FLOWERS AND ONIONS AND THE FAINTEST WHIFF OF MUSTARD.

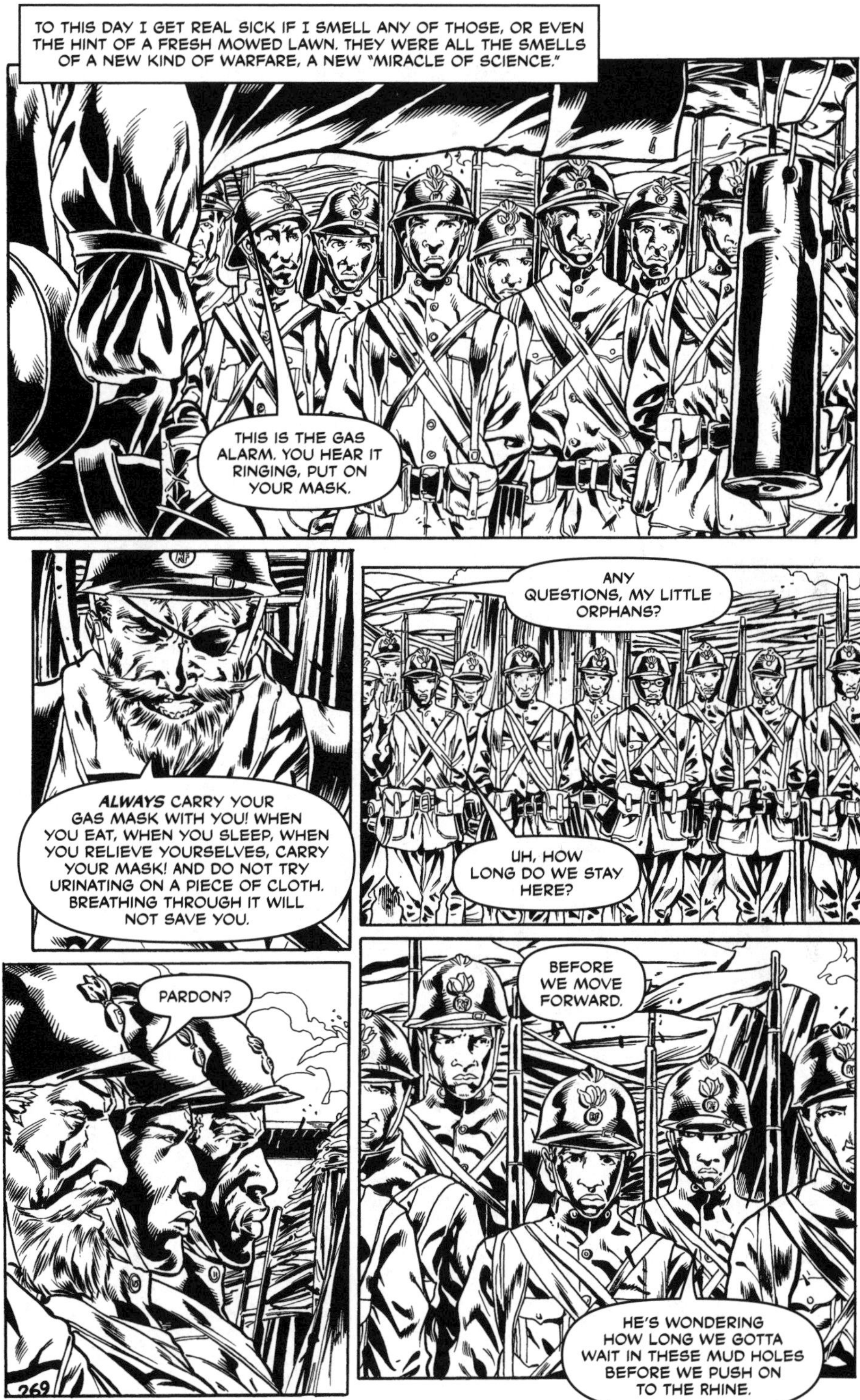
TO THIS DAY I GET REAL SICK IF I SMELL ANY OF THOSE, OR EVEN THE HINT OF A FRESH MOWED LAWN. THEY WERE ALL THE SMELLS OF A NEW KIND OF WARFARE, A NEW "MIRACLE OF SCIENCE."
THIS IS THE GAS ALARM. YOU HEAR IT RINGING, PUT ON YOUR MASK.
ALWAYS CARRY YOUR GAS MASK WITH YOU! WHEN YOU EAT, WHEN YOU SLEEP, WHEN YOU RELIEVE YOURSELVES, CARRY YOUR MASK! AND DO NOT TRY URINATING ON A PIECE OF CLOTH. BREATHING THROUGH IT WILL NOT SAVE YOU.
ANY QUESTIONS, MY LITTLE ORPHANS?
UH, HOW LONG DO WE STAY HERE?
PARDON?
HE'S WONDERING HOW LONG WE GOTTA WAIT IN THESE MUD HOLES BEFORE WE PUSH ON TO THE RHINE.
BEFORE WE MOVE FORWARD.
269

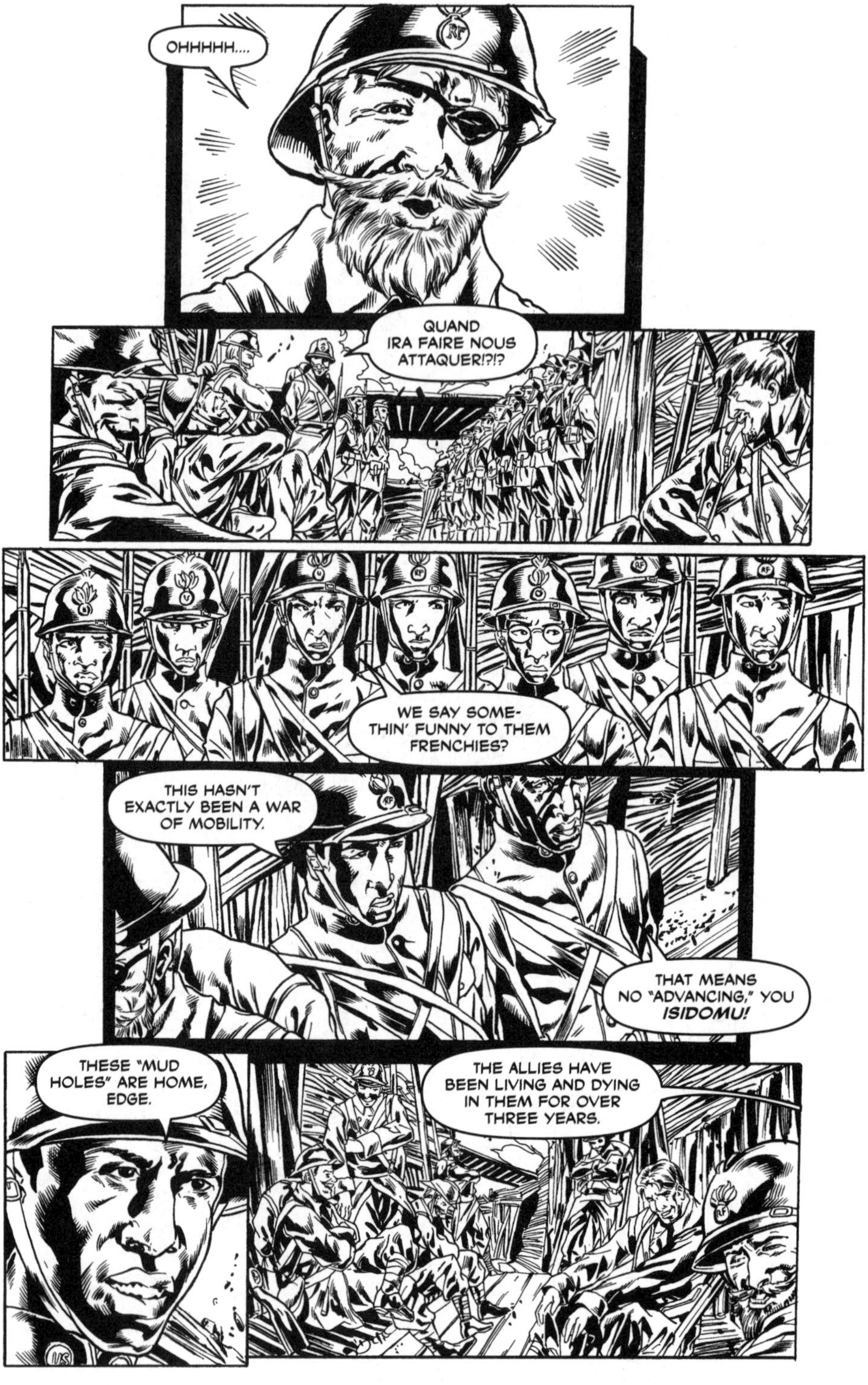
OHHHHH....
QUAND IRA FAIRE NOUS ATTAQUER!?!?
WE SAY SOME-THIN' FUNNY TO THEM FRENCHIES?
THIS HASN'T EXACTLY BEEN A WAR OF MOBILITY.
THAT MEANS NO "ADVANCING," YOU *ISIDOMU!*
THESE "MUD HOLES" ARE HOME, EDGE.
THE ALLIES HAVE BEEN LIVING AND DYING IN THEM FOR OVER THREE YEARS.

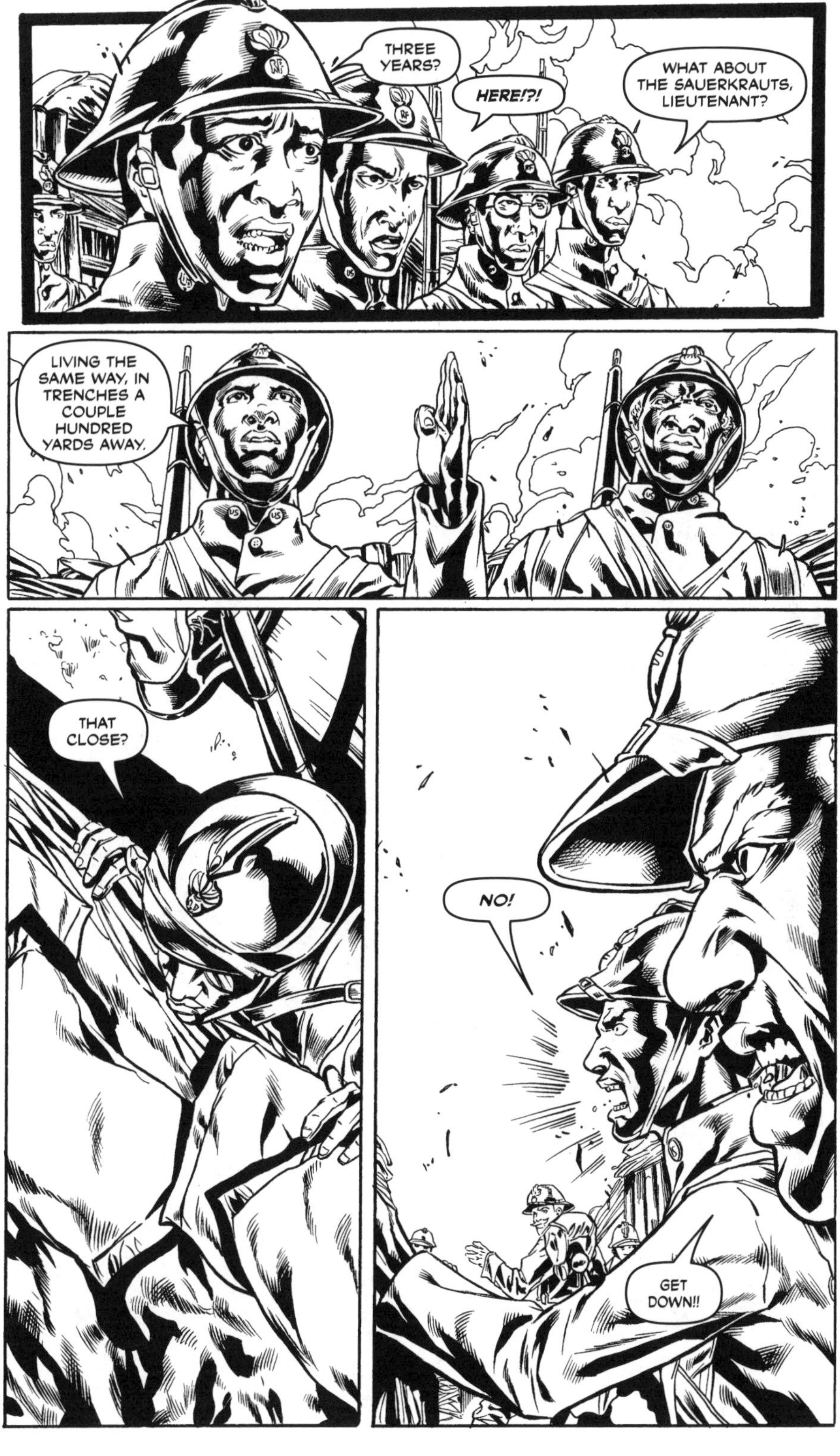
THREE YEARS?
HERE!?!
WHAT ABOUT THE SAUERKRAUTS, LIEUTENANT?
LIVING THE SAME WAY, IN TRENCHES A COUPLE HUNDRED YARDS AWAY.
THAT CLOSE?
NO!
GET DOWN!!

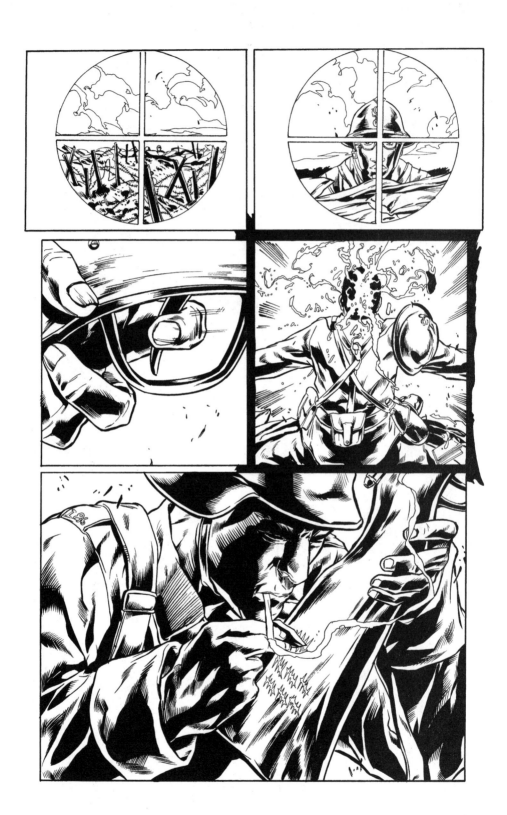

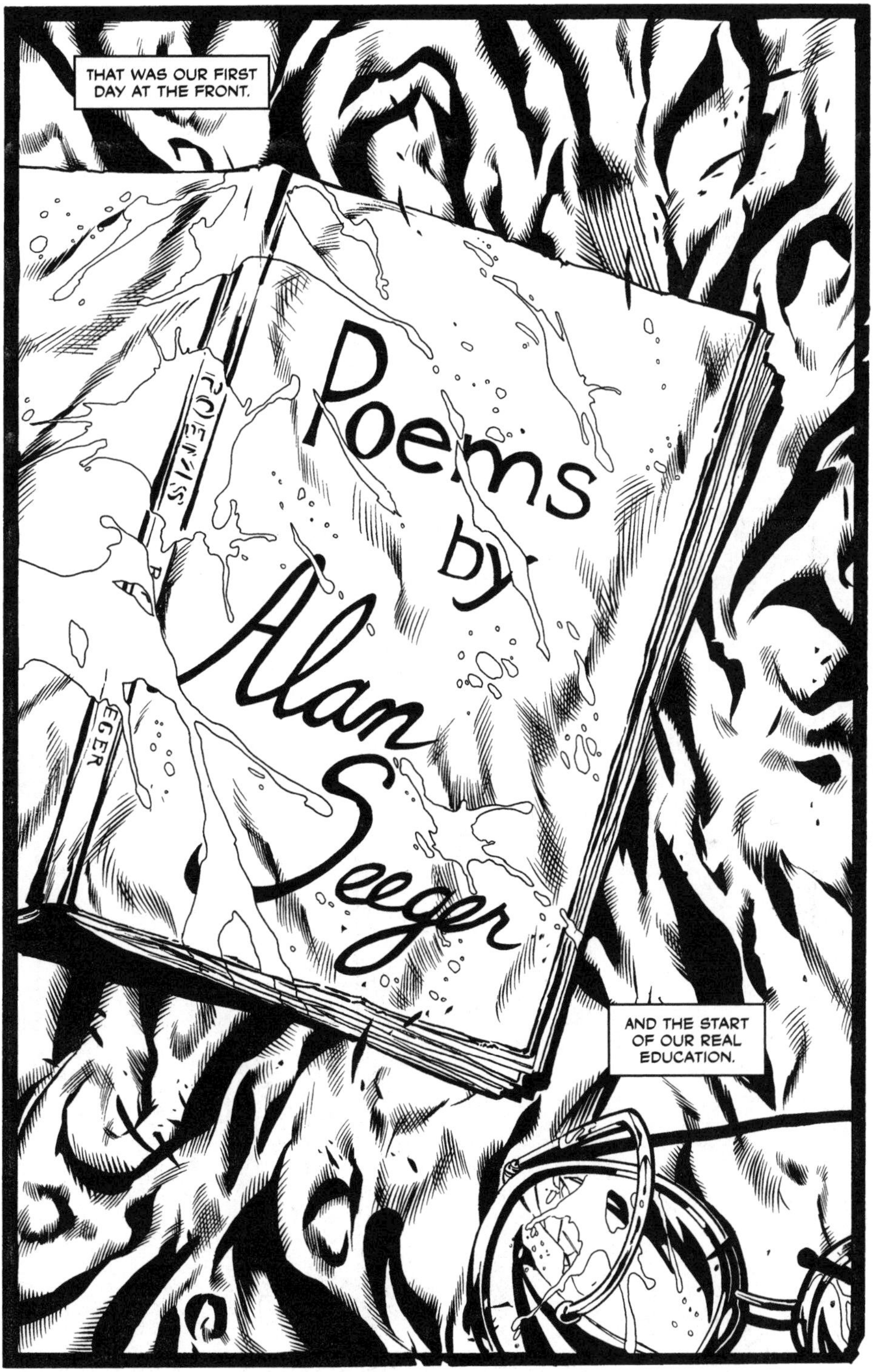
THAT WAS OUR FIRST DAY AT THE FRONT.
Poems by Alan Seeger
POEMS
SEEGER
AND THE START OF OUR REAL EDUCATION.

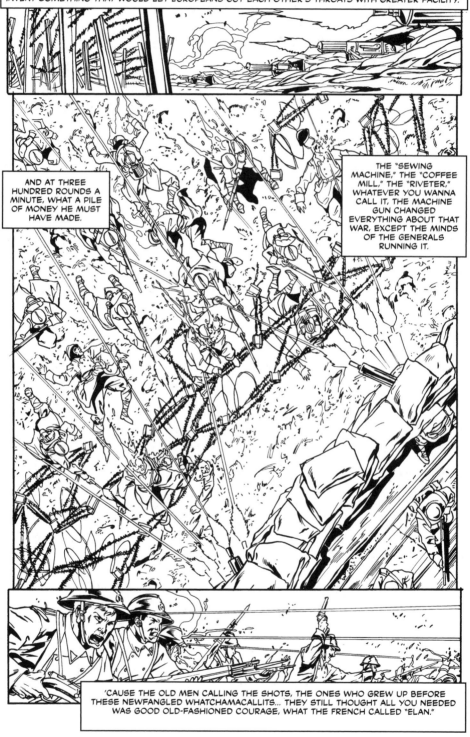

WE LEARNED ABOUT ALL THE NEW TOYS OF MODERN WARFARE; BARBED WIRE, LAND MINES, AND A REAL DOOZY, THE MACHINE GUN... THOUGHT UP BY SOME AMERICAN-BORN ENGLISHMAN WHO SUPPOSEDLY GOT THE IDEA WHEN SOMEBODY TOLD HIM, "IF YOU WANT TO MAKE A PILE OF MONEY, INVENT SOMETHING THAT WOULD LET EUROPEANS CUT EACH OTHER'S THROATS WITH GREATER FACILITY."

AND AT THREE HUNDRED ROUNDS A MINUTE, WHAT A PILE OF MONEY HE MUST HAVE MADE.

THE "SEWING MACHINE," THE "COFFEE MILL," THE "RIVETER," WHATEVER YOU WANNA CALL IT, THE MACHINE GUN CHANGED EVERYTHING ABOUT THAT WAR, EXCEPT THE MINDS OF THE GENERALS RUNNING IT.

'CAUSE THE OLD MEN CALLING THE SHOTS, THE ONES WHO GREW UP BEFORE THESE NEWFANGLED WHATCHAMACALLITS... THEY STILL THOUGHT ALL YOU NEEDED WAS GOOD OLD-FASHIONED COURAGE, WHAT THE FRENCH CALLED "ELAN."

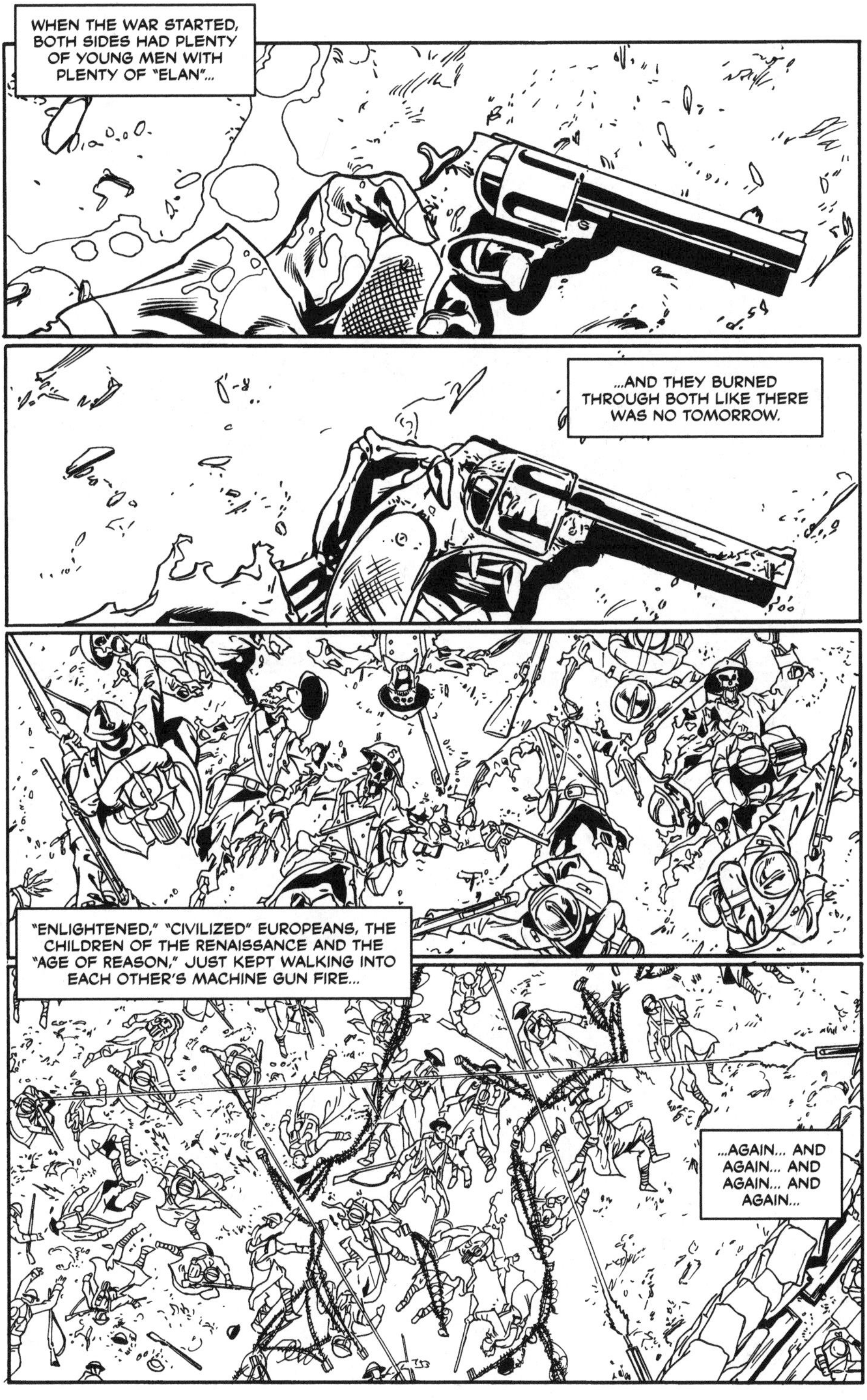
WHEN THE WAR STARTED, BOTH SIDES HAD PLENTY OF YOUNG MEN WITH PLENTY OF "ELAN"...
...AND THEY BURNED THROUGH BOTH LIKE THERE WAS NO TOMORROW.
"ENLIGHTENED," "CIVILIZED" EUROPEANS, THE CHILDREN OF THE RENAISSANCE AND THE "AGE OF REASON," JUST KEPT WALKING INTO EACH OTHER'S MACHINE GUN FIRE...
...AGAIN... AND AGAIN... AND AGAIN... AND AGAIN...

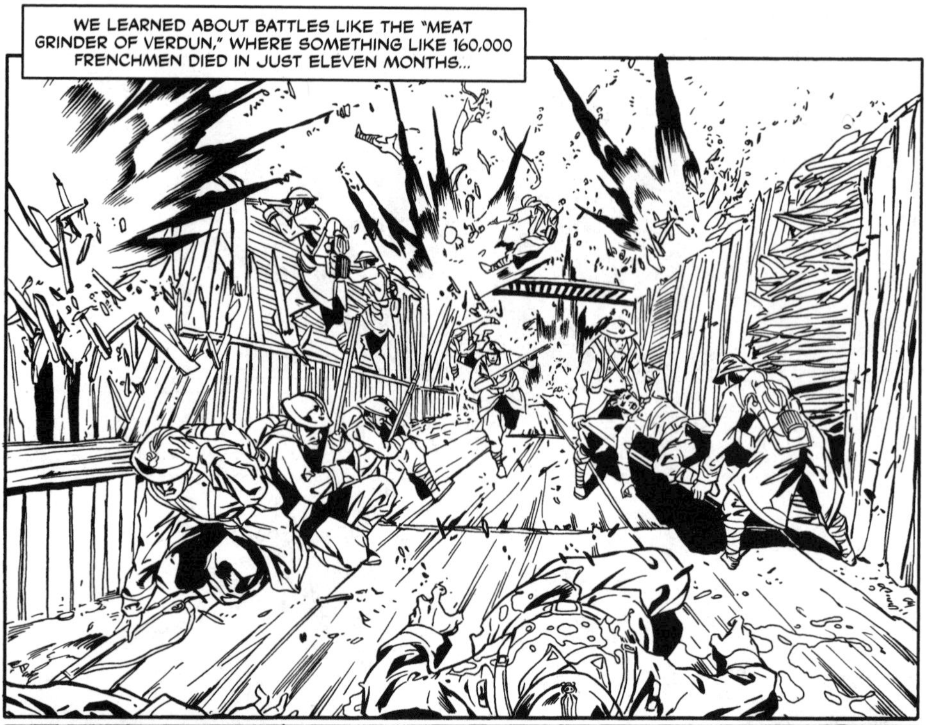
WE LEARNED ABOUT BATTLES LIKE THE "MEAT GRINDER OF VERDUN," WHERE SOMETHING LIKE 160,000 FRENCHMEN DIED IN JUST ELEVEN MONTHS...

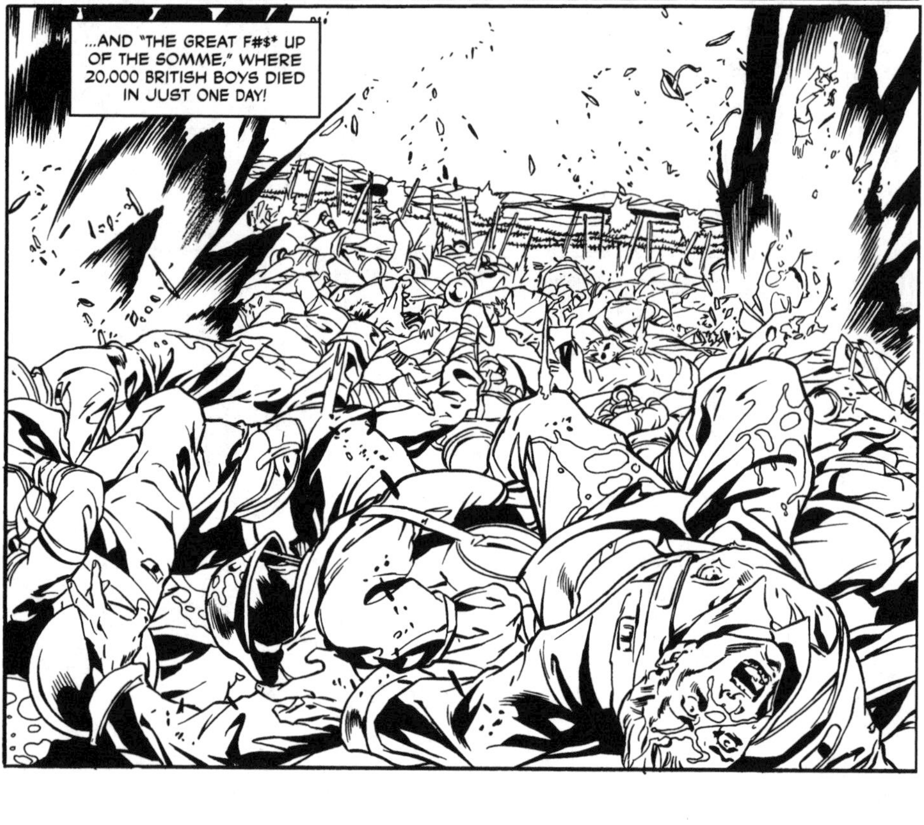
...AND "THE GREAT F#$* UP OF THE SOMME," WHERE 20,000 BRITISH BOYS DIED IN JUST ONE DAY!

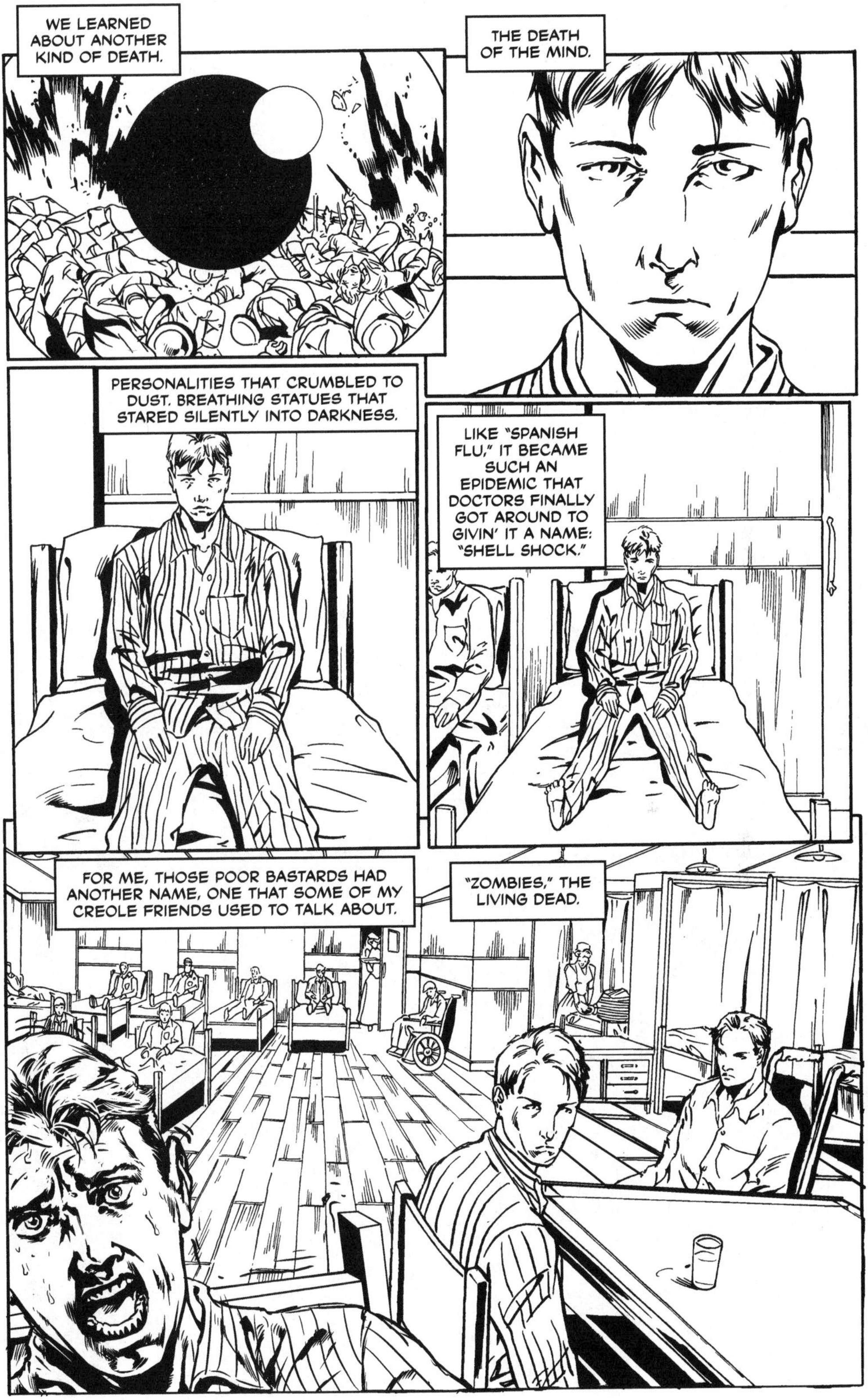
WE LEARNED ABOUT ANOTHER KIND OF DEATH.
THE DEATH OF THE MIND.
PERSONALITIES THAT CRUMBLED TO DUST. BREATHING STATUES THAT STARED SILENTLY INTO DARKNESS.
LIKE "SPANISH FLU," IT BECAME SUCH AN EPIDEMIC THAT DOCTORS FINALLY GOT AROUND TO GIVIN' IT A NAME: "SHELL SHOCK."
FOR ME, THOSE POOR BASTARDS HAD ANOTHER NAME, ONE THAT SOME OF MY CREOLE FRIENDS USED TO TALK ABOUT.
"ZOMBIES," THE LIVING DEAD.

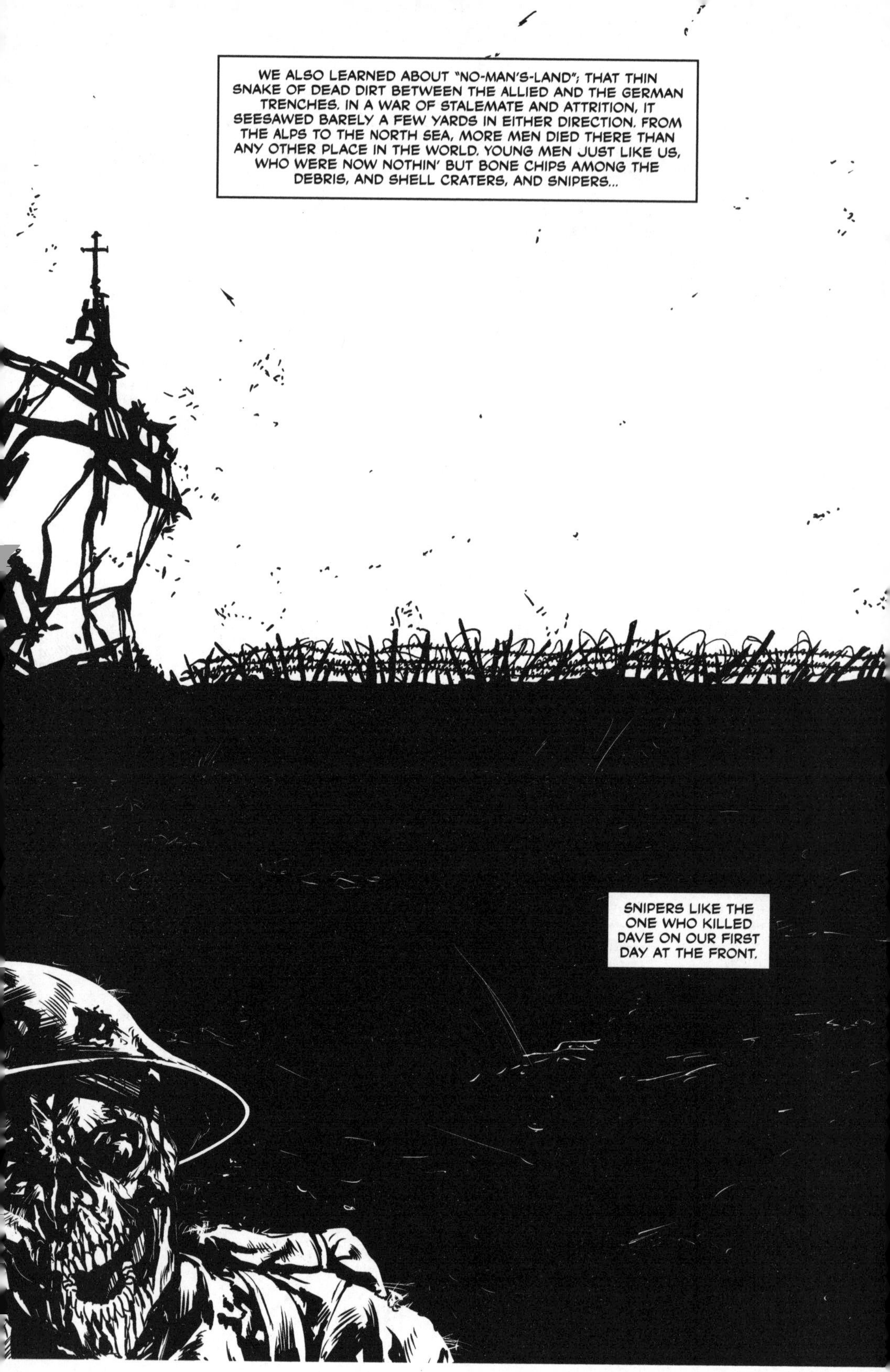
WE ALSO LEARNED ABOUT "NO-MAN'S-LAND"; THAT THIN SNAKE OF DEAD DIRT BETWEEN THE ALLIED AND THE GERMAN TRENCHES. IN A WAR OF STALEMATE AND ATTRITION, IT SEESAWED BARELY A FEW YARDS IN EITHER DIRECTION. FROM THE ALPS TO THE NORTH SEA, MORE MEN DIED THERE THAN ANY OTHER PLACE IN THE WORLD. YOUNG MEN JUST LIKE US, WHO WERE NOW NOTHIN' BUT BONE CHIPS AMONG THE DEBRIS, AND SHELL CRATERS, AND SNIPERS...
SNIPERS LIKE THE ONE WHO KILLED DAVE ON OUR FIRST DAY AT THE FRONT.

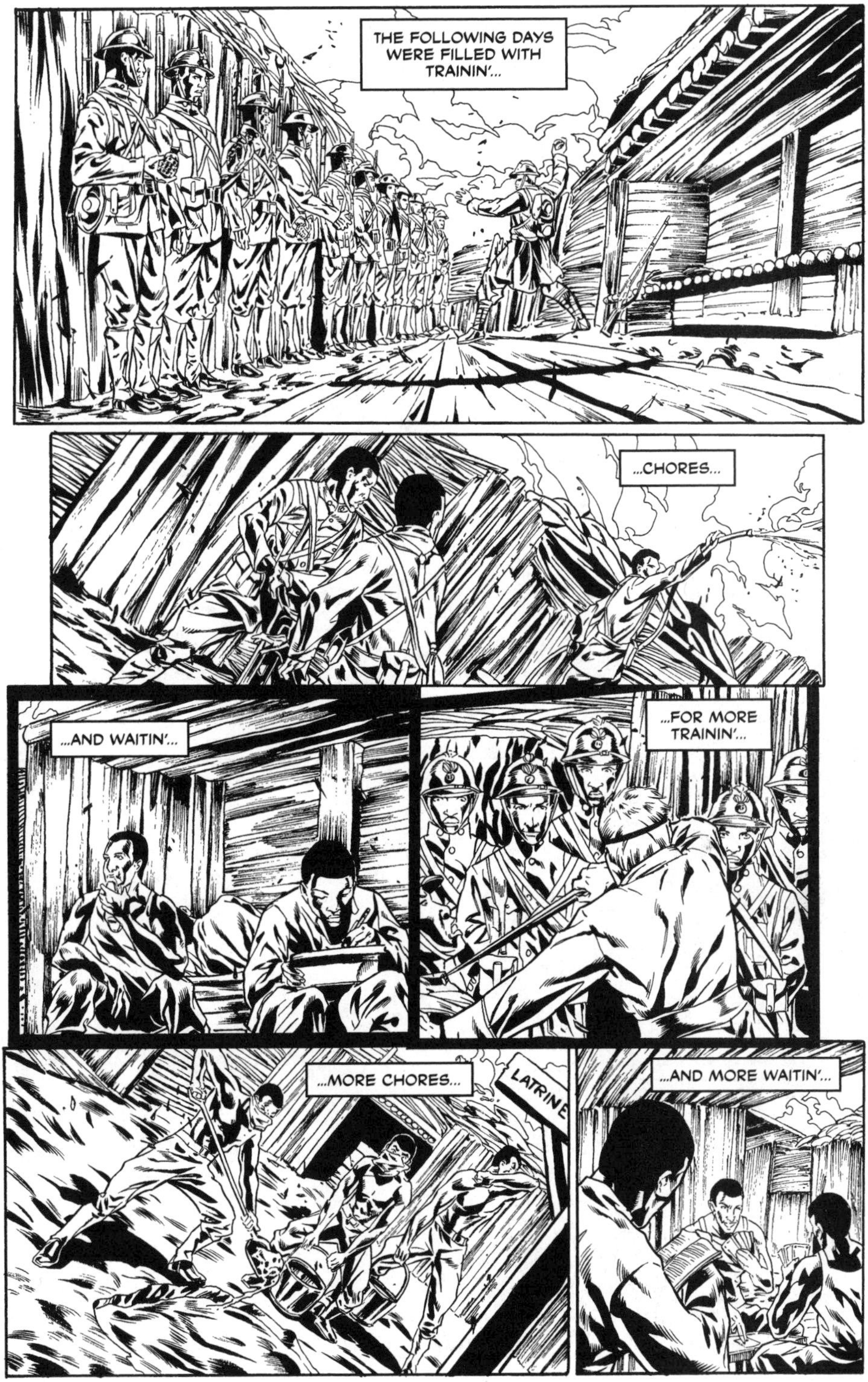
THE FOLLOWING DAYS WERE FILLED WITH TRAININ'...
...CHORES...
...AND WAITIN'...
...FOR MORE TRAININ'...
...MORE CHORES...
LATRINE
...AND MORE WAITIN'...

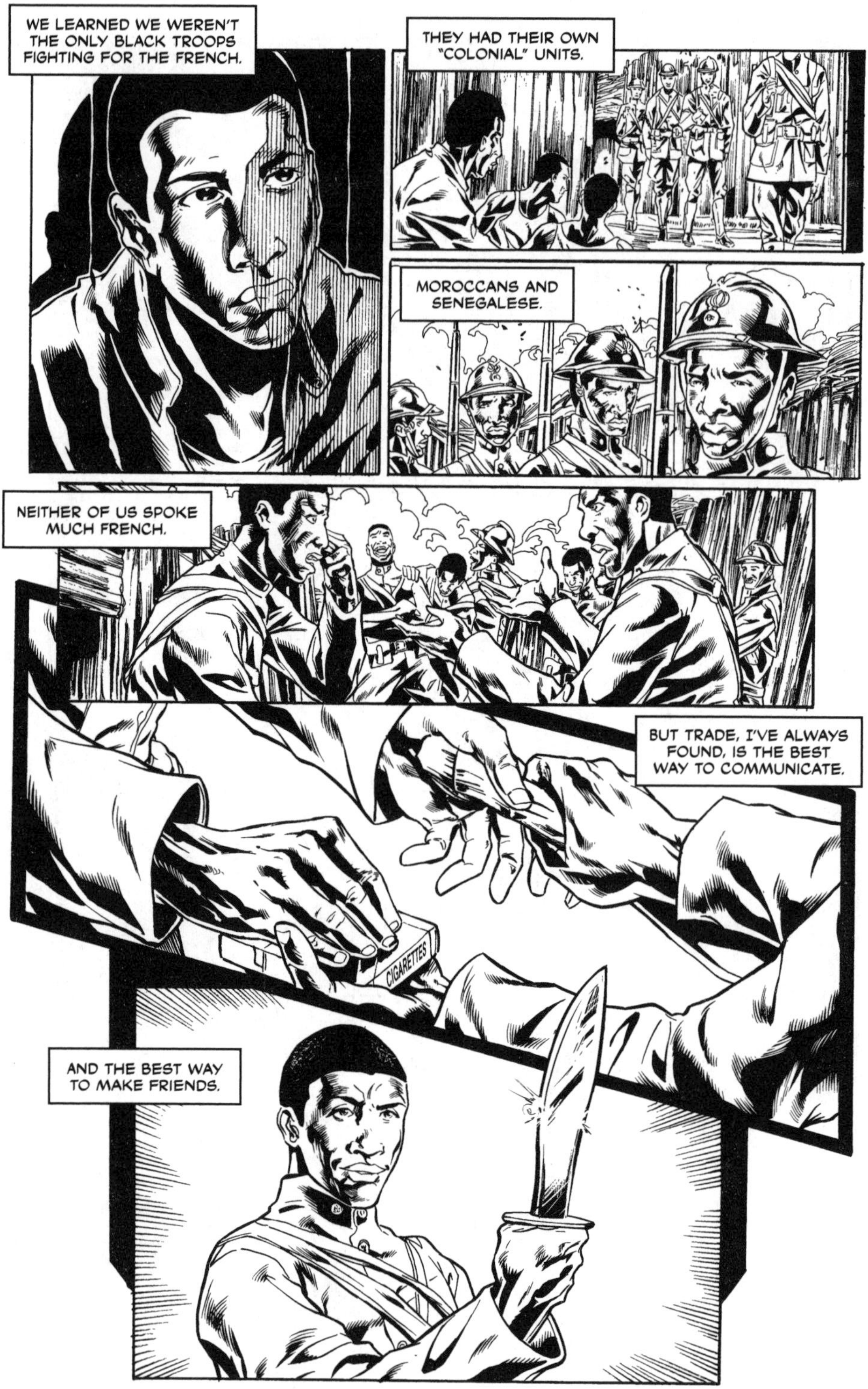
WE LEARNED WE WEREN'T THE ONLY BLACK TROOPS FIGHTING FOR THE FRENCH.
THEY HAD THEIR OWN "COLONIAL" UNITS.
MOROCCANS AND SENEGALESE.
NEITHER OF US SPOKE MUCH FRENCH.
BUT TRADE, I'VE ALWAYS FOUND, IS THE BEST WAY TO COMMUNICATE.
CIGARETTES
AND THE BEST WAY TO MAKE FRIENDS.

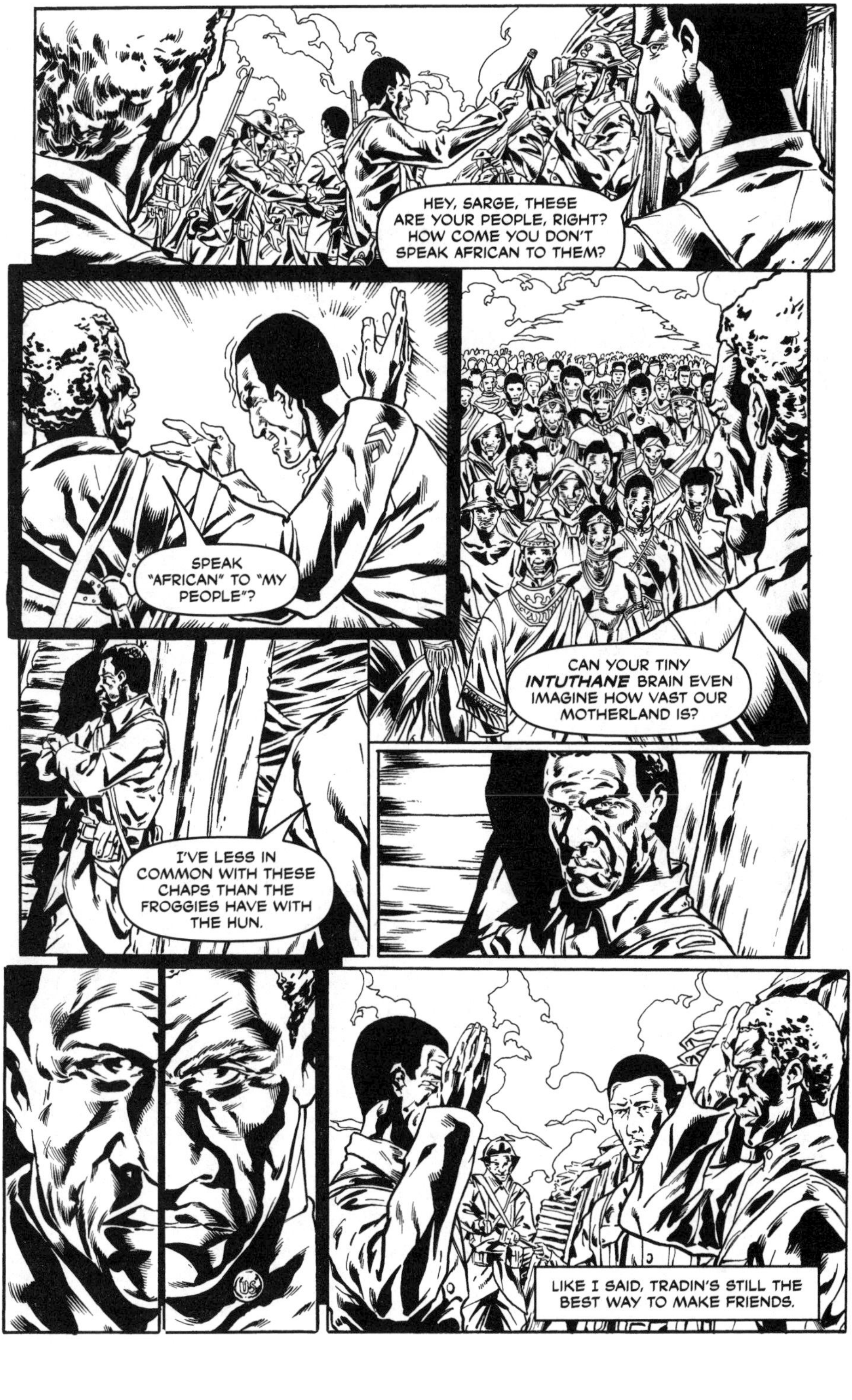
HEY, SARGE, THESE ARE YOUR PEOPLE, RIGHT? HOW COME YOU DON'T SPEAK AFRICAN TO THEM?
SPEAK "AFRICAN" TO "MY PEOPLE"?
CAN YOUR TINY INTUTHANE BRAIN EVEN IMAGINE HOW VAST OUR MOTHERLAND IS?
I'VE LESS IN COMMON WITH THESE CHAPS THAN THE FROGGIES HAVE WITH THE HUN.
LIKE I SAID, TRADIN'S STILL THE BEST WAY TO MAKE FRIENDS.

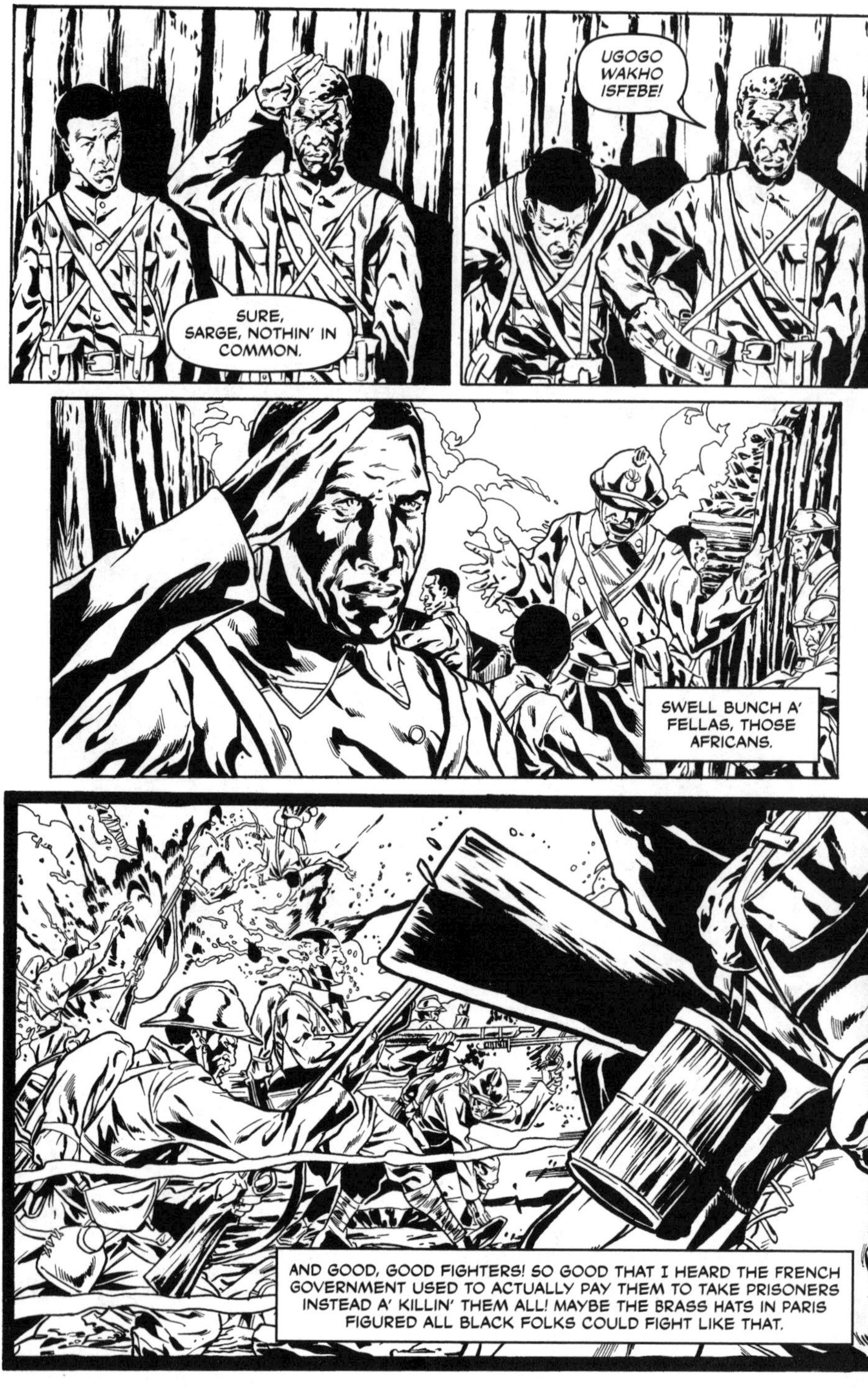
SURE, SARGE, NOTHIN' IN COMMON.
UGOGO WAKHO ISFEBE!
SWELL BUNCH A' FELLAS, THOSE AFRICANS.
AND GOOD, GOOD FIGHTERS! SO GOOD THAT I HEARD THE FRENCH GOVERNMENT USED TO ACTUALLY PAY THEM TO TAKE PRISONERS INSTEAD A' KILLIN' THEM ALL! MAYBE THE BRASS HATS IN PARIS FIGURED ALL BLACK FOLKS COULD FIGHT LIKE THAT.

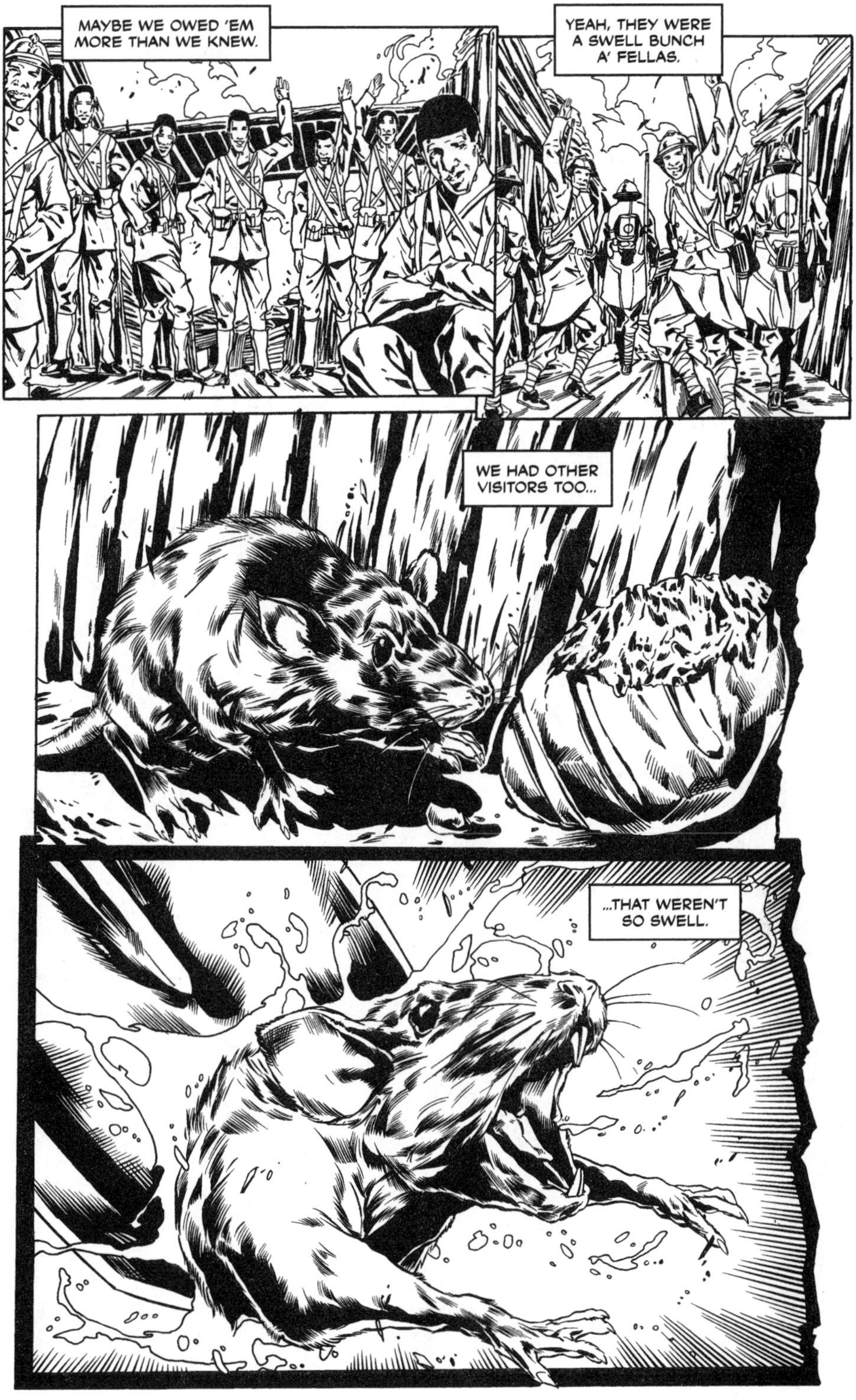
MAYBE WE OWED 'EM MORE THAN WE KNEW.
YEAH, THEY WERE A SWELL BUNCH A' FELLAS.
WE HAD OTHER VISITORS TOO...
...THAT WEREN'T SO SWELL.

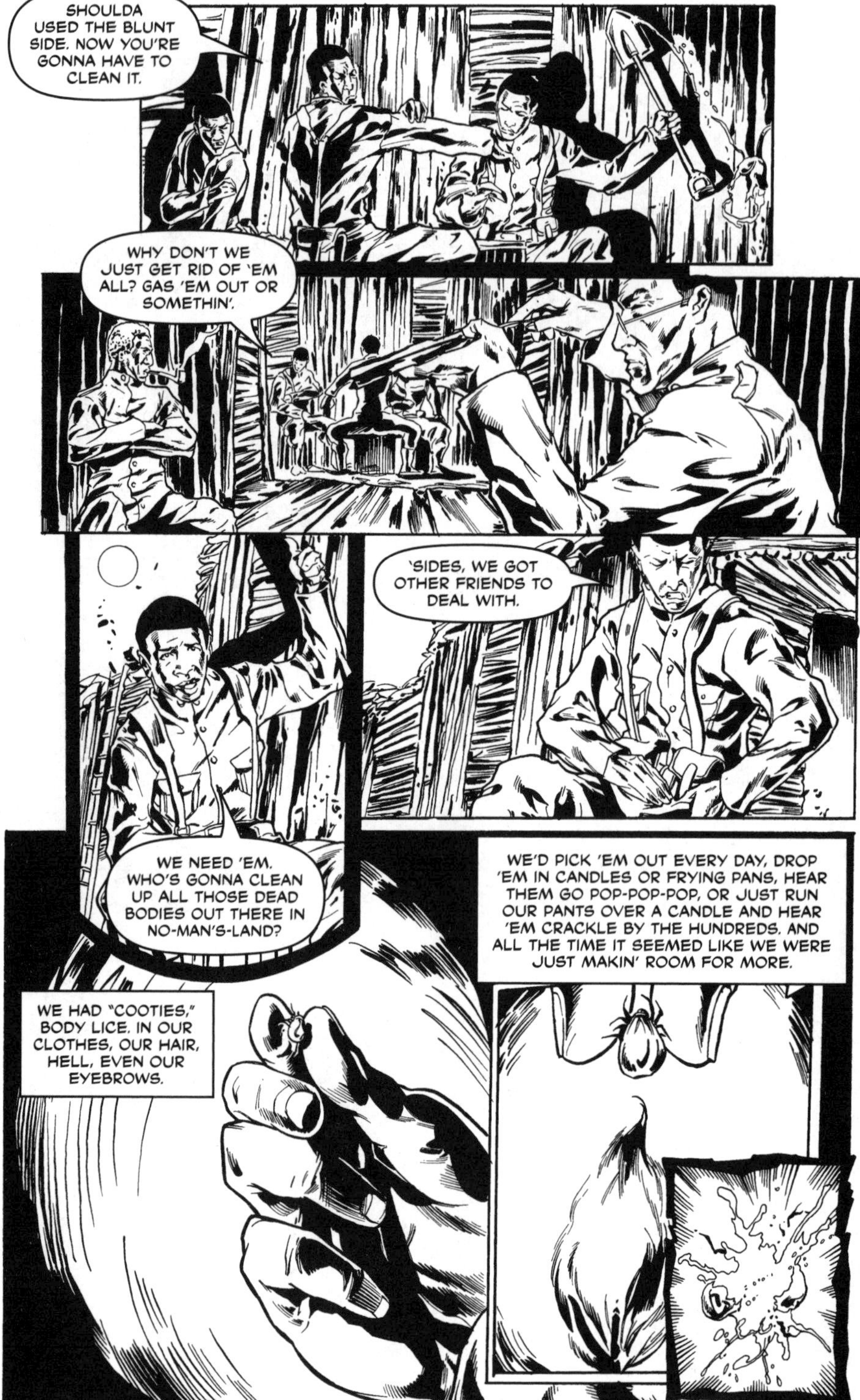
SHOULDA USED THE BLUNT SIDE. NOW YOU'RE GONNA HAVE TO CLEAN IT.
WHY DON'T WE JUST GET RID OF 'EM ALL? GAS 'EM OUT OR SOMETHIN'.
'SIDES, WE GOT OTHER FRIENDS TO DEAL WITH.
WE NEED 'EM. WHO'S GONNA CLEAN UP ALL THOSE DEAD BODIES OUT THERE IN NO-MAN'S-LAND?
WE HAD "COOTIES," BODY LICE. IN OUR CLOTHES, OUR HAIR, HELL, EVEN OUR EYEBROWS.
WE'D PICK 'EM OUT EVERY DAY, DROP 'EM IN CANDLES OR FRYING PANS, HEAR THEM GO POP-POP-POP, OR JUST RUN OUR PANTS OVER A CANDLE AND HEAR 'EM CRACKLE BY THE HUNDREDS. AND ALL THE TIME IT SEEMED LIKE WE WERE JUST MAKIN' ROOM FOR MORE.

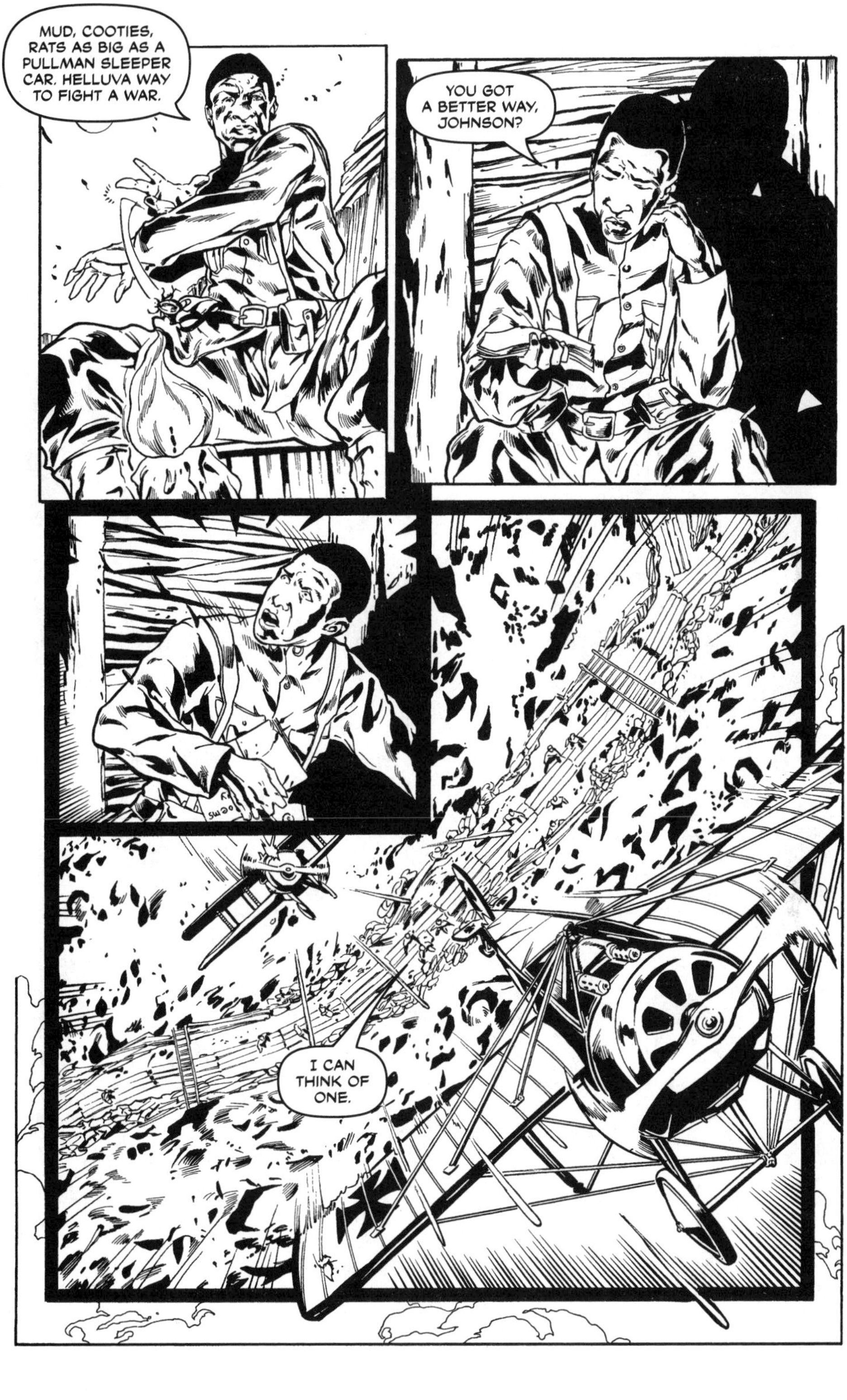
MUD, COOTIES, RATS AS BIG AS A PULLMAN SLEEPER CAR. HELLUVA WAY TO FIGHT A WAR.
YOU GOT A BETTER WAY, JOHNSON?
I CAN THINK OF ONE.

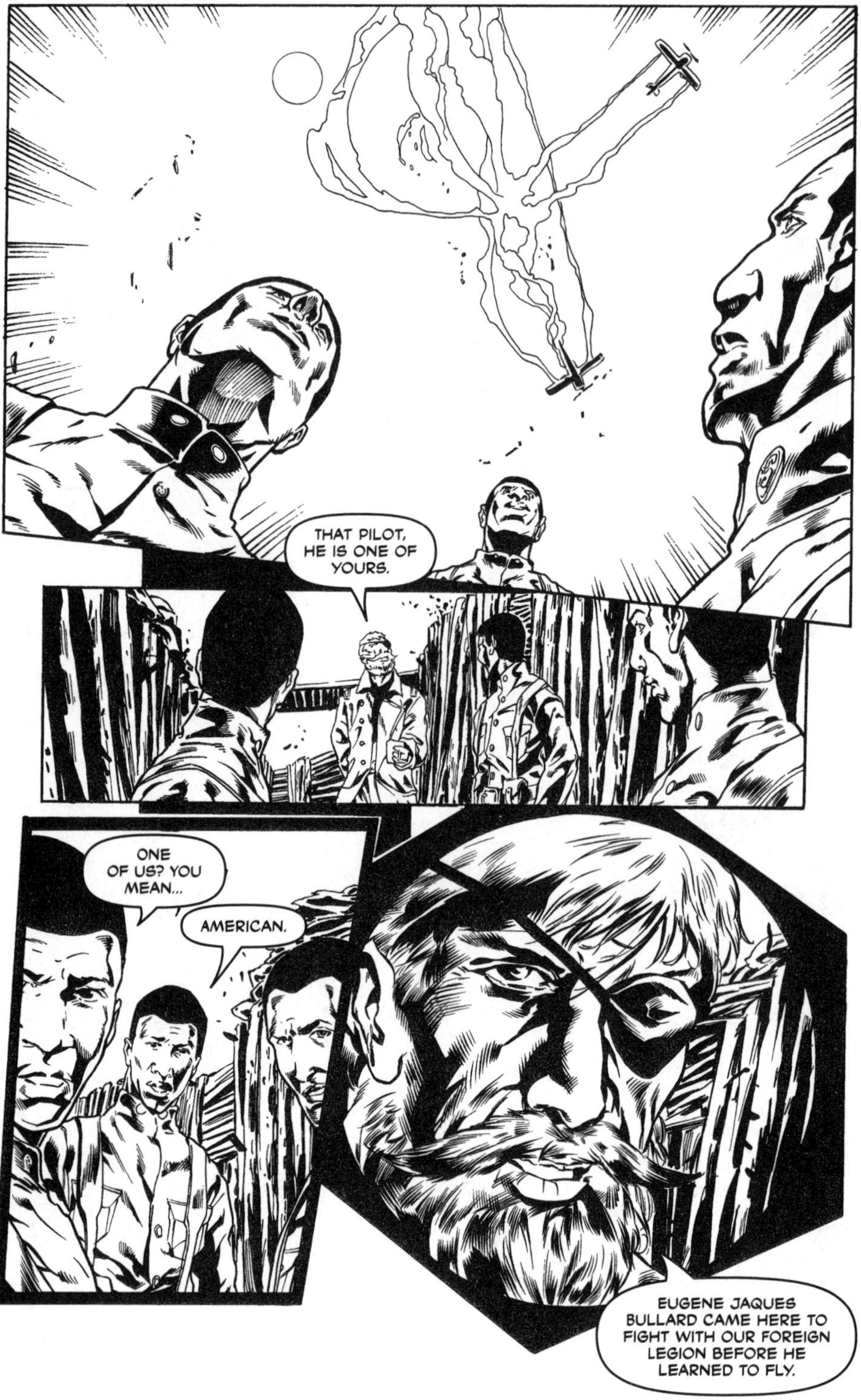
THAT PILOT, HE IS ONE OF YOURS.
ONE OF US? YOU MEAN...
AMERICAN.
EUGENE JAQUES BULLARD CAME HERE TO FIGHT WITH OUR FOREIGN LEGION BEFORE HE LEARNED TO FLY.

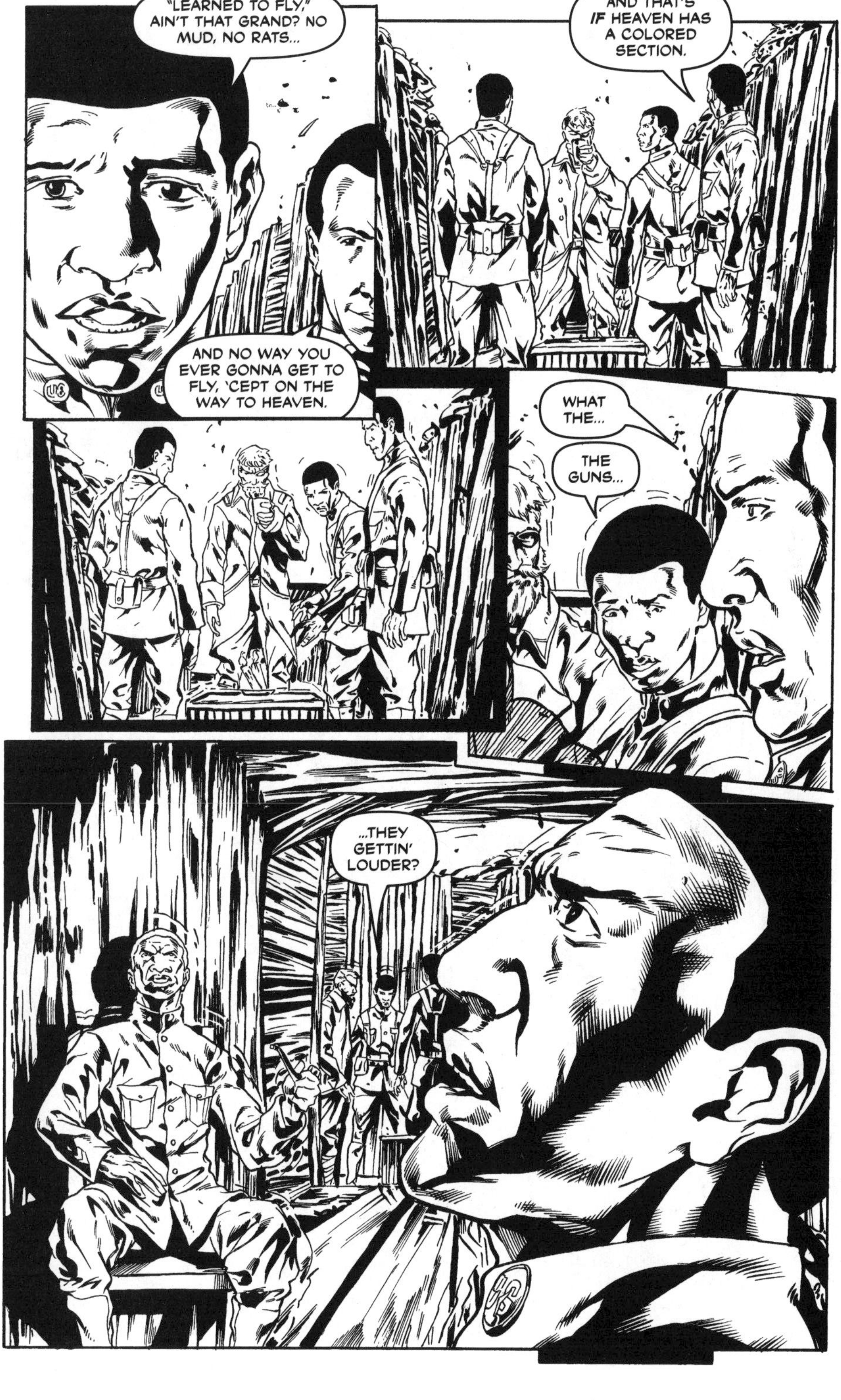
"LEARNED TO FLY," AIN'T THAT GRAND? NO MUD, NO RATS...
AND THAT'S *IF* HEAVEN HAS A COLORED SECTION.
AND NO WAY YOU EVER GONNA GET TO FLY, 'CEPT ON THE WAY TO HEAVEN.
WHAT THE...
THE GUNS...
...THEY GETTIN' LOUDER?

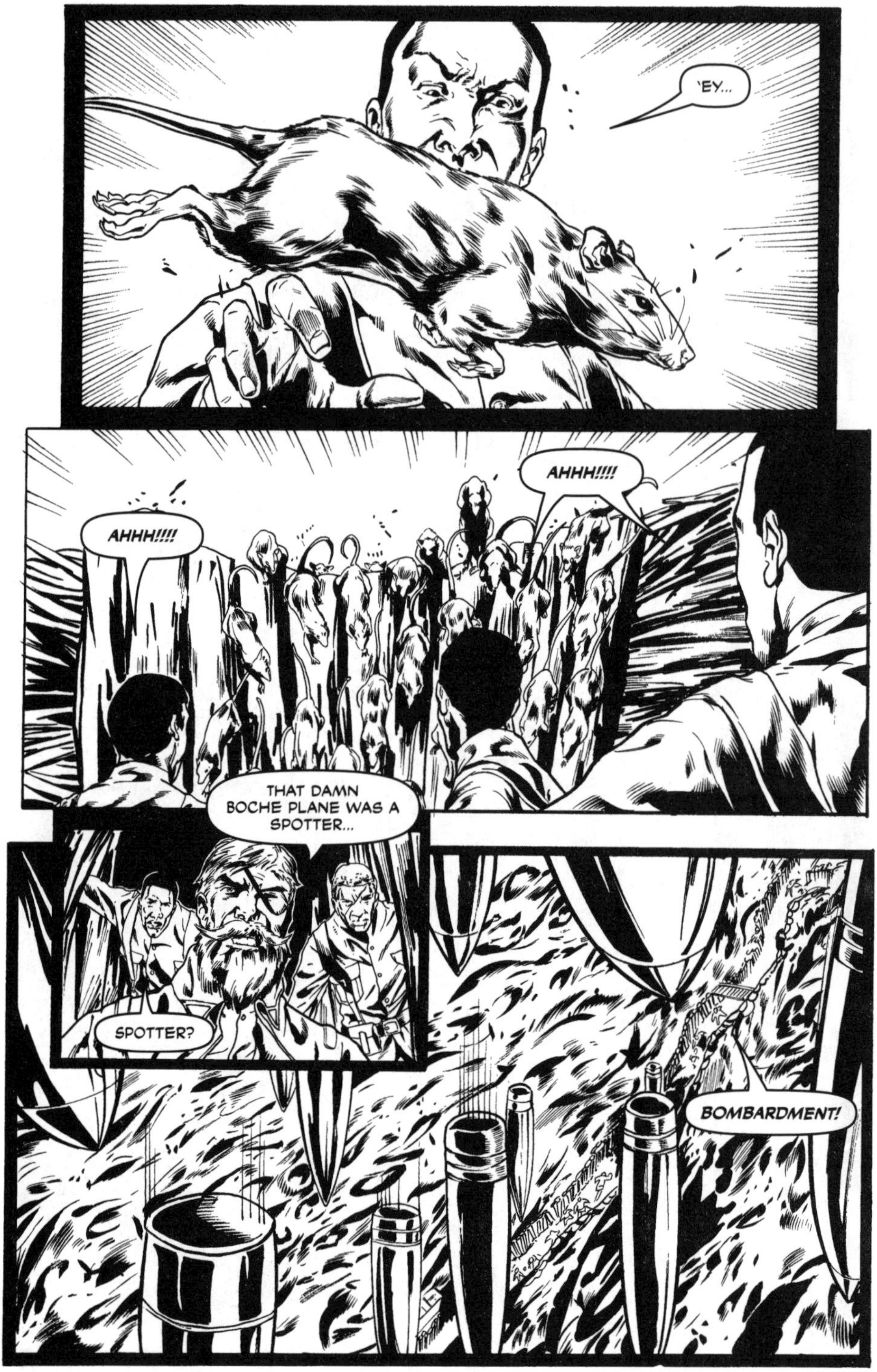
'EY...
AHHH!!!!
AHHH!!!!
THAT DAMN BOCHE PLANE WAS A SPOTTER...
SPOTTER?
BOMBARDMENT!

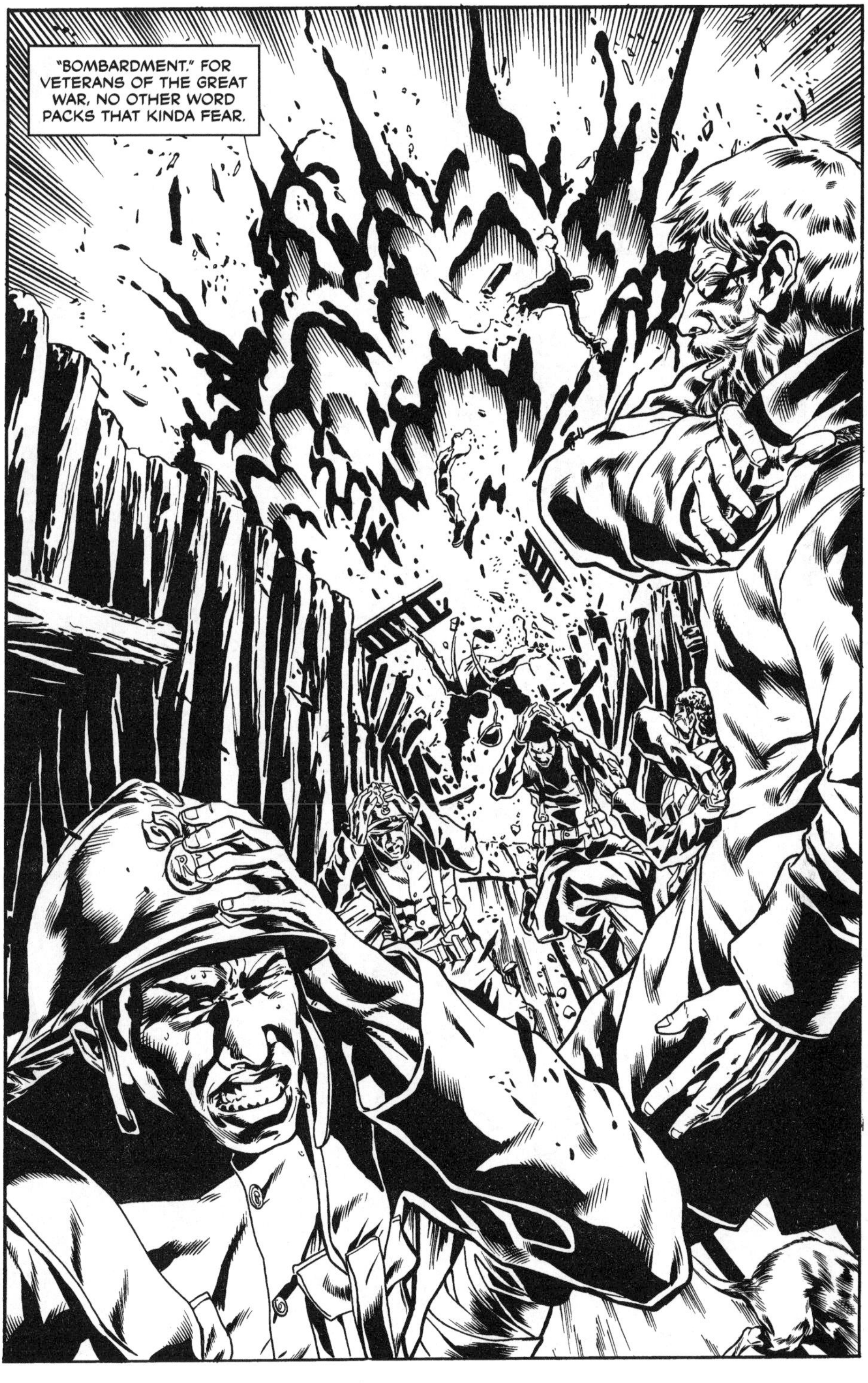
"BOMBARDMENT." FOR VETERANS OF THE GREAT WAR, NO OTHER WORD PACKS THAT KINDA FEAR.

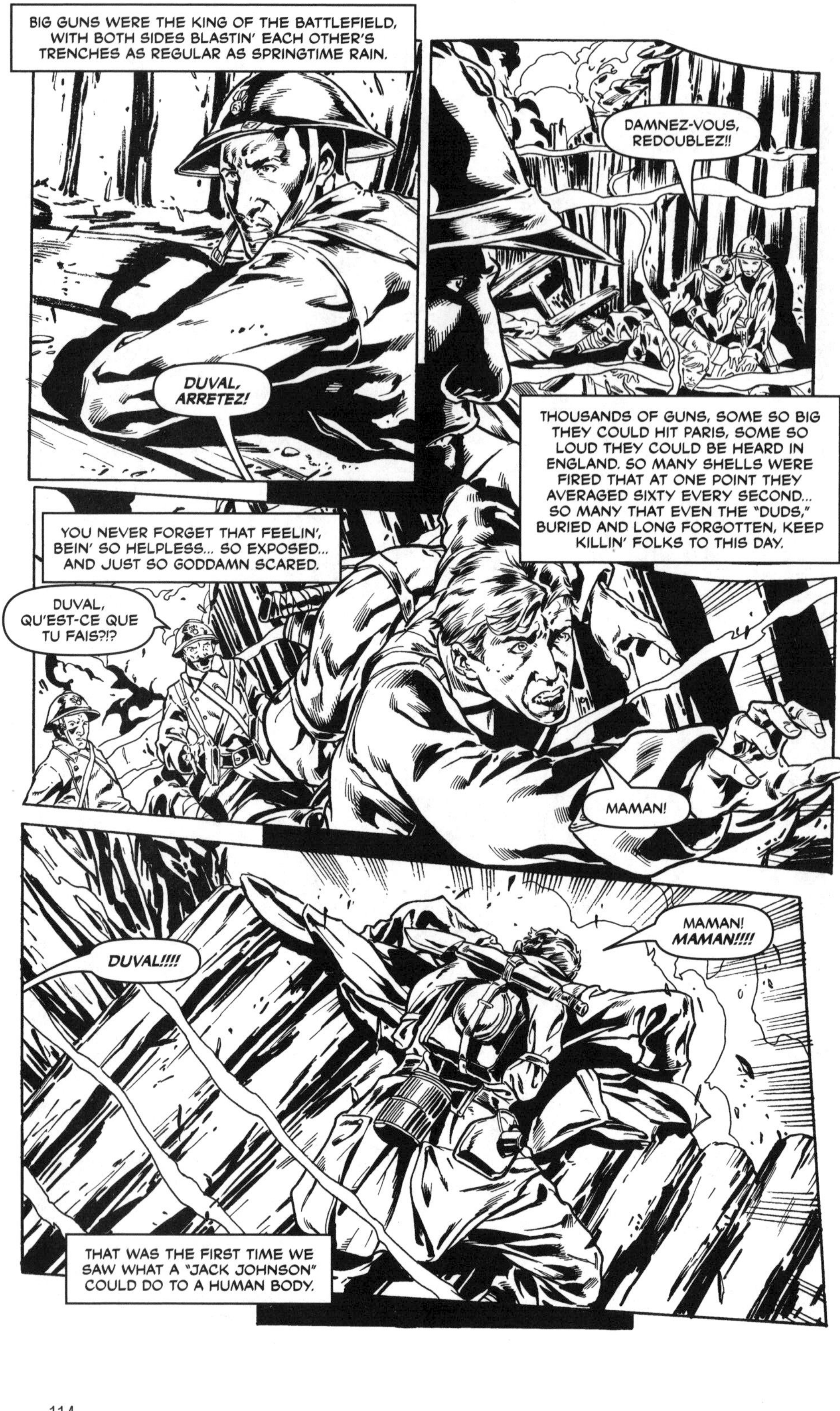
BIG GUNS WERE THE KING OF THE BATTLEFIELD, WITH BOTH SIDES BLASTIN' EACH OTHER'S TRENCHES AS REGULAR AS SPRINGTIME RAIN.
DUVAL, ARRETEZ!
DAMNEZ-VOUS, REDOUBLEZ!!
THOUSANDS OF GUNS, SOME SO BIG THEY COULD HIT PARIS, SOME SO LOUD THEY COULD BE HEARD IN ENGLAND. SO MANY SHELLS WERE FIRED THAT AT ONE POINT THEY AVERAGED SIXTY EVERY SECOND... SO MANY THAT EVEN THE "DUDS," BURIED AND LONG FORGOTTEN, KEEP KILLIN' FOLKS TO THIS DAY.
YOU NEVER FORGET THAT FEELIN', BEIN' SO HELPLESS... SO EXPOSED... AND JUST SO GODDAMN SCARED.
DUVAL, QU'EST-CE QUE TU FAIS?!?
MAMAN!
DUVAL!!!!
MAMAN! MAMAN!!!!
THAT WAS THE FIRST TIME WE SAW WHAT A "JACK JOHNSON" COULD DO TO A HUMAN BODY.

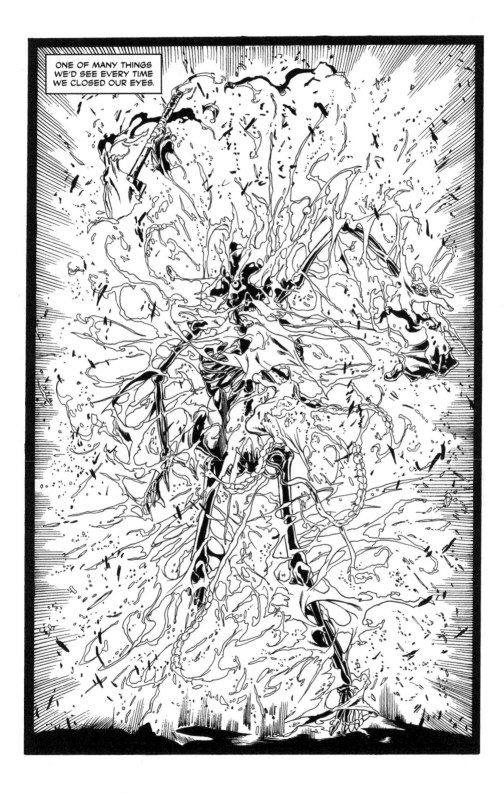

ONE OF MANY THINGS WE'D SEE EVERY TIME WE CLOSED OUR EYES.

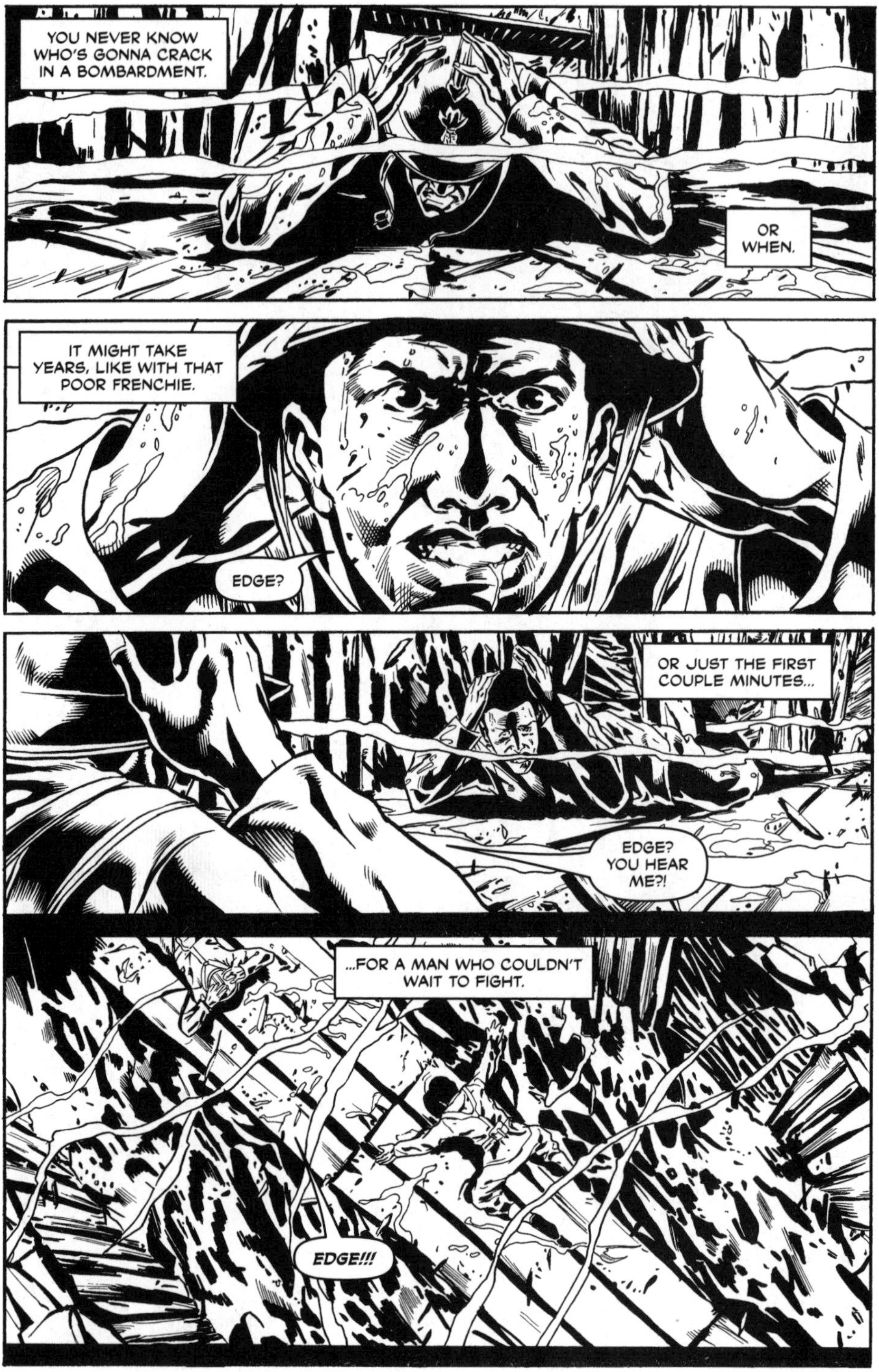
YOU NEVER KNOW WHO'S GONNA CRACK IN A BOMBARDMENT.
OR WHEN.
IT MIGHT TAKE YEARS, LIKE WITH THAT POOR FRENCHIE.
EDGE?
OR JUST THE FIRST COUPLE MINUTES...
EDGE? YOU HEAR ME?!
...FOR A MAN WHO COULDN'T WAIT TO FIGHT.
EDGE!!!

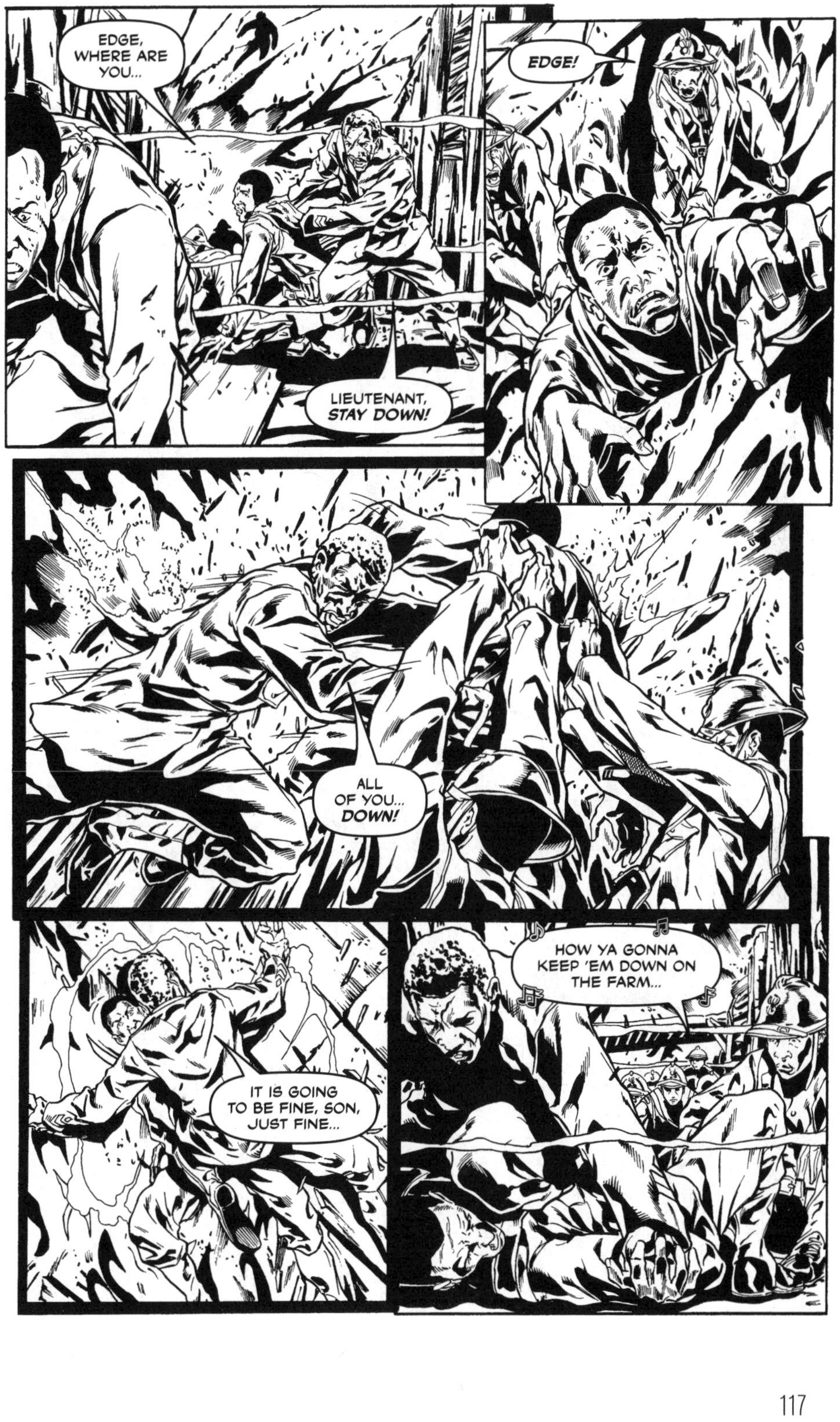
EDGE, WHERE ARE YOU...
LIEUTENANT, STAY DOWN!
EDGE!
ALL OF YOU... DOWN!
IT IS GOING TO BE FINE, SON, JUST FINE...
HOW YA GONNA KEEP 'EM DOWN ON THE FARM...

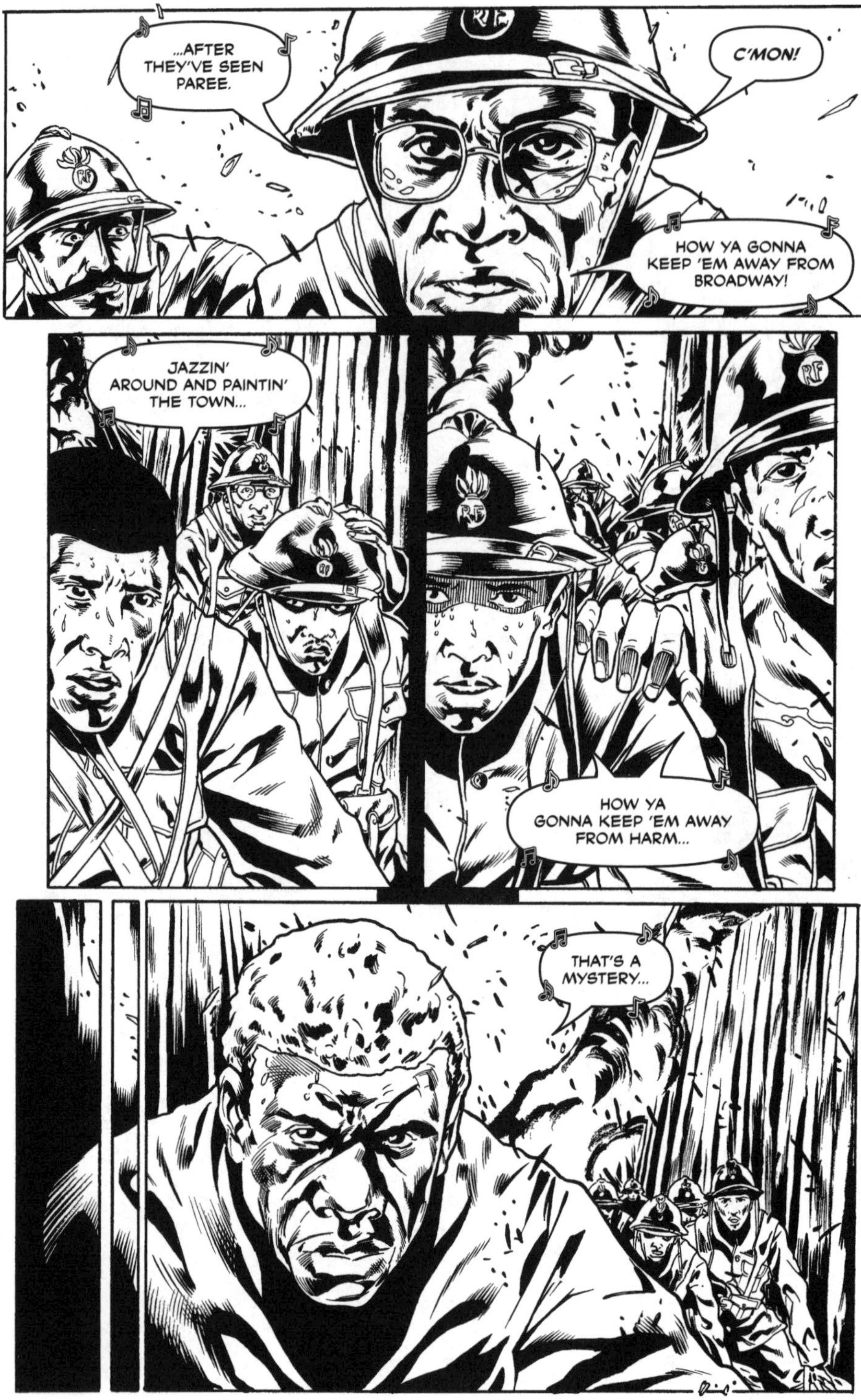
...AFTER THEY'VE SEEN PAREE.
C'MON!
HOW YA GONNA KEEP 'EM AWAY FROM BROADWAY!
JAZZIN' AROUND AND PAINTIN' THE TOWN...
HOW YA GONNA KEEP 'EM AWAY FROM HARM...
THAT'S A MYSTERY...

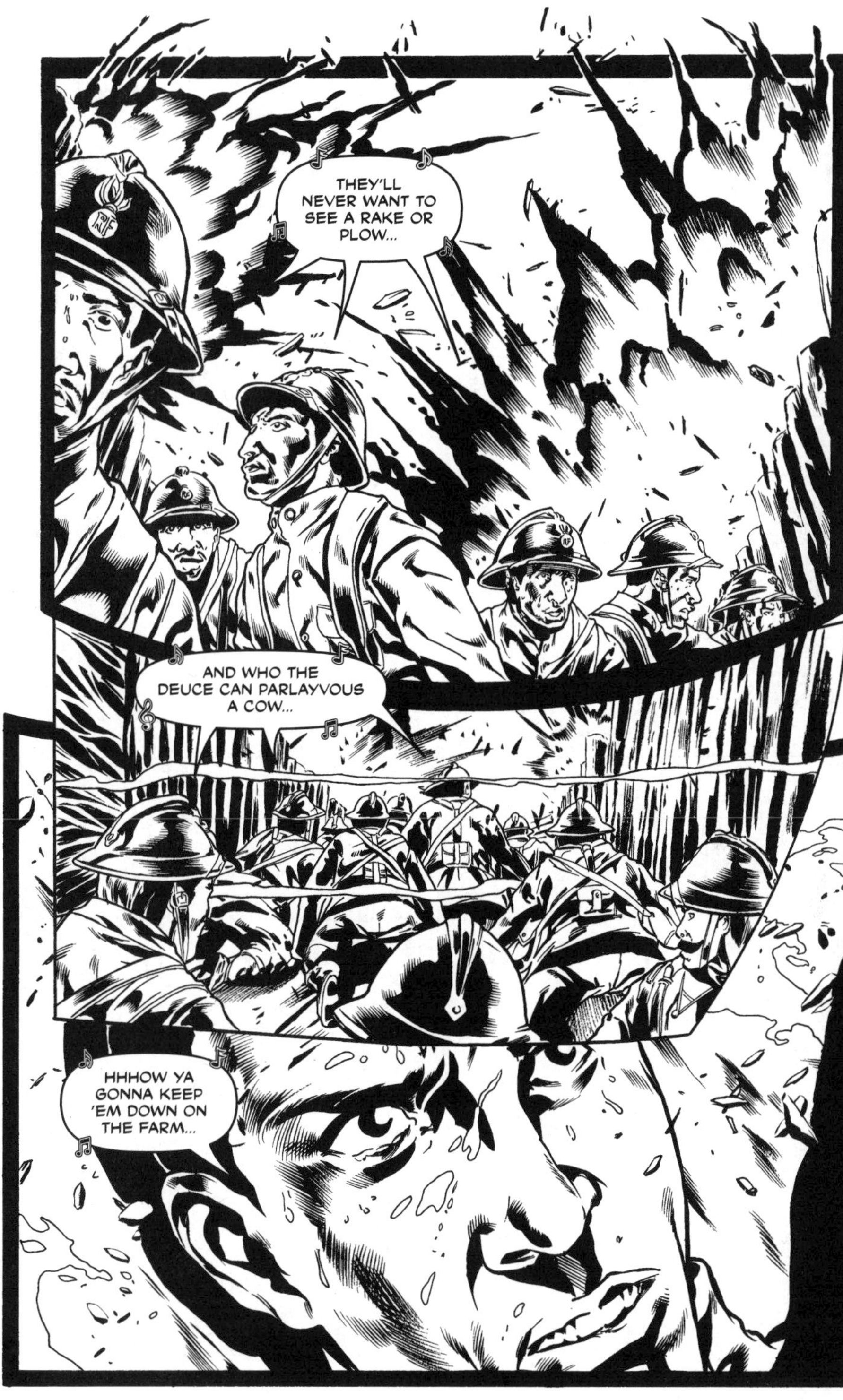
THEY'LL NEVER WANT TO SEE A RAKE OR PLOW...
AND WHO THE DEUCE CAN PARLAYVOUS A COW...
HHHOW YA GONNA KEEP 'EM DOWN ON THE FARM...

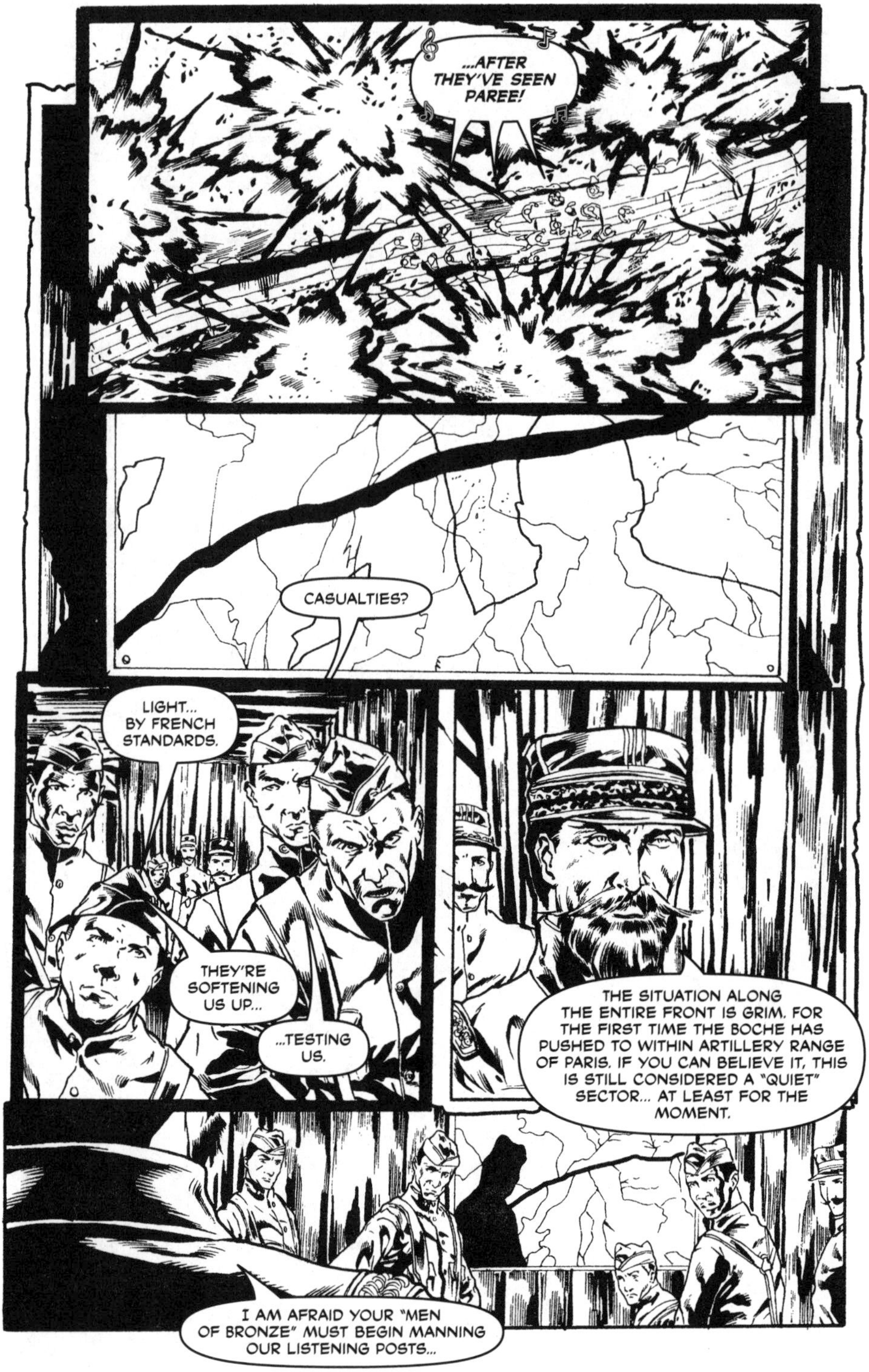
...AFTER THEY'VE SEEN PAREE!
CASUALTIES?
LIGHT... BY FRENCH STANDARDS.
THEY'RE SOFTENING US UP...
...TESTING US.
THE SITUATION ALONG THE ENTIRE FRONT IS GRIM. FOR THE FIRST TIME THE BOCHE HAS PUSHED TO WITHIN ARTILLERY RANGE OF PARIS. IF YOU CAN BELIEVE IT, THIS IS STILL CONSIDERED A "QUIET" SECTOR... AT LEAST FOR THE MOMENT.
I AM AFRAID YOUR "MEN OF BRONZE" MUST BEGIN MANNING OUR LISTENING POSTS...

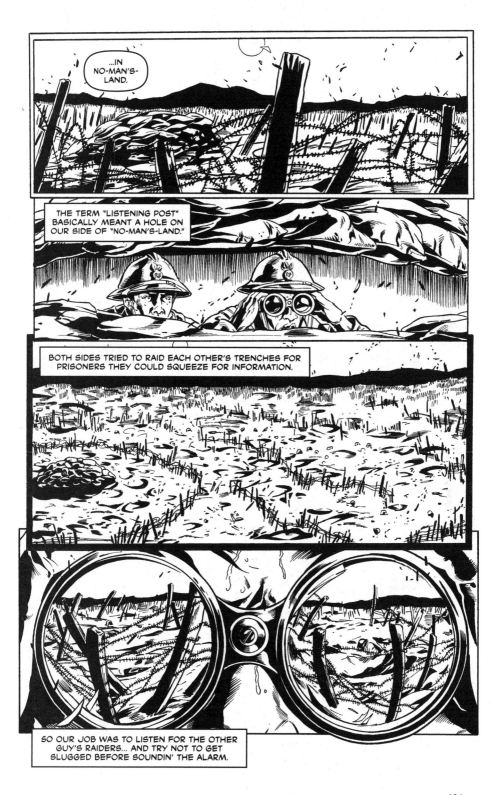

...IN NO-MAN'S-LAND.

THE TERM "LISTENING POST" BASICALLY MEANT A HOLE ON OUR SIDE OF "NO-MAN'S-LAND."

BOTH SIDES TRIED TO RAID EACH OTHER'S TRENCHES FOR PRISONERS THEY COULD SQUEEZE FOR INFORMATION.

SO OUR JOB WAS TO LISTEN FOR THE OTHER GUY'S RAIDERS... AND TRY NOT TO GET SLUGGED BEFORE SOUNDIN' THE ALARM.

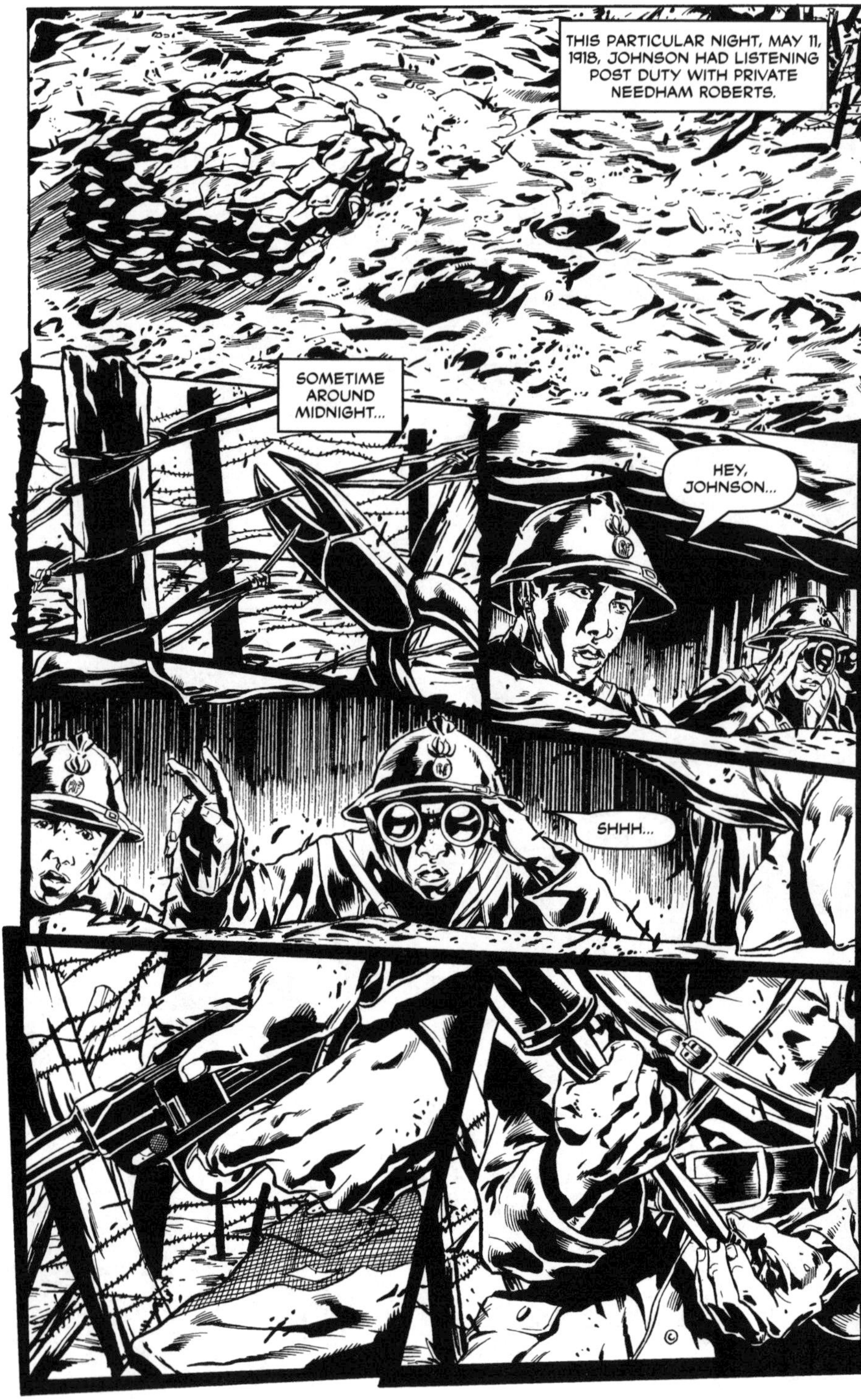
THIS PARTICULAR NIGHT, MAY 11, 1918, JOHNSON HAD LISTENING POST DUTY WITH PRIVATE NEEDHAM ROBERTS.
SOMETIME AROUND MIDNIGHT...
HEY, JOHNSON...
SHHH...

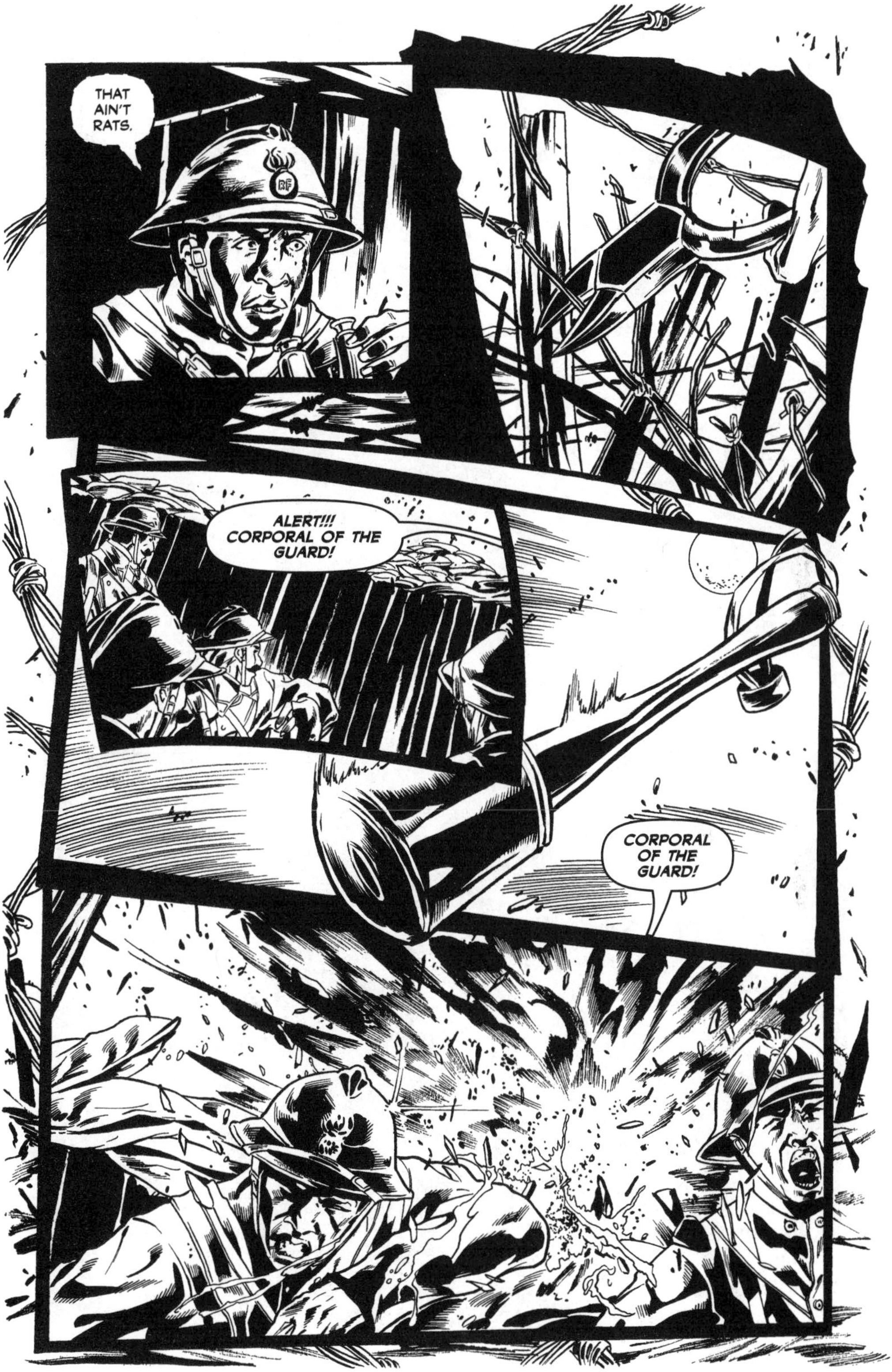
THAT AIN'T RATS.
ALERT!!! CORPORAL OF THE GUARD!
CORPORAL OF THE GUARD!

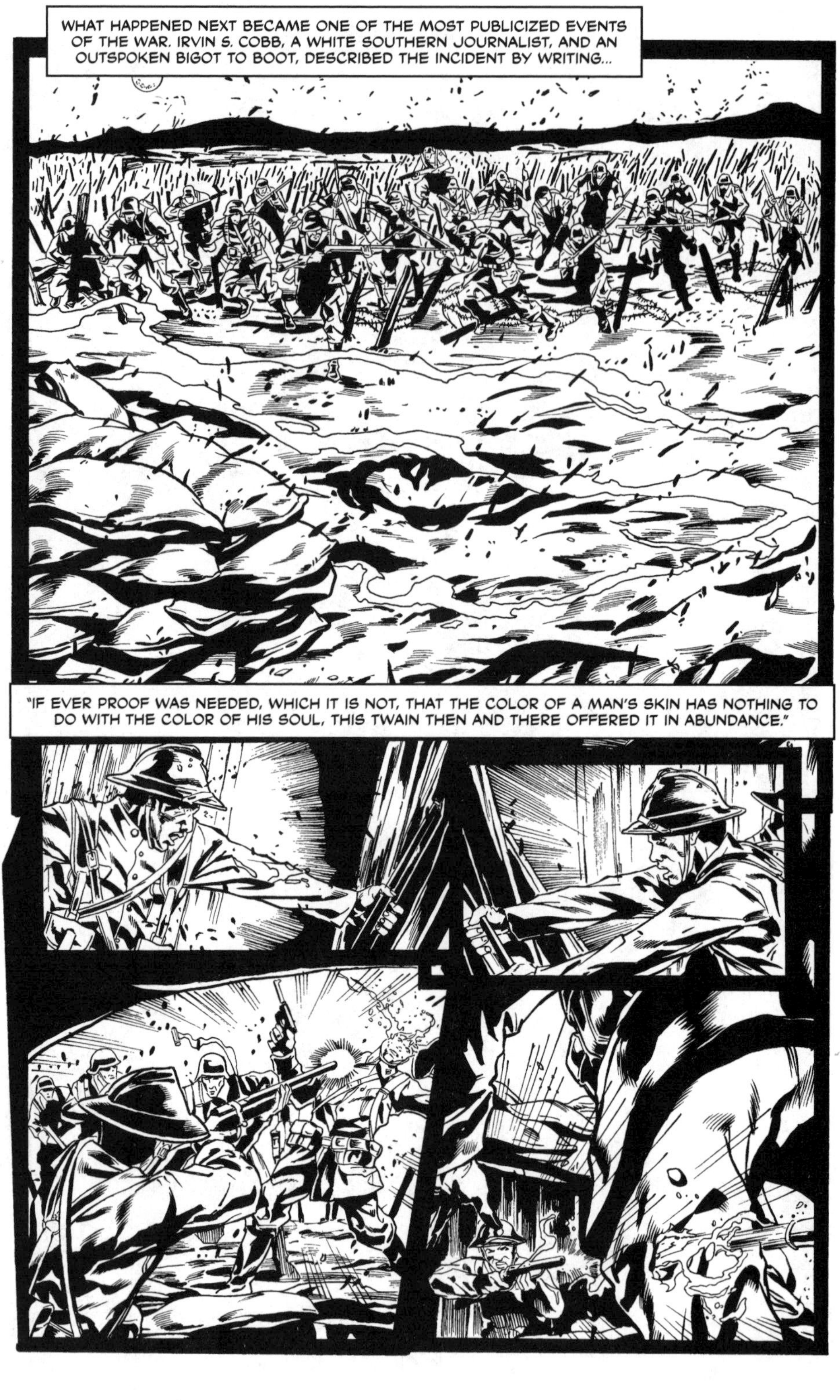
WHAT HAPPENED NEXT BECAME ONE OF THE MOST PUBLICIZED EVENTS OF THE WAR. IRVIN S. COBB, A WHITE SOUTHERN JOURNALIST, AND AN OUTSPOKEN BIGOT TO BOOT, DESCRIBED THE INCIDENT BY WRITING...
"IF EVER PROOF WAS NEEDED, WHICH IT IS NOT, THAT THE COLOR OF A MAN'S SKIN HAS NOTHING TO DO WITH THE COLOR OF HIS SOUL, THIS TWAIN THEN AND THERE OFFERED IT IN ABUNDANCE."

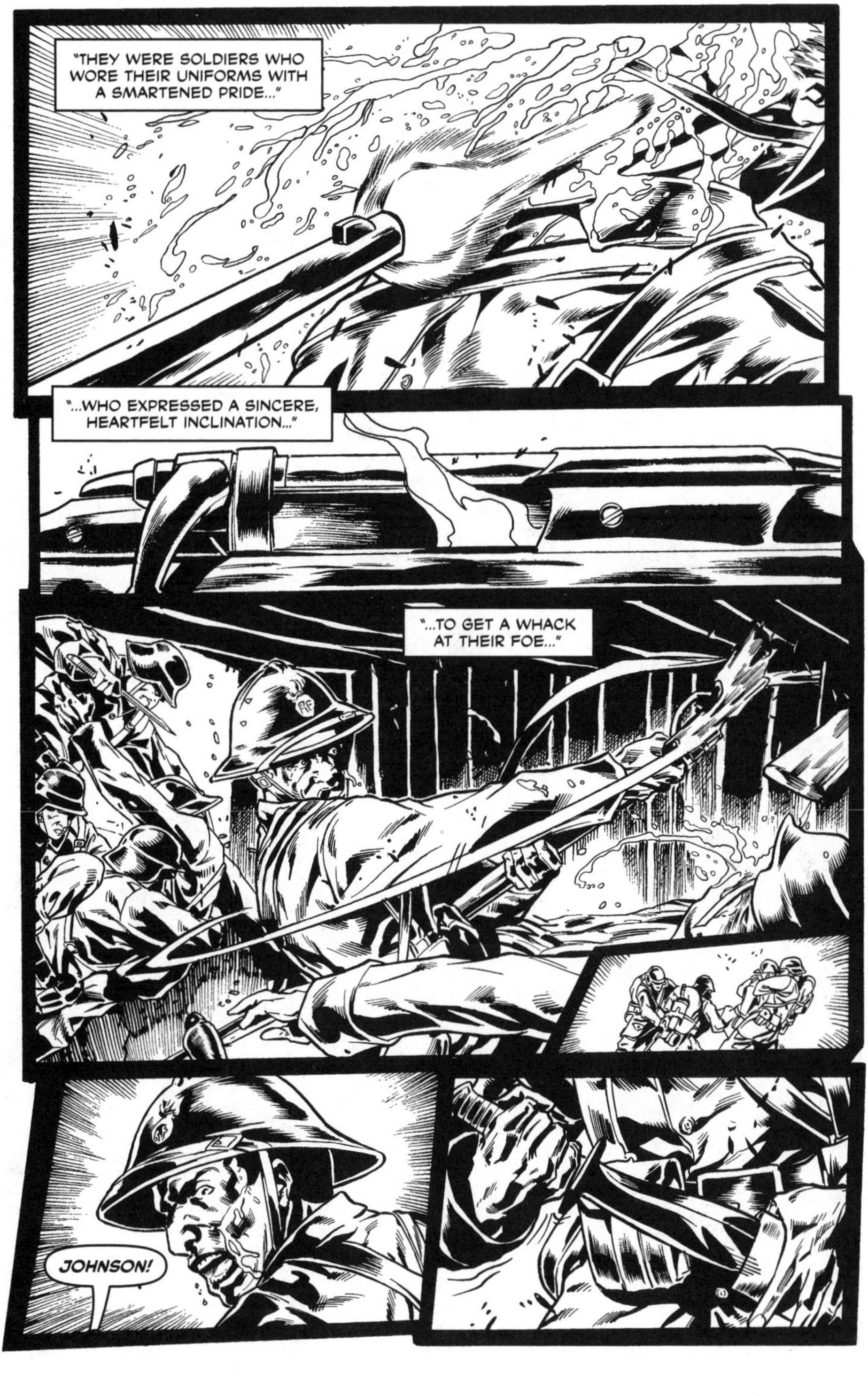
"THEY WERE SOLDIERS WHO WORE THEIR UNIFORMS WITH A SMARTENED PRIDE..."
"...WHO EXPRESSED A SINCERE, HEARTFELT INCLINATION..."
"...TO GET A WHACK AT THEIR FOE..."
JOHNSON!

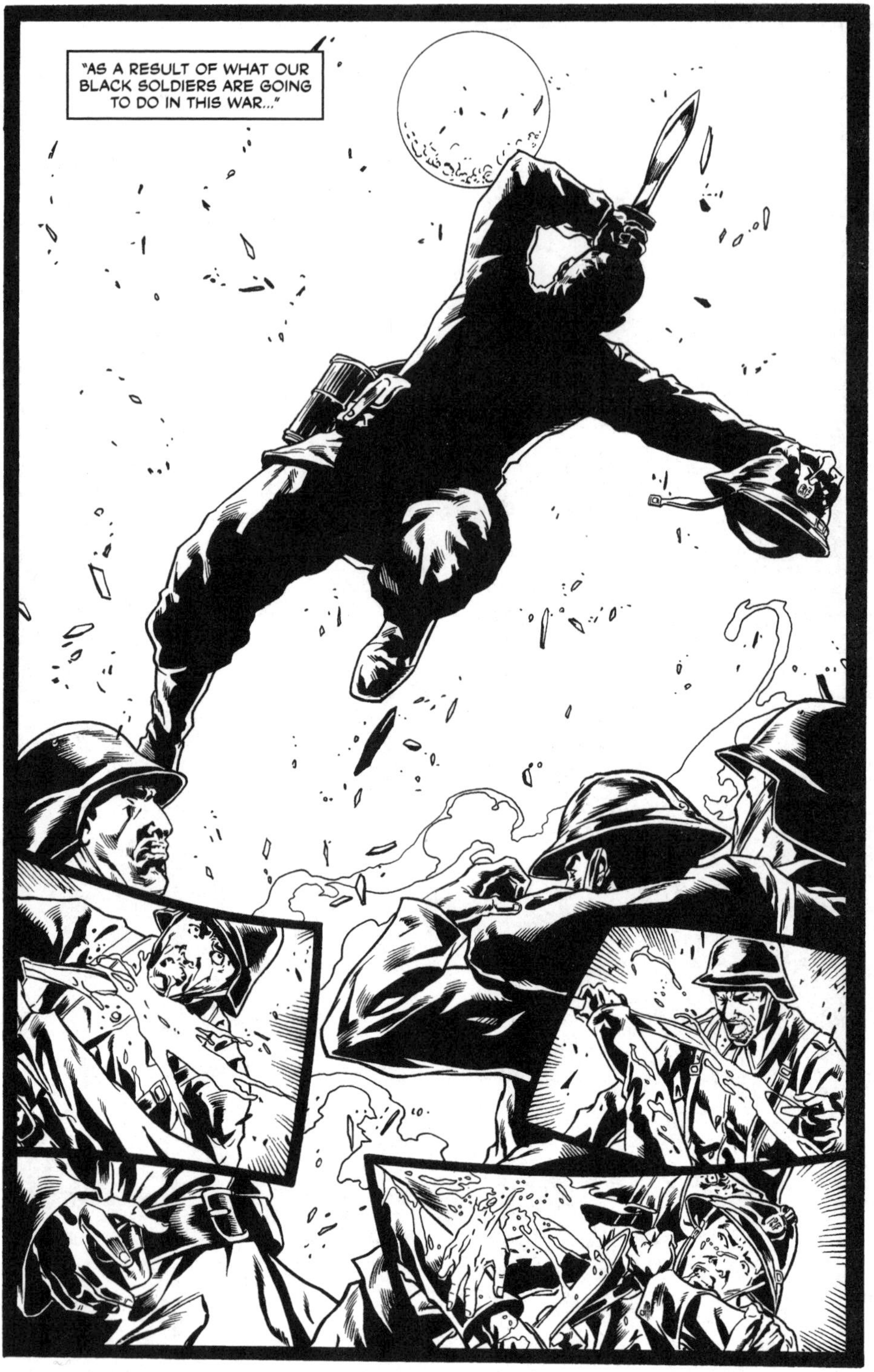
"AS A RESULT OF WHAT OUR BLACK SOLDIERS ARE GOING TO DO IN THIS WAR..."

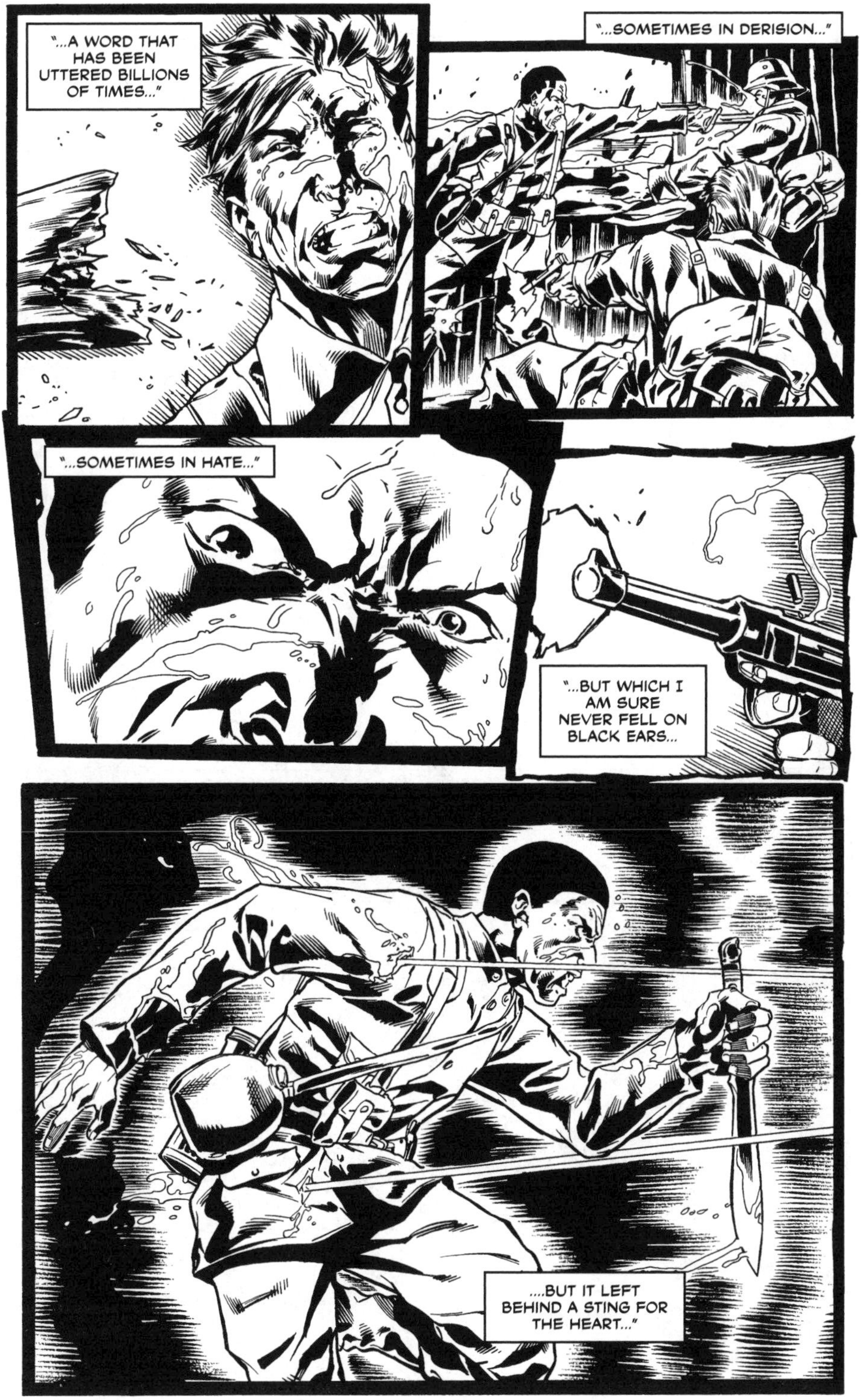
"...A WORD THAT HAS BEEN UTTERED BILLIONS OF TIMES..."
"...SOMETIMES IN DERISION..."
"...SOMETIMES IN HATE..."
"...BUT WHICH I AM SURE NEVER FELL ON BLACK EARS...
....BUT IT LEFT BEHIND A STING FOR THE HEART..."

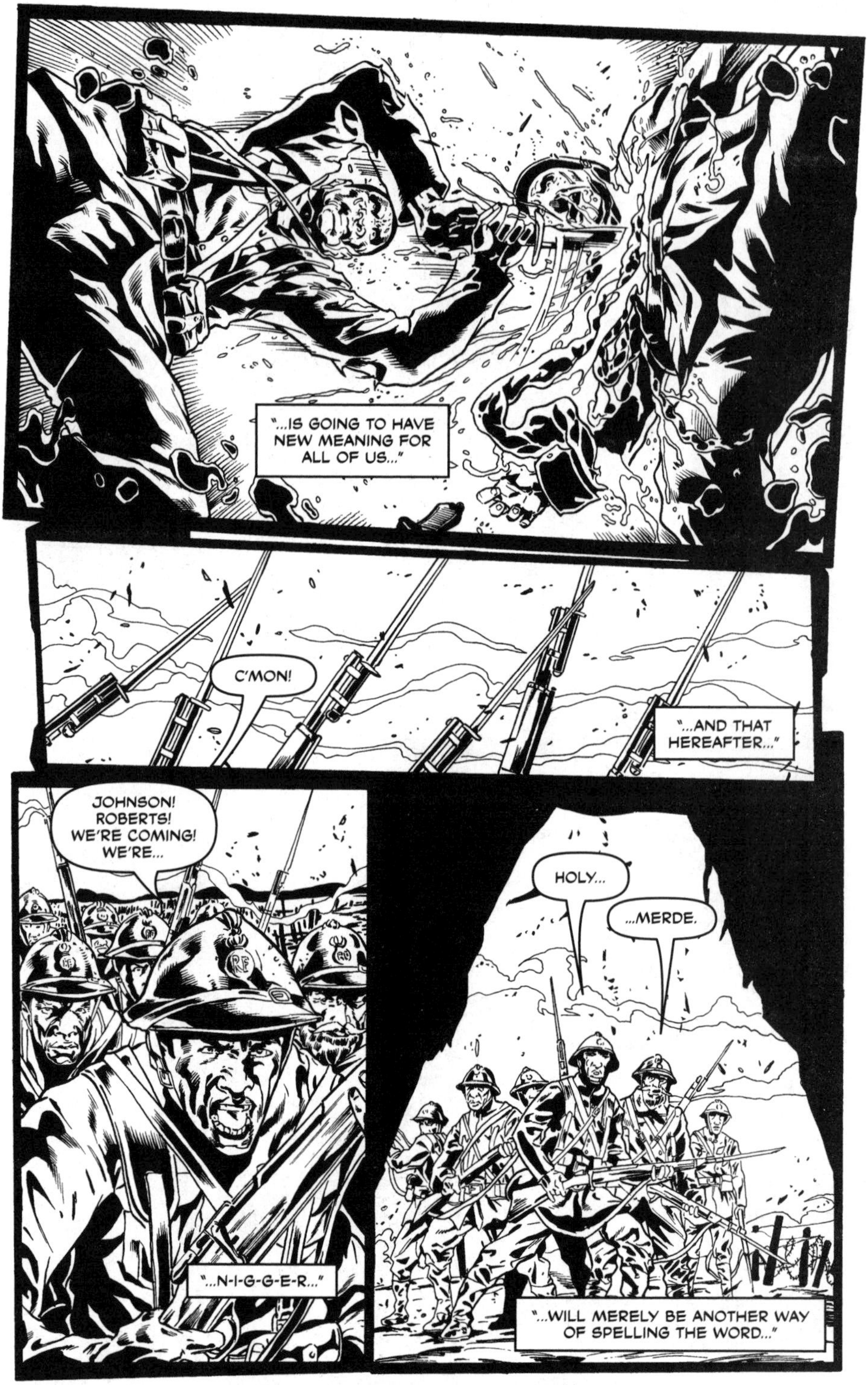
"...IS GOING TO HAVE NEW MEANING FOR ALL OF US..."
C'MON!
"...AND THAT HEREAFTER..."
JOHNSON! ROBERTS! WE'RE COMING! WE'RE...
"...N-I-G-G-E-R..."
HOLY...
...MERDE.
"...WILL MERELY BE ANOTHER WAY OF SPELLING THE WORD..."

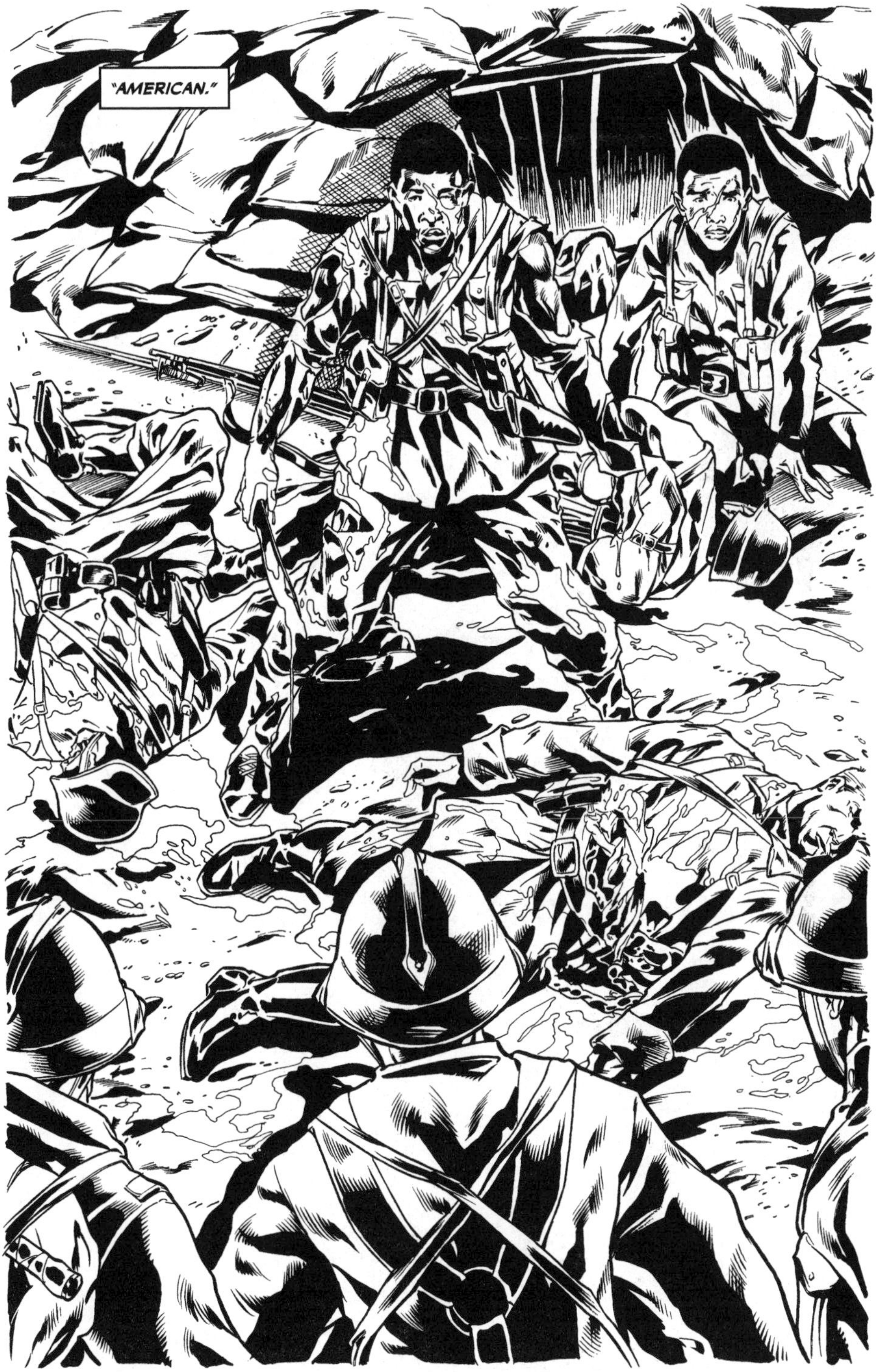
"AMERICAN."

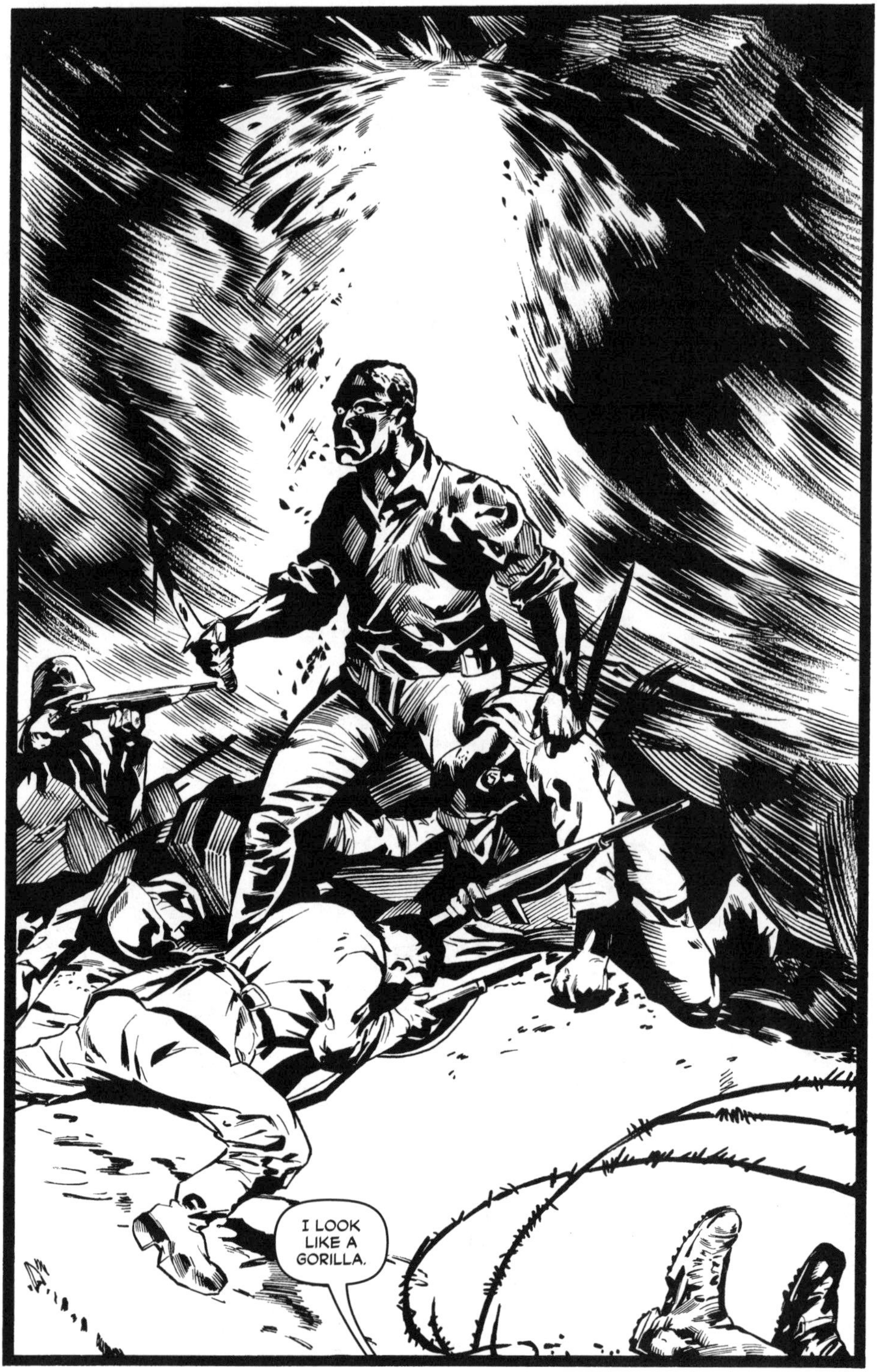
I LOOK LIKE A GORILLA.

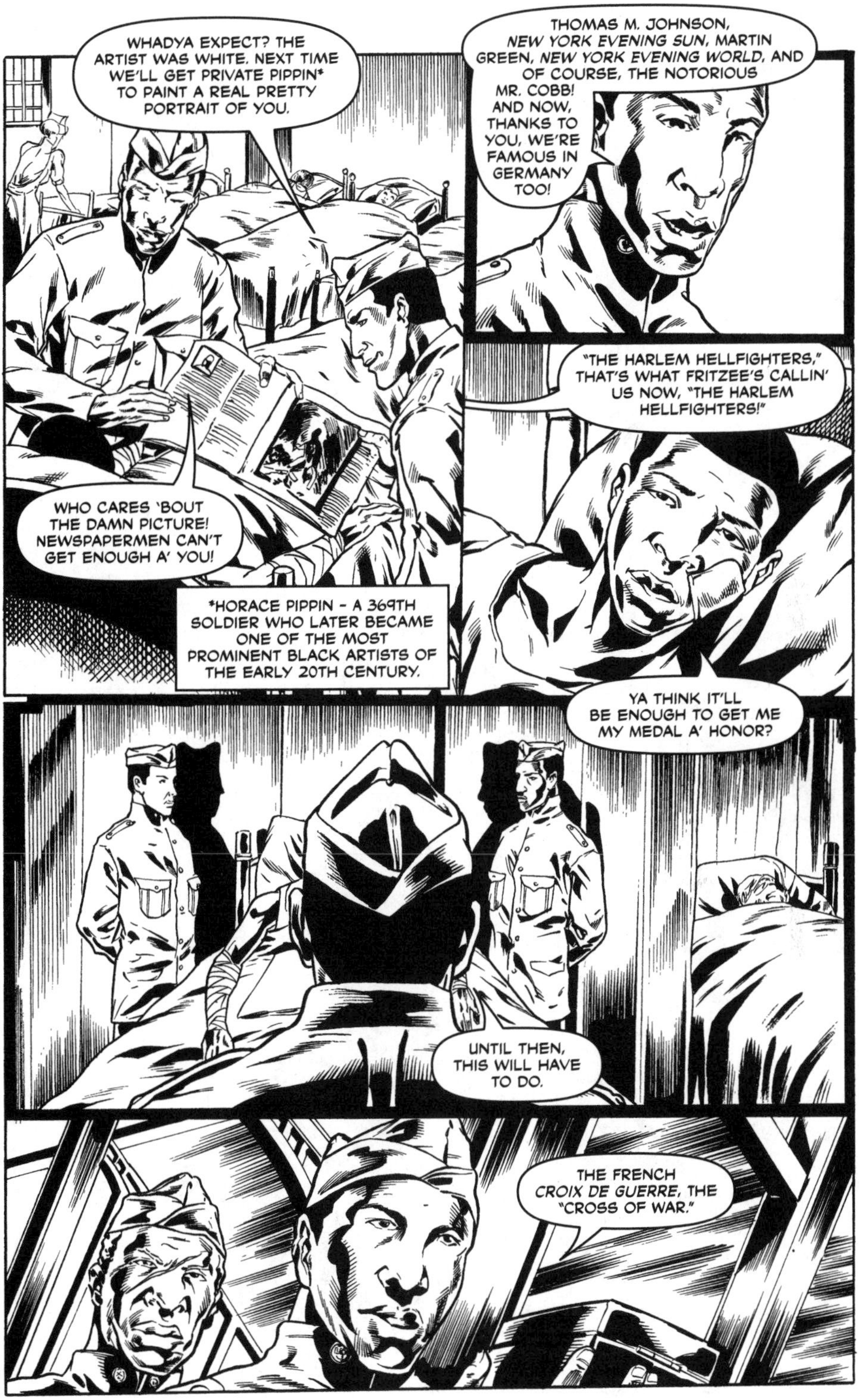
WHADYA EXPECT? THE ARTIST WAS WHITE. NEXT TIME WE'LL GET PRIVATE PIPPIN* TO PAINT A REAL PRETTY PORTRAIT OF YOU.
WHO CARES 'BOUT THE DAMN PICTURE! NEWSPAPERMEN CAN'T GET ENOUGH A' YOU!
*HORACE PIPPIN - A 369TH SOLDIER WHO LATER BECAME ONE OF THE MOST PROMINENT BLACK ARTISTS OF THE EARLY 20TH CENTURY.
THOMAS M. JOHNSON, *NEW YORK EVENING SUN*, MARTIN GREEN, *NEW YORK EVENING WORLD*, AND OF COURSE, THE NOTORIOUS MR. COBB! AND NOW, THANKS TO YOU, WE'RE FAMOUS IN GERMANY TOO!
"THE HARLEM HELLFIGHTERS," THAT'S WHAT FRITZEE'S CALLIN' US NOW, "THE HARLEM HELLFIGHTERS!"
YA THINK IT'LL BE ENOUGH TO GET ME MY MEDAL A' HONOR?
UNTIL THEN, THIS WILL HAVE TO DO.
THE FRENCH *CROIX DE GUERRE*, THE "CROSS OF WAR."

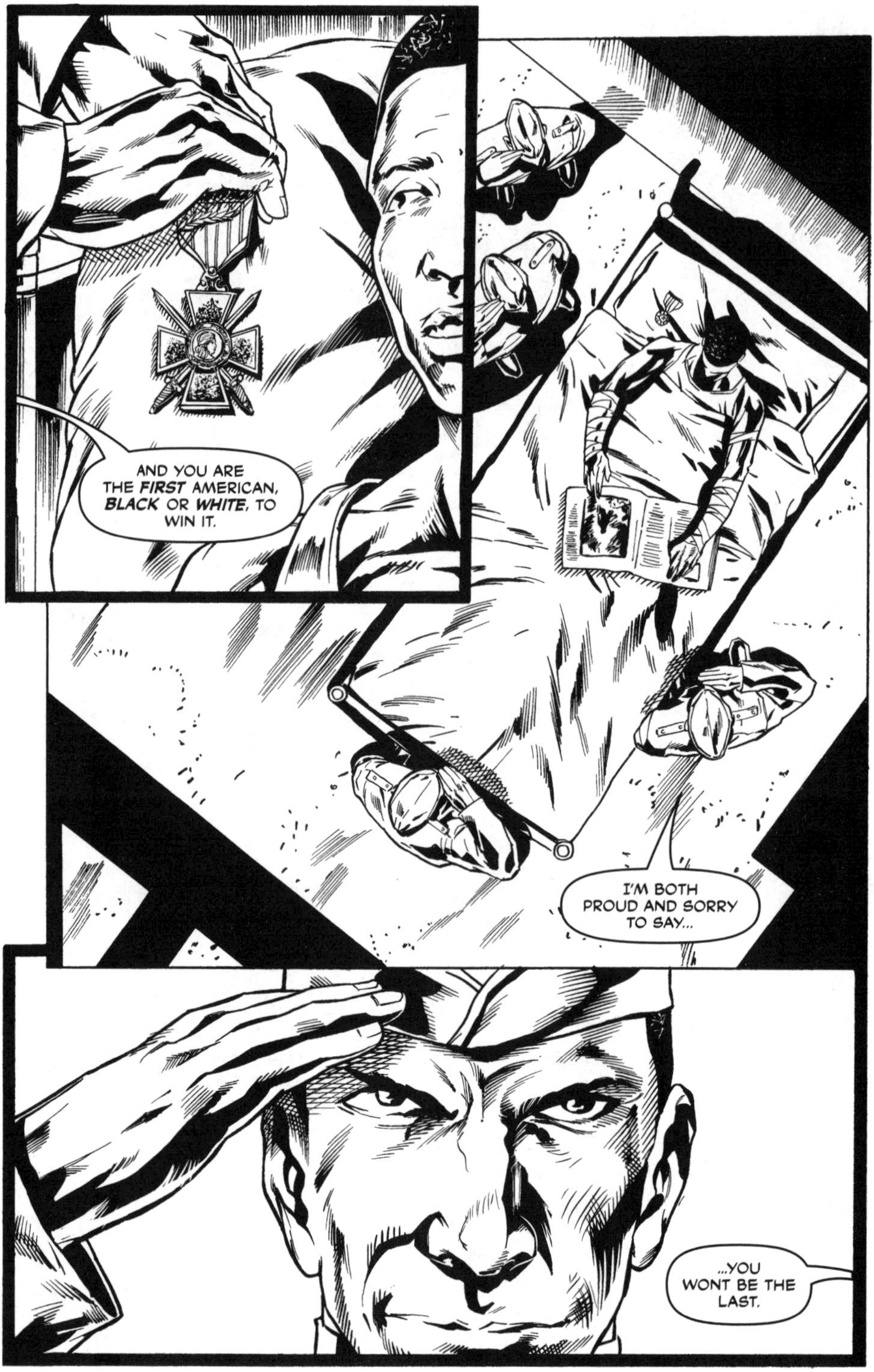
AND YOU ARE THE FIRST AMERICAN, BLACK OR WHITE, TO WIN IT.
I'M BOTH PROUD AND SORRY TO SAY...
...YOU WONT BE THE LAST.

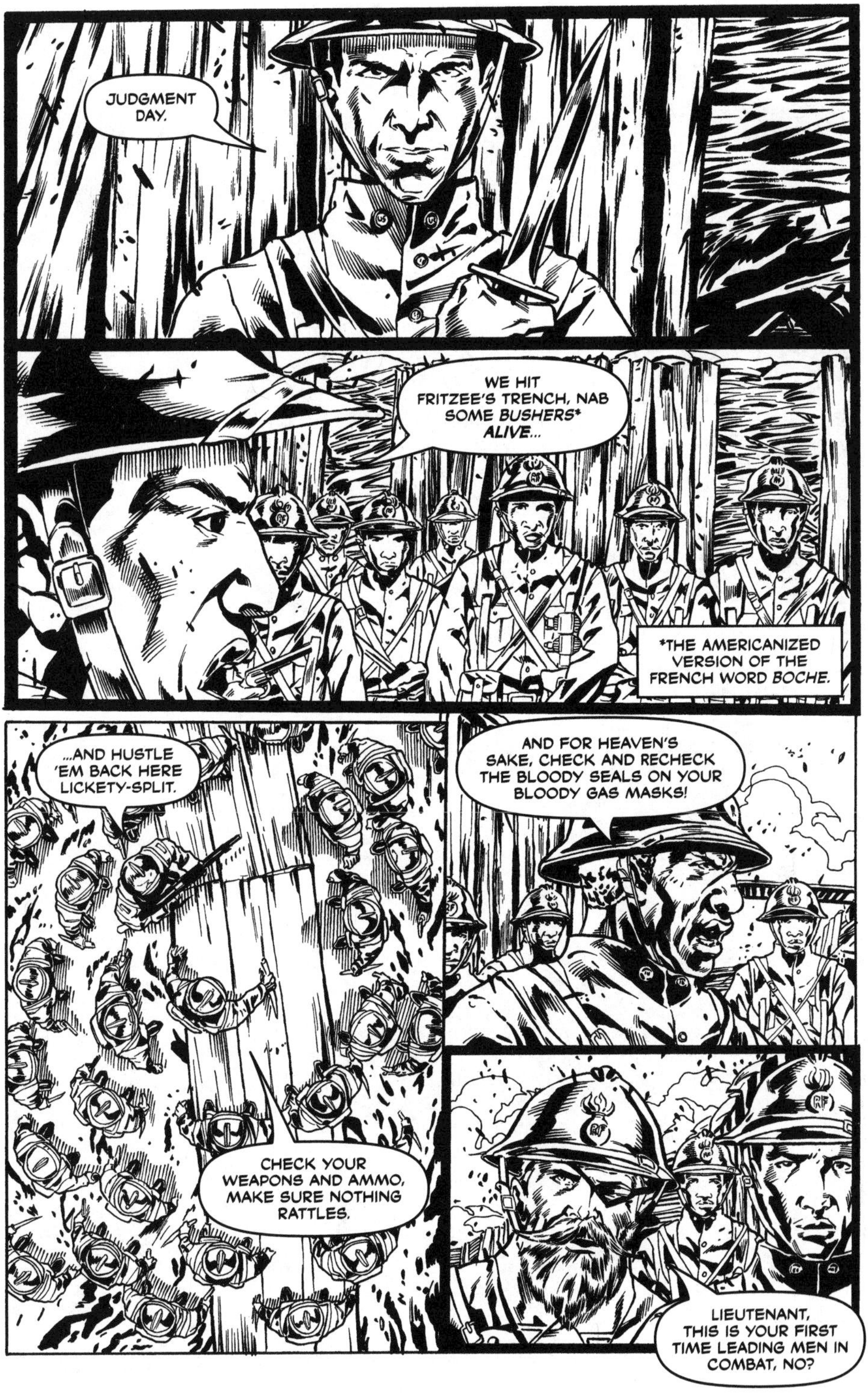
JUDGMENT DAY.
WE HIT FRITZEE'S TRENCH, NAB SOME *BUSHERS** *ALIVE*...
*THE AMERICANIZED VERSION OF THE FRENCH WORD *BOCHE*.
...AND HUSTLE 'EM BACK HERE LICKETY-SPLIT.
CHECK YOUR WEAPONS AND AMMO, MAKE SURE NOTHING RATTLES.
AND FOR HEAVEN'S SAKE, CHECK AND RECHECK THE BLOODY SEALS ON YOUR BLOODY GAS MASKS!
LIEUTENANT, THIS IS YOUR FIRST TIME LEADING MEN IN COMBAT, NO?

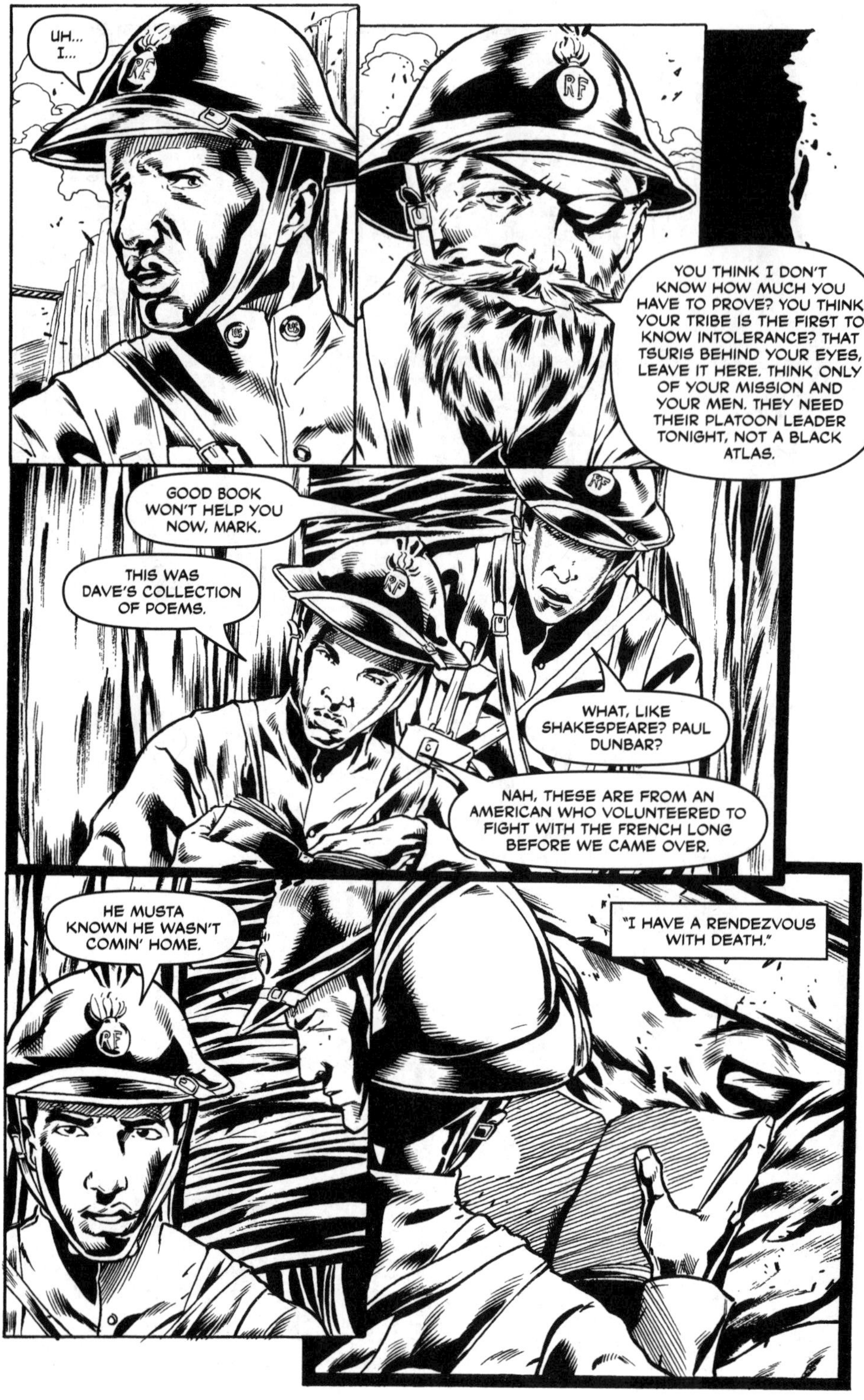
UH... I...
YOU THINK I DON'T KNOW HOW MUCH YOU HAVE TO PROVE? YOU THINK YOUR TRIBE IS THE FIRST TO KNOW INTOLERANCE? THAT TSURIS BEHIND YOUR EYES, LEAVE IT HERE. THINK ONLY OF YOUR MISSION AND YOUR MEN. THEY NEED THEIR PLATOON LEADER TONIGHT, NOT A BLACK ATLAS.
GOOD BOOK WON'T HELP YOU NOW, MARK.
THIS WAS DAVE'S COLLECTION OF POEMS.
WHAT, LIKE SHAKESPEARE? PAUL DUNBAR?
NAH, THESE ARE FROM AN AMERICAN WHO VOLUNTEERED TO FIGHT WITH THE FRENCH LONG BEFORE WE CAME OVER.
HE MUSTA KNOWN HE WASN'T COMIN' HOME.
"I HAVE A RENDEZVOUS WITH DEATH."

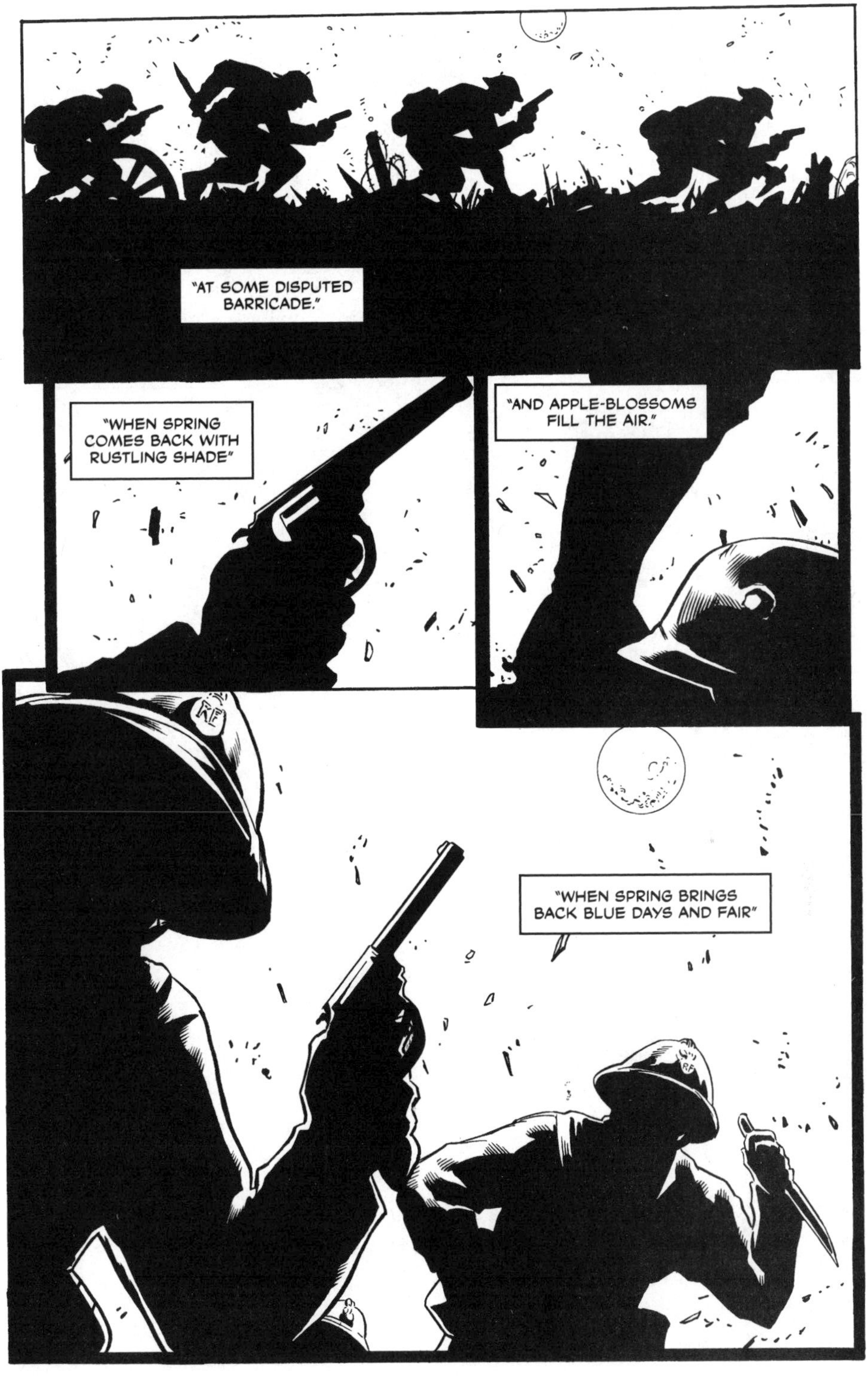
"AT SOME DISPUTED BARRICADE."
"WHEN SPRING COMES BACK WITH RUSTLING SHADE"
"AND APPLE-BLOSSOMS FILL THE AIR."
"WHEN SPRING BRINGS BACK BLUE DAYS AND FAIR"

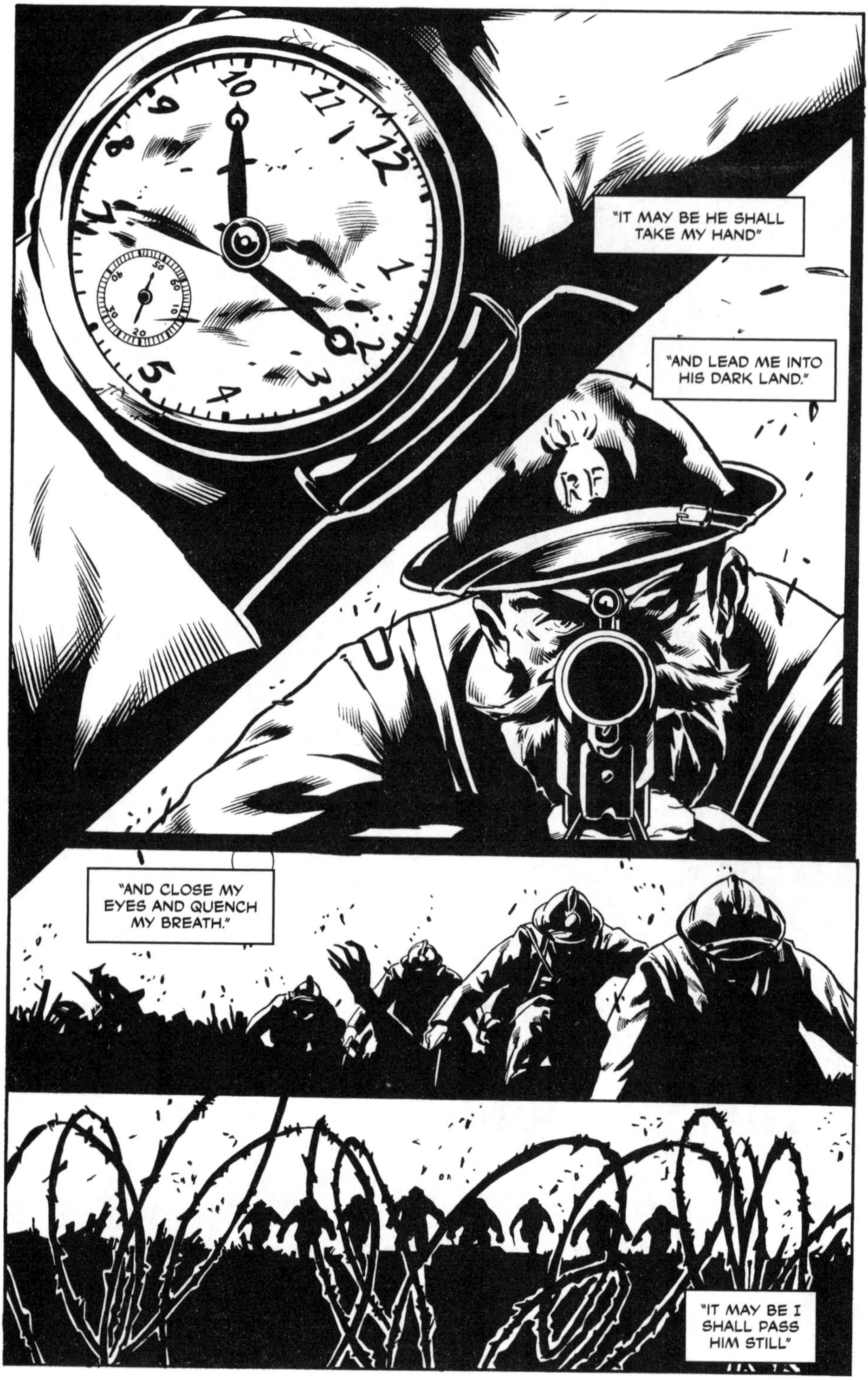
"IT MAY BE HE SHALL TAKE MY HAND"
"AND LEAD ME INTO HIS DARK LAND."
"AND CLOSE MY EYES AND QUENCH MY BREATH."
"IT MAY BE I SHALL PASS HIM STILL"

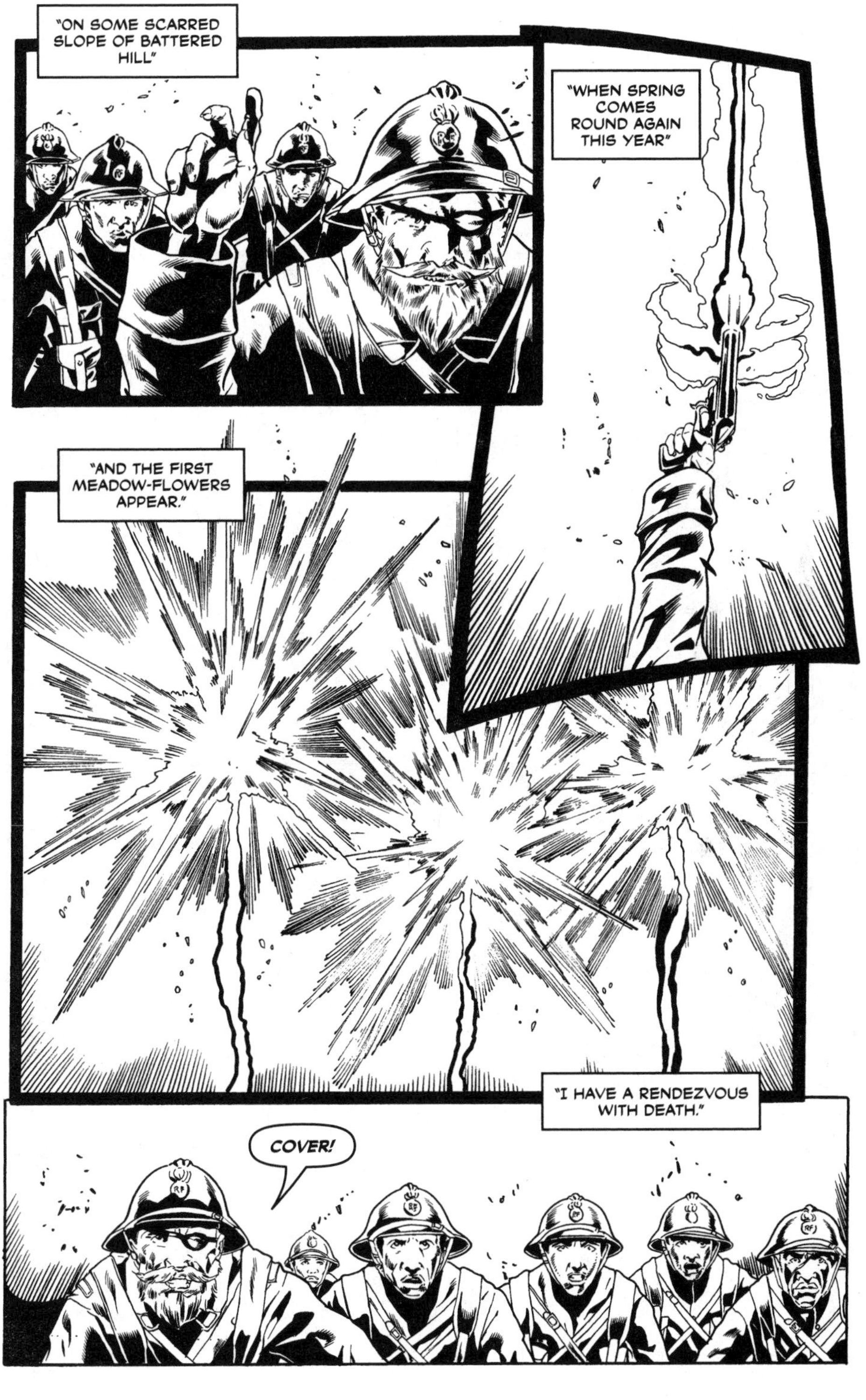
"ON SOME SCARRED SLOPE OF BATTERED HILL"
"WHEN SPRING COMES ROUND AGAIN THIS YEAR"
"AND THE FIRST MEADOW-FLOWERS APPEAR."
"I HAVE A RENDEZVOUS WITH DEATH."
COVER!

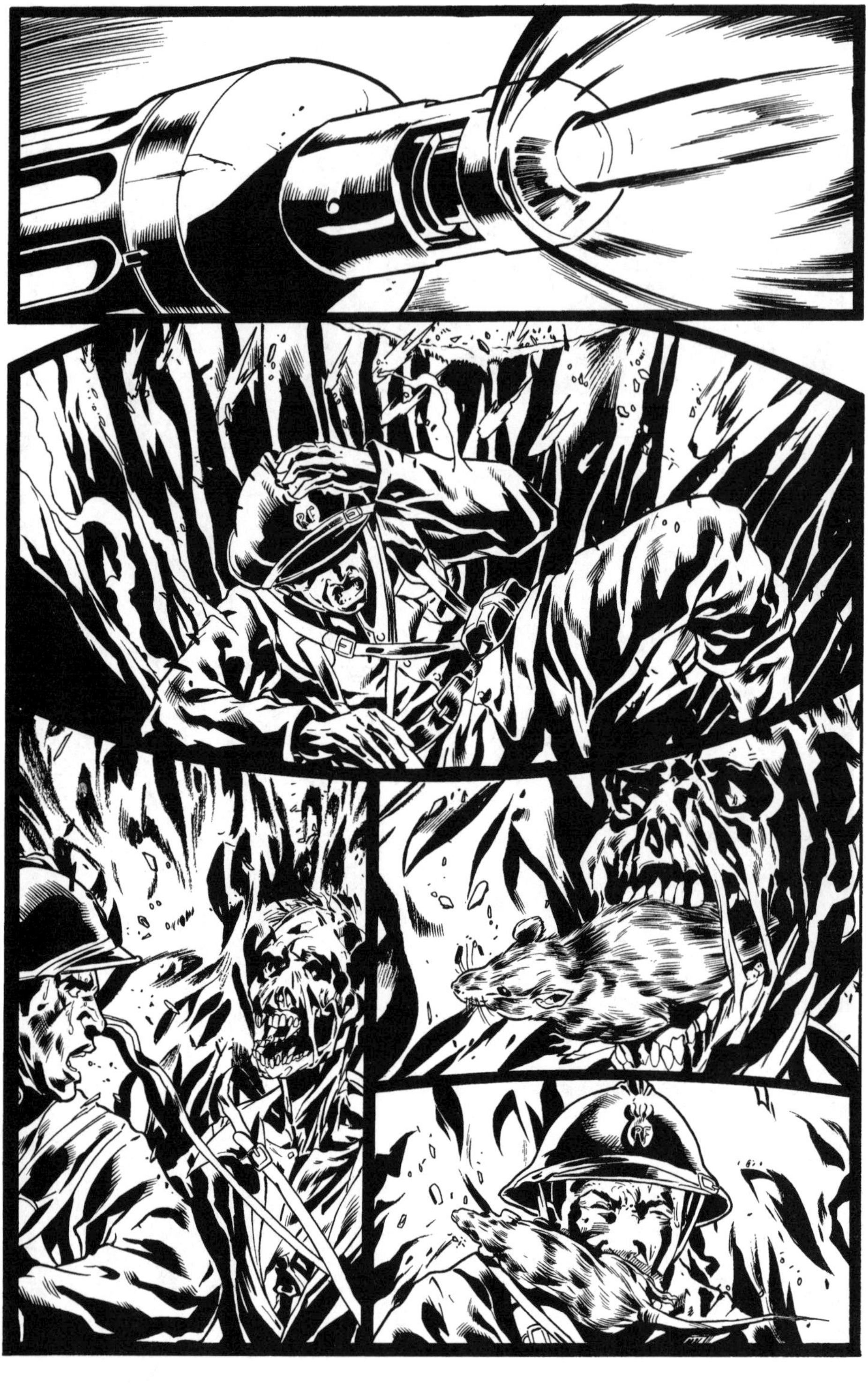

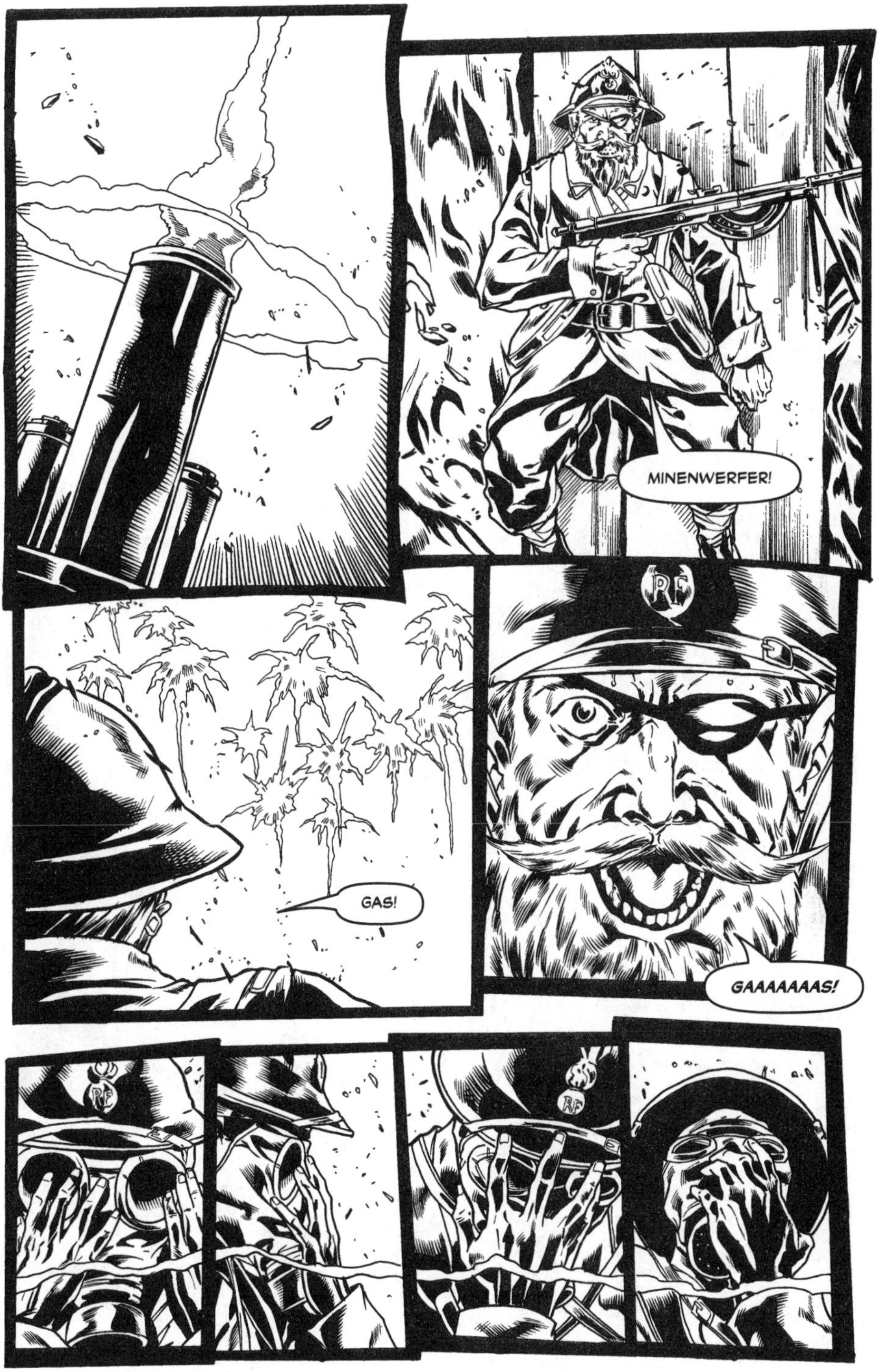
MINENWERFER!
GAS!
GAAAAAAAS!

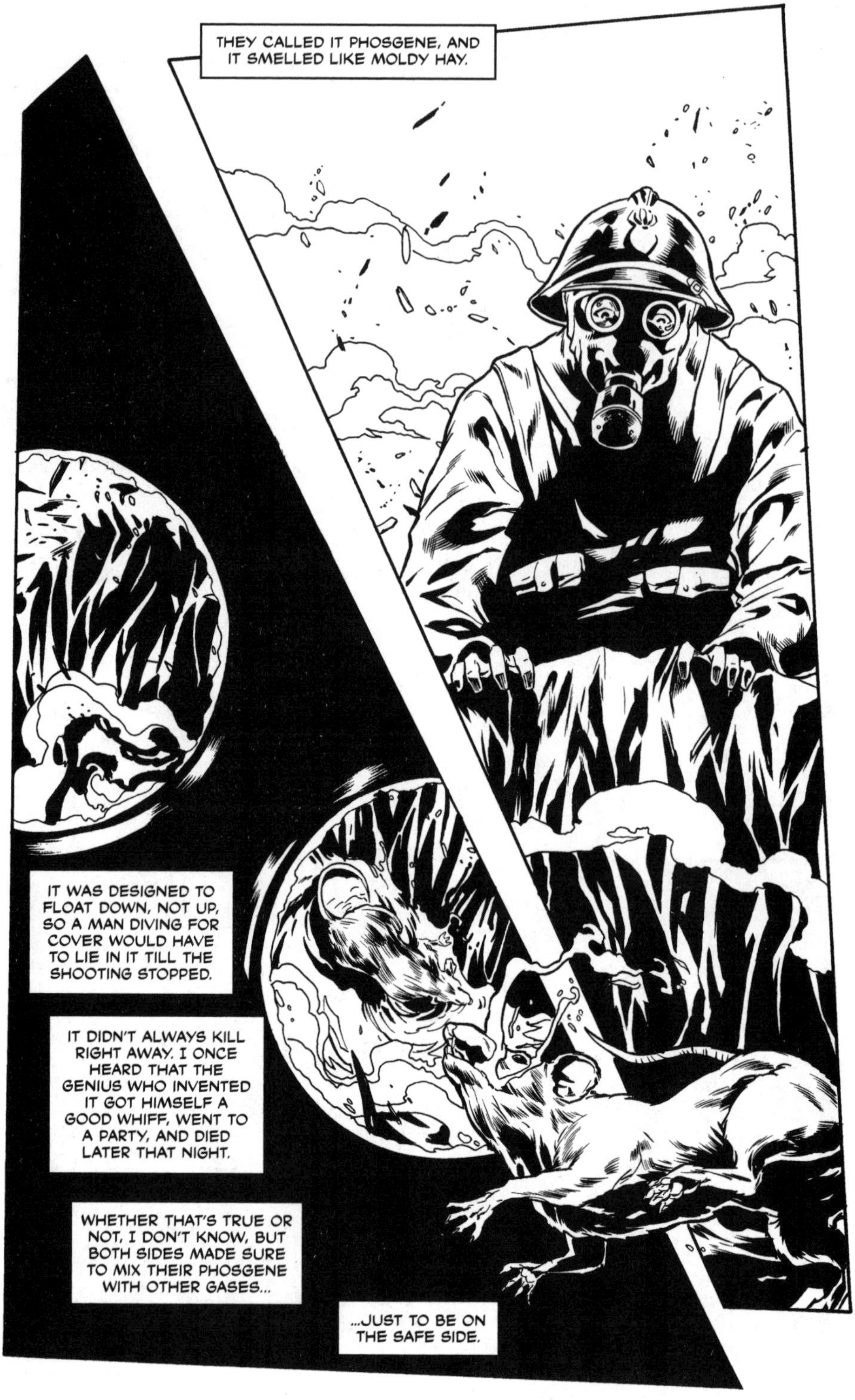
THEY CALLED IT PHOSGENE, AND IT SMELLED LIKE MOLDY HAY.
IT WAS DESIGNED TO FLOAT DOWN, NOT UP, SO A MAN DIVING FOR COVER WOULD HAVE TO LIE IN IT TILL THE SHOOTING STOPPED.
IT DIDN'T ALWAYS KILL RIGHT AWAY. I ONCE HEARD THAT THE GENIUS WHO INVENTED IT GOT HIMSELF A GOOD WHIFF, WENT TO A PARTY, AND DIED LATER THAT NIGHT.
WHETHER THAT'S TRUE OR NOT, I DON'T KNOW, BUT BOTH SIDES MADE SURE TO MIX THEIR PHOSGENE WITH OTHER GASES...
...JUST TO BE ON THE SAFE SIDE.

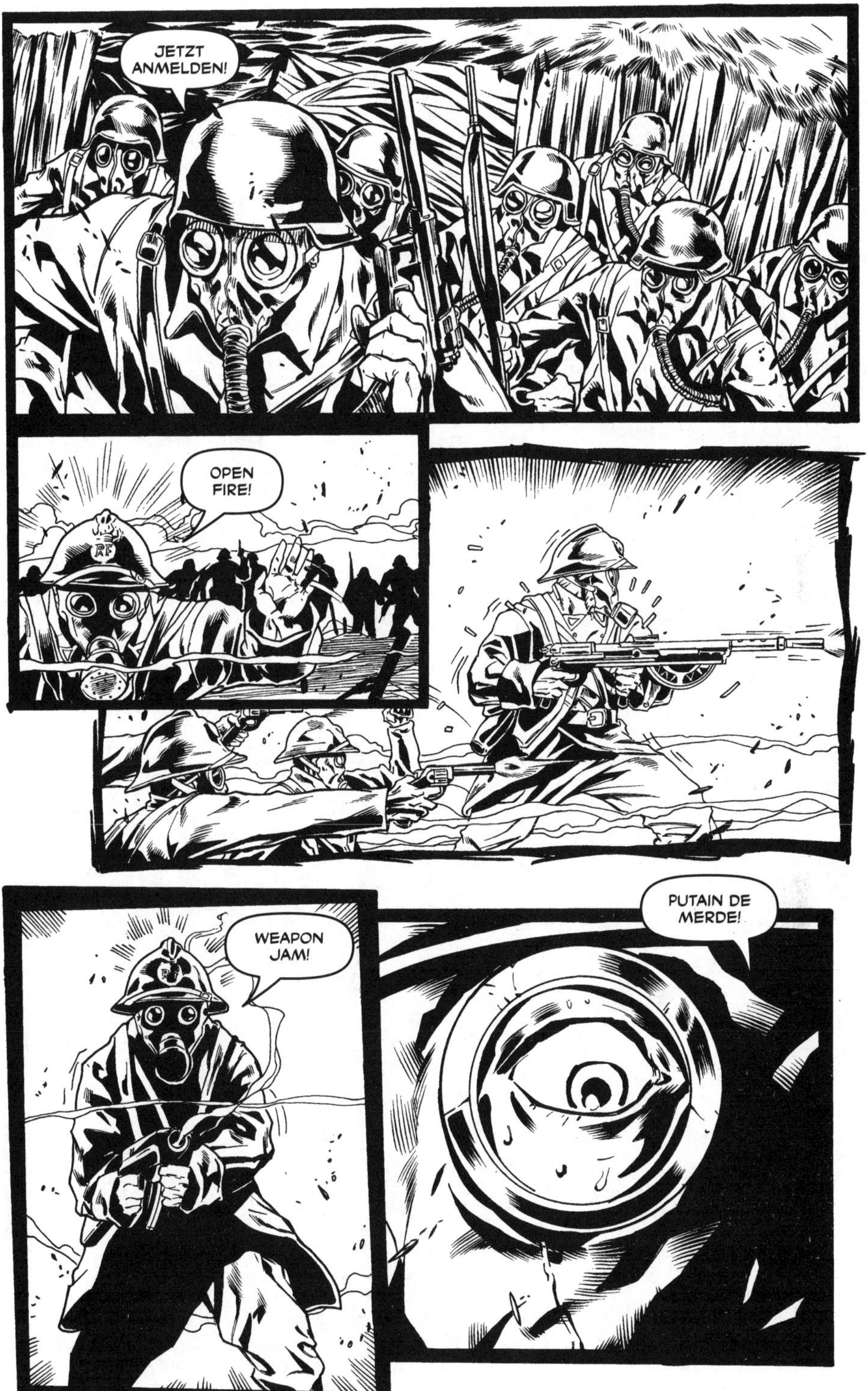
JETZT ANMELDEN!
OPEN FIRE!
WEAPON JAM!
PUTAIN DE MERDE!

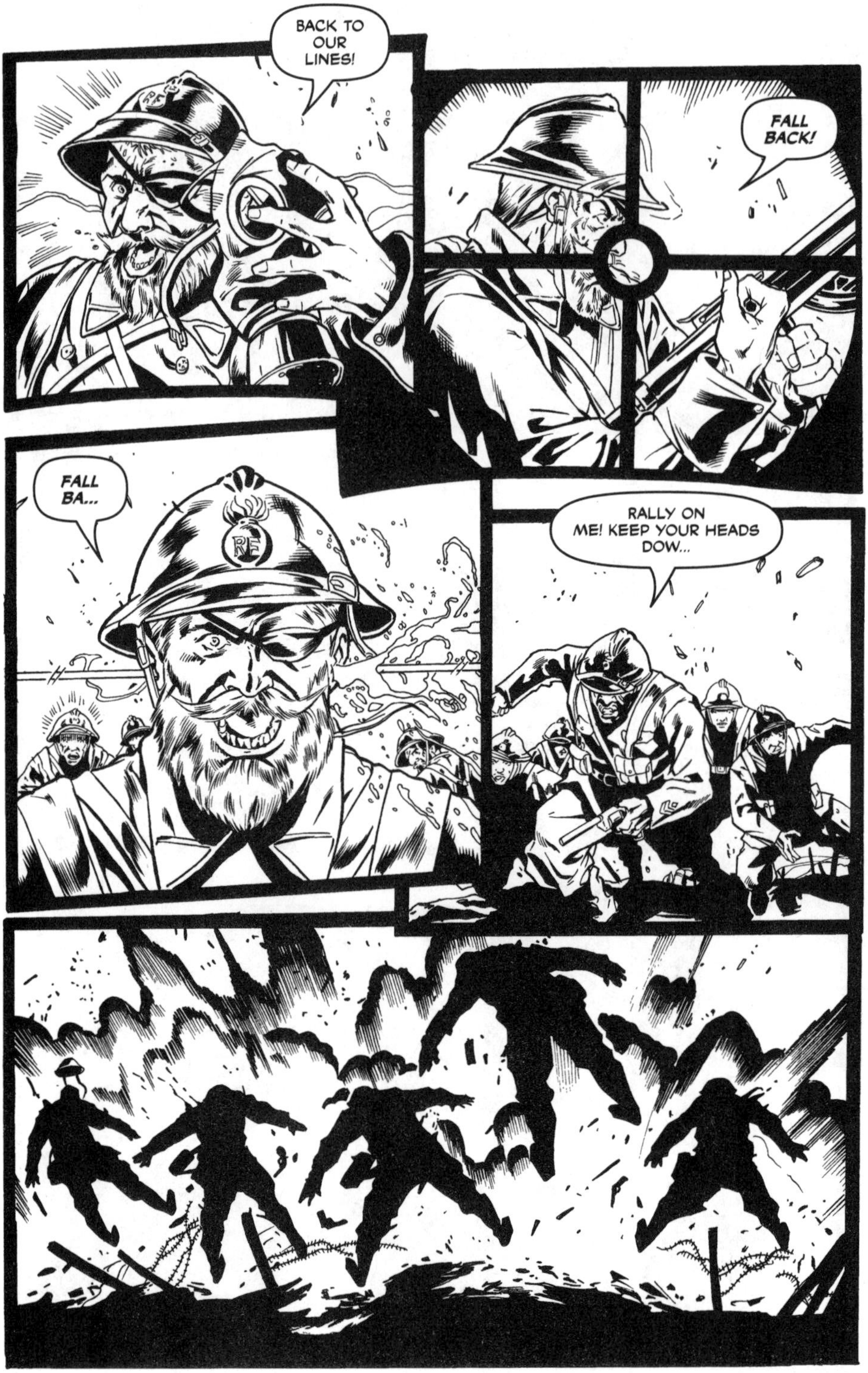
BACK TO OUR LINES!
FALL BACK!
FALL BA...
RALLY ON ME! KEEP YOUR HEADS DOW...

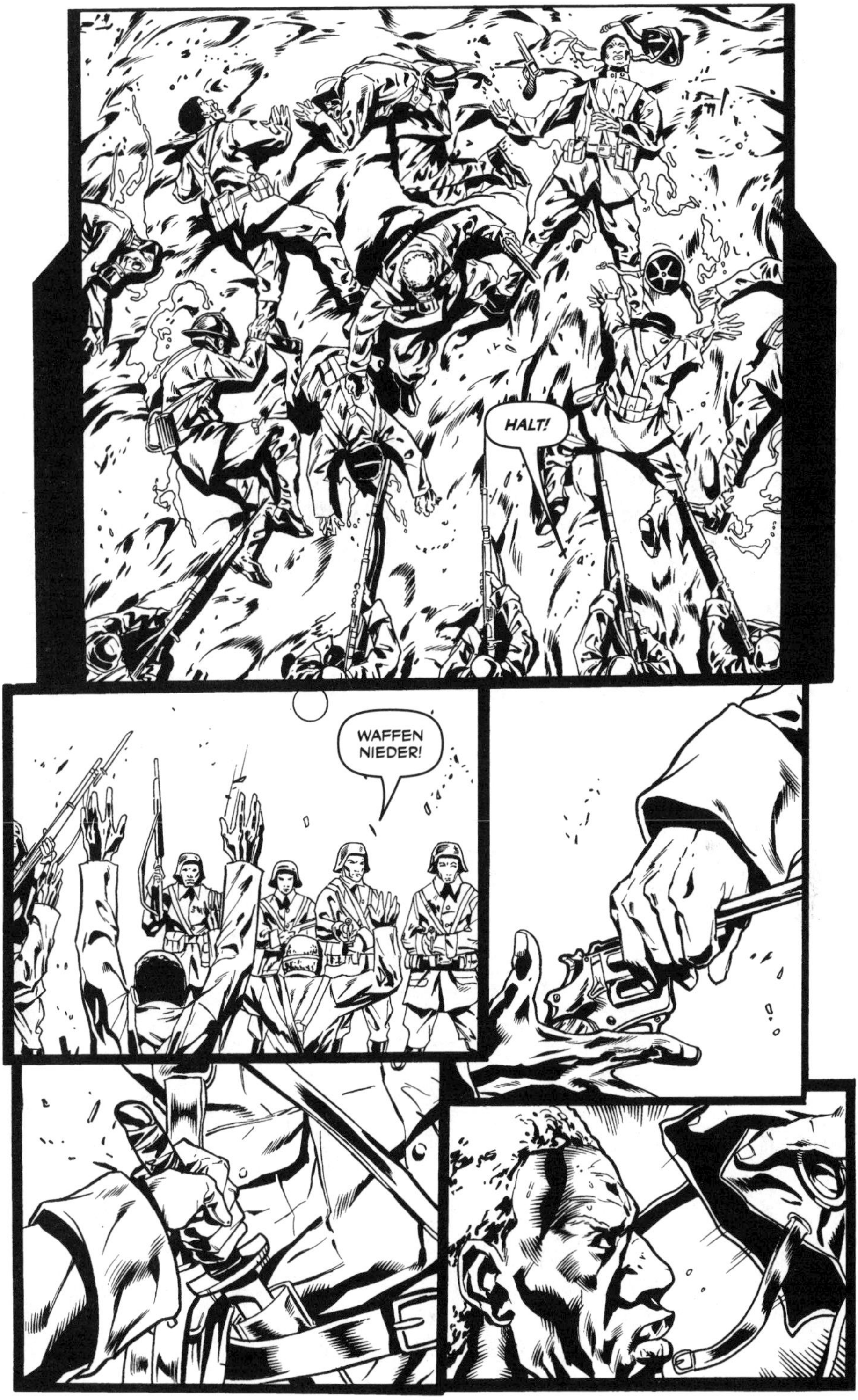
HALT!
WAFFEN NIEDER!

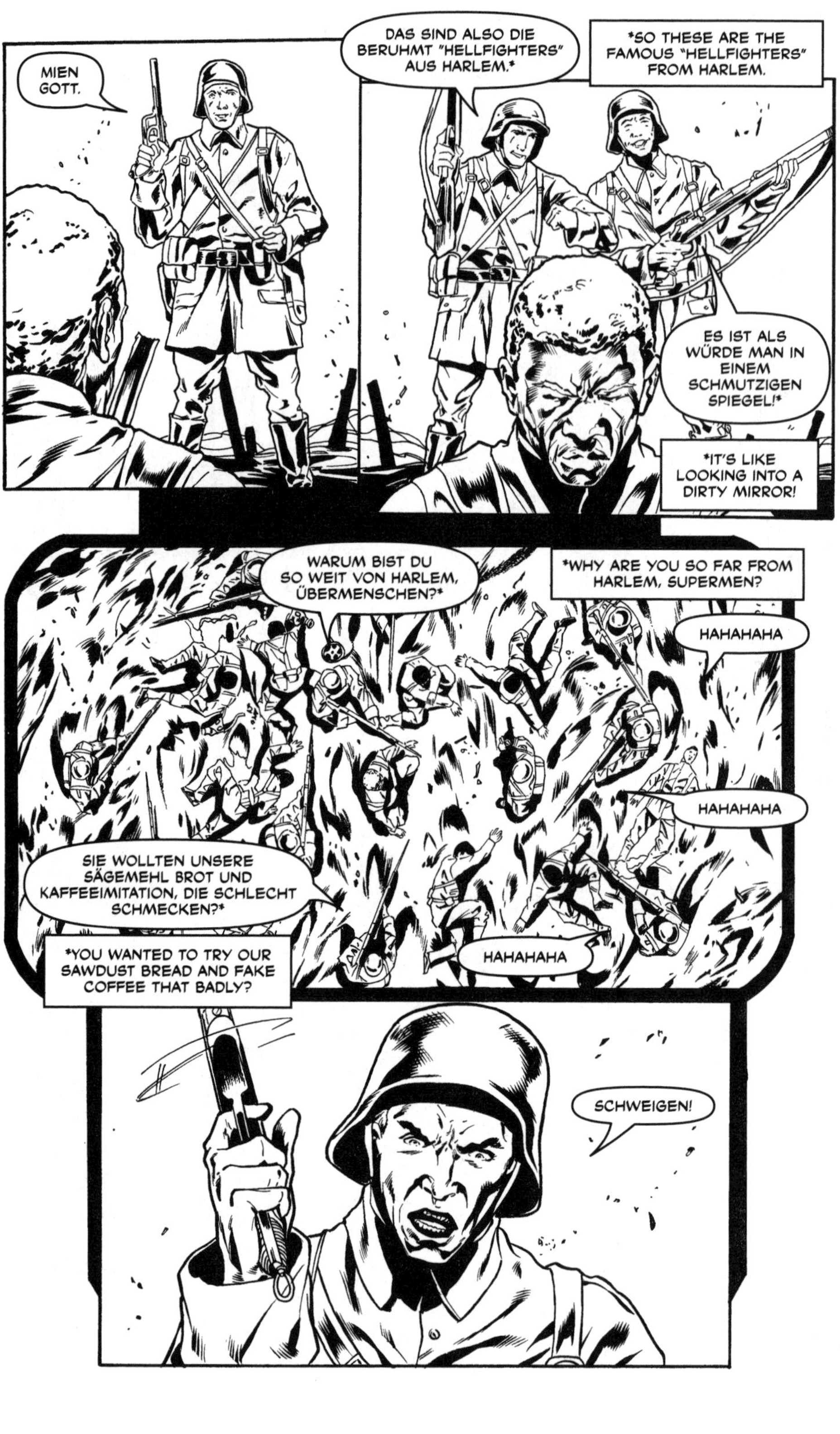
MIEN GOTT.
DAS SIND ALSO DIE BERUHMT "HELLFIGHTERS" AUS HARLEM.*
*SO THESE ARE THE FAMOUS "HELLFIGHTERS" FROM HARLEM.
ES IST ALS WÜRDE MAN IN EINEM SCHMUTZIGEN SPIEGEL!*
*IT'S LIKE LOOKING INTO A DIRTY MIRROR!
WARUM BIST DU SO WEIT VON HARLEM, ÜBERMENSCHEN?*
*WHY ARE YOU SO FAR FROM HARLEM, SUPERMEN?
HAHAHAHA
HAHAHAHA
SIE WOLLTEN UNSERE SÄGEMEHL BROT UND KAFFEEIMITATION, DIE SCHLECHT SCHMECKEN?*
*YOU WANTED TO TRY OUR SAWDUST BREAD AND FAKE COFFEE THAT BADLY?
HAHAHAHA
SCHWEIGEN!

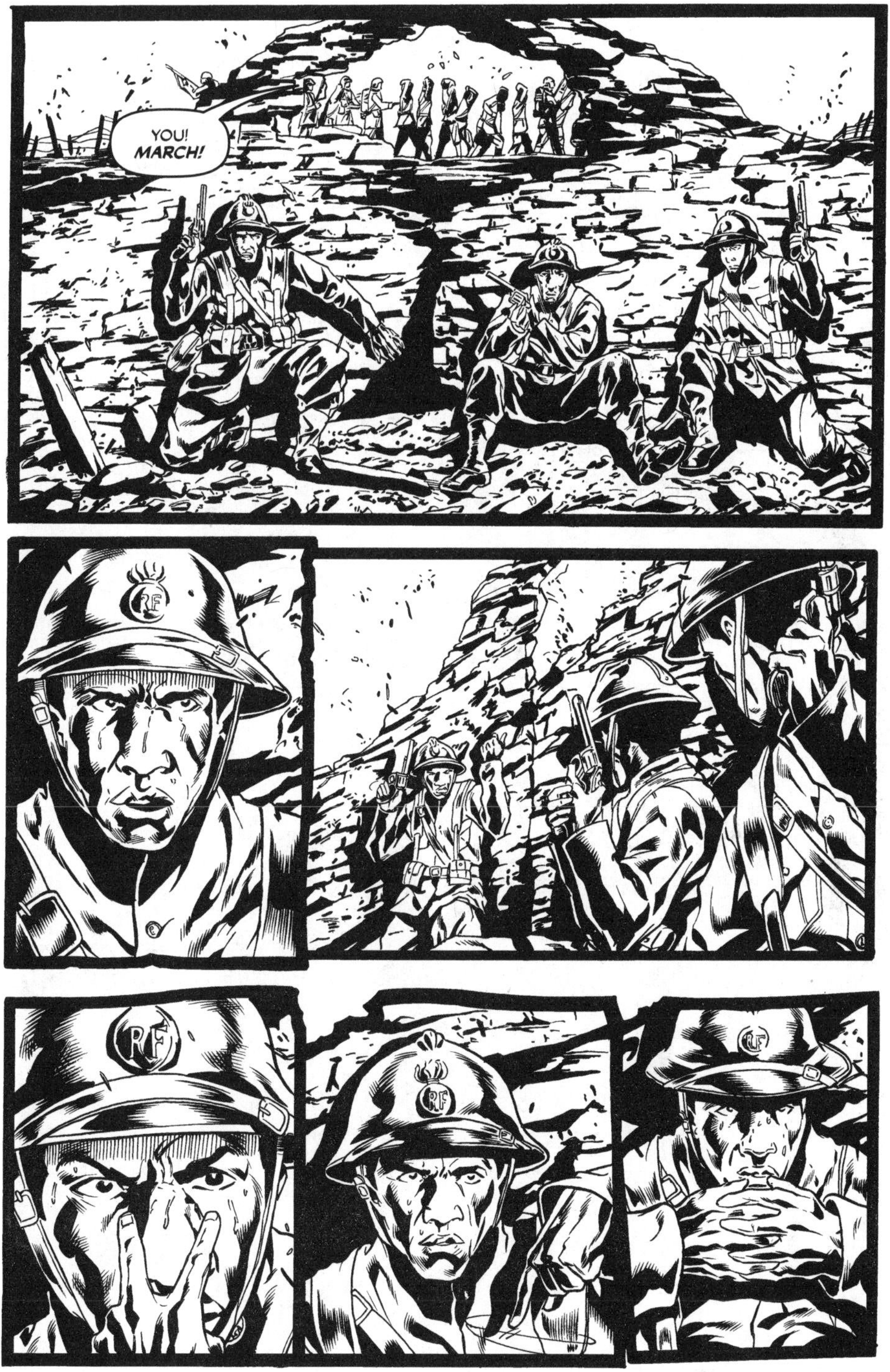
YOU! MARCH!

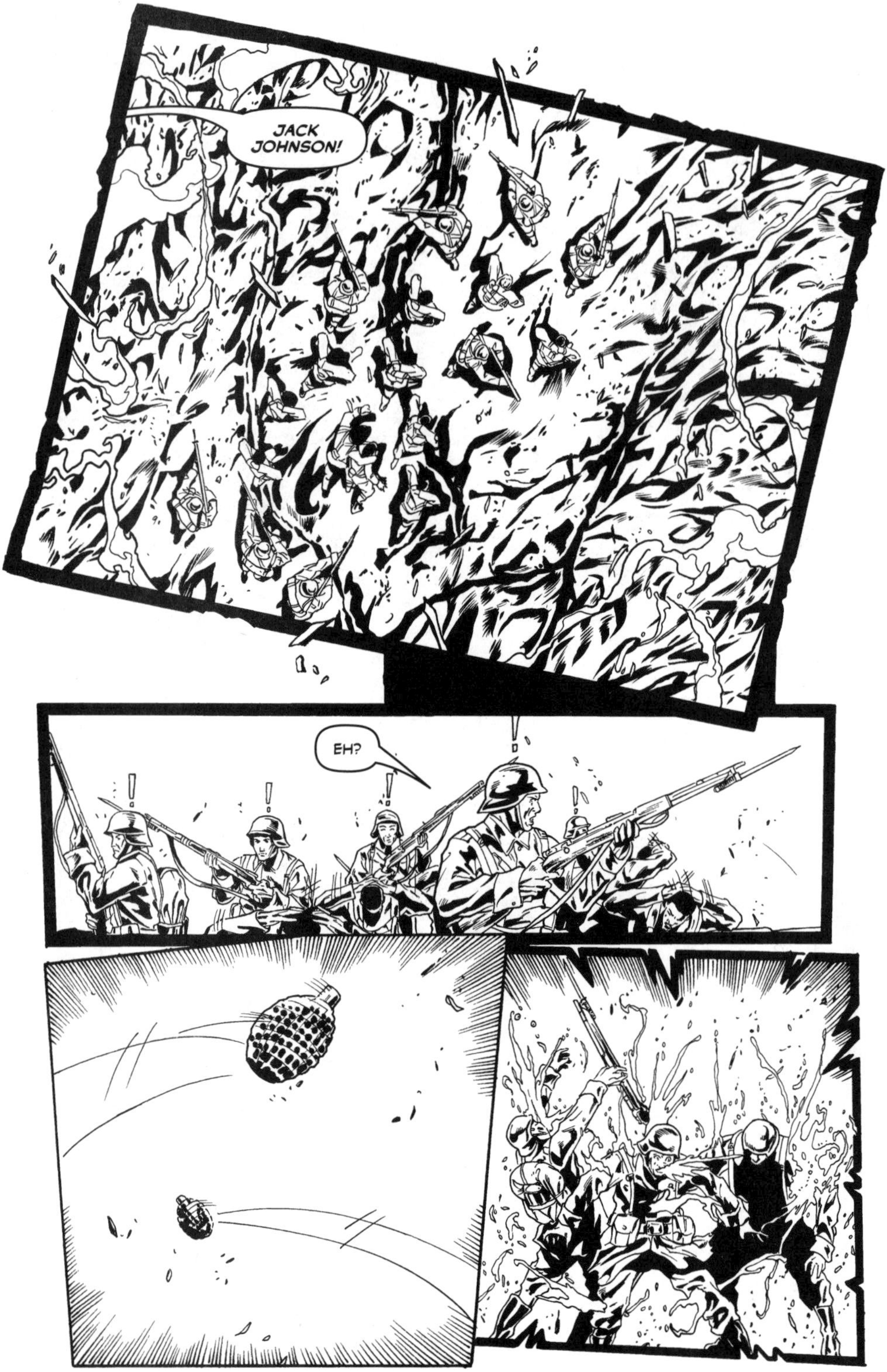
JACK JOHNSON!
EH?

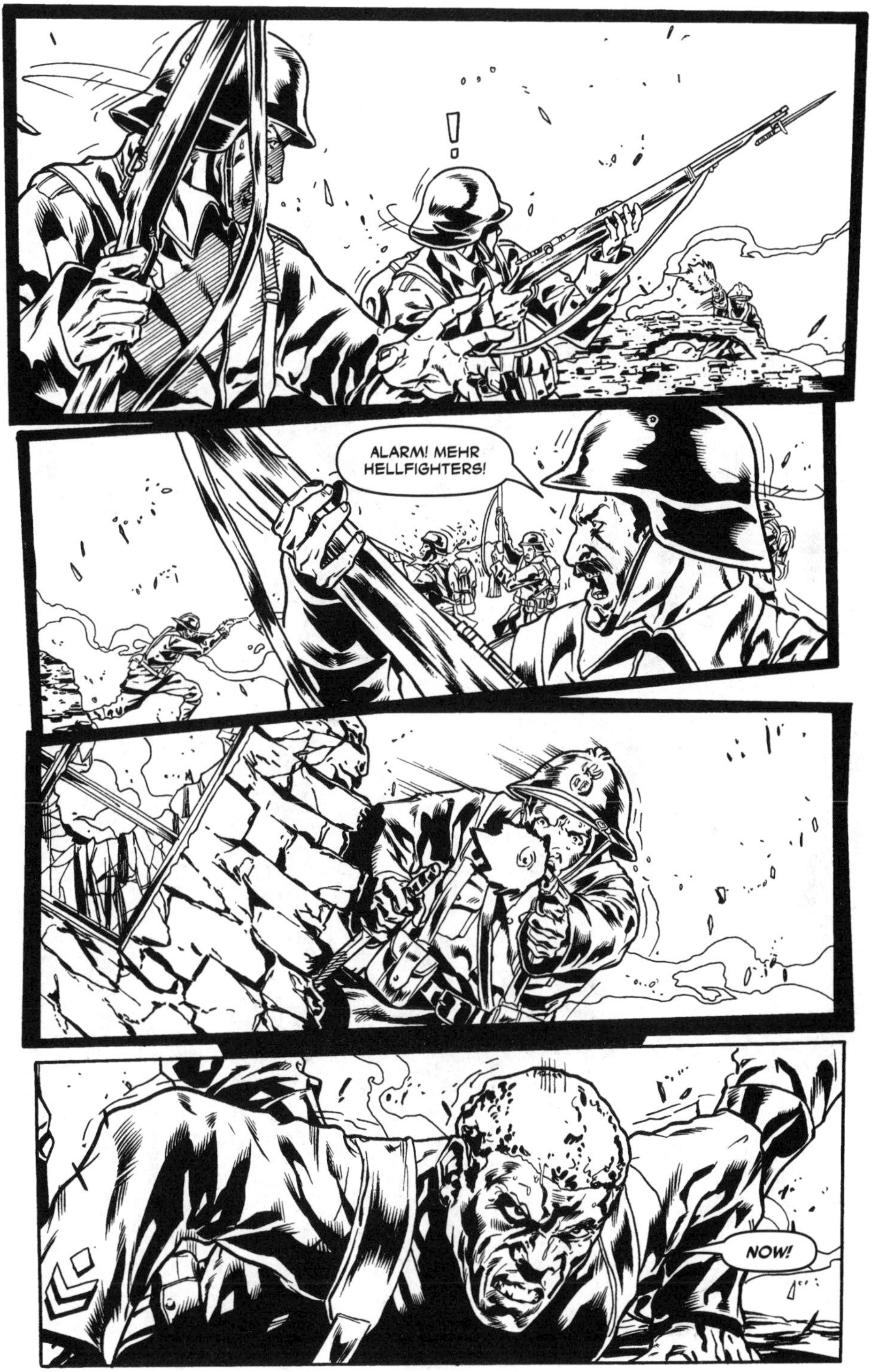
!
ALARM! MEHR HELLFIGHTERS!
NOW!

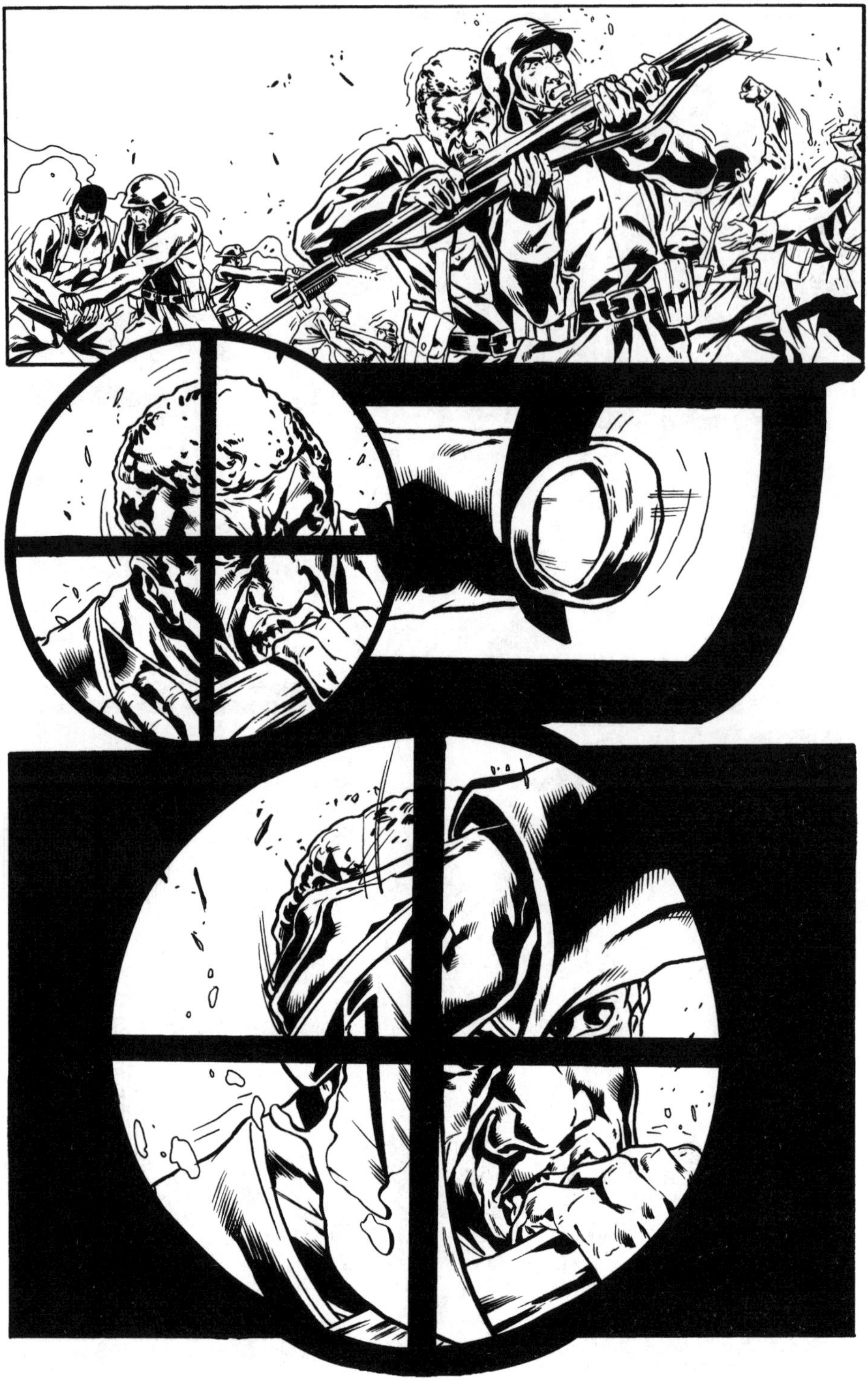

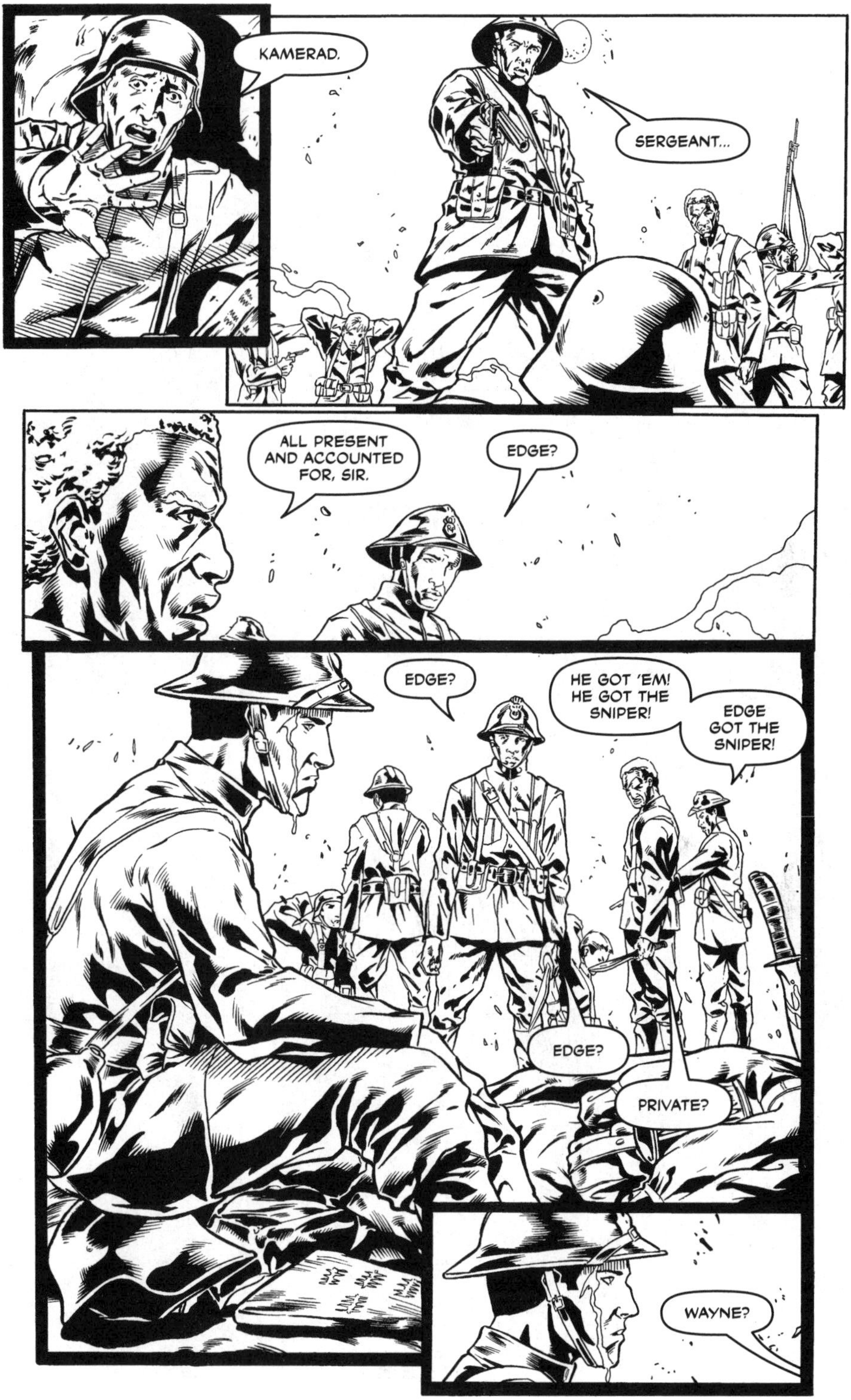
KAMERAD.
SERGEANT...
ALL PRESENT AND ACCOUNTED FOR, SIR.
EDGE?
EDGE?
HE GOT 'EM! HE GOT THE SNIPER!
EDGE GOT THE SNIPER!
EDGE?
PRIVATE?
WAYNE?

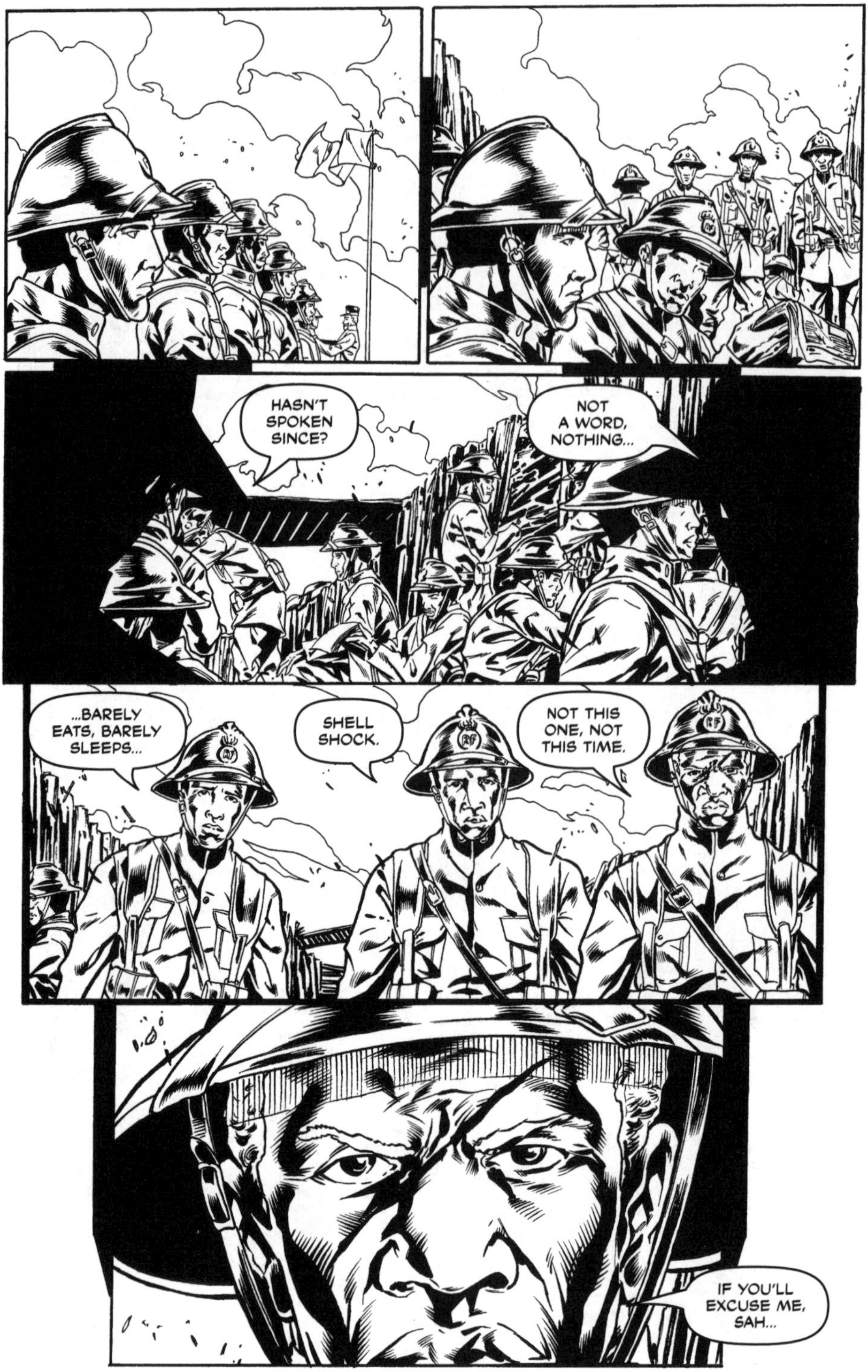
HASN'T SPOKEN SINCE?
NOT A WORD, NOTHING...
...BARELY EATS, BARELY SLEEPS...
SHELL SHOCK.
NOT THIS ONE, NOT THIS TIME.
IF YOU'LL EXCUSE ME, SAH...

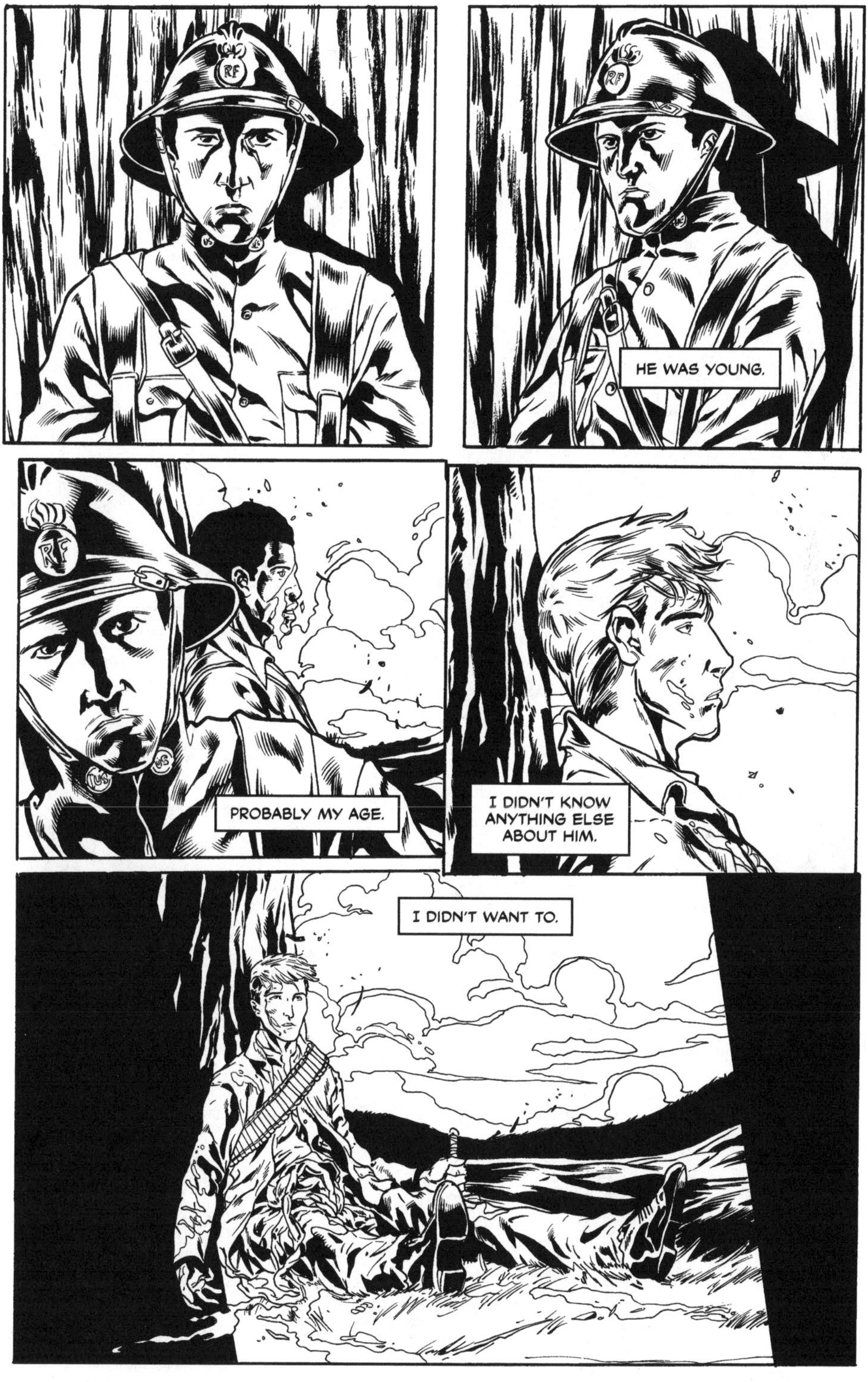
HE WAS YOUNG.
PROBABLY MY AGE.
I DIDN'T KNOW ANYTHING ELSE ABOUT HIM.
I DIDN'T WANT TO.

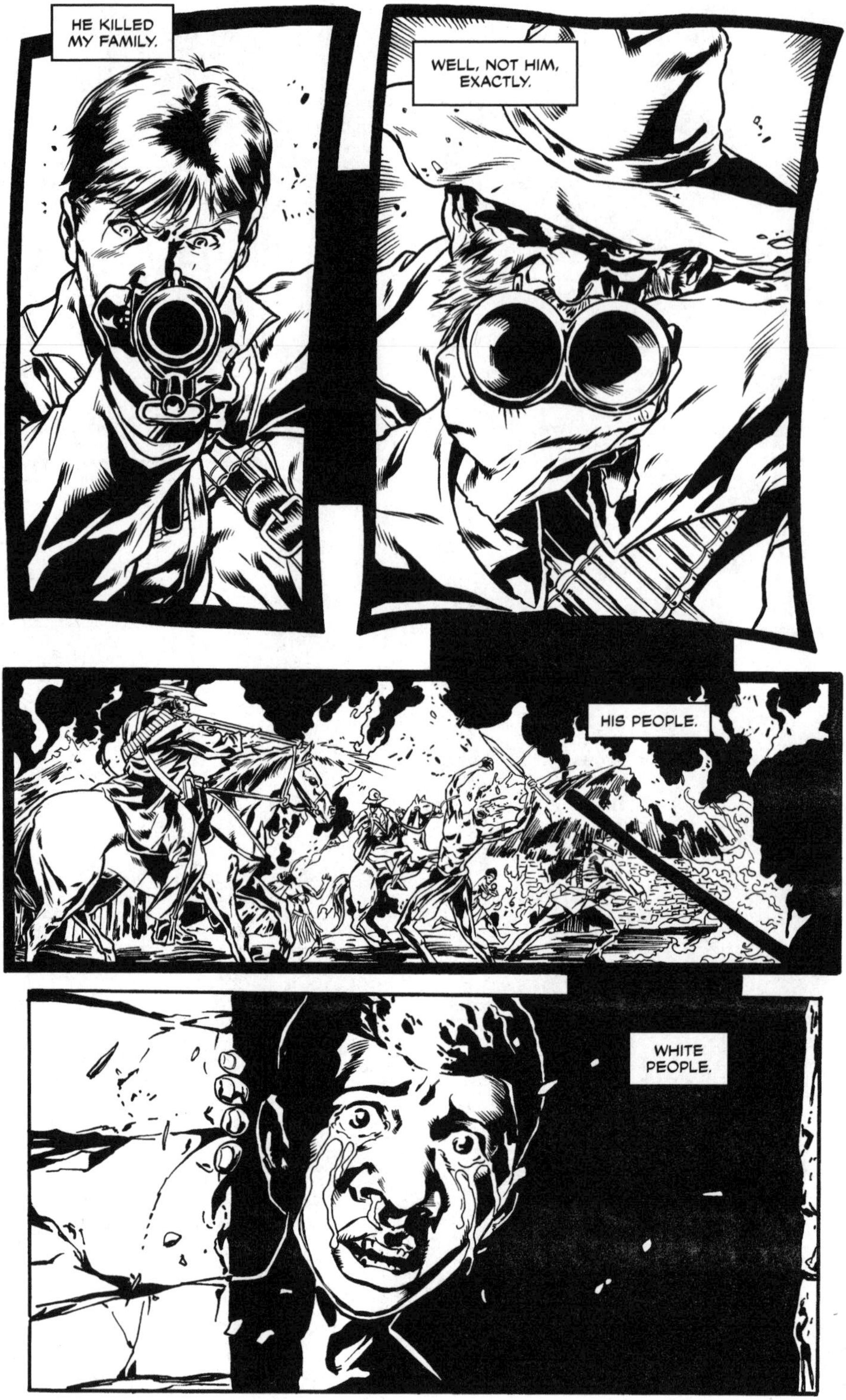
HE KILLED MY FAMILY.
WELL, NOT HIM, EXACTLY.
HIS PEOPLE.
WHITE PEOPLE.

I KNEW I WOULD DRAW THEIR BLOOD SOME DAY.

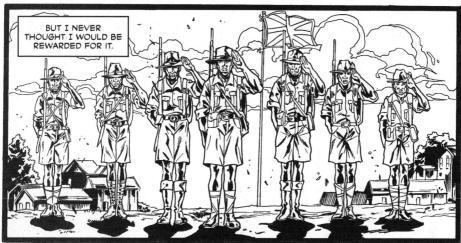

BUT I NEVER THOUGHT I WOULD BE REWARDED FOR IT.

"WHITE FOLKS PAYING ME TO KILL OTHER WHITE FOLKS."

"GLORY HALLELUJAH."

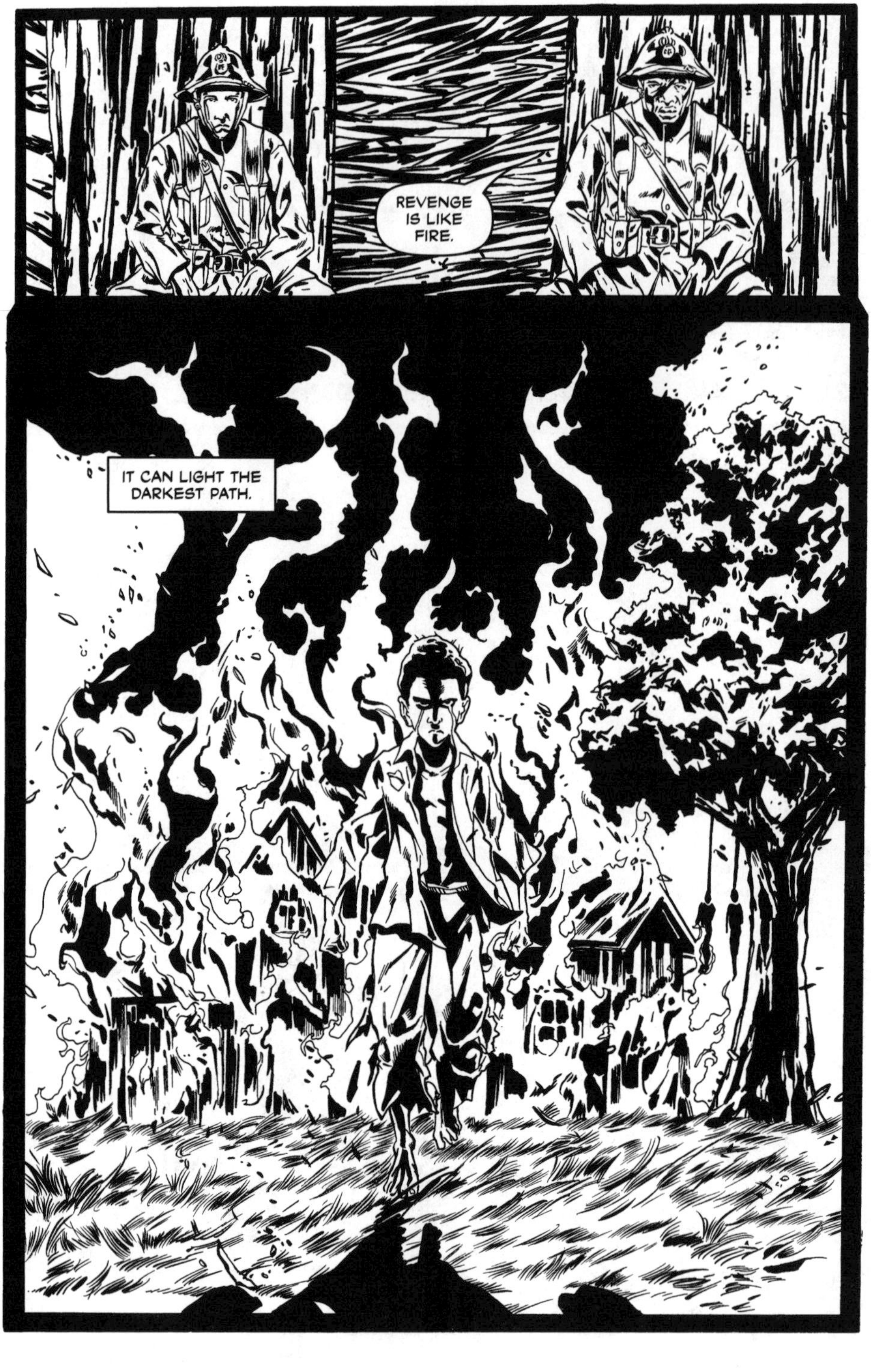
REVENGE IS LIKE FIRE.
IT CAN LIGHT THE DARKEST PATH.

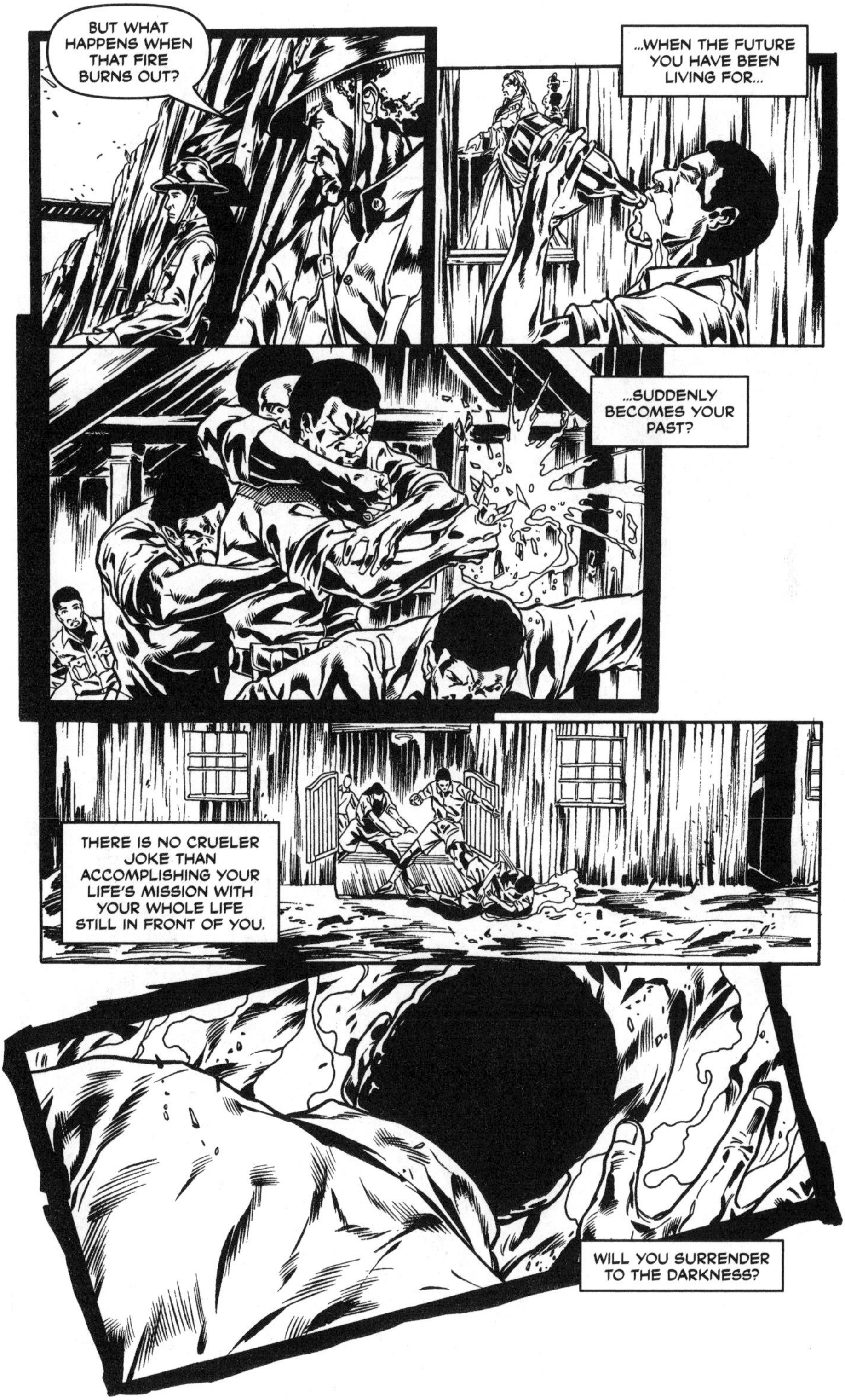
BUT WHAT HAPPENS WHEN THAT FIRE BURNS OUT?
...WHEN THE FUTURE YOU HAVE BEEN LIVING FOR...
...SUDDENLY BECOMES YOUR PAST?
THERE IS NO CRUELER JOKE THAN ACCOMPLISHING YOUR LIFE'S MISSION WITH YOUR WHOLE LIFE STILL IN FRONT OF YOU.
WILL YOU SURRENDER TO THE DARKNESS?

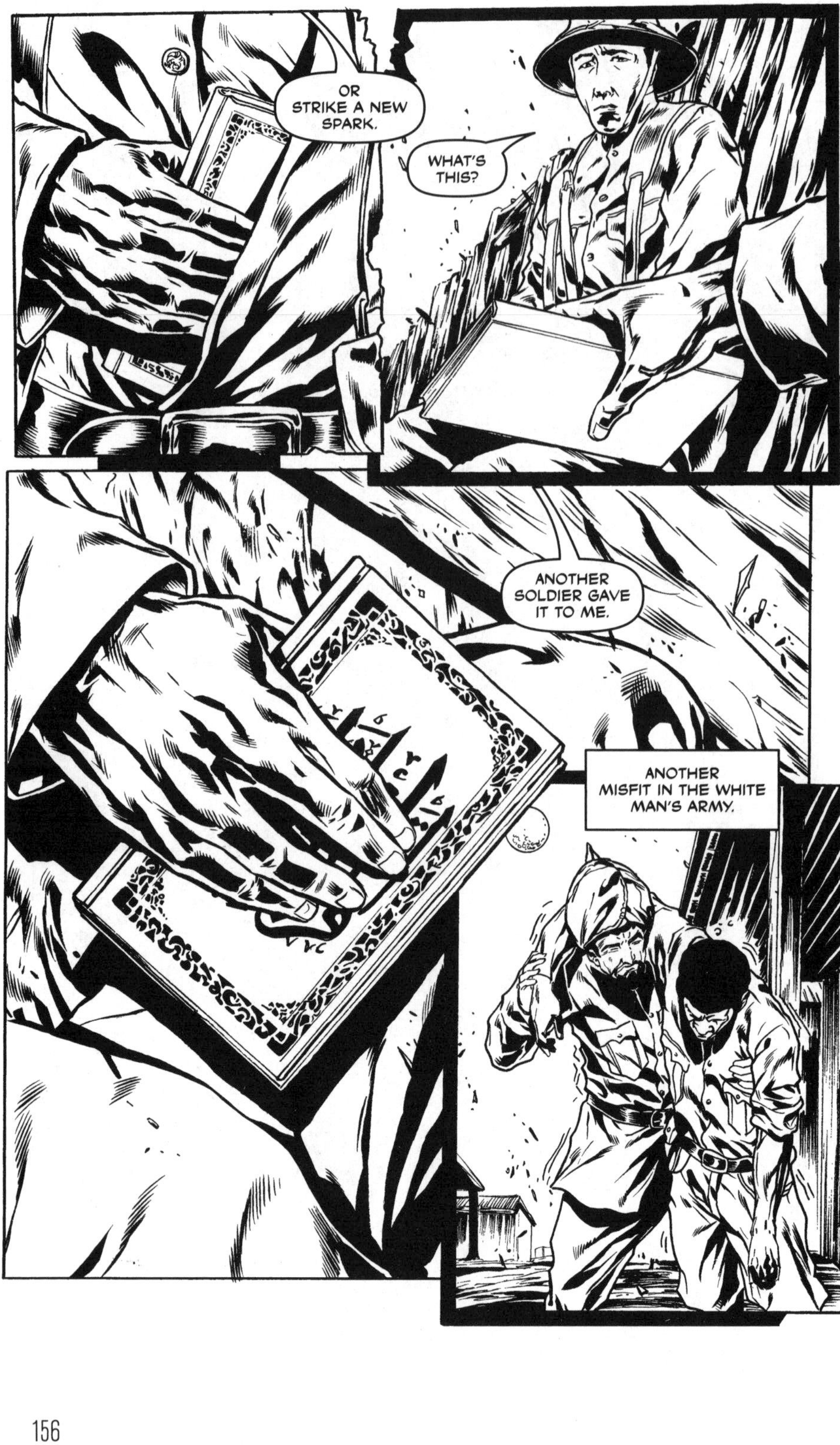
OR STRIKE A NEW SPARK.
WHAT'S THIS?
ANOTHER SOLDIER GAVE IT TO ME.
ANOTHER MISFIT IN THE WHITE MAN'S ARMY.

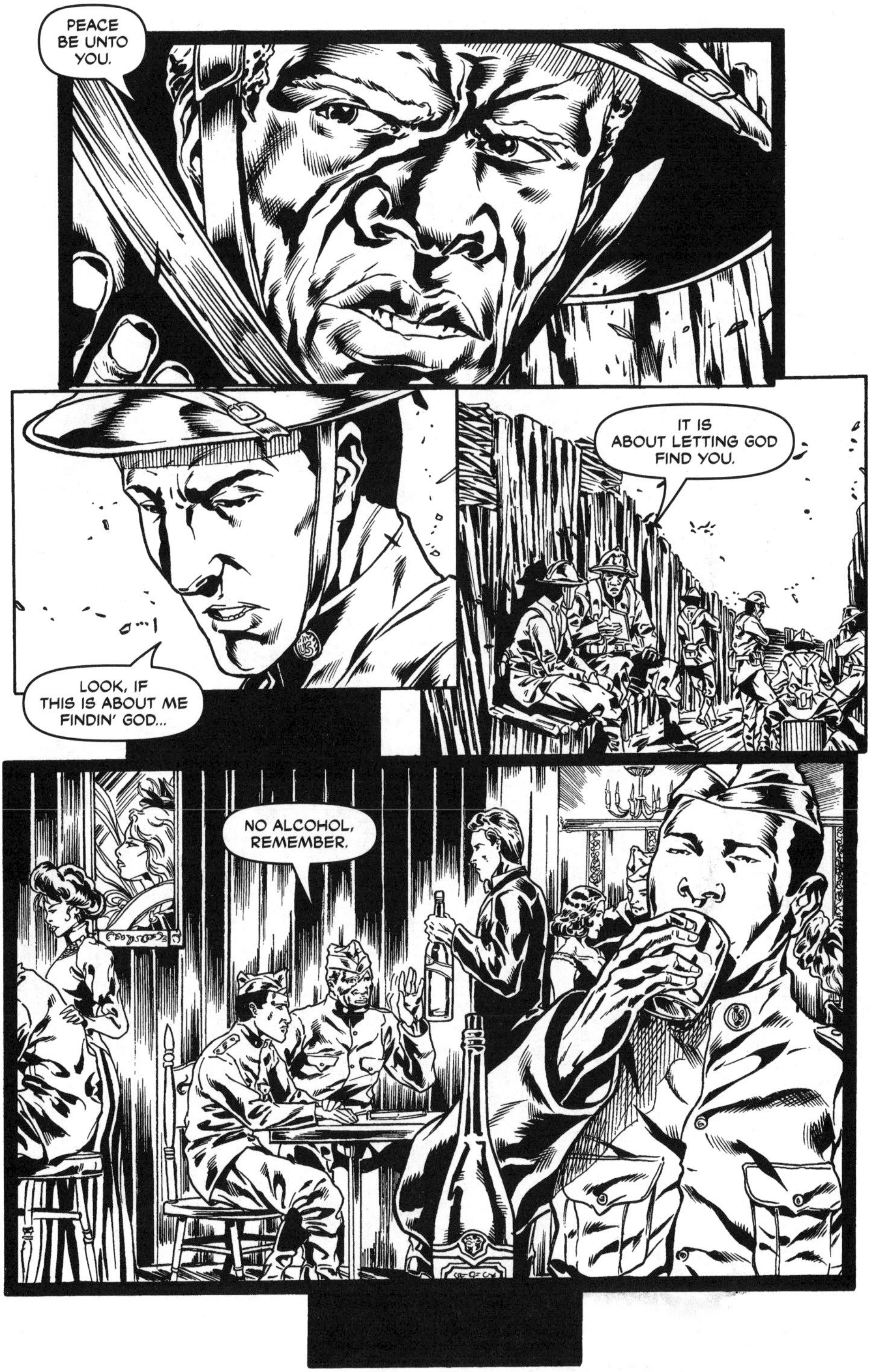
PEACE BE UNTO YOU.
LOOK, IF THIS IS ABOUT ME FINDIN' GOD...
IT IS ABOUT LETTING GOD FIND YOU.
NO ALCOHOL, REMEMBER.

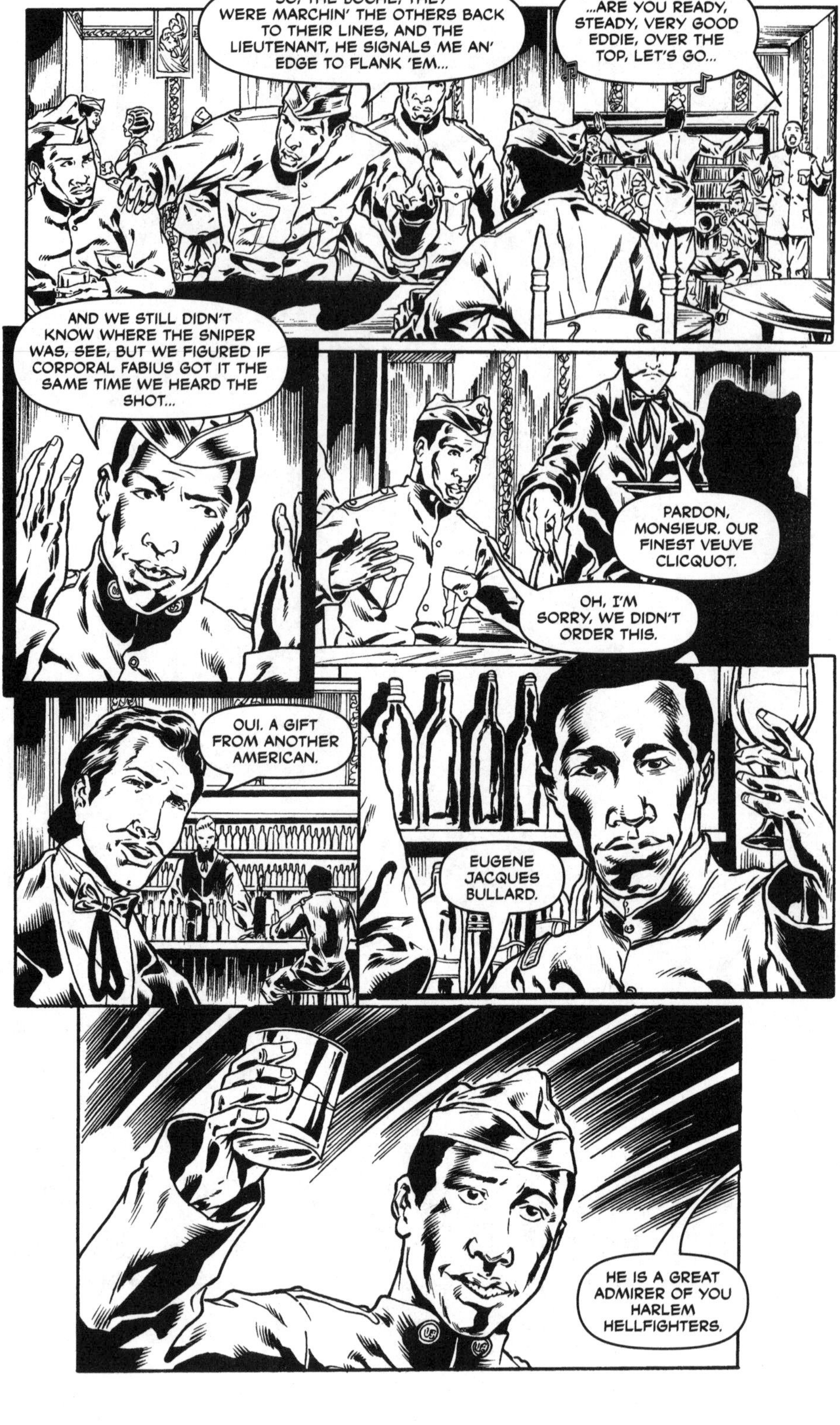
SO, THE BOCHE, THEY WERE MARCHIN' THE OTHERS BACK TO THEIR LINES, AND THE LIEUTENANT, HE SIGNALS ME AN' EDGE TO FLANK 'EM...
...ARE YOU READY, STEADY, VERY GOOD EDDIE, OVER THE TOP, LET'S GO...
AND WE STILL DIDN'T KNOW WHERE THE SNIPER WAS, SEE, BUT WE FIGURED IF CORPORAL FABIUS GOT IT THE SAME TIME WE HEARD THE SHOT...
PARDON, MONSIEUR. OUR FINEST VEUVE CLICQUOT.
OH, I'M SORRY, WE DIDN'T ORDER THIS.
OUI. A GIFT FROM ANOTHER AMERICAN.
EUGENE JACQUES BULLARD.
HE IS A GREAT ADMIRER OF YOU HARLEM HELLFIGHTERS.

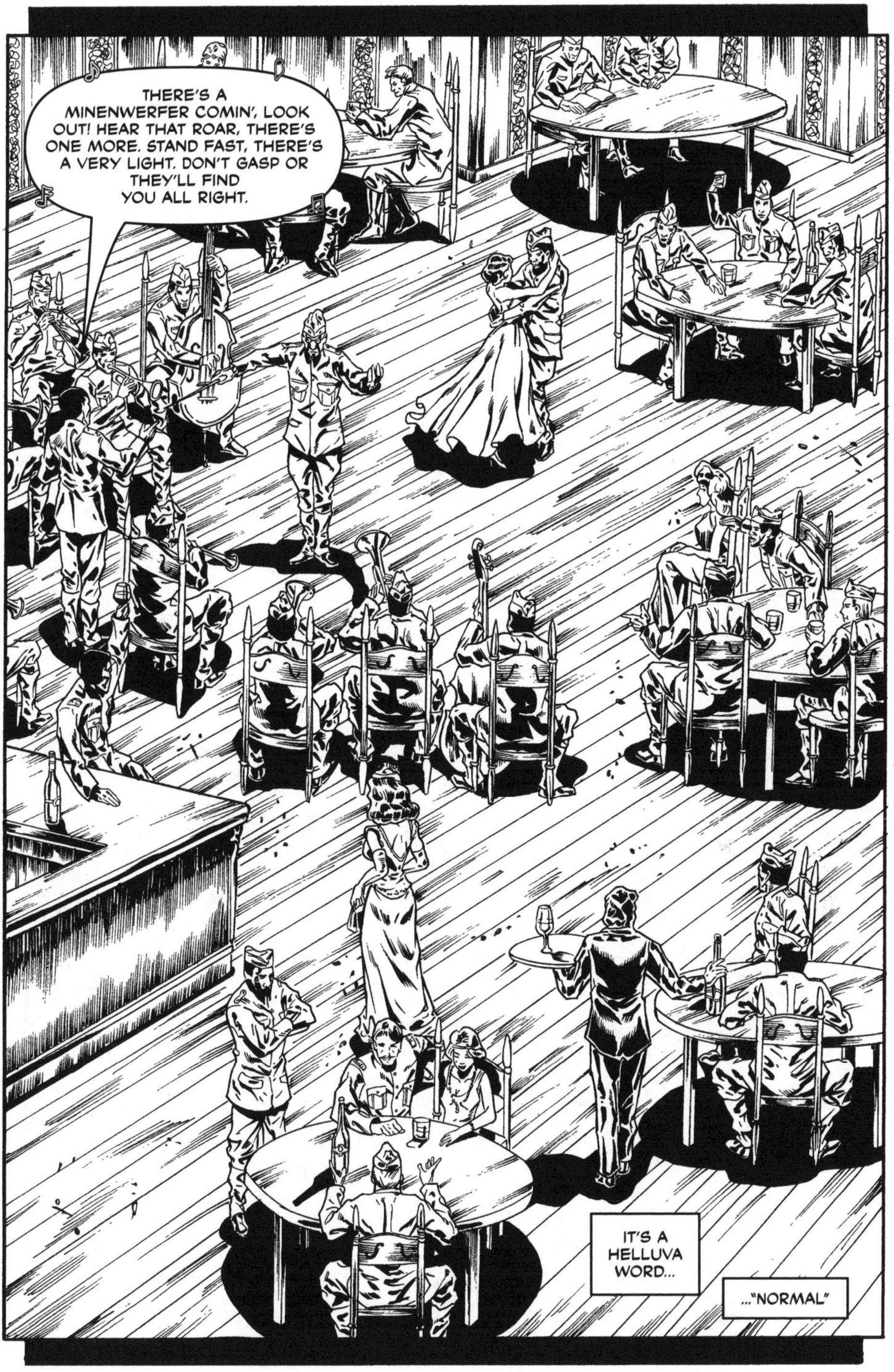

THERE'S A MINENWERFER COMIN', LOOK OUT! HEAR THAT ROAR, THERE'S ONE MORE. STAND FAST, THERE'S A VERY LIGHT. DON'T GASP OR THEY'LL FIND YOU ALL RIGHT.
IT'S A HELLUVA WORD...
..."NORMAL"

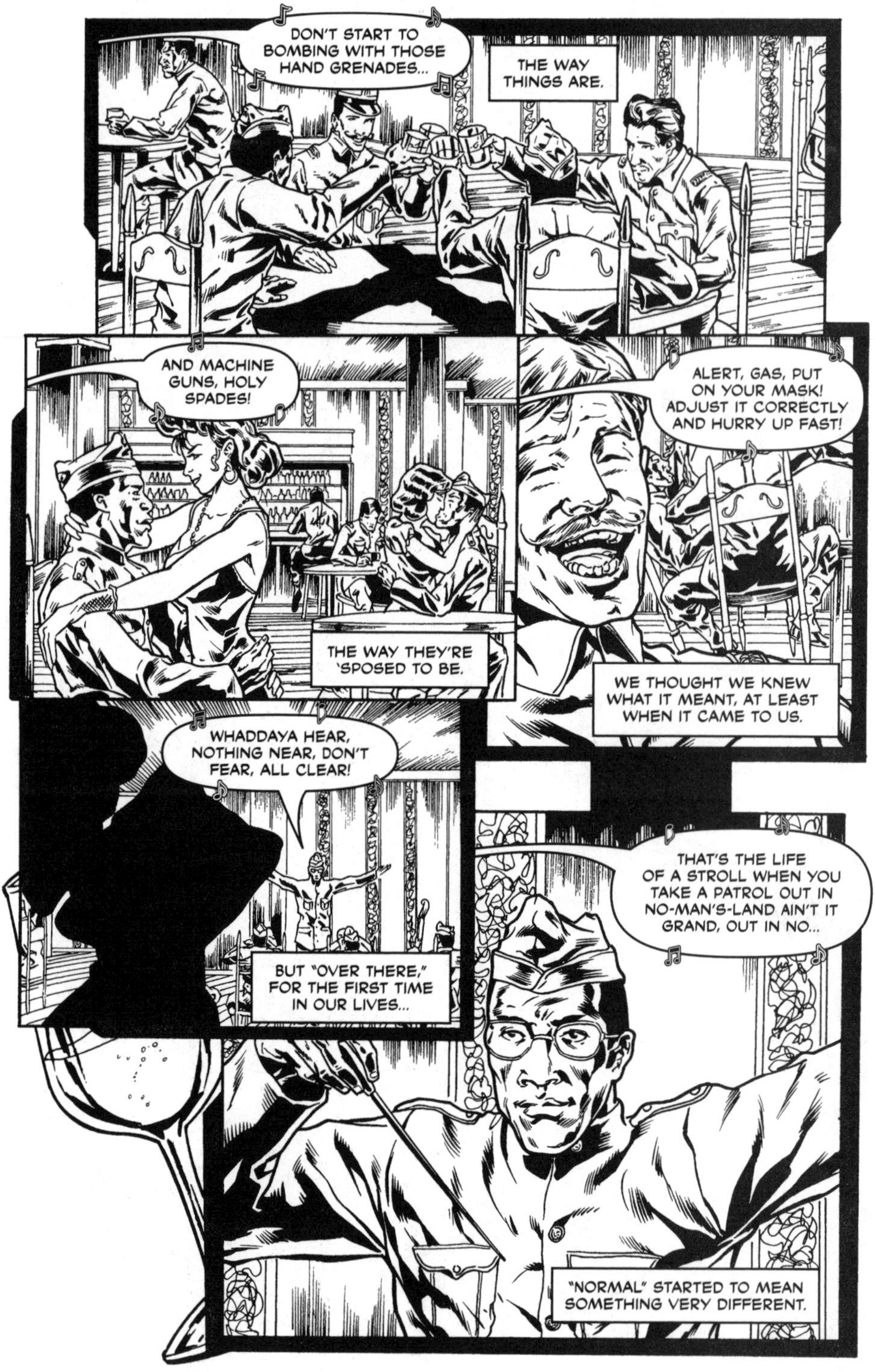
DON'T START TO BOMBING WITH THOSE HAND GRENADES...
THE WAY THINGS ARE.
AND MACHINE GUNS, HOLY SPADES!
THE WAY THEY'RE 'SPOSED TO BE.
ALERT, GAS, PUT ON YOUR MASK! ADJUST IT CORRECTLY AND HURRY UP FAST!
WE THOUGHT WE KNEW WHAT IT MEANT, AT LEAST WHEN IT CAME TO US.
WHADDAYA HEAR, NOTHING NEAR, DON'T FEAR, ALL CLEAR!
BUT "OVER THERE," FOR THE FIRST TIME IN OUR LIVES...
THAT'S THE LIFE OF A STROLL WHEN YOU TAKE A PATROL OUT IN NO-MAN'S-LAND AIN'T IT GRAND, OUT IN NO...
"NORMAL" STARTED TO MEAN SOMETHING VERY DIFFERENT.

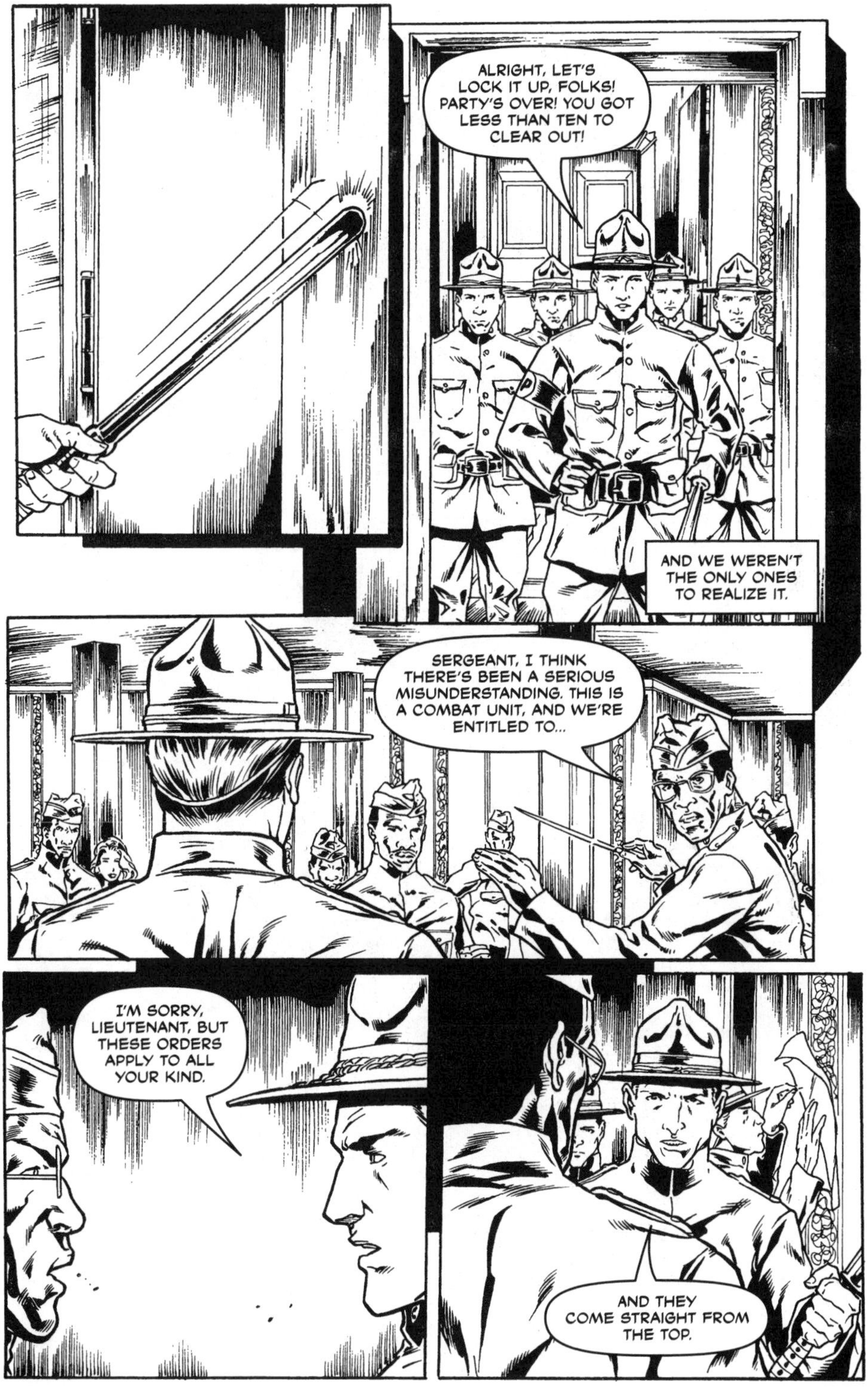
ALRIGHT, LET'S LOCK IT UP, FOLKS! PARTY'S OVER! YOU GOT LESS THAN TEN TO CLEAR OUT!
AND WE WEREN'T THE ONLY ONES TO REALIZE IT.
SERGEANT, I THINK THERE'S BEEN A SERIOUS MISUNDERSTANDING. THIS IS A COMBAT UNIT, AND WE'RE ENTITLED TO...
I'M SORRY, LIEUTENANT, BUT THESE ORDERS APPLY TO ALL YOUR KIND.
AND THEY COME STRAIGHT FROM THE TOP.

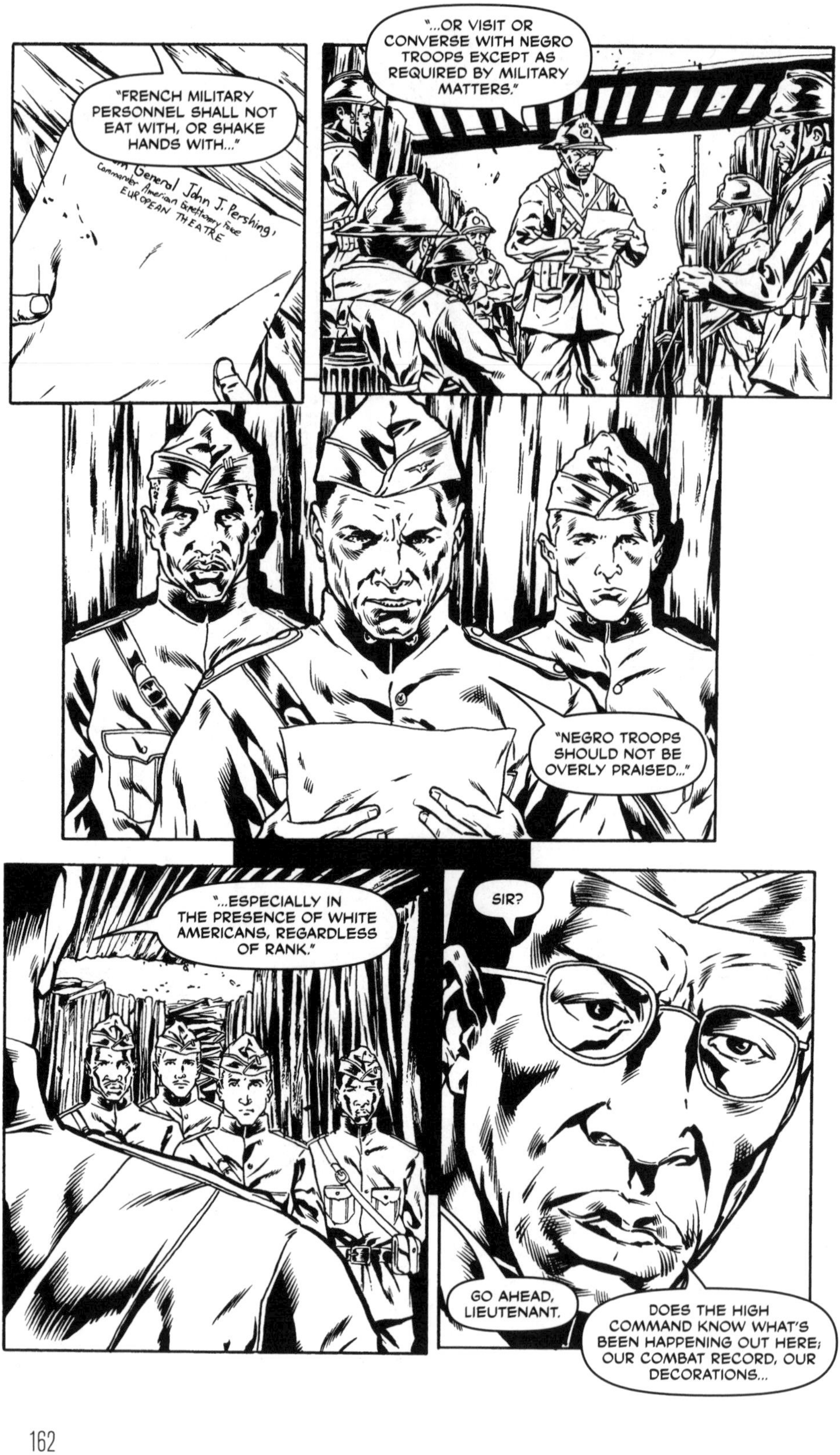
"FRENCH MILITARY PERSONNEL SHALL NOT EAT WITH, OR SHAKE HANDS WITH..."
General John J. Pershing,
EUROPEAN THEATRE
"...OR VISIT OR CONVERSE WITH NEGRO TROOPS EXCEPT AS REQUIRED BY MILITARY MATTERS."
"NEGRO TROOPS SHOULD NOT BE OVERLY PRAISED..."
"...ESPECIALLY IN THE PRESENCE OF WHITE AMERICANS, REGARDLESS OF RANK."
SIR?
GO AHEAD, LIEUTENANT.
DOES THE HIGH COMMAND KNOW WHAT'S BEEN HAPPENING OUT HERE; OUR COMBAT RECORD, OUR DECORATIONS...

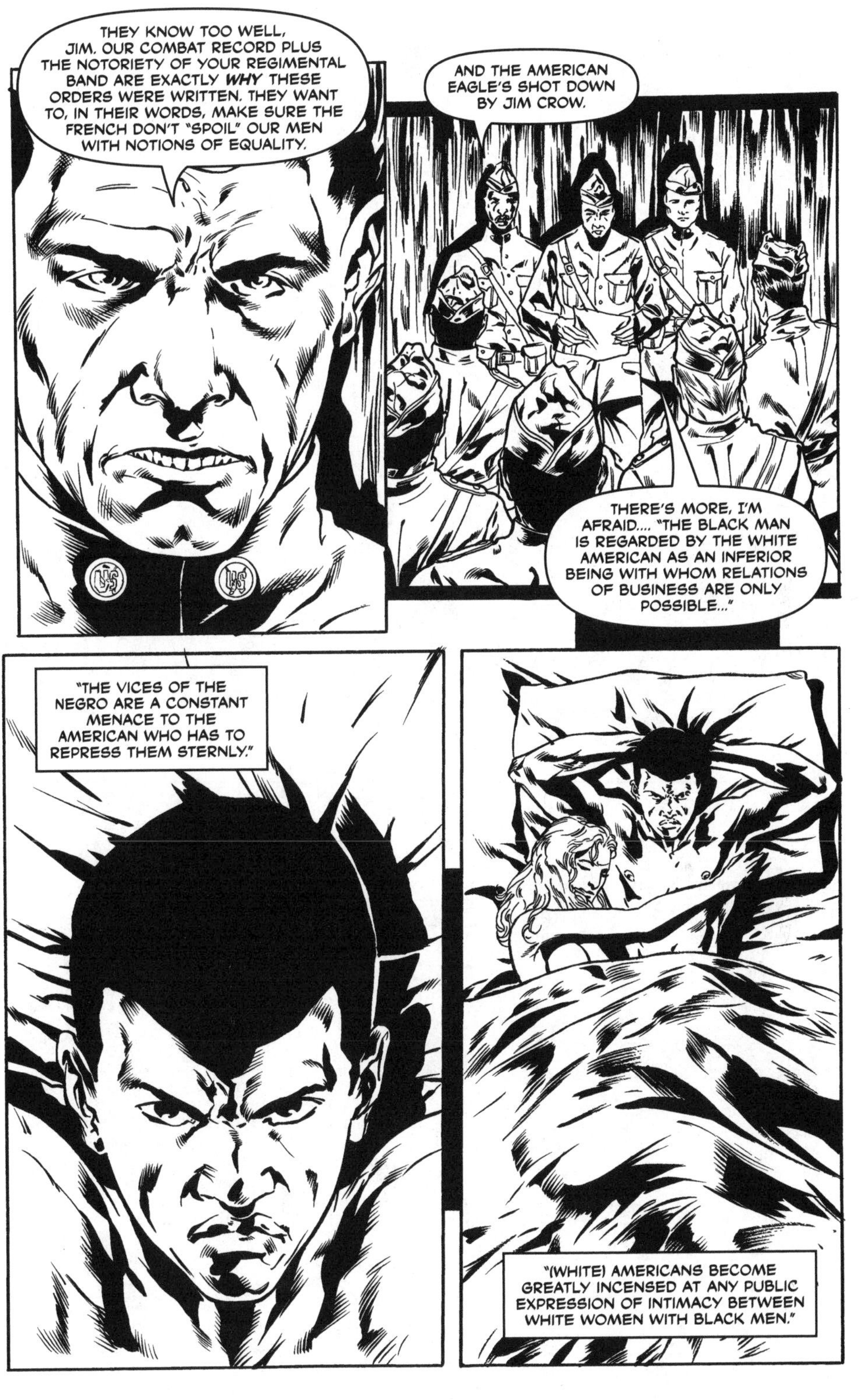

THEY KNOW TOO WELL, JIM. OUR COMBAT RECORD PLUS THE NOTORIETY OF YOUR REGIMENTAL BAND ARE EXACTLY ***WHY*** THESE ORDERS WERE WRITTEN. THEY WANT TO, IN THEIR WORDS, MAKE SURE THE FRENCH DON'T "SPOIL" OUR MEN WITH NOTIONS OF EQUALITY.
AND THE AMERICAN EAGLE'S SHOT DOWN BY JIM CROW.
THERE'S MORE, I'M AFRAID.... "THE BLACK MAN IS REGARDED BY THE WHITE AMERICAN AS AN INFERIOR BEING WITH WHOM RELATIONS OF BUSINESS ARE ONLY POSSIBLE..."
"THE VICES OF THE NEGRO ARE A CONSTANT MENACE TO THE AMERICAN WHO HAS TO REPRESS THEM STERNLY."
"(WHITE) AMERICANS BECOME GREATLY INCENSED AT ANY PUBLIC EXPRESSION OF INTIMACY BETWEEN WHITE WOMEN WITH BLACK MEN."

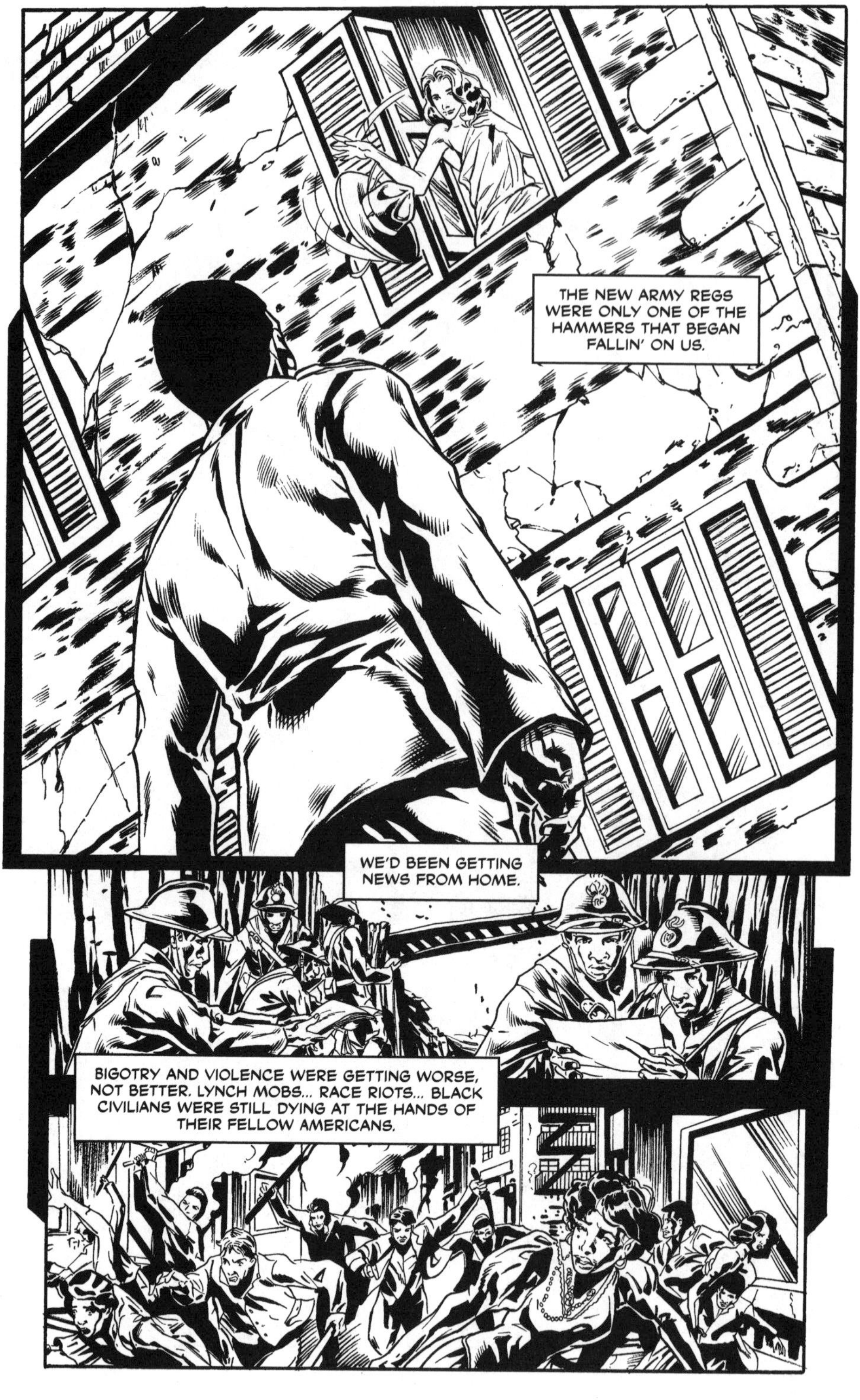
THE NEW ARMY REGS WERE ONLY ONE OF THE HAMMERS THAT BEGAN FALLIN' ON US.
WE'D BEEN GETTING NEWS FROM HOME.
BIGOTRY AND VIOLENCE WERE GETTING WORSE, NOT BETTER. LYNCH MOBS... RACE RIOTS... BLACK CIVILIANS WERE STILL DYING AT THE HANDS OF THEIR FELLOW AMERICANS.

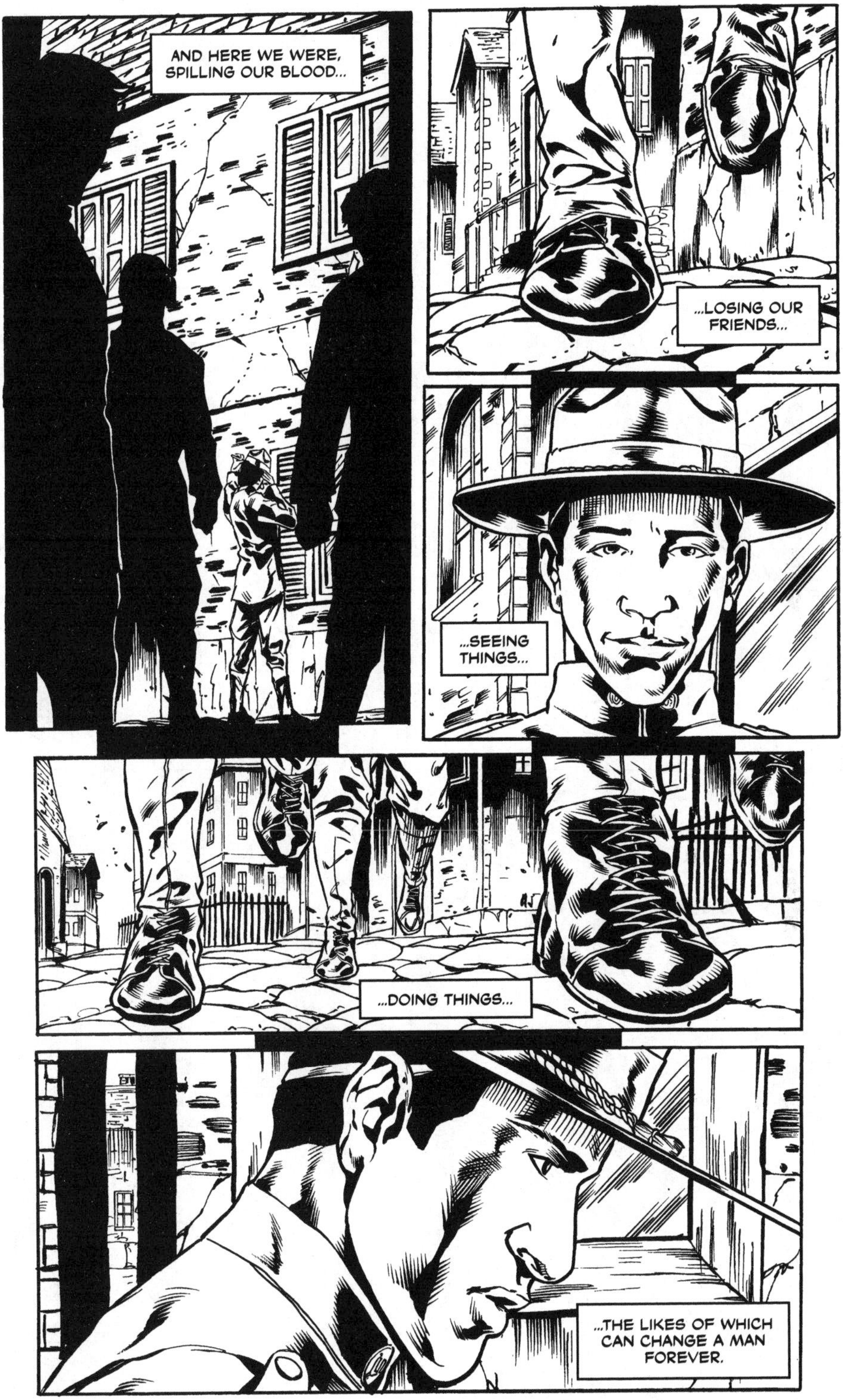
AND HERE WE WERE, SPILLING OUR BLOOD...
...LOSING OUR FRIENDS...
...SEEING THINGS...
...DOING THINGS...
...THE LIKES OF WHICH CAN CHANGE A MAN FOREVER.

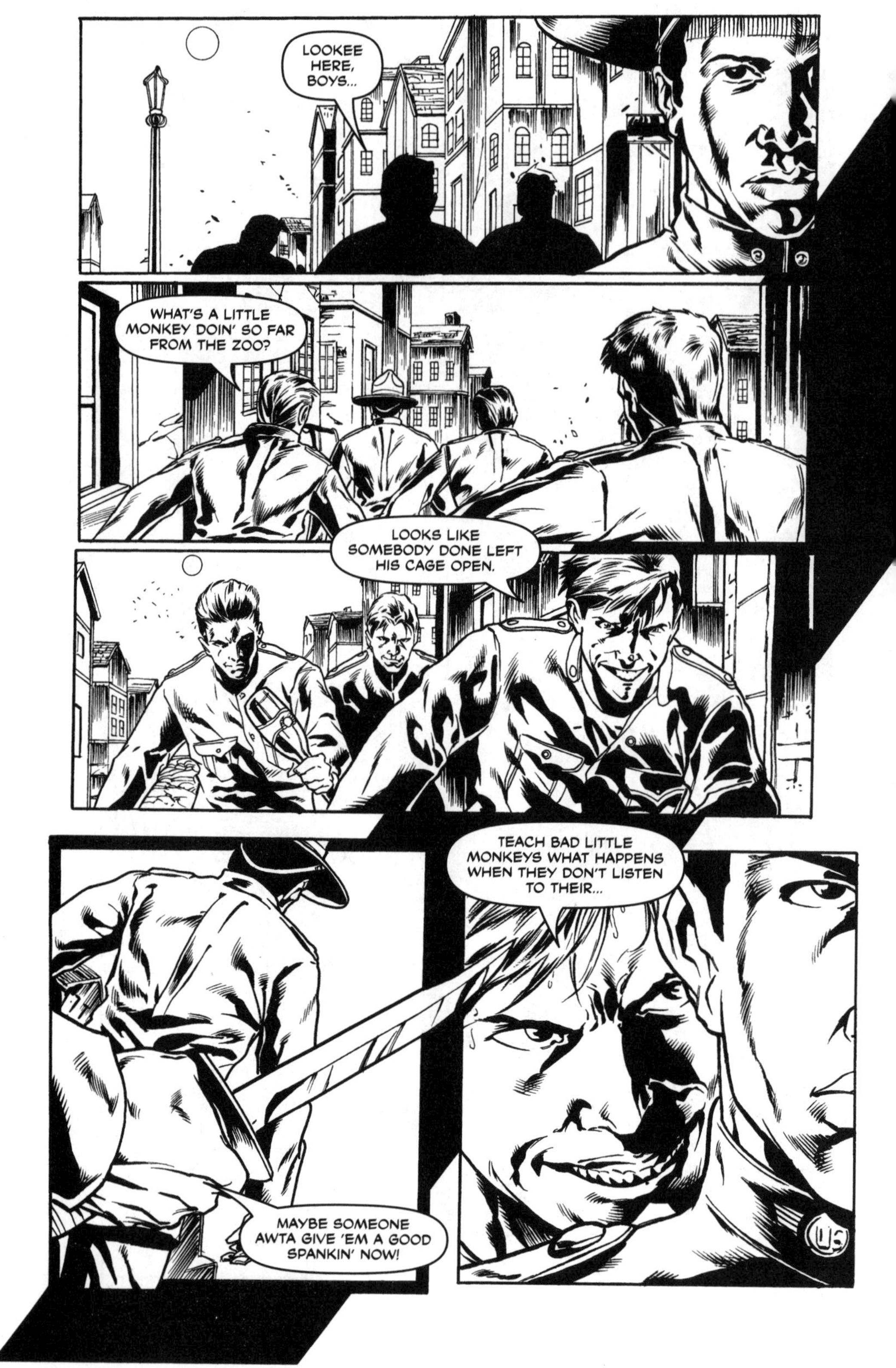
LOOKEE HERE, BOYS...
WHAT'S A LITTLE MONKEY DOIN' SO FAR FROM THE ZOO?
LOOKS LIKE SOMEBODY DONE LEFT HIS CAGE OPEN.
TEACH BAD LITTLE MONKEYS WHAT HAPPENS WHEN THEY DON'T LISTEN TO THEIR...
MAYBE SOMEONE AWTA GIVE 'EM A GOOD SPANKIN' NOW!

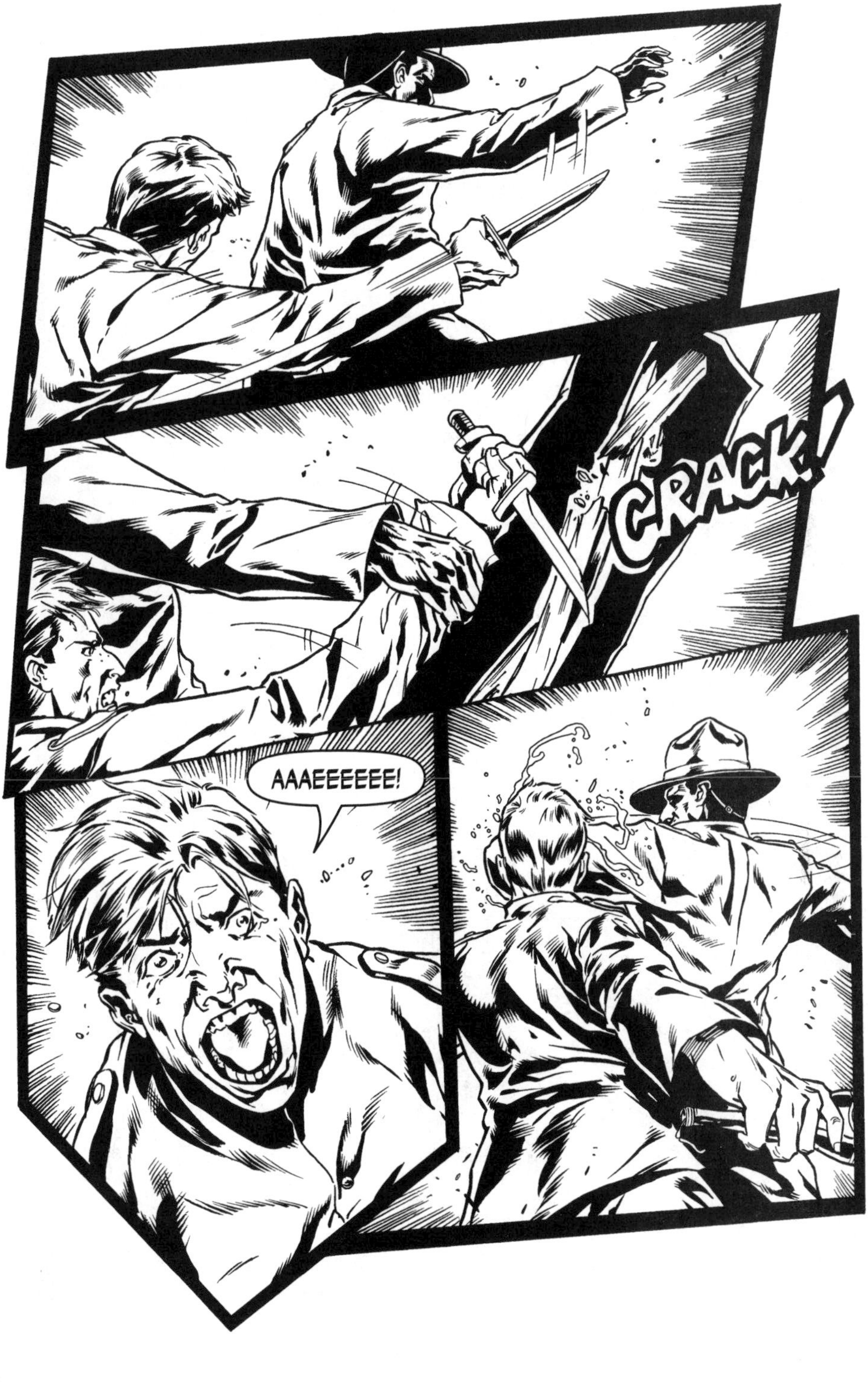
CRACK!
AAAEEEEEEE!

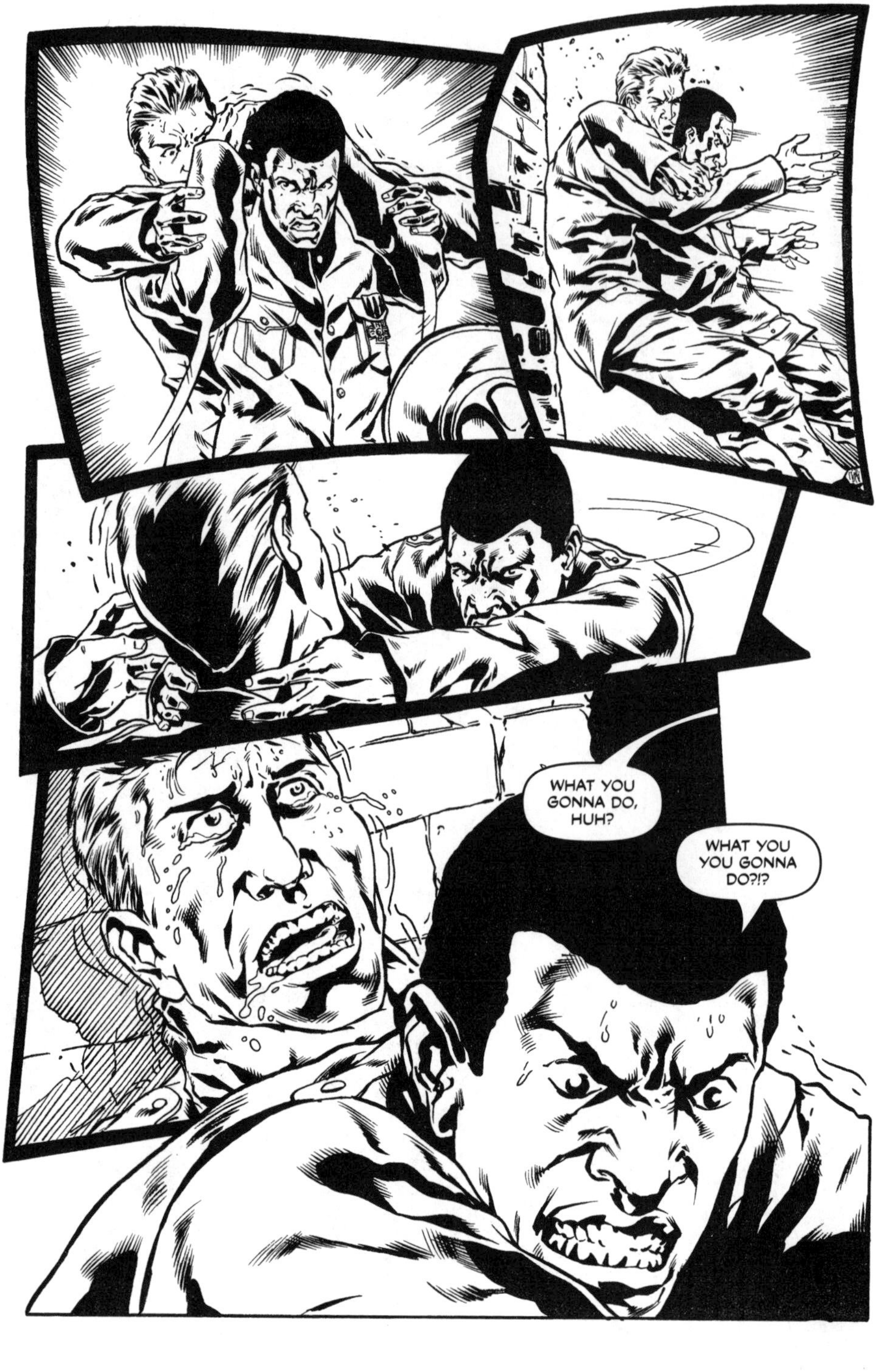
WHAT YOU GONNA DO, HUH?
WHAT YOU YOU GONNA DO?!?

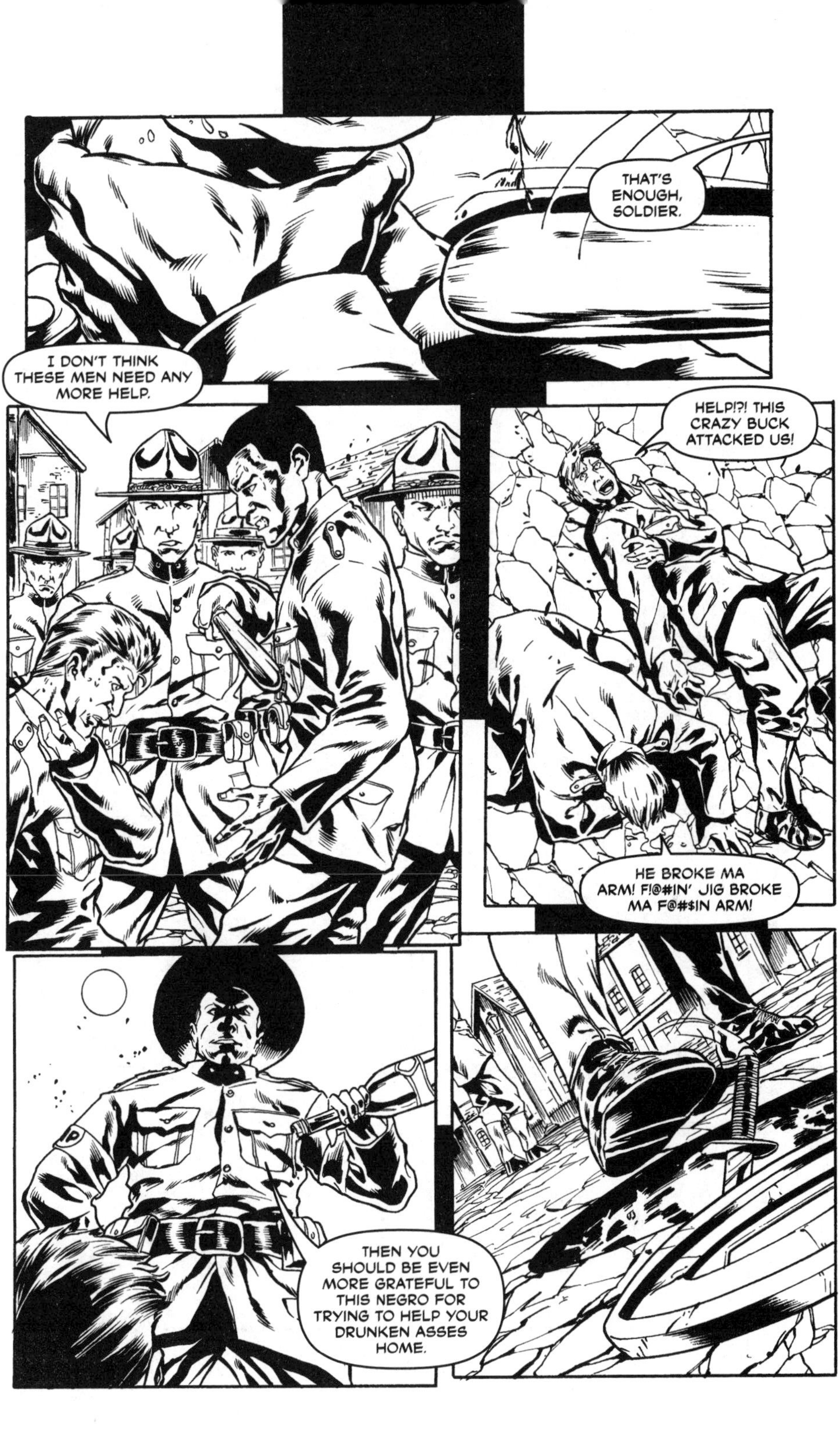
THAT'S ENOUGH, SOLDIER.
I DON'T THINK THESE MEN NEED ANY MORE HELP.
HELP!?! THIS CRAZY BUCK ATTACKED US!
HE BROKE MA ARM! F!@#IN' JIG BROKE MA F@#$IN ARM!
THEN YOU SHOULD BE EVEN MORE GRATEFUL TO THIS NEGRO FOR TRYING TO HELP YOUR DRUNKEN ASSES HOME.

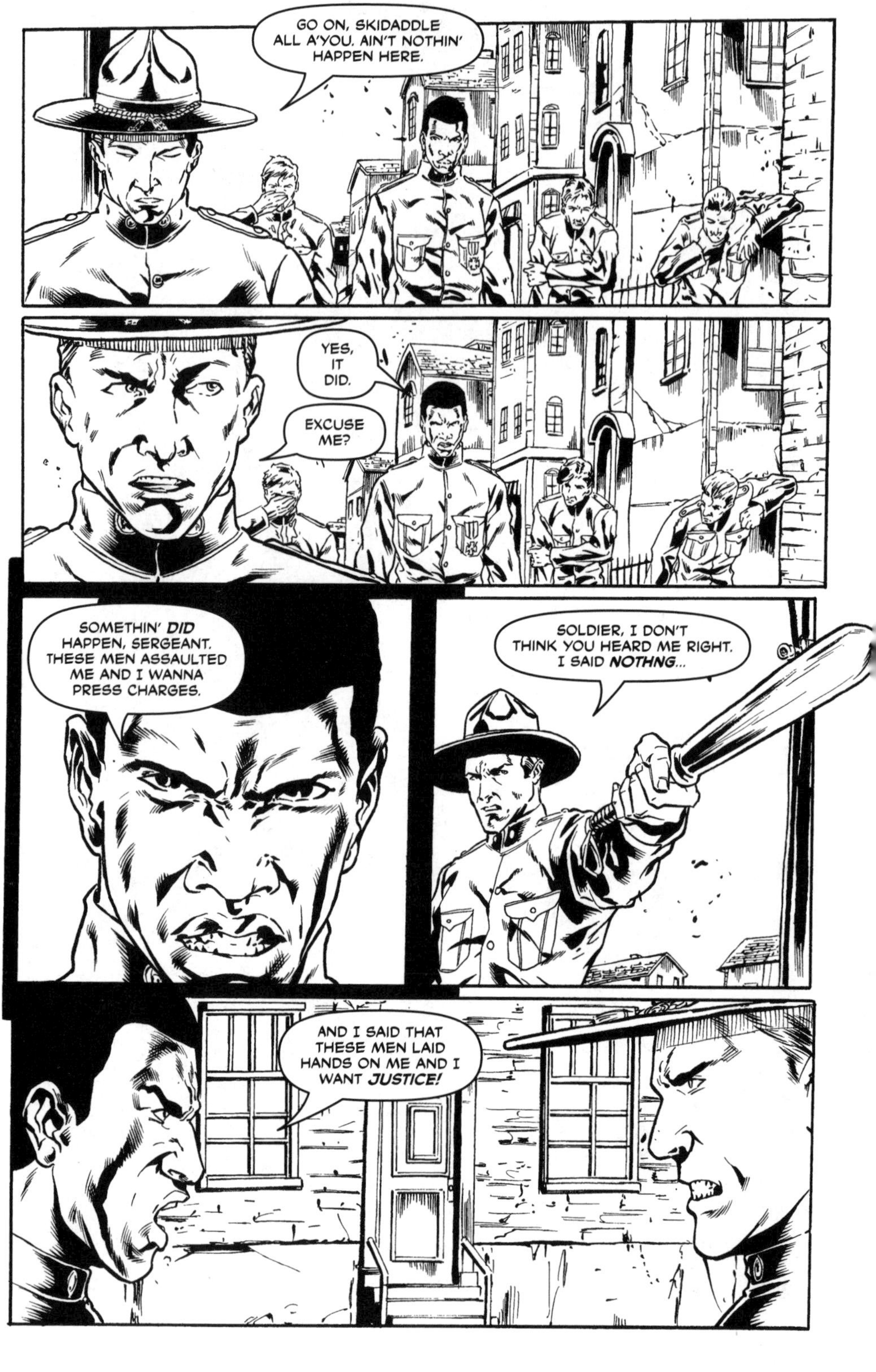
GO ON, SKIDADDLE ALL A'YOU. AIN'T NOTHIN' HAPPEN HERE.
YES, IT DID.
EXCUSE ME?
SOMETHIN' *DID* HAPPEN, SERGEANT. THESE MEN ASSAULTED ME AND I WANNA PRESS CHARGES.
SOLDIER, I DON'T THINK YOU HEARD ME RIGHT. I SAID *NOTHING*...
AND I SAID THAT THESE MEN LAID HANDS ON ME AND I WANT *JUSTICE!*

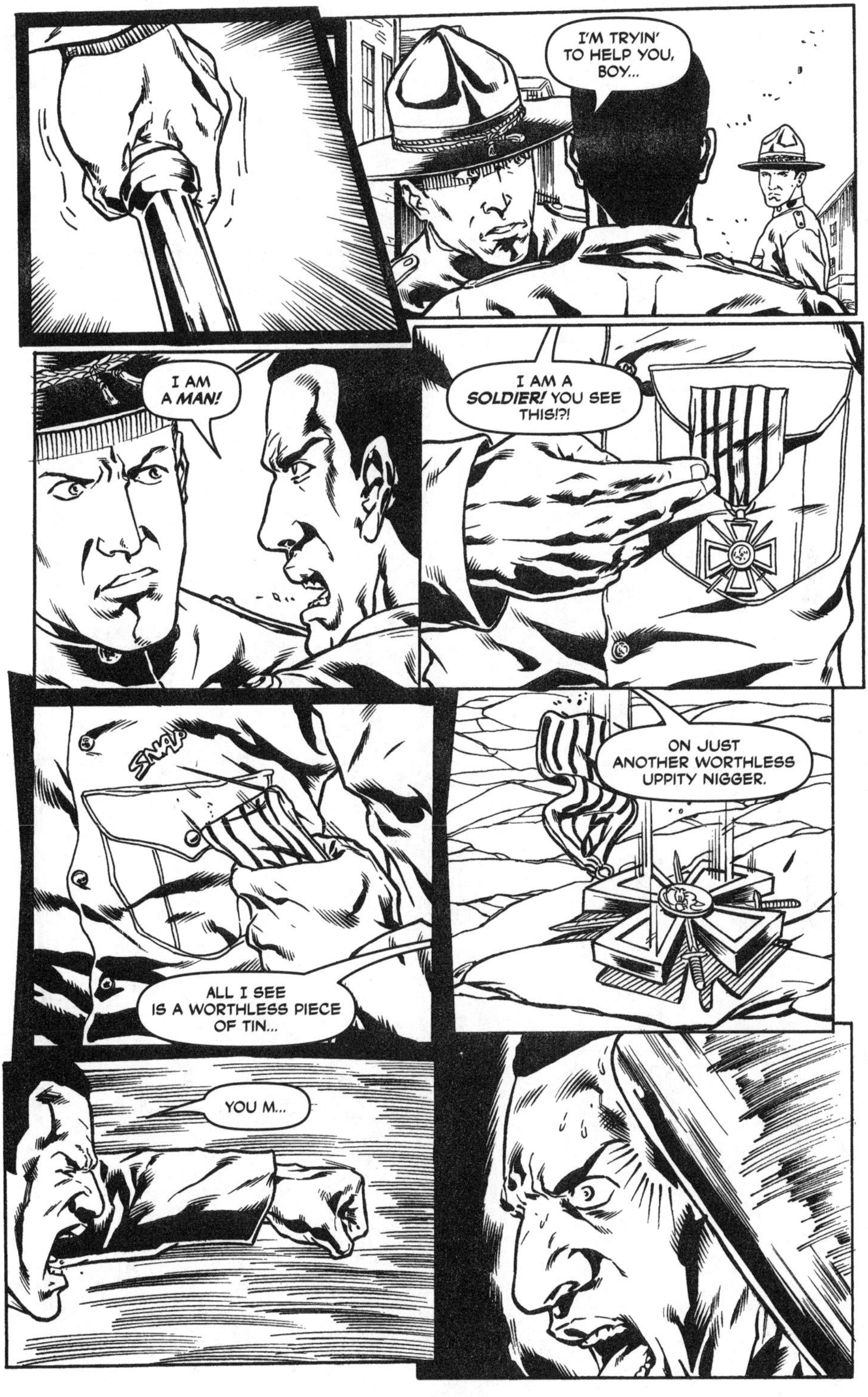
I'M TRYIN' TO HELP YOU, BOY...
I AM A *MAN!*
I AM A *SOLDIER!* YOU SEE THIS!?!
SNAP
ALL I SEE IS A WORTHLESS PIECE OF TIN...
ON JUST ANOTHER WORTHLESS UPPITY NIGGER.
YOU M...

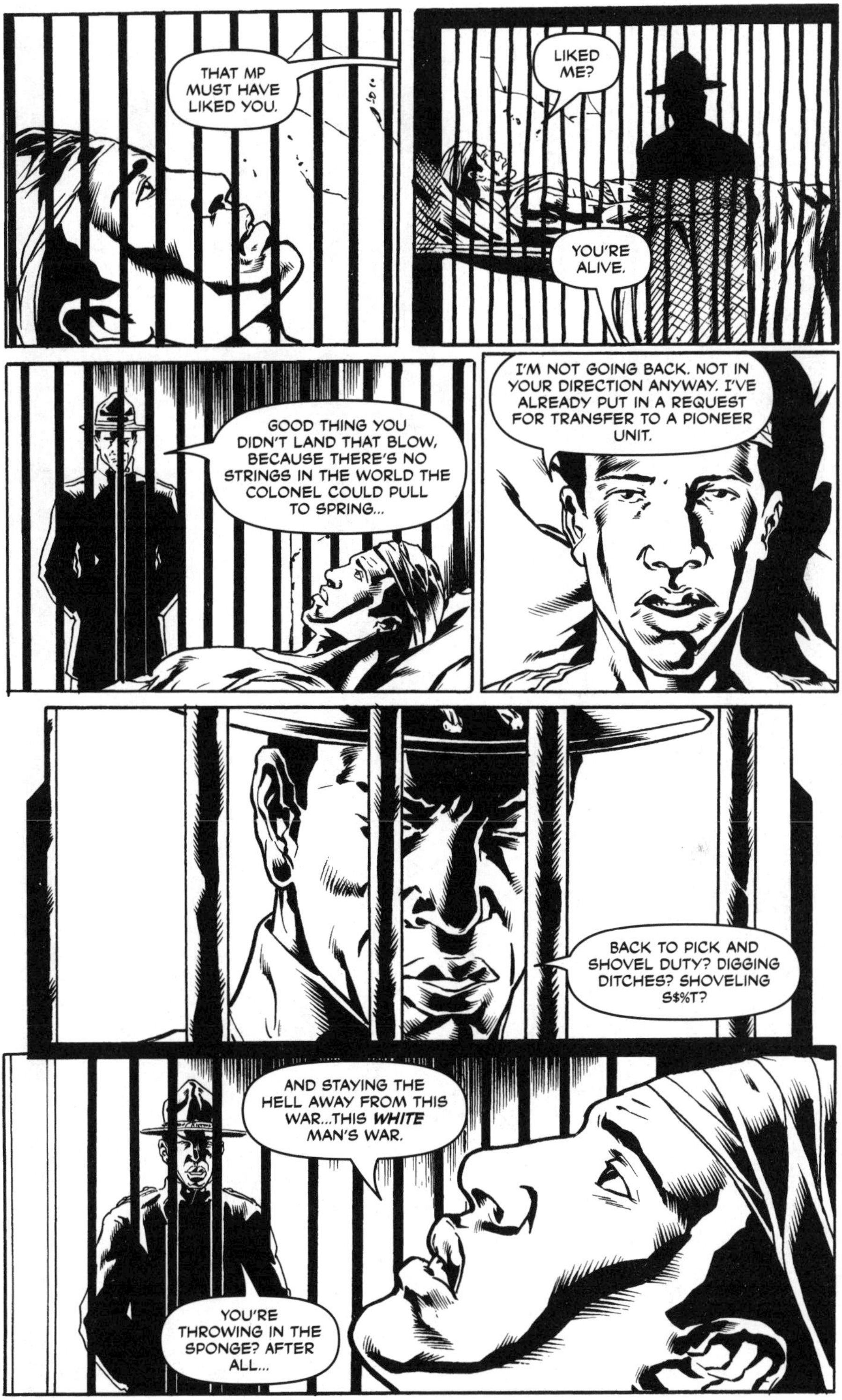
THAT MP MUST HAVE LIKED YOU.
LIKED ME?
YOU'RE ALIVE.
GOOD THING YOU DIDN'T LAND THAT BLOW, BECAUSE THERE'S NO STRINGS IN THE WORLD THE COLONEL COULD PULL TO SPRING...
I'M NOT GOING BACK. NOT IN YOUR DIRECTION ANYWAY. I'VE ALREADY PUT IN A REQUEST FOR TRANSFER TO A PIONEER UNIT.
BACK TO PICK AND SHOVEL DUTY? DIGGING DITCHES? SHOVELING S$%T?
AND STAYING THE HELL AWAY FROM THIS WAR...THIS *WHITE* MAN'S WAR.
YOU'RE THROWING IN THE SPONGE? AFTER ALL...

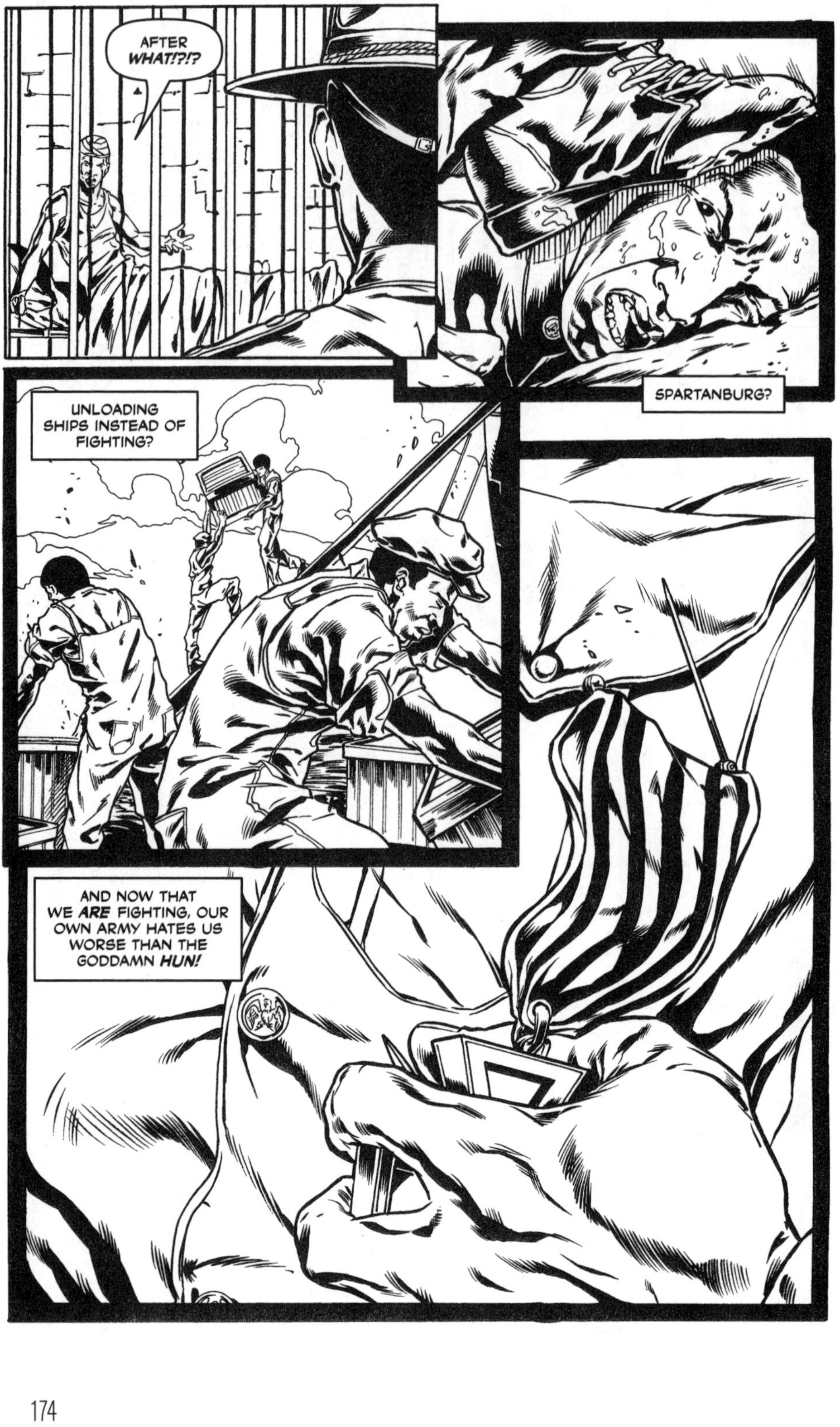
AFTER WHAT!?!?
SPARTANBURG?
UNLOADING SHIPS INSTEAD OF FIGHTING?
AND NOW THAT WE *ARE* FIGHTING, OUR OWN ARMY HATES US WORSE THAN THE GODDAMN *HUN!*

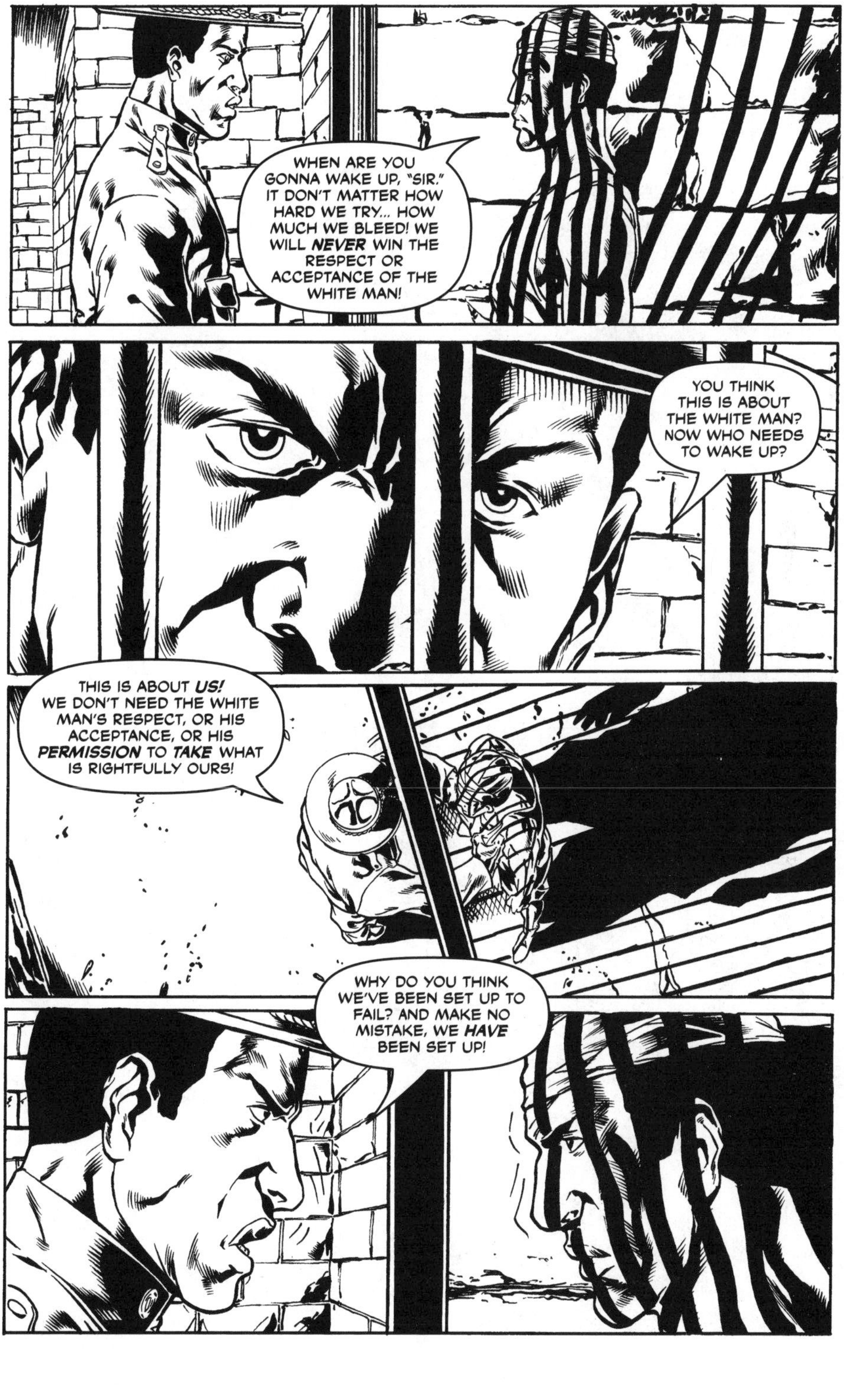
WHEN ARE YOU GONNA WAKE UP, "SIR." IT DON'T MATTER HOW HARD WE TRY... HOW MUCH WE BLEED! WE WILL **NEVER** WIN THE RESPECT OR ACCEPTANCE OF THE WHITE MAN!
YOU THINK THIS IS ABOUT THE WHITE MAN? NOW WHO NEEDS TO WAKE UP?
THIS IS ABOUT **US!** WE DON'T NEED THE WHITE MAN'S RESPECT, OR HIS ACCEPTANCE, OR HIS **PERMISSION** TO **TAKE** WHAT IS RIGHTFULLY OURS!
WHY DO YOU THINK WE'VE BEEN SET UP TO FAIL? AND MAKE NO MISTAKE, WE **HAVE** BEEN SET UP!

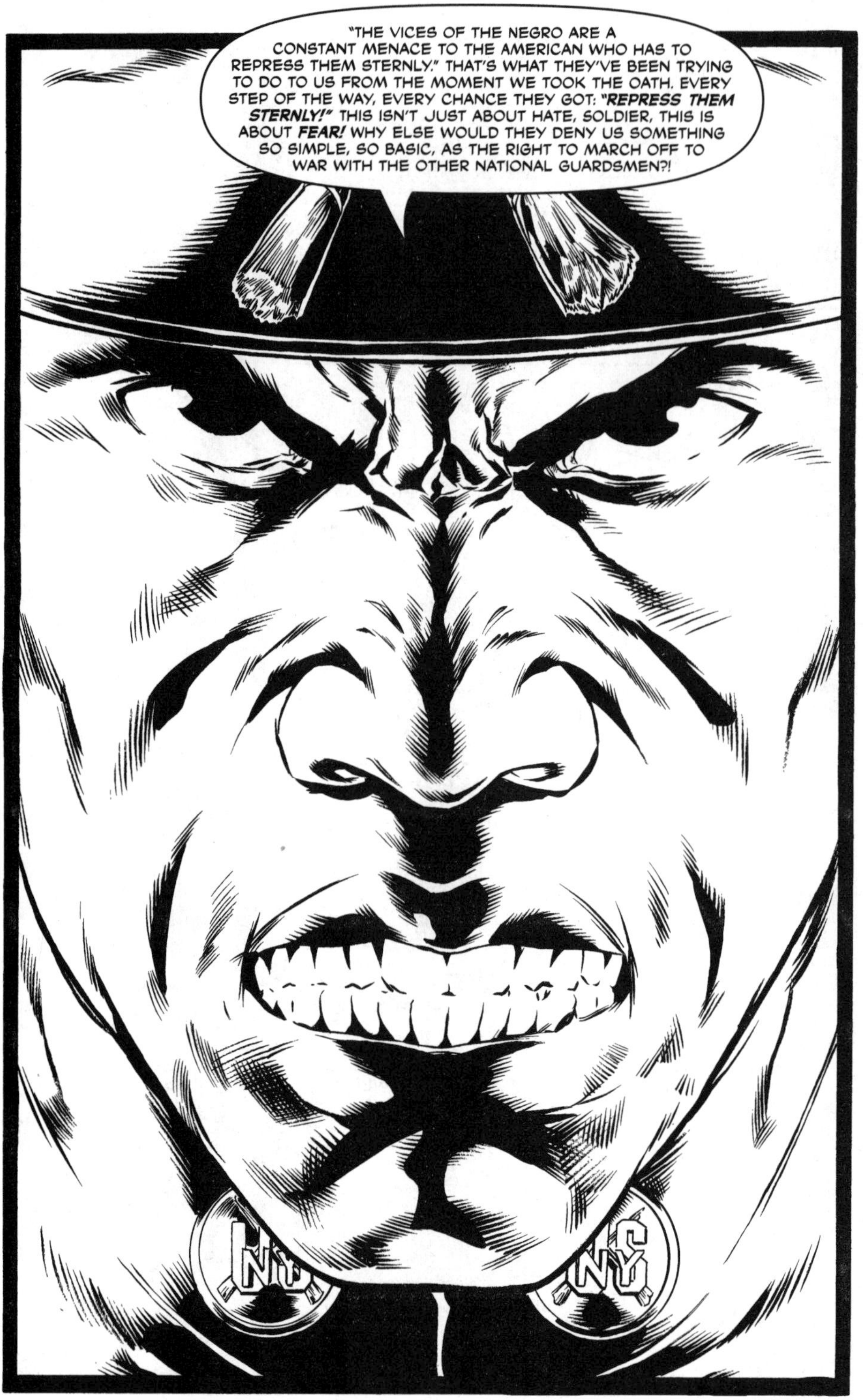
"THE VICES OF THE NEGRO ARE A CONSTANT MENACE TO THE AMERICAN WHO HAS TO REPRESS THEM STERNLY." THAT'S WHAT THEY'VE BEEN TRYING TO DO TO US FROM THE MOMENT WE TOOK THE OATH. EVERY STEP OF THE WAY, EVERY CHANCE THEY GOT: *"REPRESS THEM STERNLY!"* THIS ISN'T JUST ABOUT HATE, SOLDIER, THIS IS ABOUT *FEAR!* WHY ELSE WOULD THEY DENY US SOMETHING SO SIMPLE, SO BASIC, AS THE RIGHT TO MARCH OFF TO WAR WITH THE OTHER NATIONAL GUARDSMEN?!
NY
NY

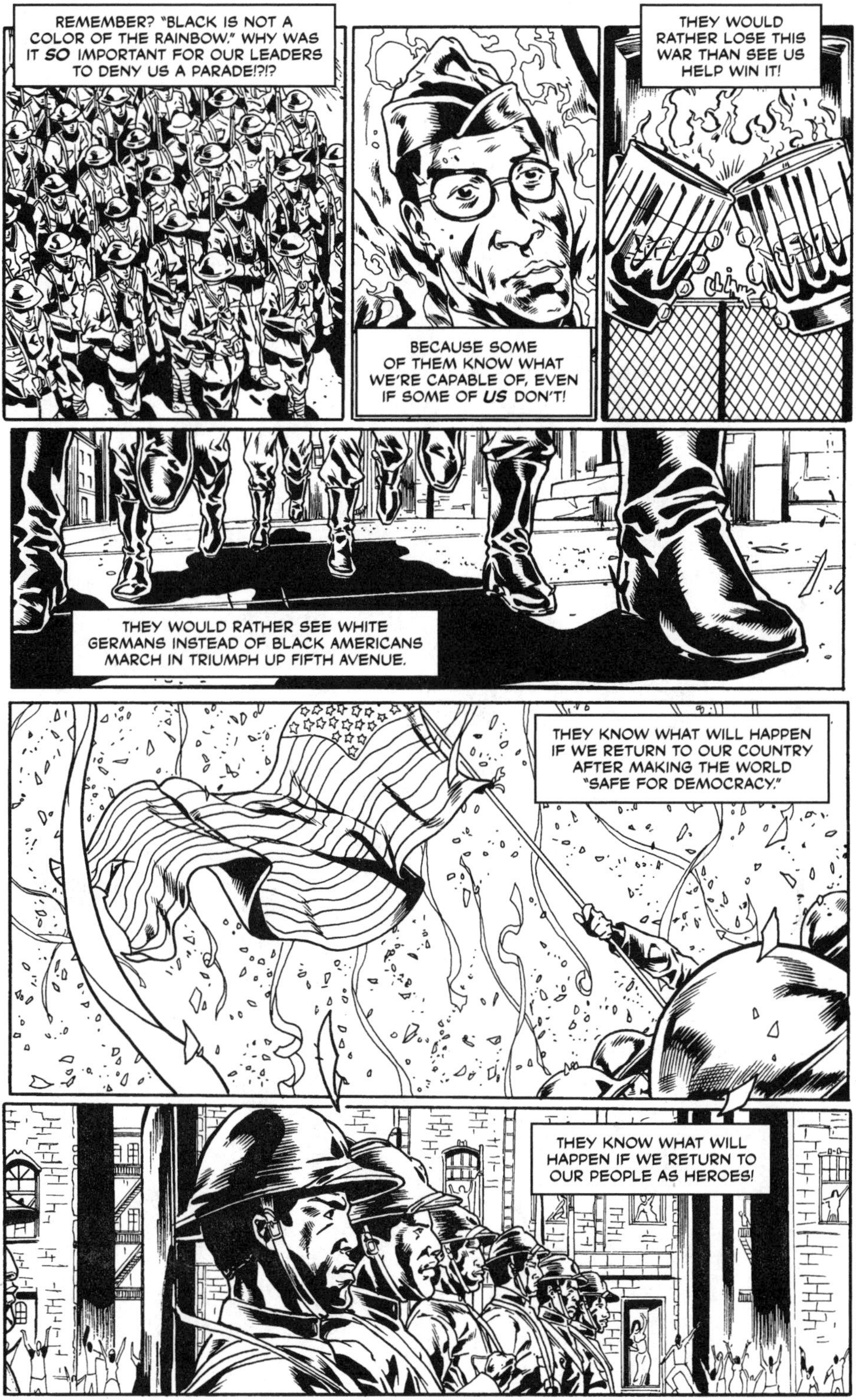
REMEMBER? "BLACK IS NOT A COLOR OF THE RAINBOW." WHY WAS IT SO IMPORTANT FOR OUR LEADERS TO DENY US A PARADE!?!?
BECAUSE SOME OF THEM KNOW WHAT WE'RE CAPABLE OF, EVEN IF SOME OF US DON'T!
THEY WOULD RATHER LOSE THIS WAR THAN SEE US HELP WIN IT!
THEY WOULD RATHER SEE WHITE GERMANS INSTEAD OF BLACK AMERICANS MARCH IN TRIUMPH UP FIFTH AVENUE.
THEY KNOW WHAT WILL HAPPEN IF WE RETURN TO OUR COUNTRY AFTER MAKING THE WORLD "SAFE FOR DEMOCRACY."
THEY KNOW WHAT WILL HAPPEN IF WE RETURN TO OUR PEOPLE AS HEROES!

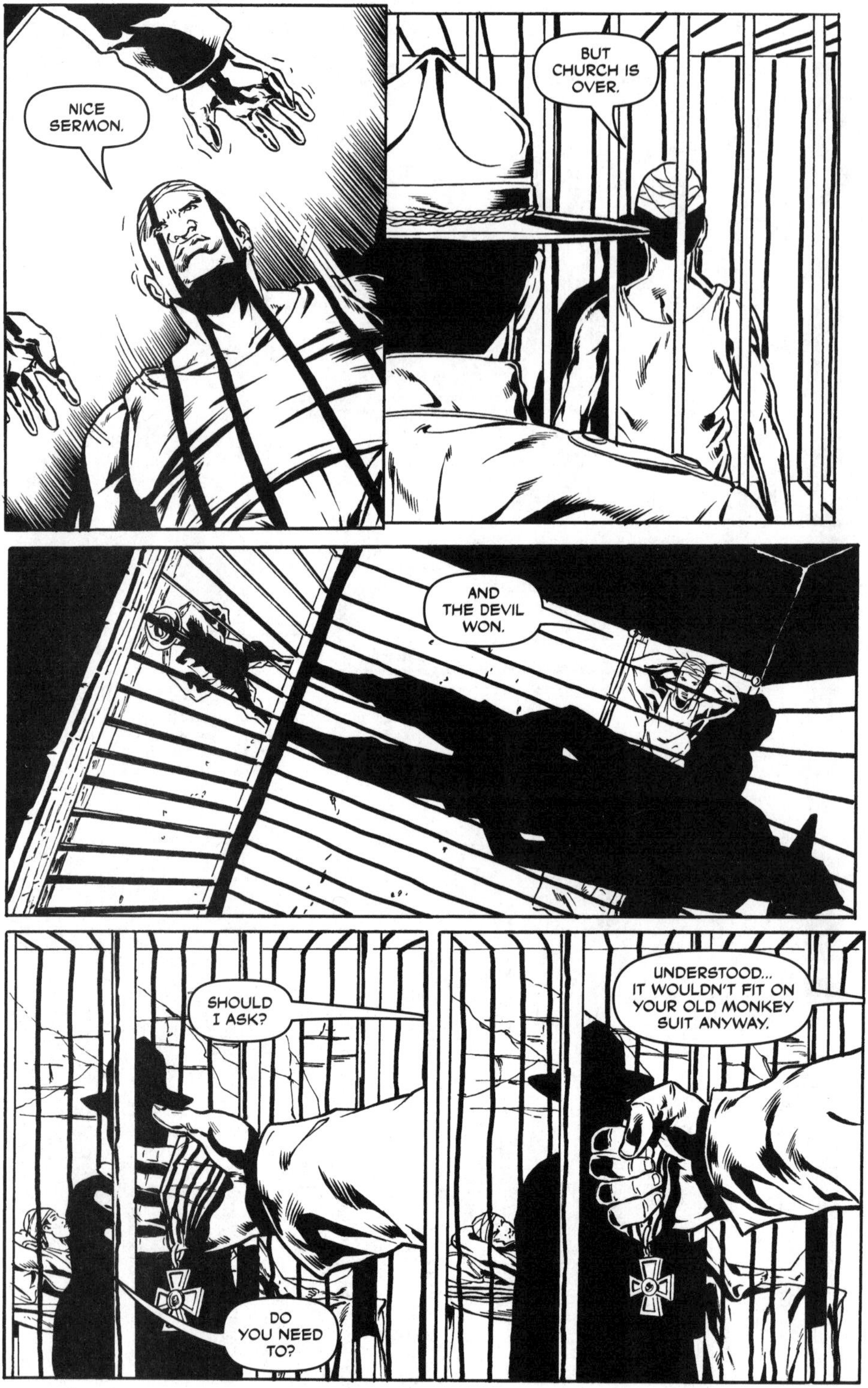
NICE SERMON.
BUT CHURCH IS OVER.
AND THE DEVIL WON.
SHOULD I ASK?
DO YOU NEED TO?
UNDERSTOOD... IT WOULDN'T FIT ON YOUR OLD MONKEY SUIT ANYWAY.

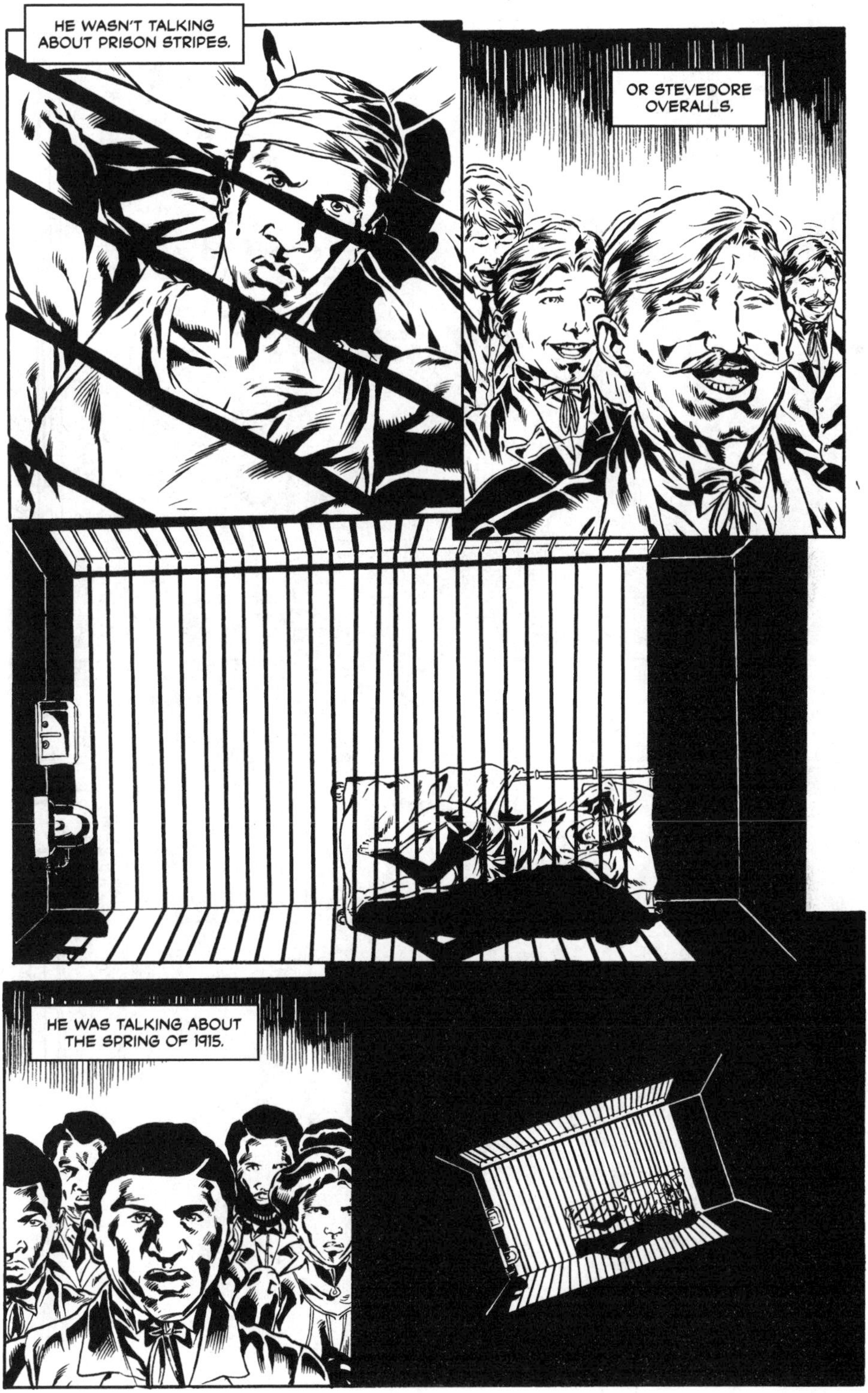
HE WASN'T TALKING ABOUT PRISON STRIPES.
OR STEVEDORE OVERALLS.
HE WAS TALKING ABOUT THE SPRING OF 1915.

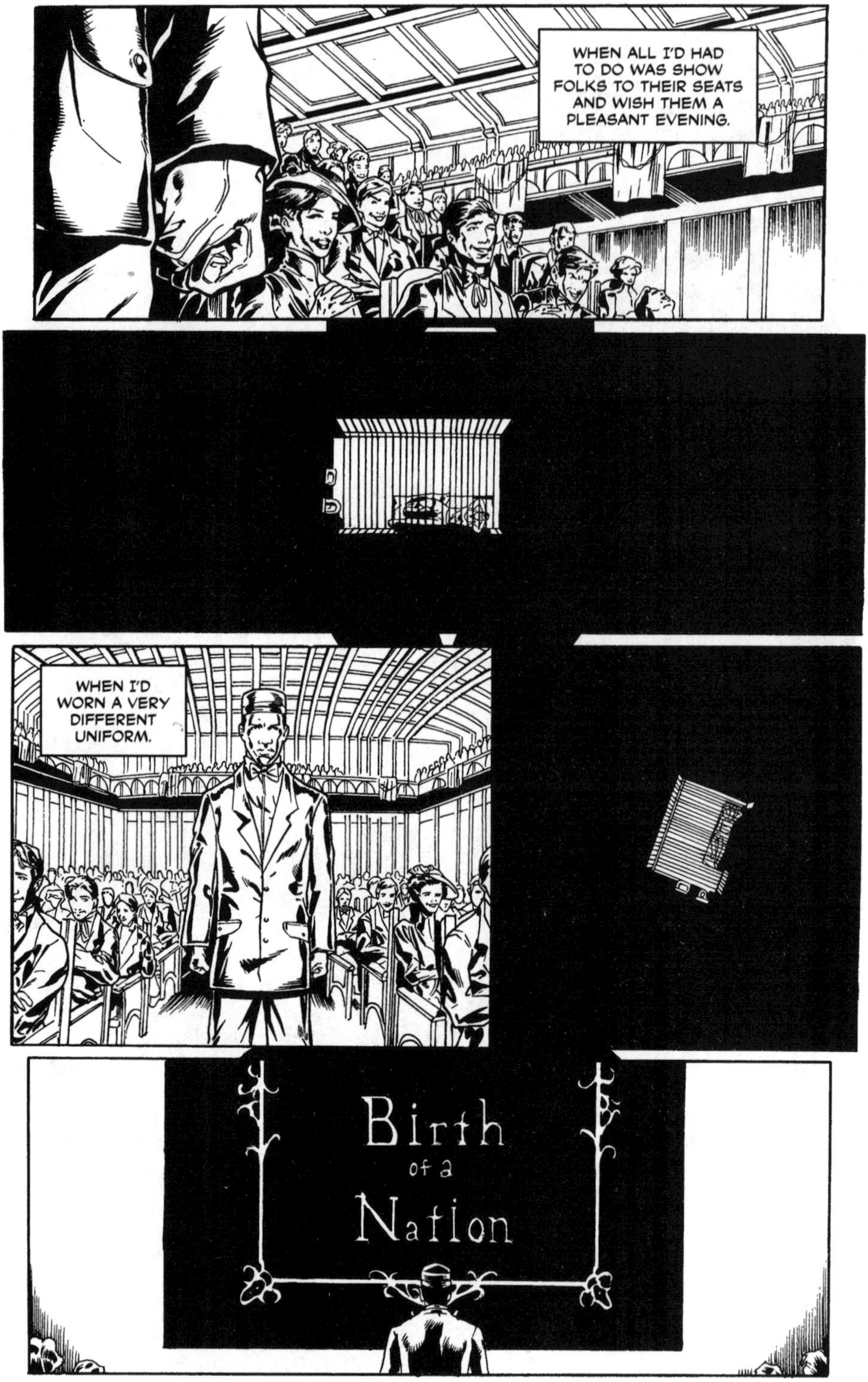
WHEN ALL I'D HAD TO DO WAS SHOW FOLKS TO THEIR SEATS AND WISH THEM A PLEASANT EVENING.
WHEN I'D WORN A VERY DIFFERENT UNIFORM.
Birth of a Nation

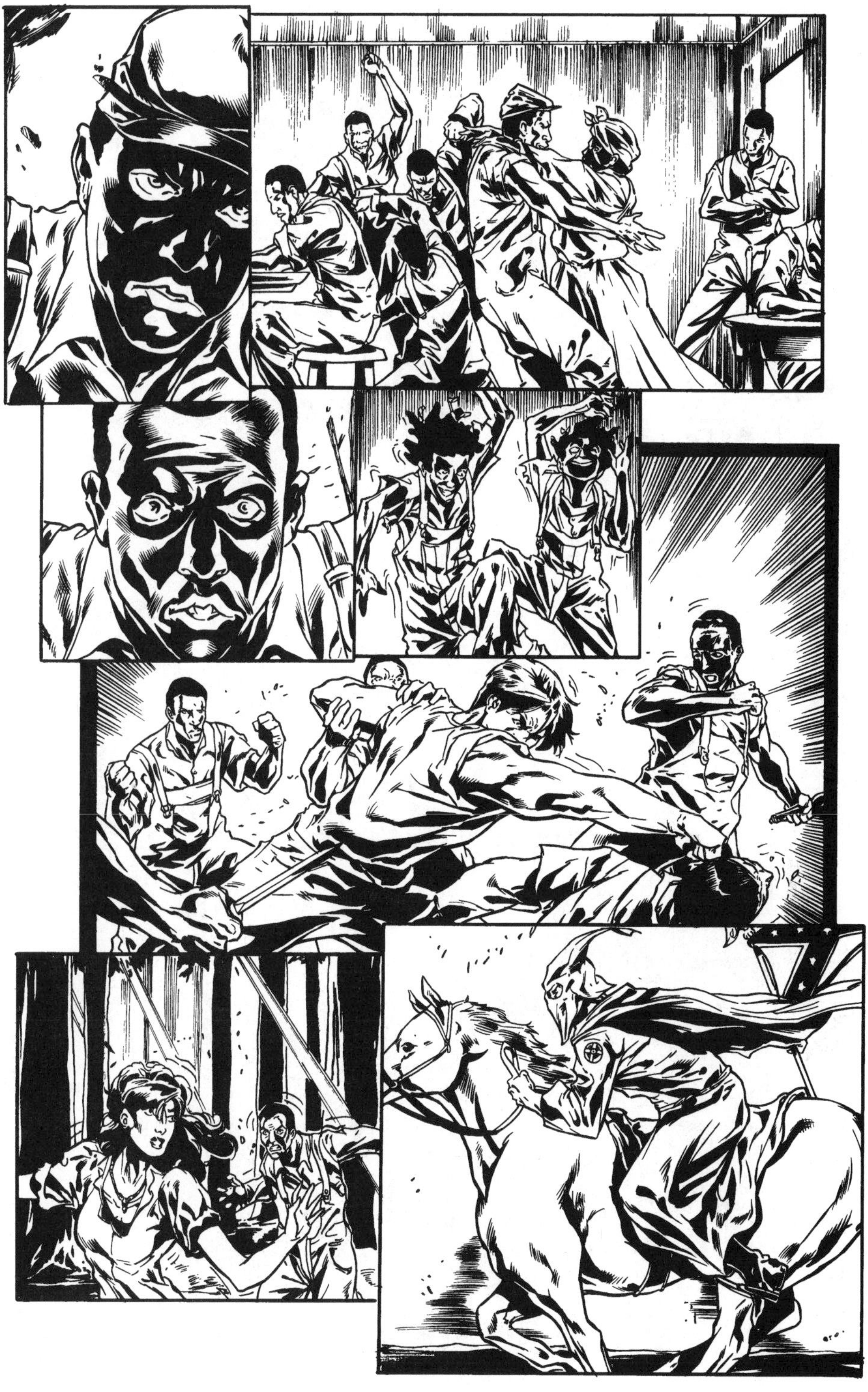

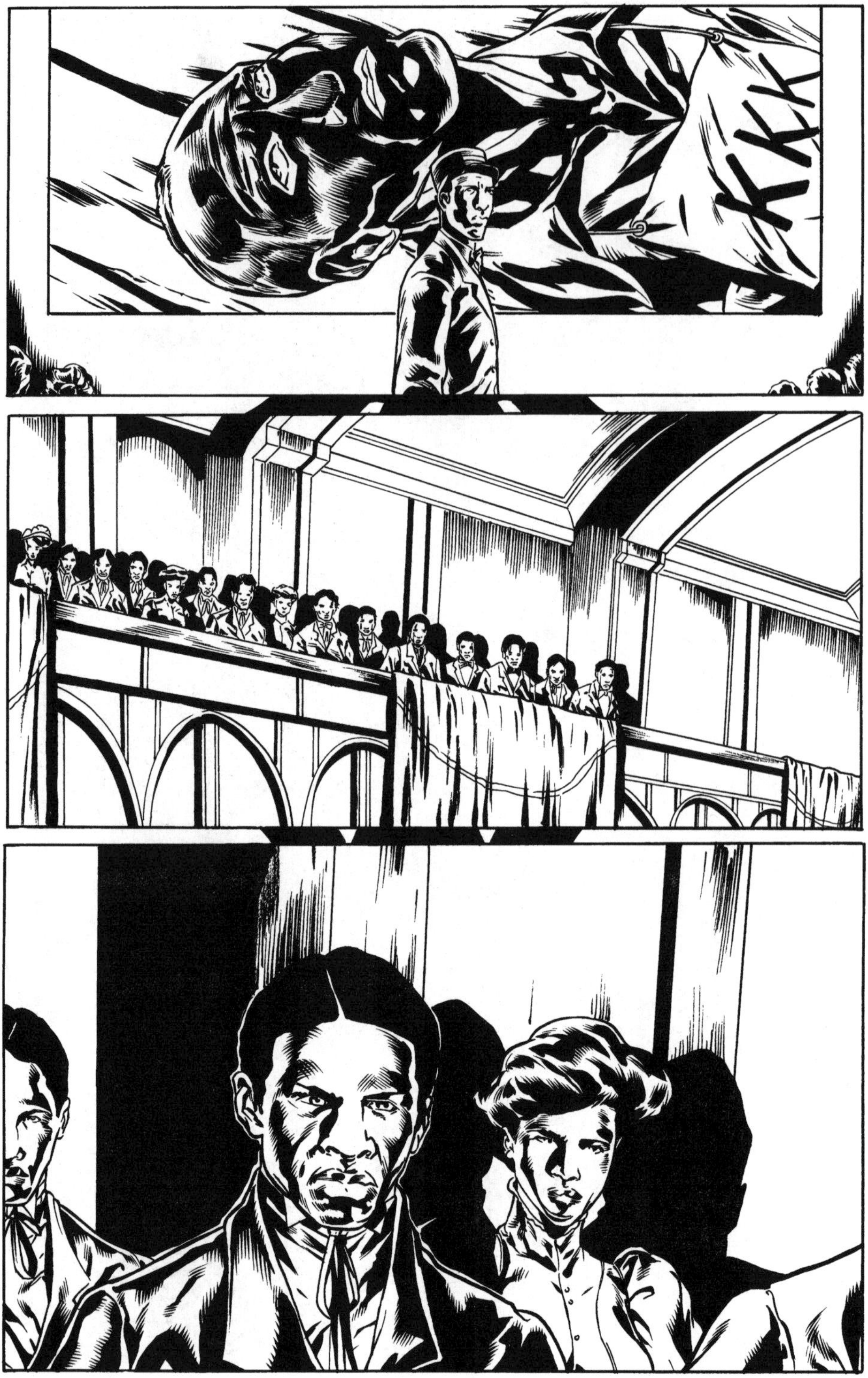
KKK

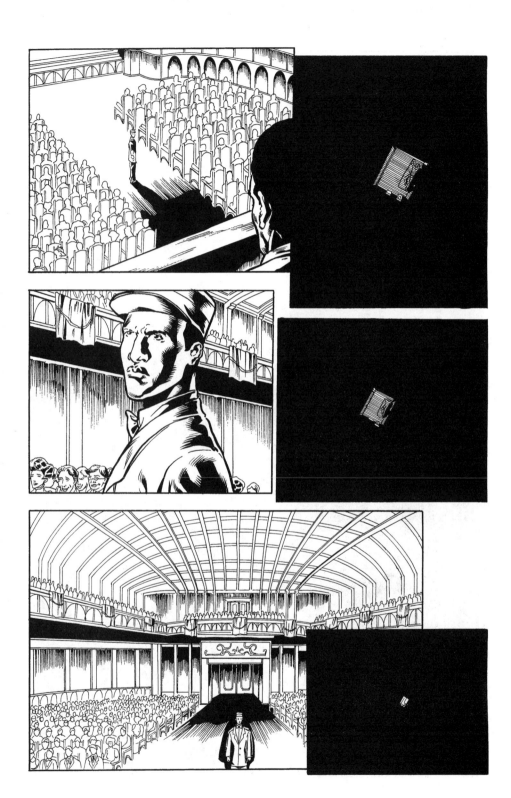

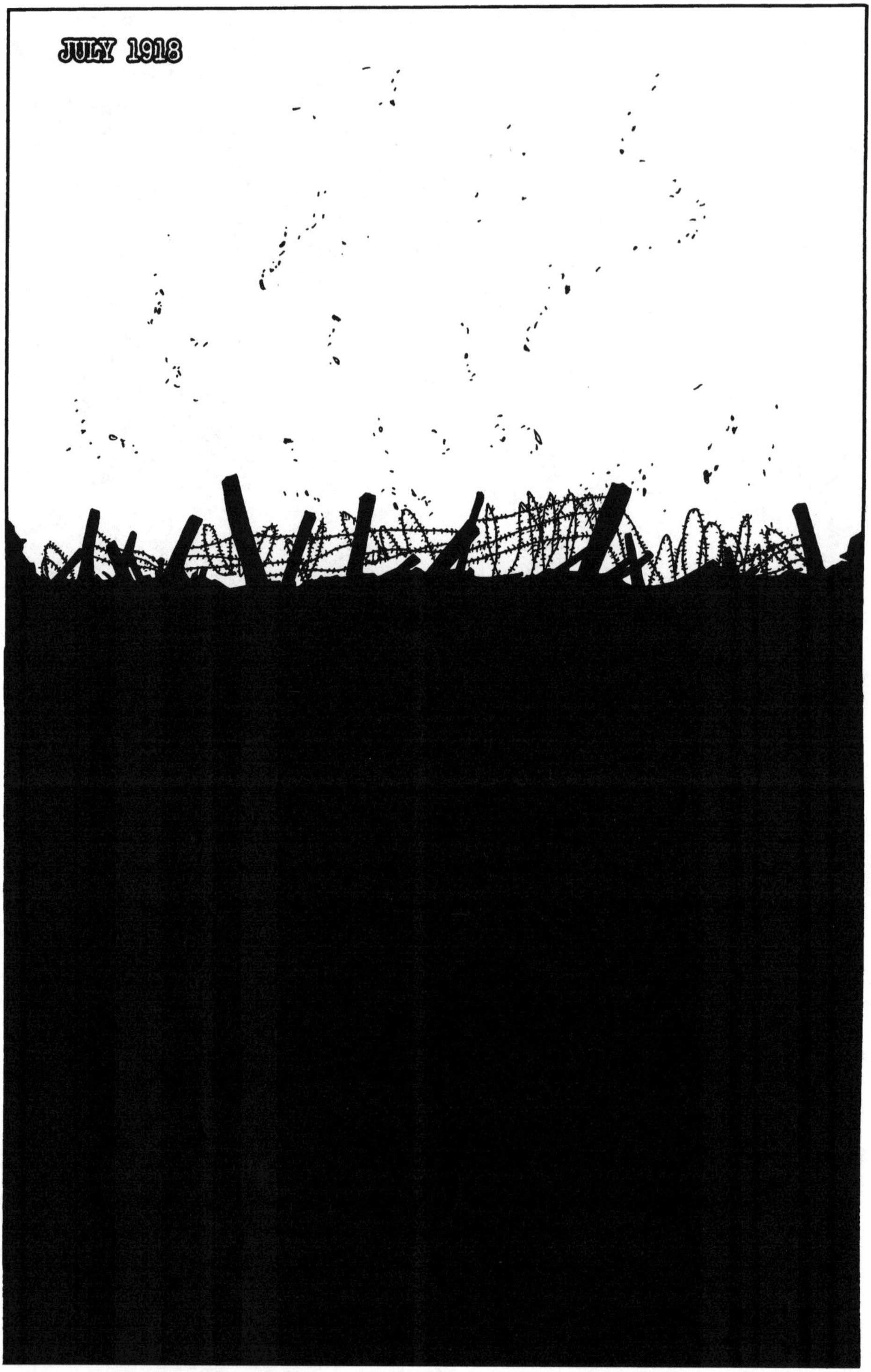
JULY 1918

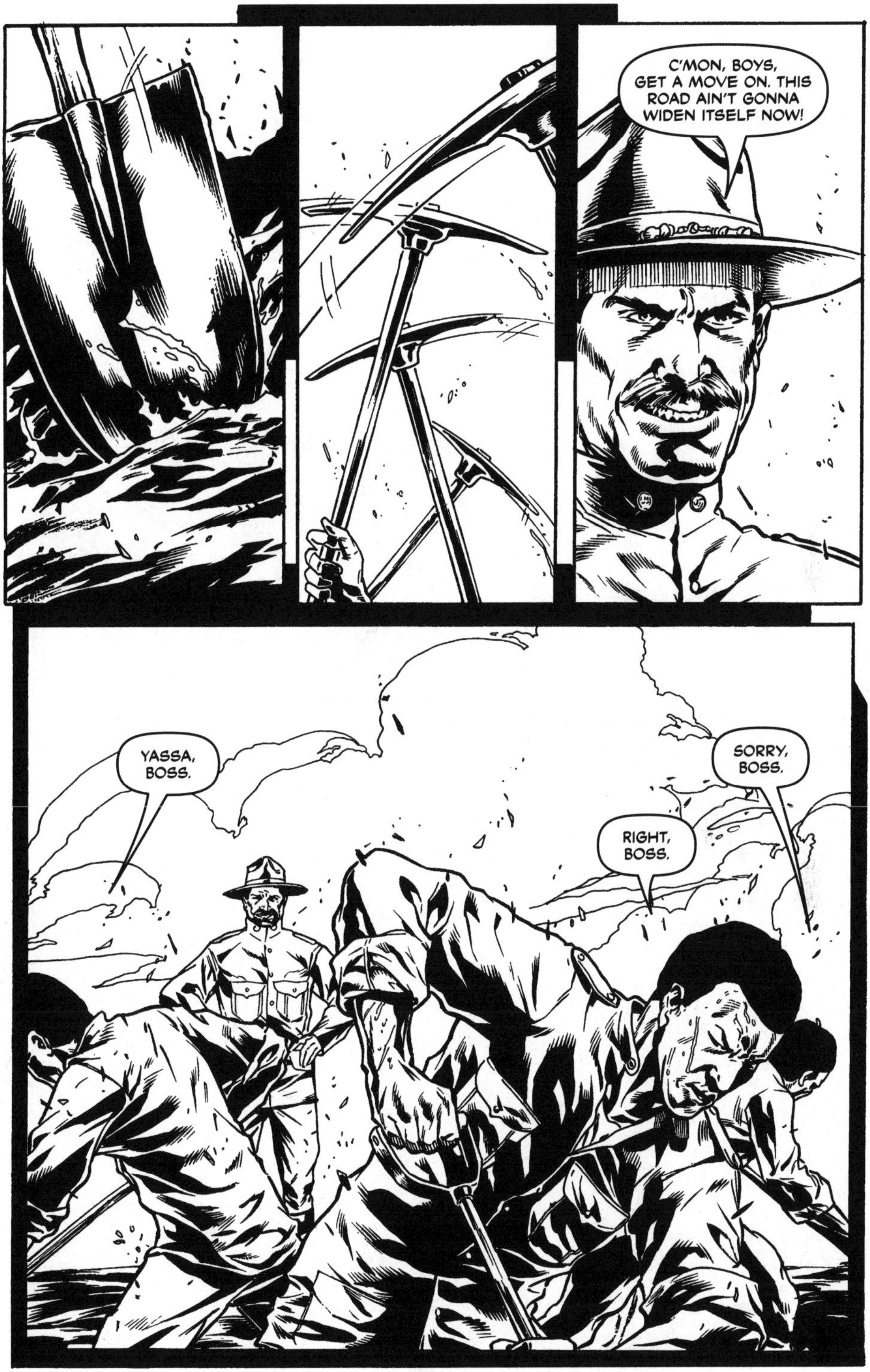
C'MON, BOYS, GET A MOVE ON. THIS ROAD AIN'T GONNA WIDEN ITSELF NOW!
YASSA, BOSS.
RIGHT, BOSS.
SORRY, BOSS.

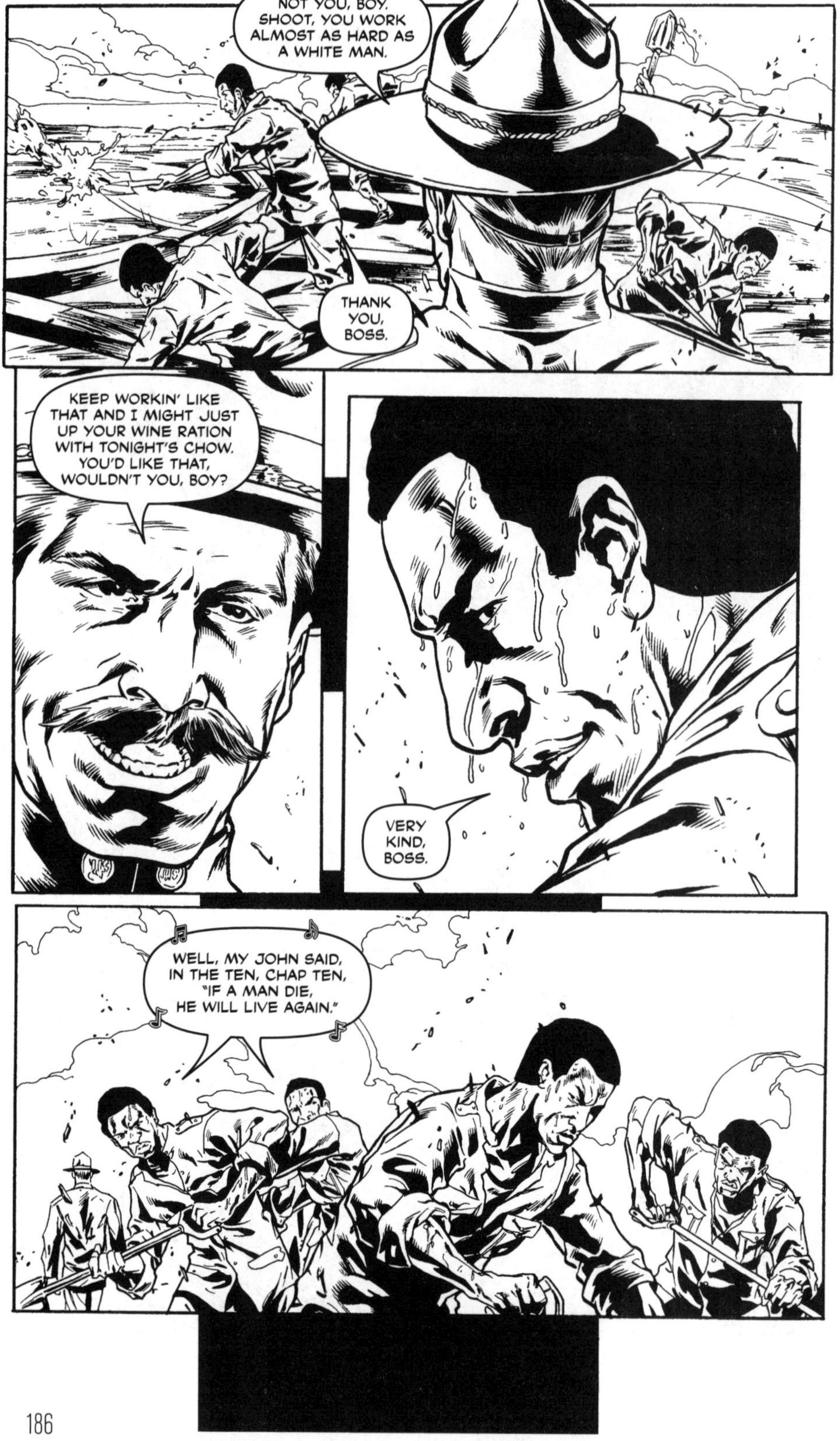
NOT YOU, BOY. SHOOT, YOU WORK ALMOST AS HARD AS A WHITE MAN.
THANK YOU, BOSS.
KEEP WORKIN' LIKE THAT AND I MIGHT JUST UP YOUR WINE RATION WITH TONIGHT'S CHOW. YOU'D LIKE THAT, WOULDN'T YOU, BOY?
VERY KIND, BOSS.
WELL, MY JOHN SAID, IN THE TEN, CHAP TEN, "IF A MAN DIE, HE WILL LIVE AGAIN."

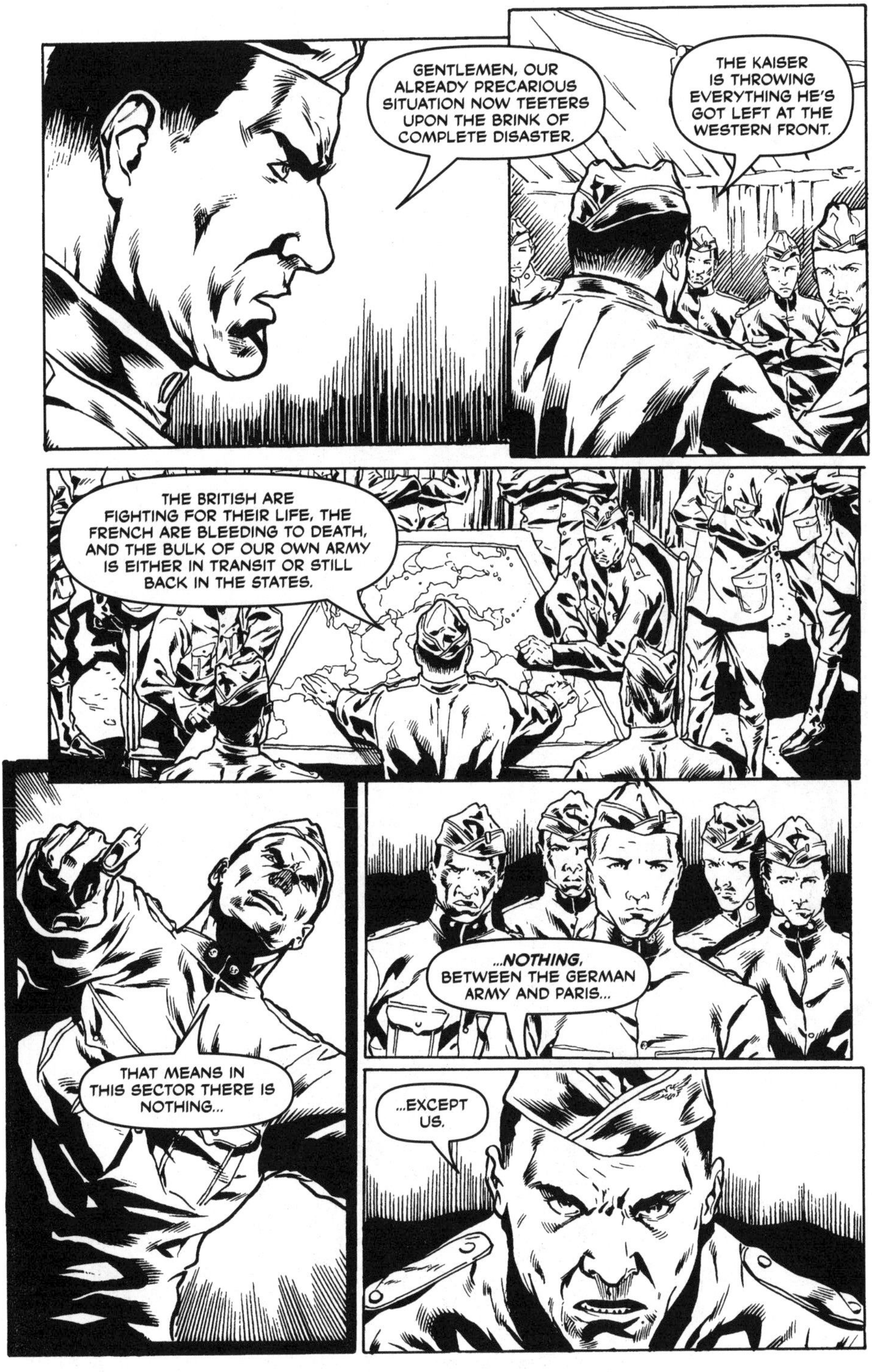
GENTLEMEN, OUR ALREADY PRECARIOUS SITUATION NOW TEETERS UPON THE BRINK OF COMPLETE DISASTER.
THE KAISER IS THROWING EVERYTHING HE'S GOT LEFT AT THE WESTERN FRONT.
THE BRITISH ARE FIGHTING FOR THEIR LIFE, THE FRENCH ARE BLEEDING TO DEATH, AND THE BULK OF OUR OWN ARMY IS EITHER IN TRANSIT OR STILL BACK IN THE STATES.
THAT MEANS IN THIS SECTOR THERE IS NOTHING...
...*NOTHING*, BETWEEN THE GERMAN ARMY AND PARIS...
...EXCEPT US.

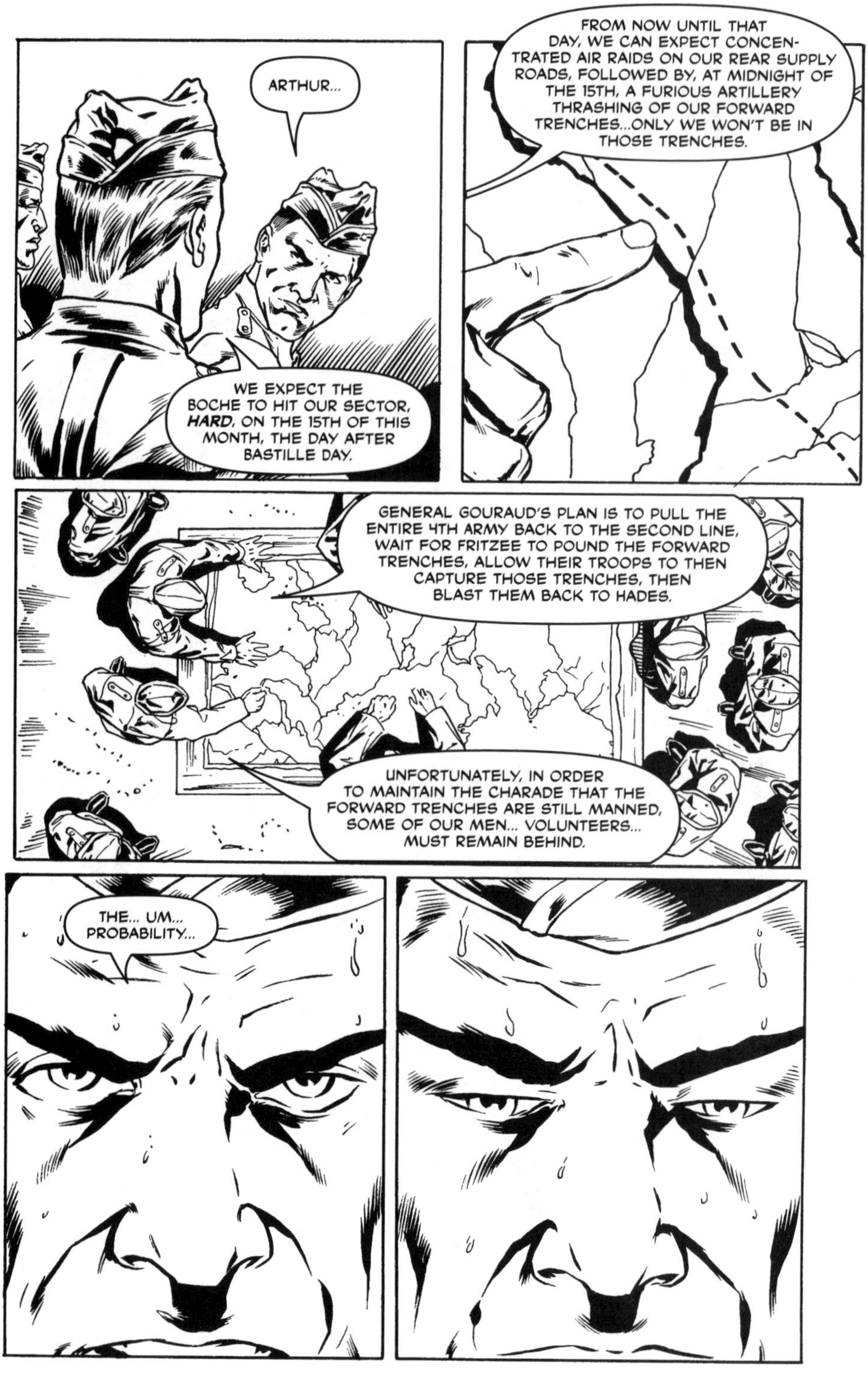
ARTHUR...
WE EXPECT THE BOCHE TO HIT OUR SECTOR, **HARD**, ON THE 15TH OF THIS MONTH, THE DAY AFTER BASTILLE DAY.
FROM NOW UNTIL THAT DAY, WE CAN EXPECT CONCEN-TRATED AIR RAIDS ON OUR REAR SUPPLY ROADS, FOLLOWED BY, AT MIDNIGHT OF THE 15TH, A FURIOUS ARTILLERY THRASHING OF OUR FORWARD TRENCHES...ONLY WE WON'T BE IN THOSE TRENCHES.
GENERAL GOURAUD'S PLAN IS TO PULL THE ENTIRE 4TH ARMY BACK TO THE SECOND LINE, WAIT FOR FRITZEE TO POUND THE FORWARD TRENCHES, ALLOW THEIR TROOPS TO THEN CAPTURE THOSE TRENCHES, THEN BLAST THEM BACK TO HADES.
UNFORTUNATELY, IN ORDER TO MAINTAIN THE CHARADE THAT THE FORWARD TRENCHES ARE STILL MANNED, SOME OF OUR MEN... VOLUNTEERS... MUST REMAIN BEHIND.
THE... UM... PROBABILITY...

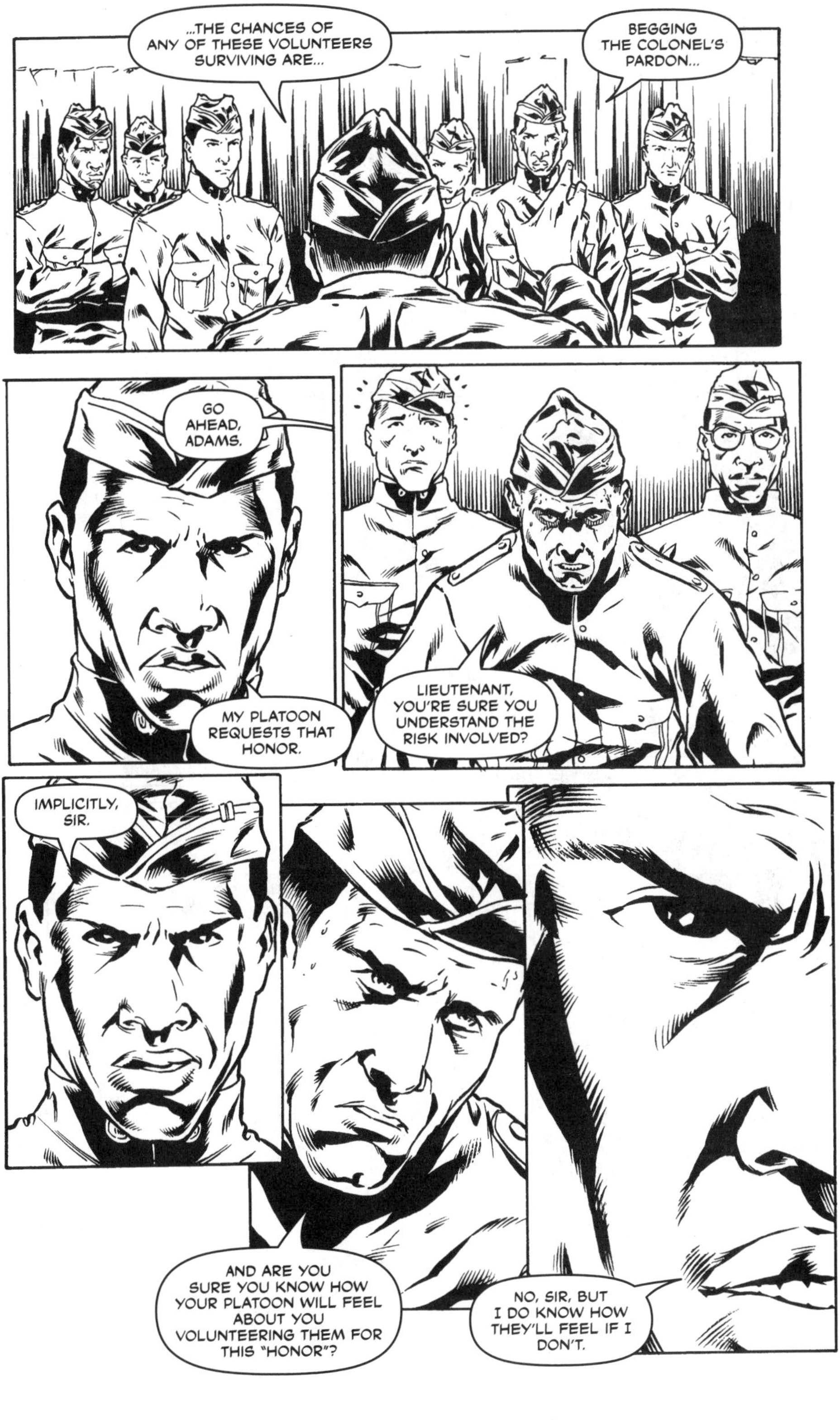
...THE CHANCES OF ANY OF THESE VOLUNTEERS SURVIVING ARE...
BEGGING THE COLONEL'S PARDON...
GO AHEAD, ADAMS.
MY PLATOON REQUESTS THAT HONOR.
LIEUTENANT, YOU'RE SURE YOU UNDERSTAND THE RISK INVOLVED?
IMPLICITLY, SIR.
AND ARE YOU SURE YOU KNOW HOW YOUR PLATOON WILL FEEL ABOUT YOU VOLUNTEERING THEM FOR THIS "HONOR"?
NO, SIR, BUT I DO KNOW HOW THEY'LL FEEL IF I DON'T.

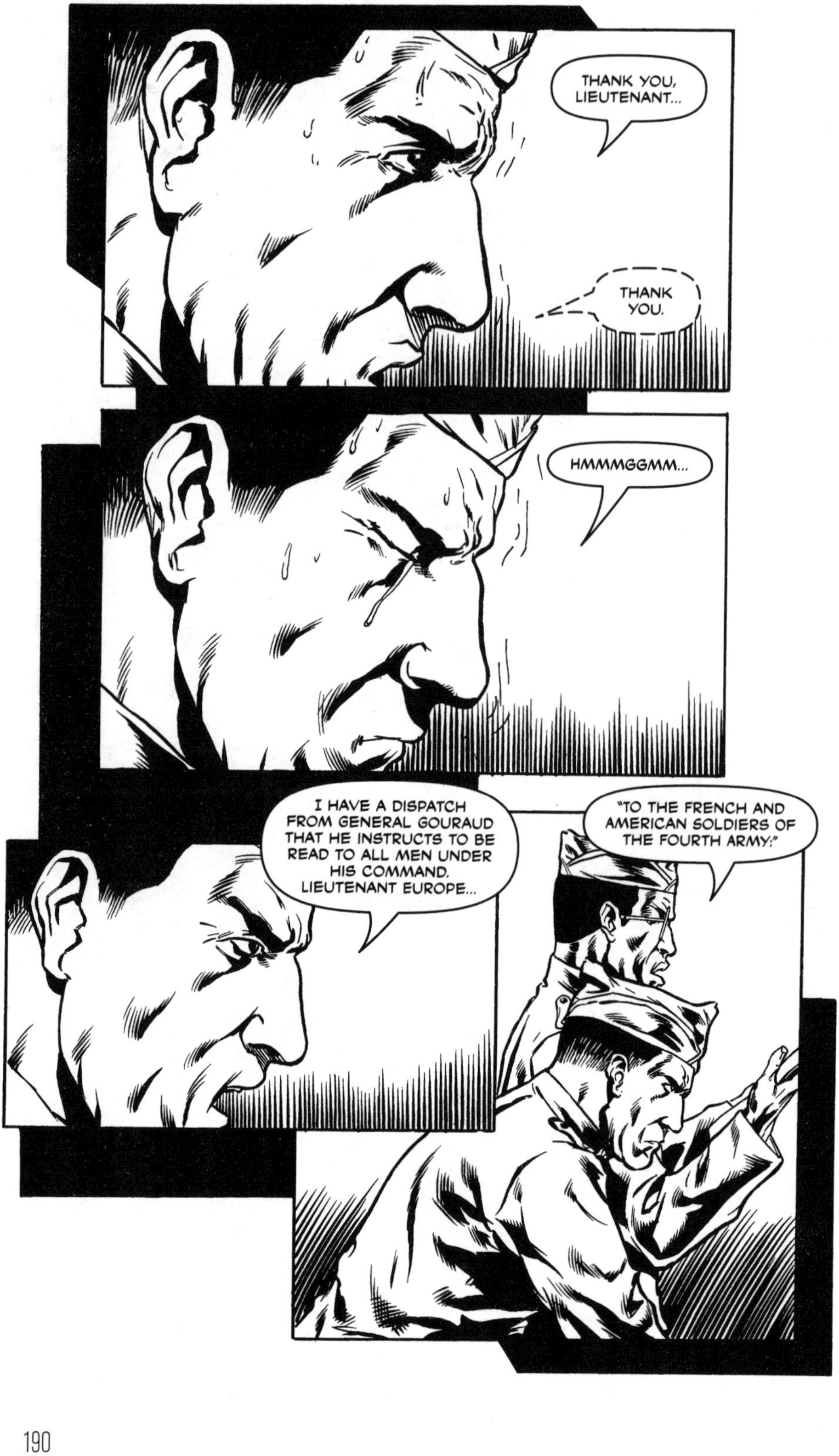
THANK YOU, LIEUTENANT...
THANK YOU.
HMMMGGMM...
I HAVE A DISPATCH FROM GENERAL GOURAUD THAT HE INSTRUCTS TO BE READ TO ALL MEN UNDER HIS COMMAND, LIEUTENANT EUROPE...
"TO THE FRENCH AND AMERICAN SOLDIERS OF THE FOURTH ARMY:"

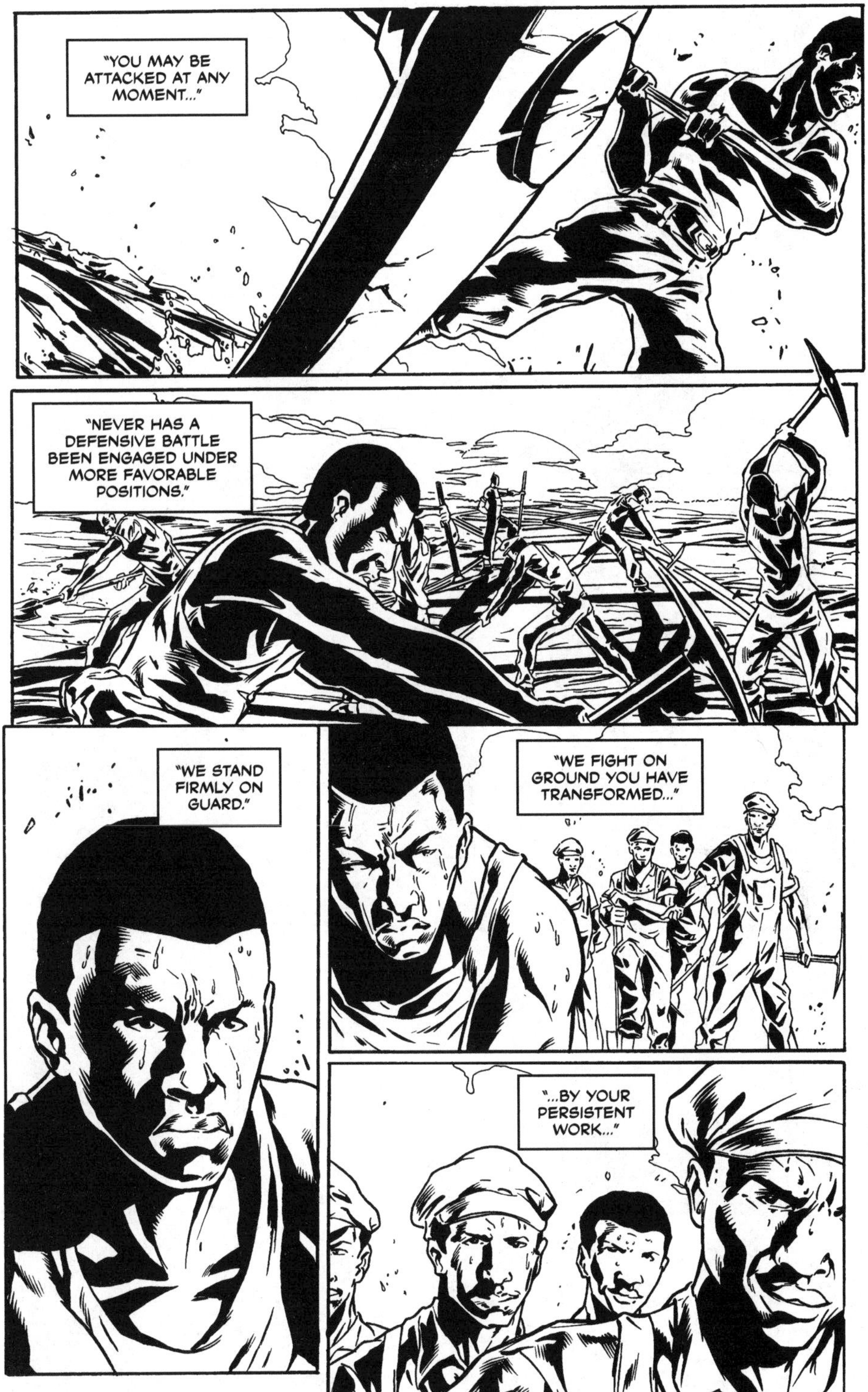
"YOU MAY BE ATTACKED AT ANY MOMENT..."
"NEVER HAS A DEFENSIVE BATTLE BEEN ENGAGED UNDER MORE FAVORABLE POSITIONS."
"WE STAND FIRMLY ON GUARD."
"WE FIGHT ON GROUND YOU HAVE TRANSFORMED..."
"...BY YOUR PERSISTENT WORK..."

"...INTO A FORMIDABLE FORTRESS..."

"...WHERE ALL PASSAGES ARE WELL GUARDED."

"THE BOMBARDMENT WILL BE TERRIBLE."

"YOU WILL STAND IT WITHOUT LOSING COURAGE."

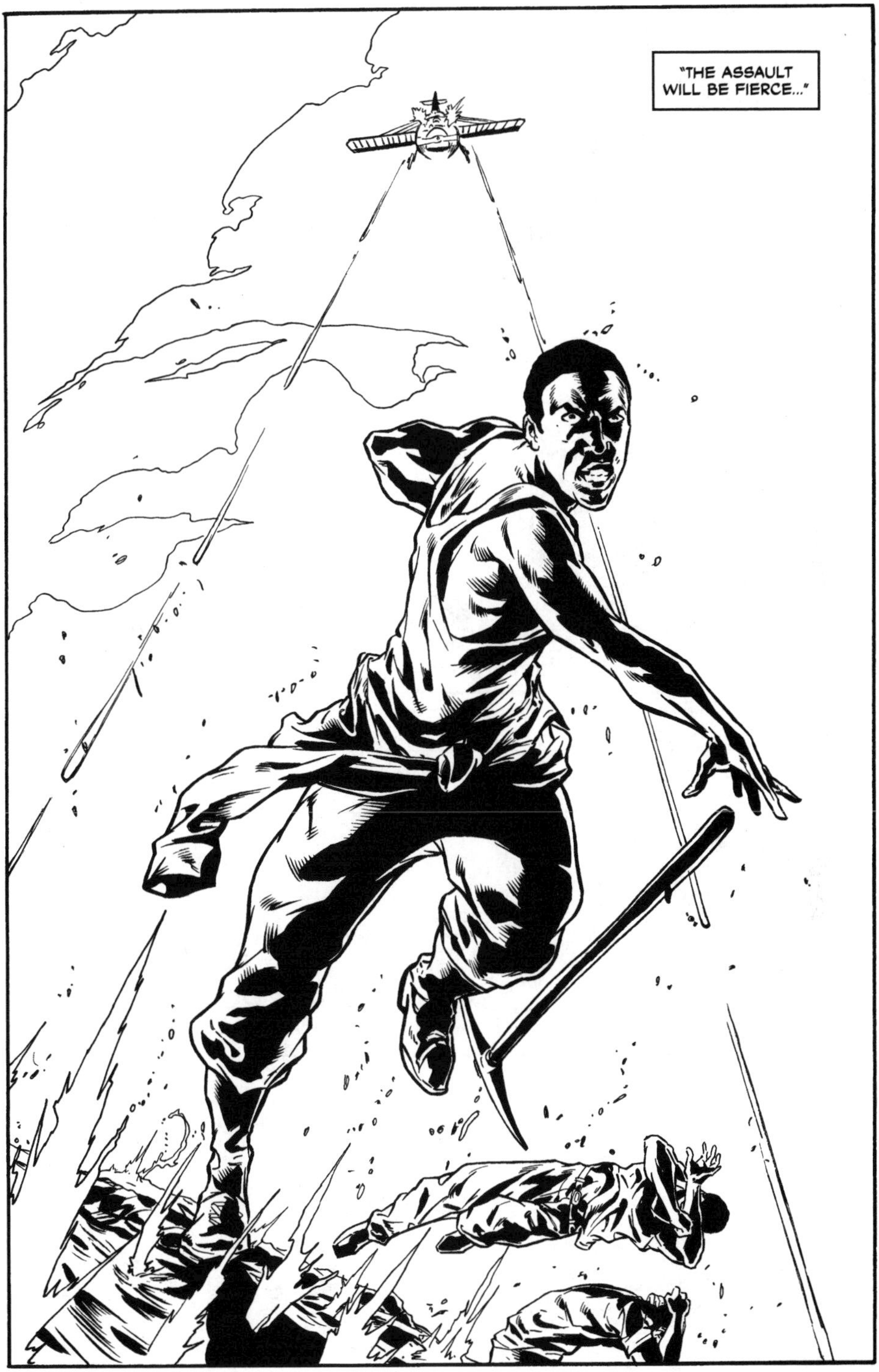
"THE ASSAULT
WILL BE FIERCE..."

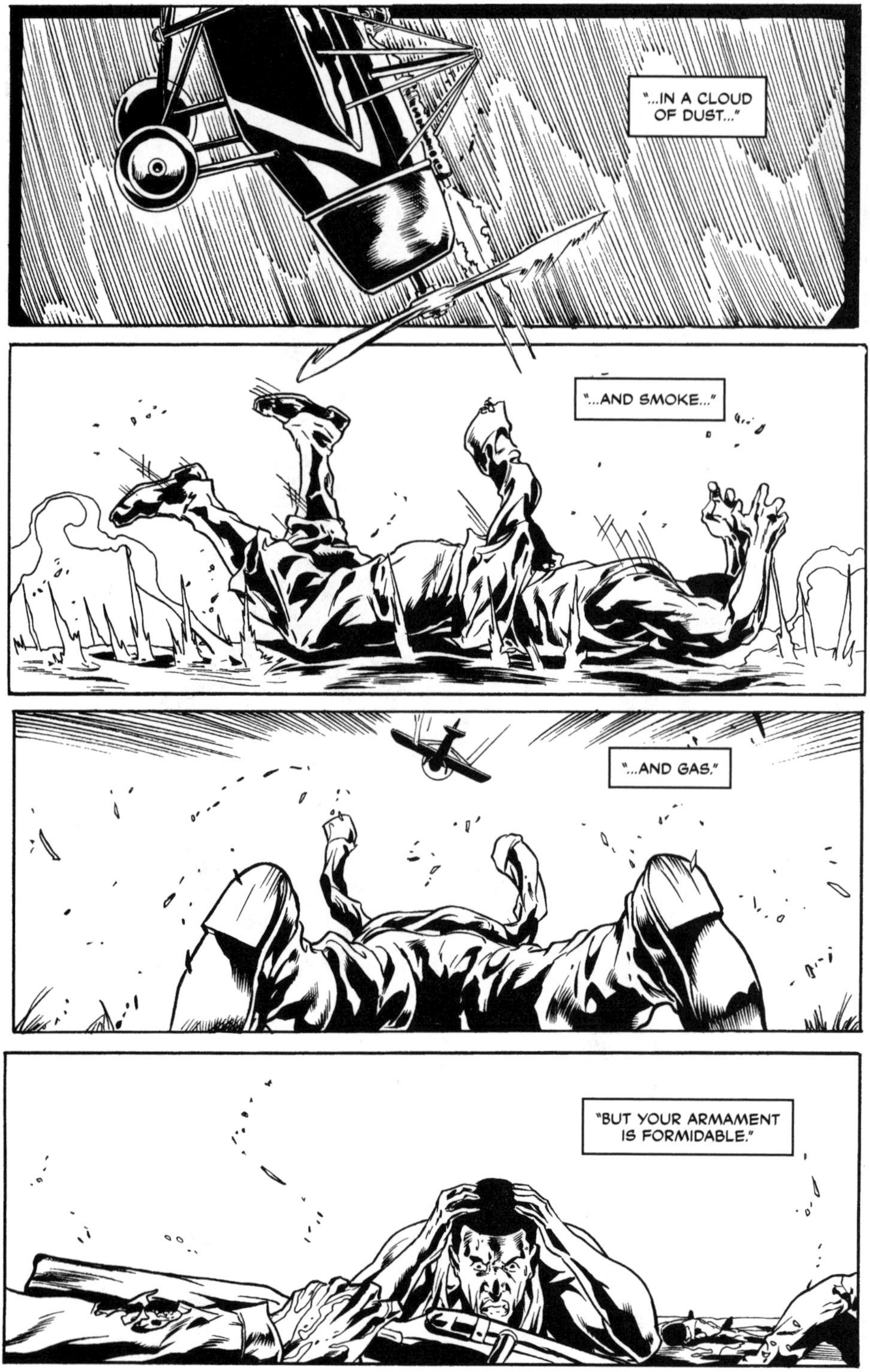
"...IN A CLOUD OF DUST..."
"...AND SMOKE..."
"...AND GAS."
"BUT YOUR ARMAMENT IS FORMIDABLE."

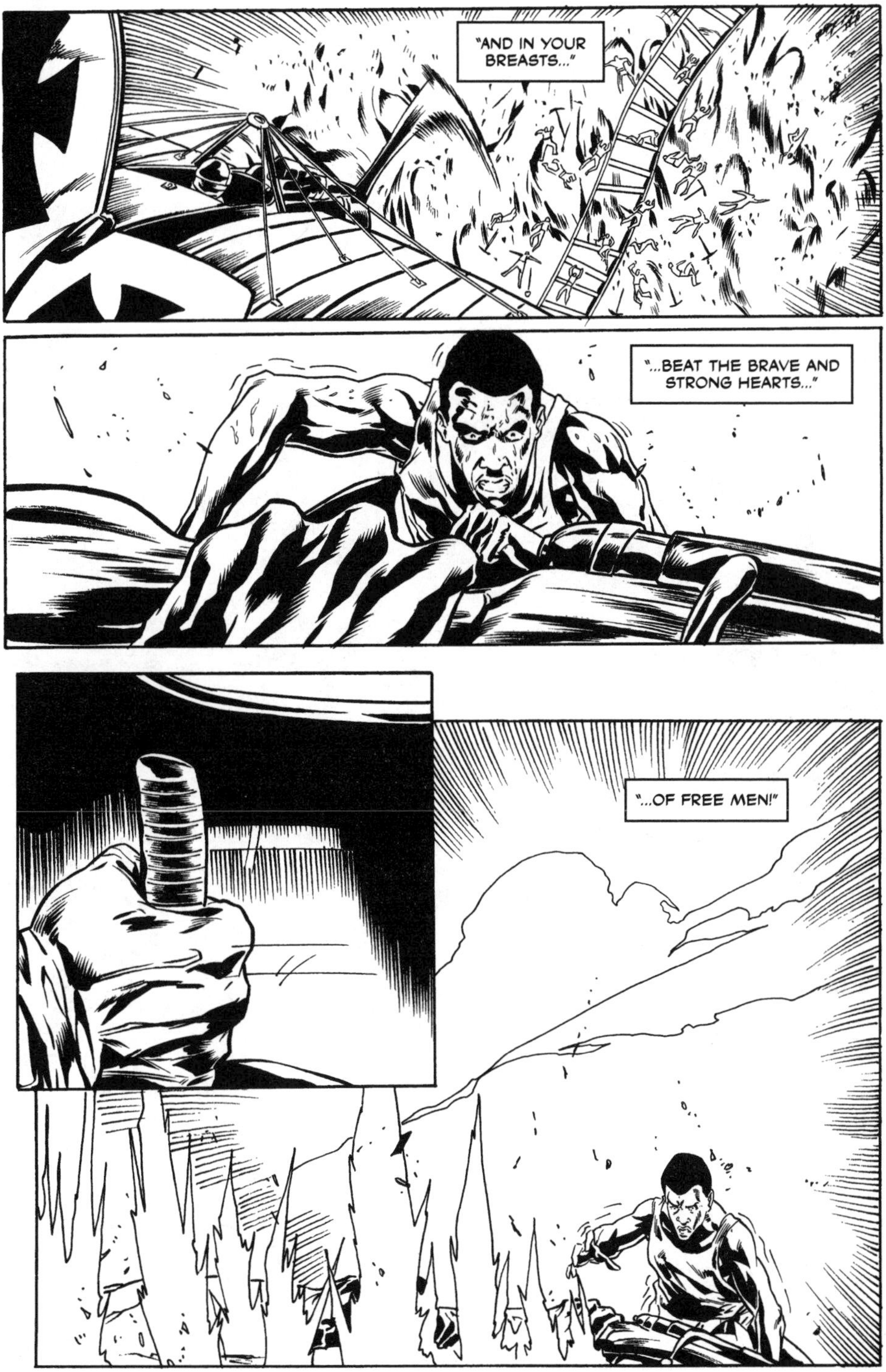
"AND IN YOUR BREASTS..."
"...BEAT THE BRAVE AND STRONG HEARTS..."
"...OF FREE MEN!"

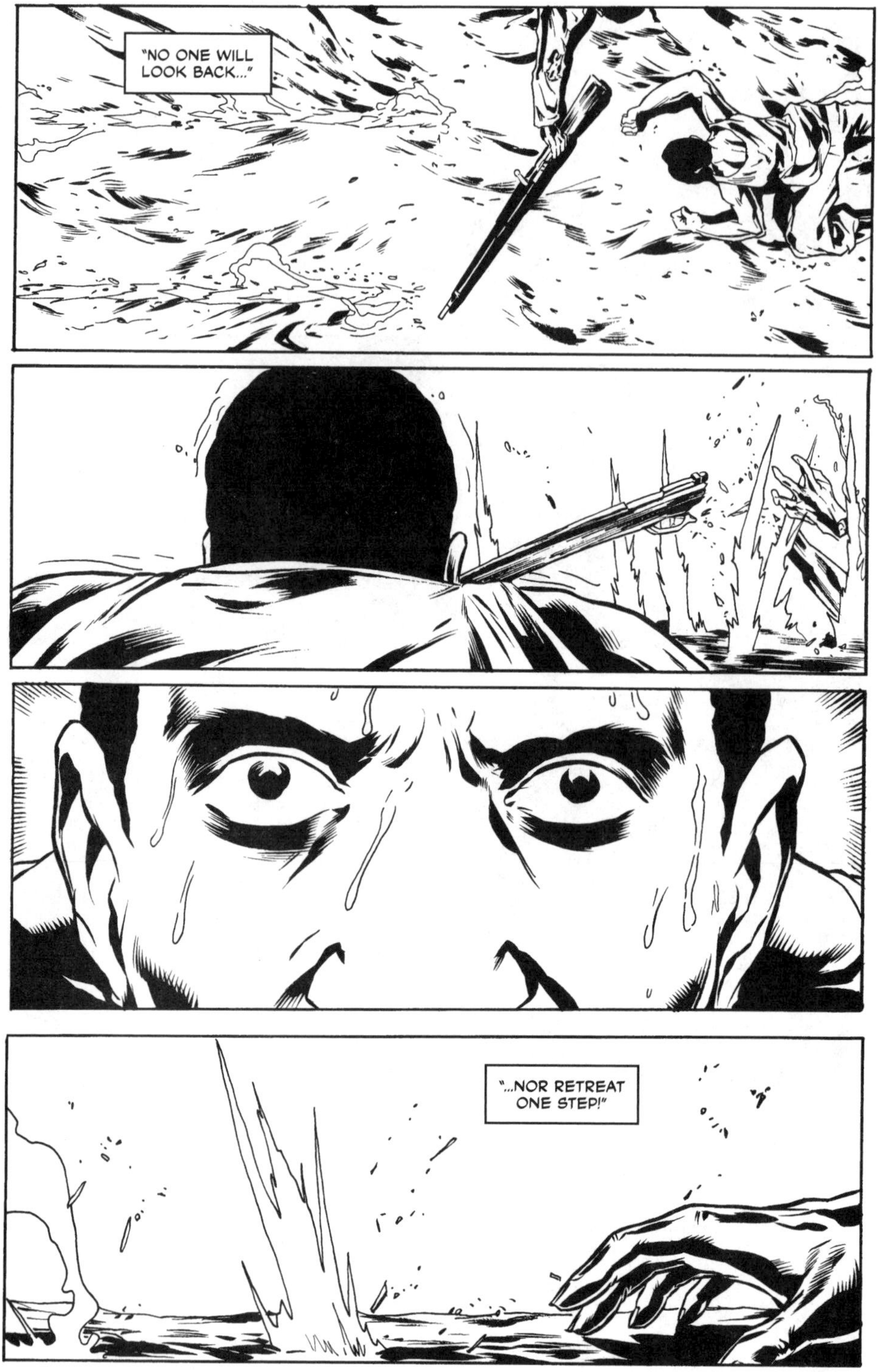
"NO ONE WILL LOOK BACK..."
"...NOR RETREAT ONE STEP!"

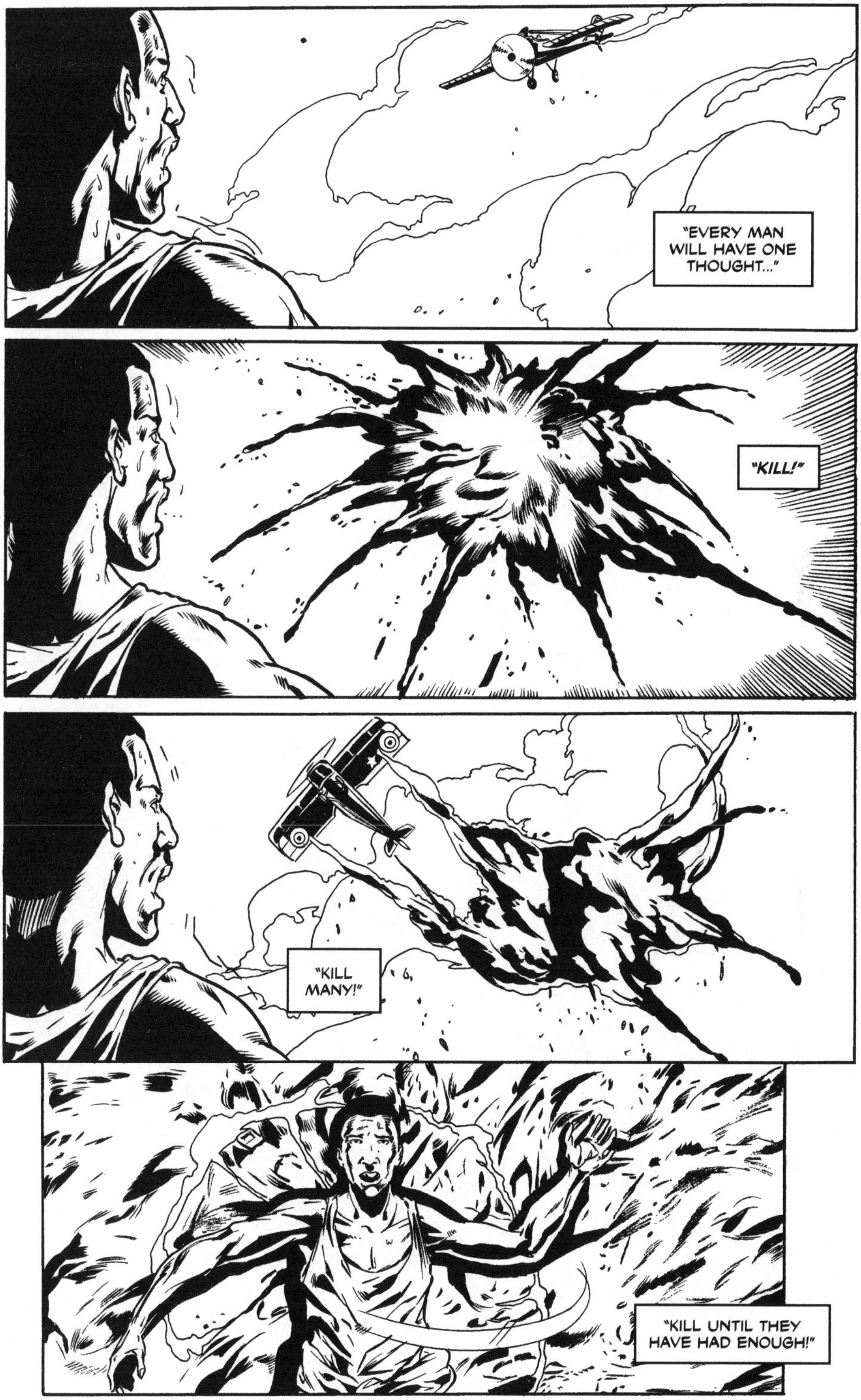
"EVERY MAN WILL HAVE ONE THOUGHT..."
"KILL!"
"KILL MANY!"
"KILL UNTIL THEY HAVE HAD ENOUGH!"

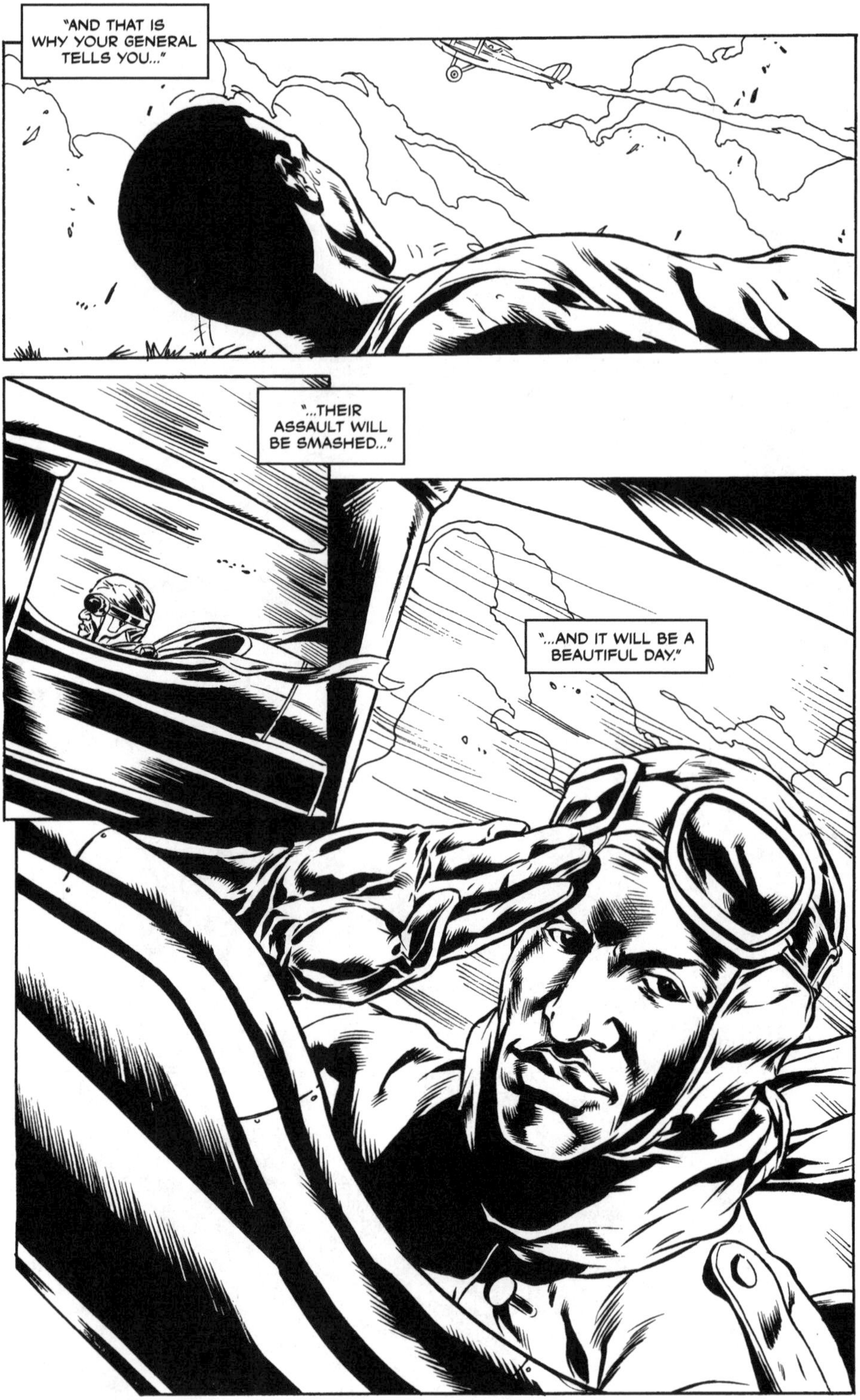
"AND THAT IS WHY YOUR GENERAL TELLS YOU..."
"...THEIR ASSAULT WILL BE SMASHED..."
"...AND IT WILL BE A BEAUTIFUL DAY."

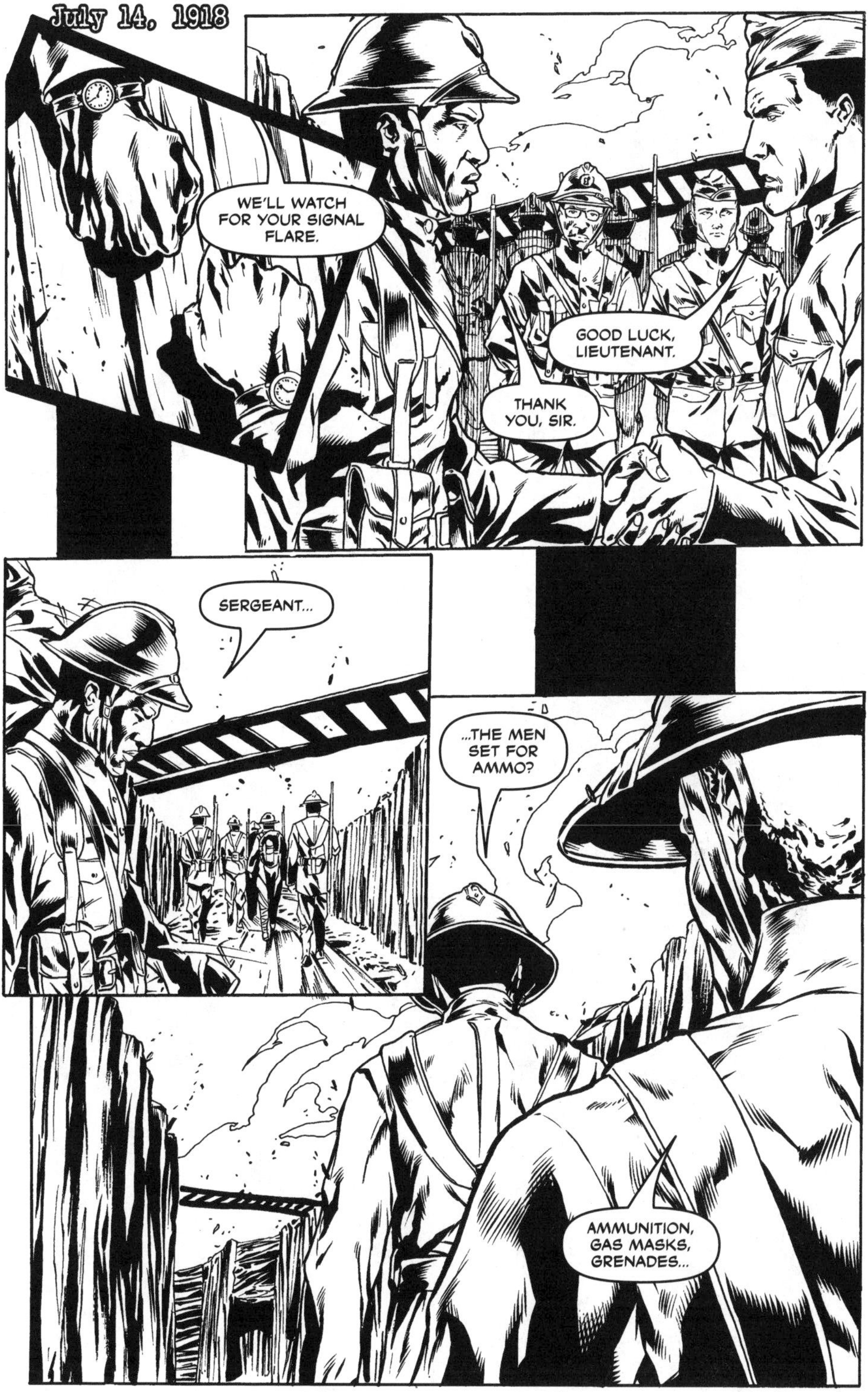
July 14, 1918
WE'LL WATCH FOR YOUR SIGNAL FLARE.
GOOD LUCK, LIEUTENANT.
THANK YOU, SIR.
SERGEANT...
...THE MEN SET FOR AMMO?
AMMUNITION, GAS MASKS, GRENADES...

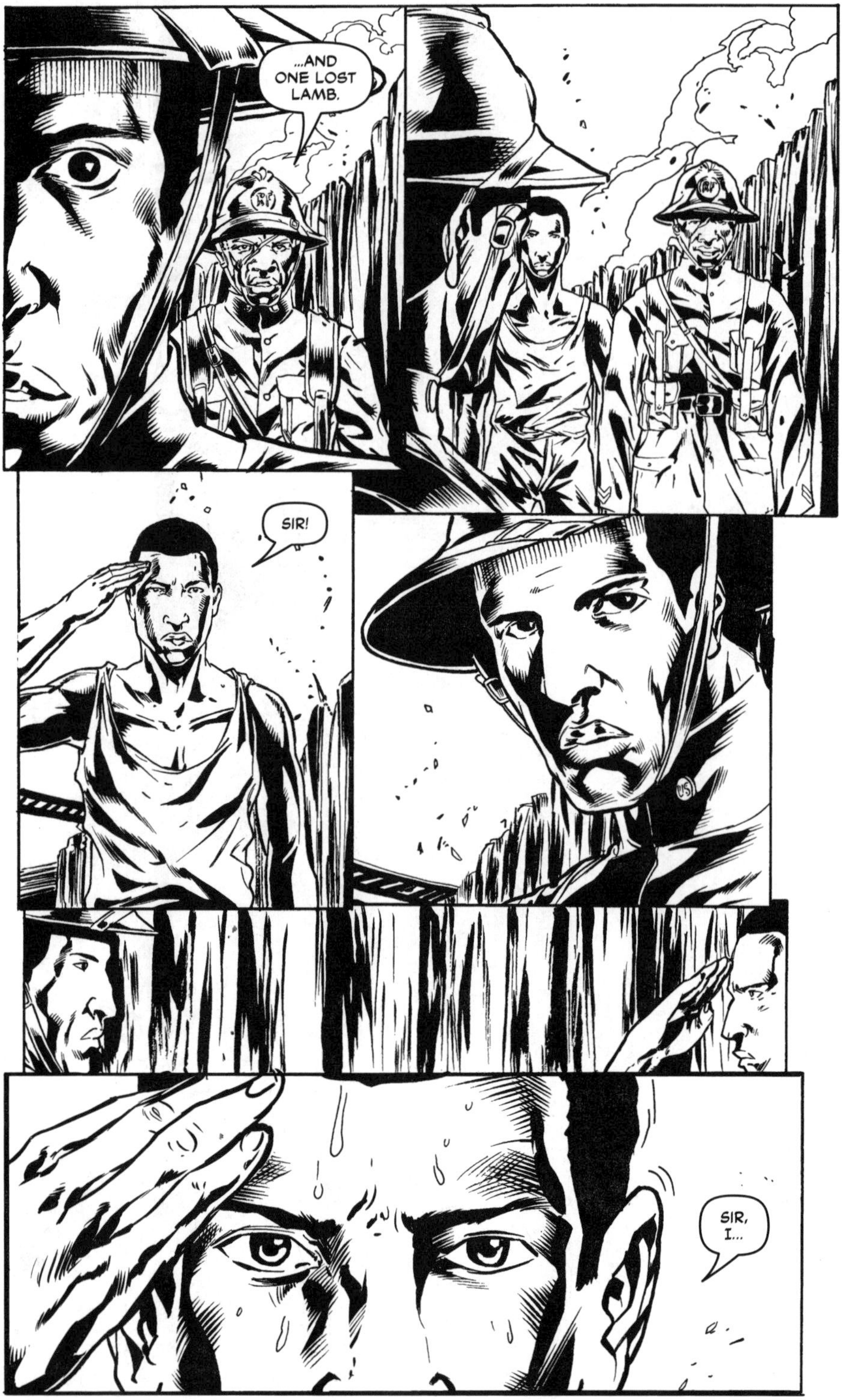
...AND ONE LOST LAMB.
SIR!
SIR, I...

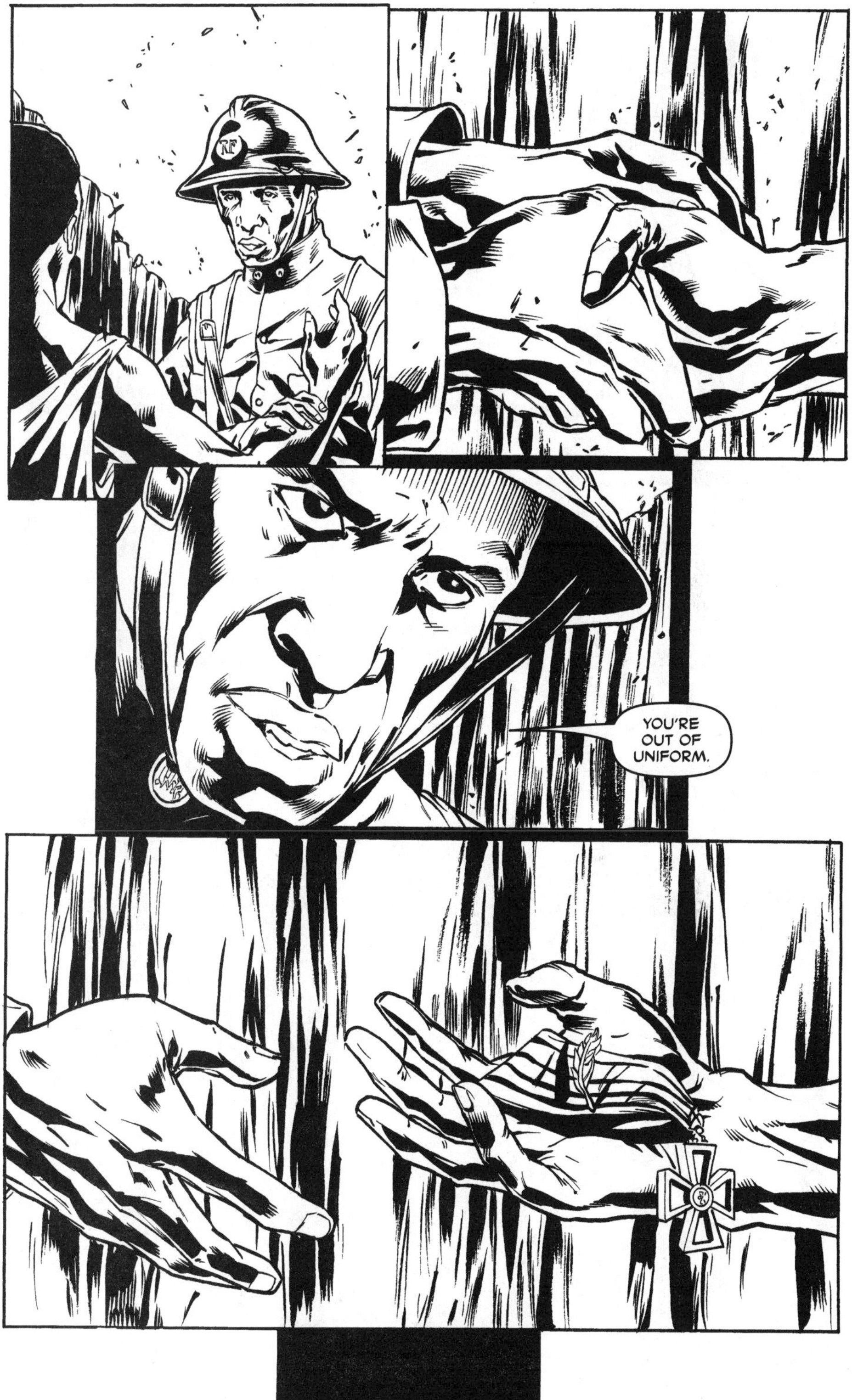
YOU'RE OUT OF UNIFORM.

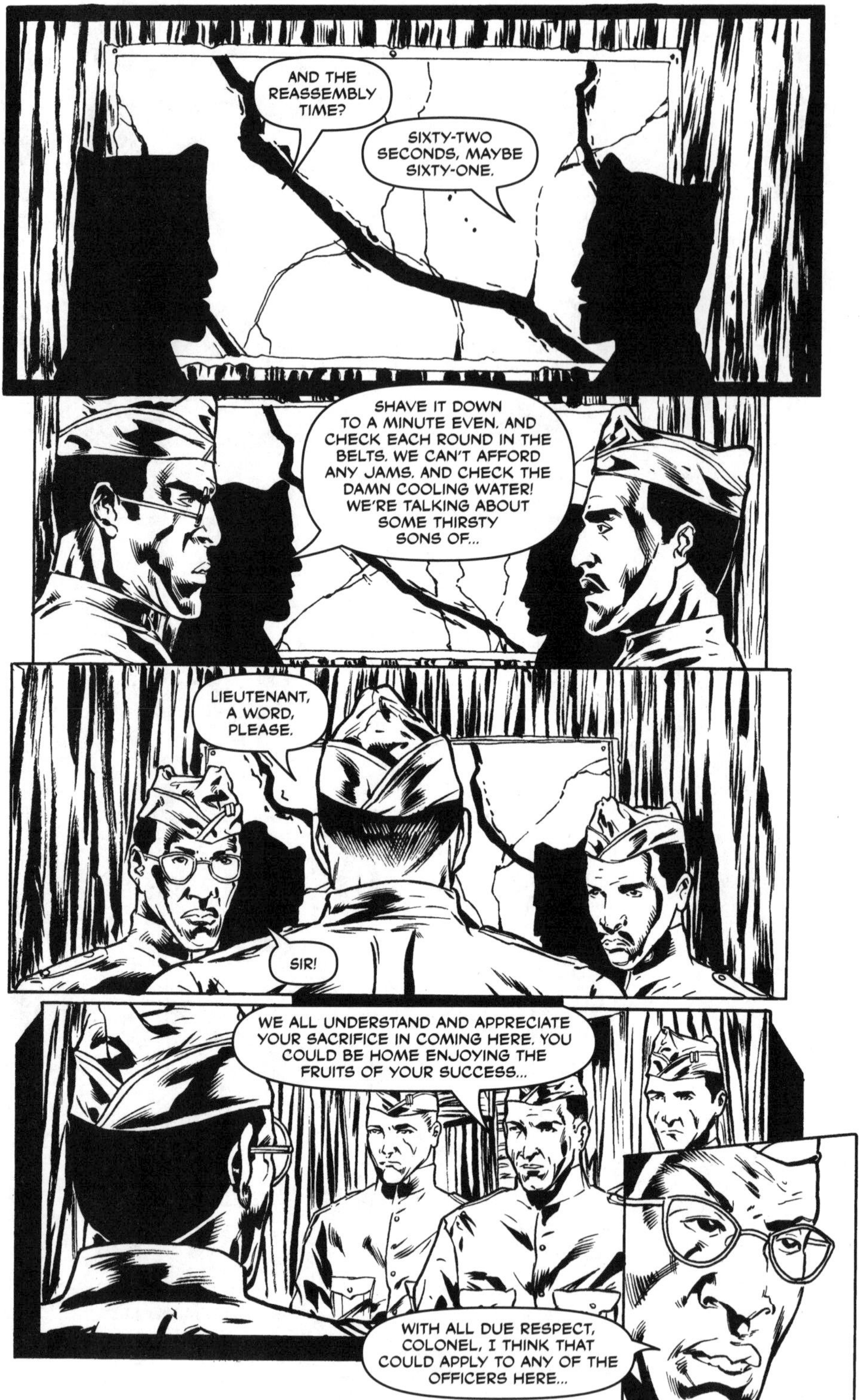
AND THE REASSEMBLY TIME?
SIXTY-TWO SECONDS, MAYBE SIXTY-ONE.
SHAVE IT DOWN TO A MINUTE EVEN, AND CHECK EACH ROUND IN THE BELTS. WE CAN'T AFFORD ANY JAMS. AND CHECK THE DAMN COOLING WATER! WE'RE TALKING ABOUT SOME THIRSTY SONS OF...
LIEUTENANT, A WORD, PLEASE.
SIR!
WE ALL UNDERSTAND AND APPRECIATE YOUR SACRIFICE IN COMING HERE. YOU COULD BE HOME ENJOYING THE FRUITS OF YOUR SUCCESS...
WITH ALL DUE RESPECT, COLONEL, I THINK THAT COULD APPLY TO ANY OF THE OFFICERS HERE...

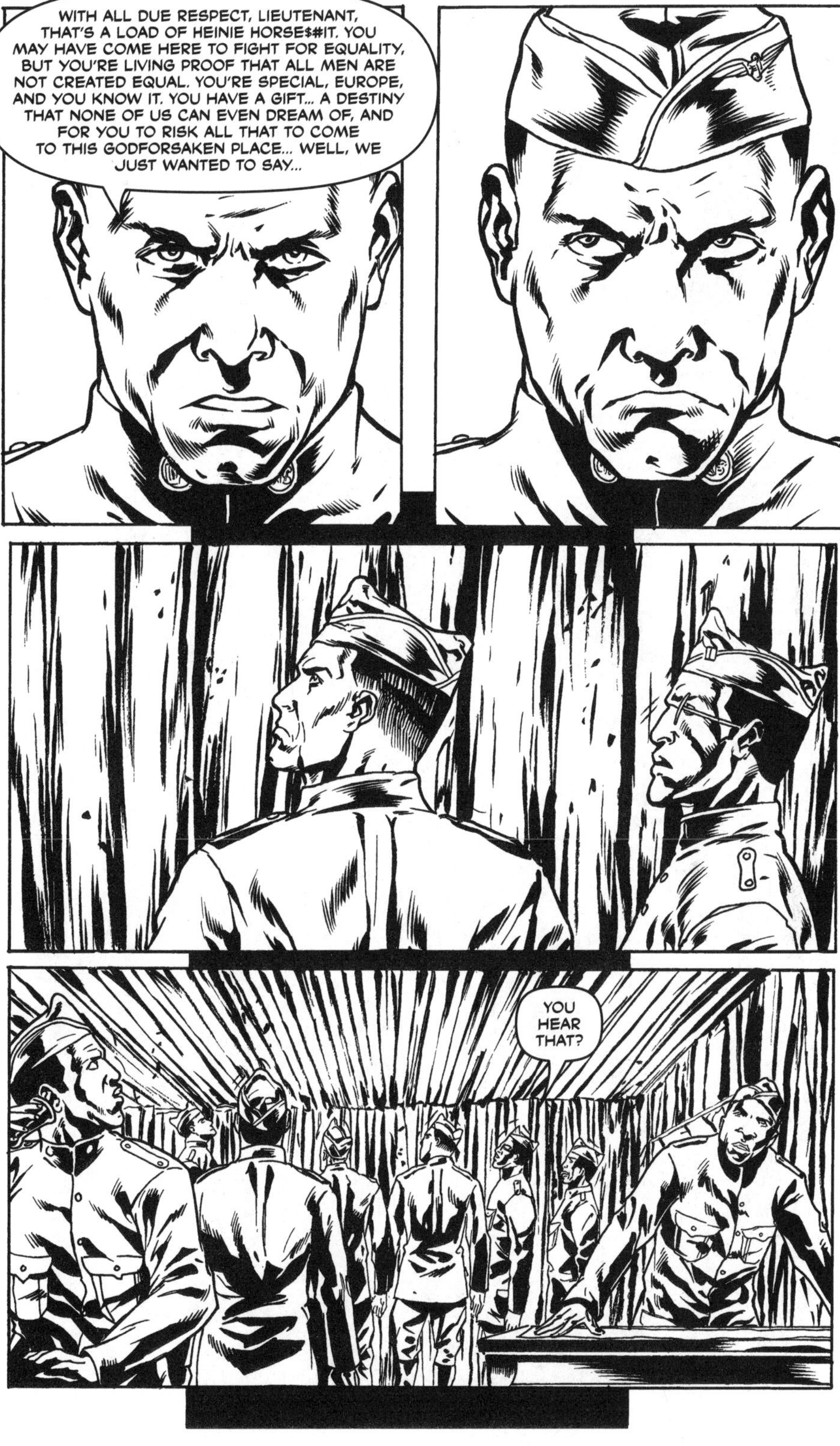
WITH ALL DUE RESPECT, LIEUTENANT, THAT'S A LOAD OF HEINIE HORSE$#IT. YOU MAY HAVE COME HERE TO FIGHT FOR EQUALITY, BUT YOU'RE LIVING PROOF THAT ALL MEN ARE NOT CREATED EQUAL. YOU'RE SPECIAL, EUROPE, AND YOU KNOW IT. YOU HAVE A GIFT... A DESTINY THAT NONE OF US CAN EVEN DREAM OF, AND FOR YOU TO RISK ALL THAT TO COME TO THIS GODFORSAKEN PLACE... WELL, WE JUST WANTED TO SAY...
YOU HEAR THAT?

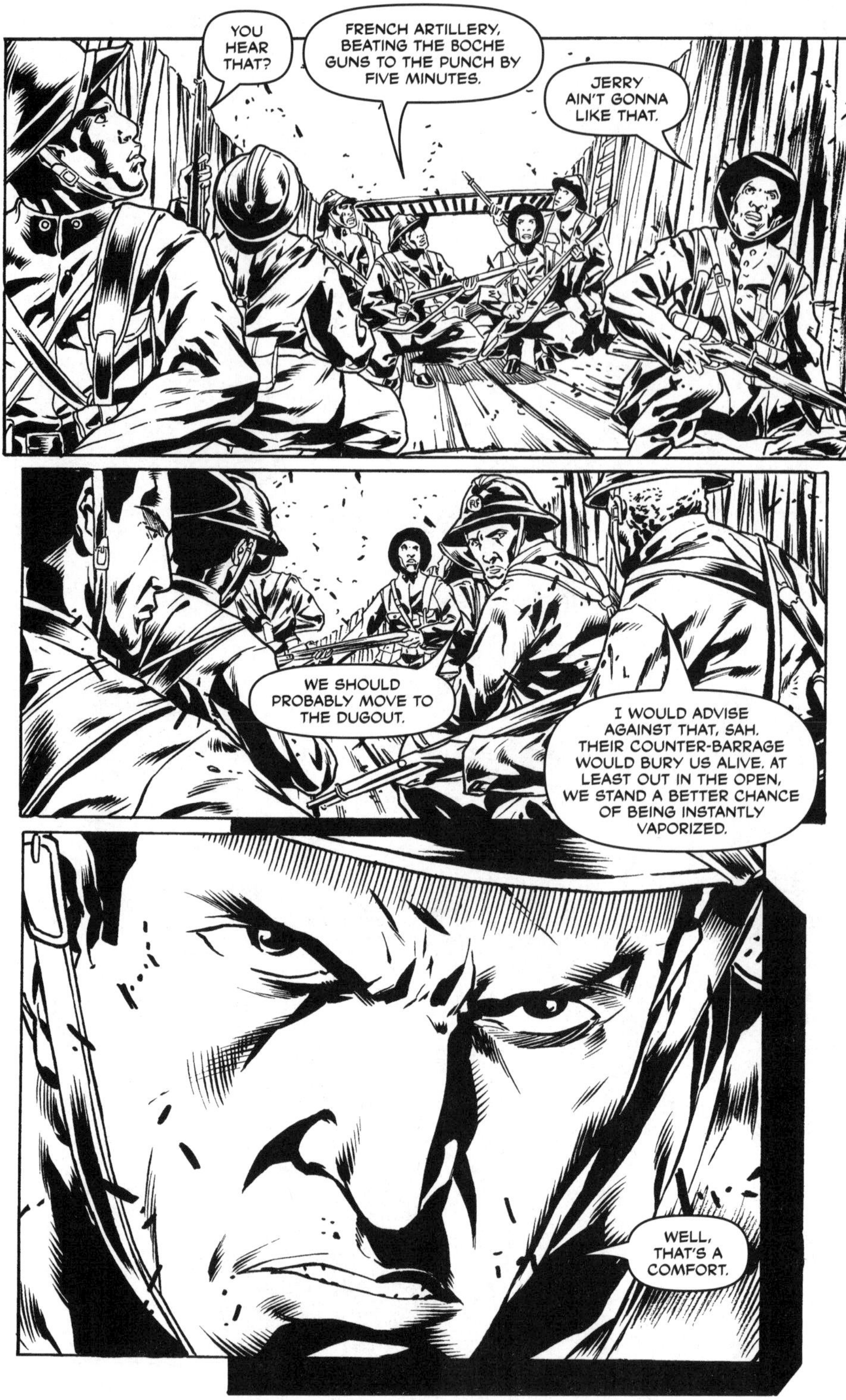
YOU HEAR THAT?
FRENCH ARTILLERY, BEATING THE BOCHE GUNS TO THE PUNCH BY FIVE MINUTES.
JERRY AIN'T GONNA LIKE THAT.
WE SHOULD PROBABLY MOVE TO THE DUGOUT.
I WOULD ADVISE AGAINST THAT, SAH. THEIR COUNTER-BARRAGE WOULD BURY US ALIVE. AT LEAST OUT IN THE OPEN, WE STAND A BETTER CHANCE OF BEING INSTANTLY VAPORIZED.
WELL, THAT'S A COMFORT.

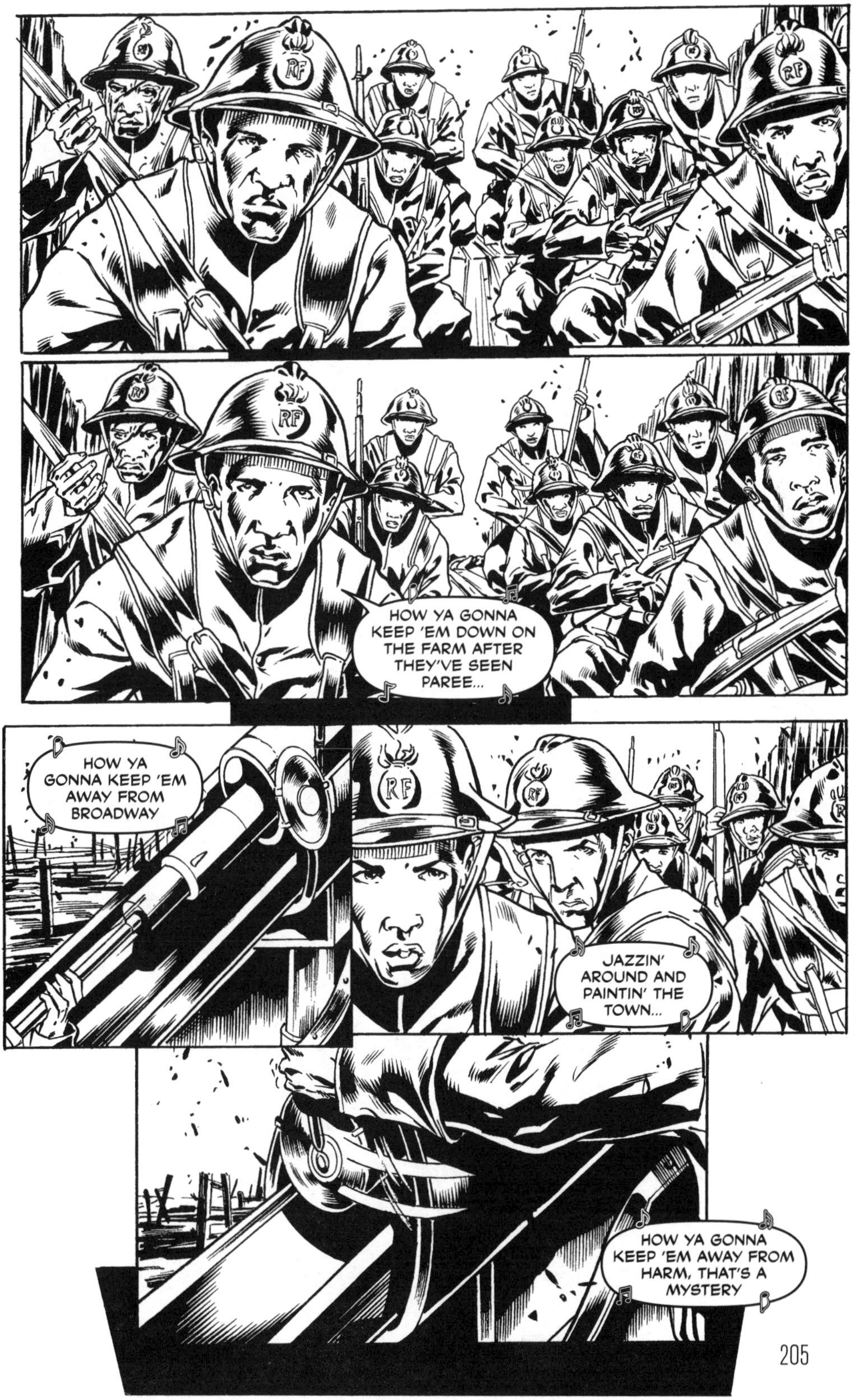
HOW YA GONNA KEEP 'EM DOWN ON THE FARM AFTER THEY'VE SEEN PAREE...
HOW YA GONNA KEEP 'EM AWAY FROM BROADWAY
JAZZIN' AROUND AND PAINTIN' THE TOWN...
HOW YA GONNA KEEP 'EM AWAY FROM HARM, THAT'S A MYSTERY

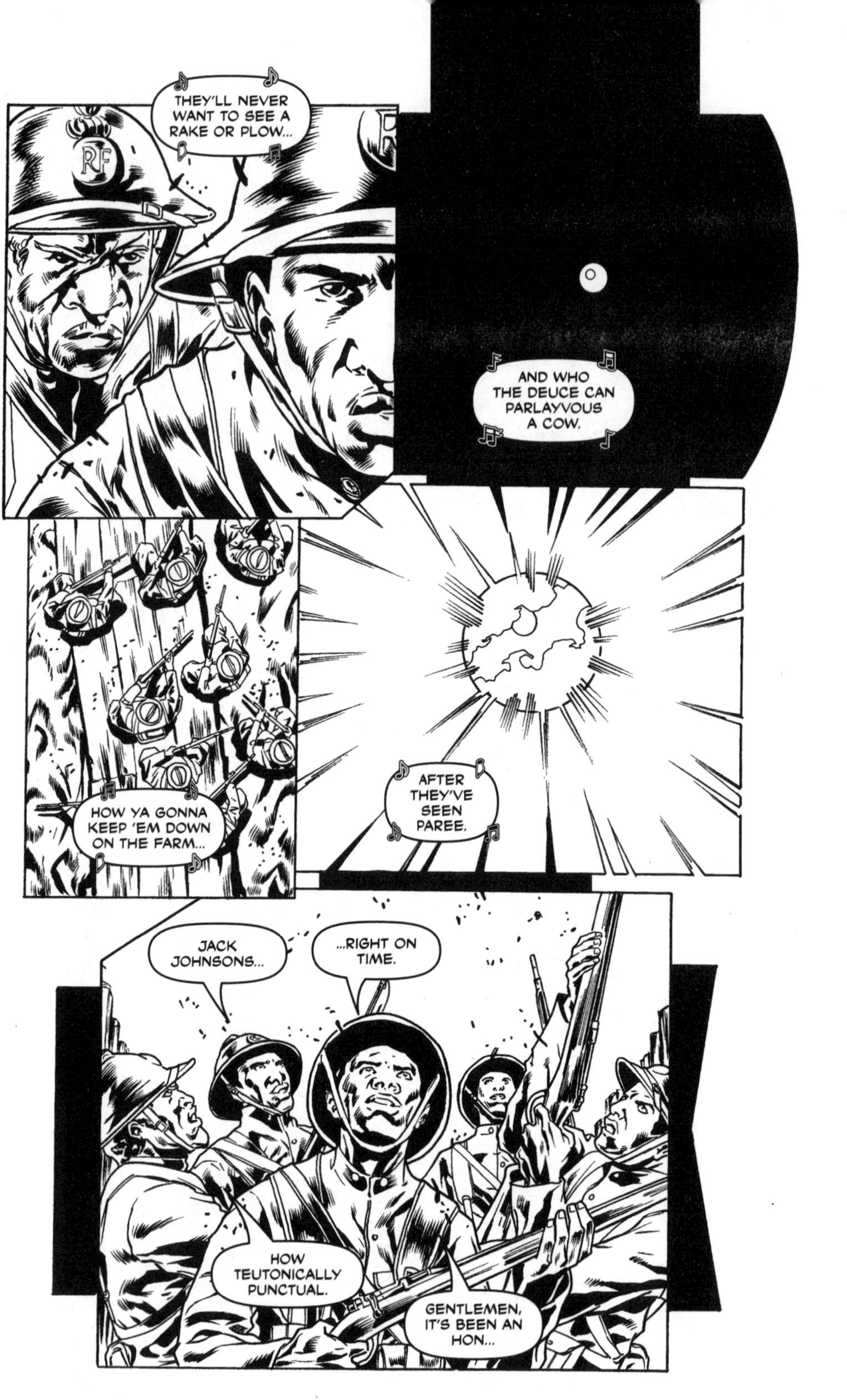
THEY'LL NEVER WANT TO SEE A RAKE OR PLOW...
AND WHO THE DEUCE CAN PARLAYVOUS A COW.
HOW YA GONNA KEEP 'EM DOWN ON THE FARM...
AFTER THEY'VE SEEN PAREE.
JACK JOHNSONS...
...RIGHT ON TIME.
HOW TEUTONICALLY PUNCTUAL.
GENTLEMEN, IT'S BEEN AN HON...

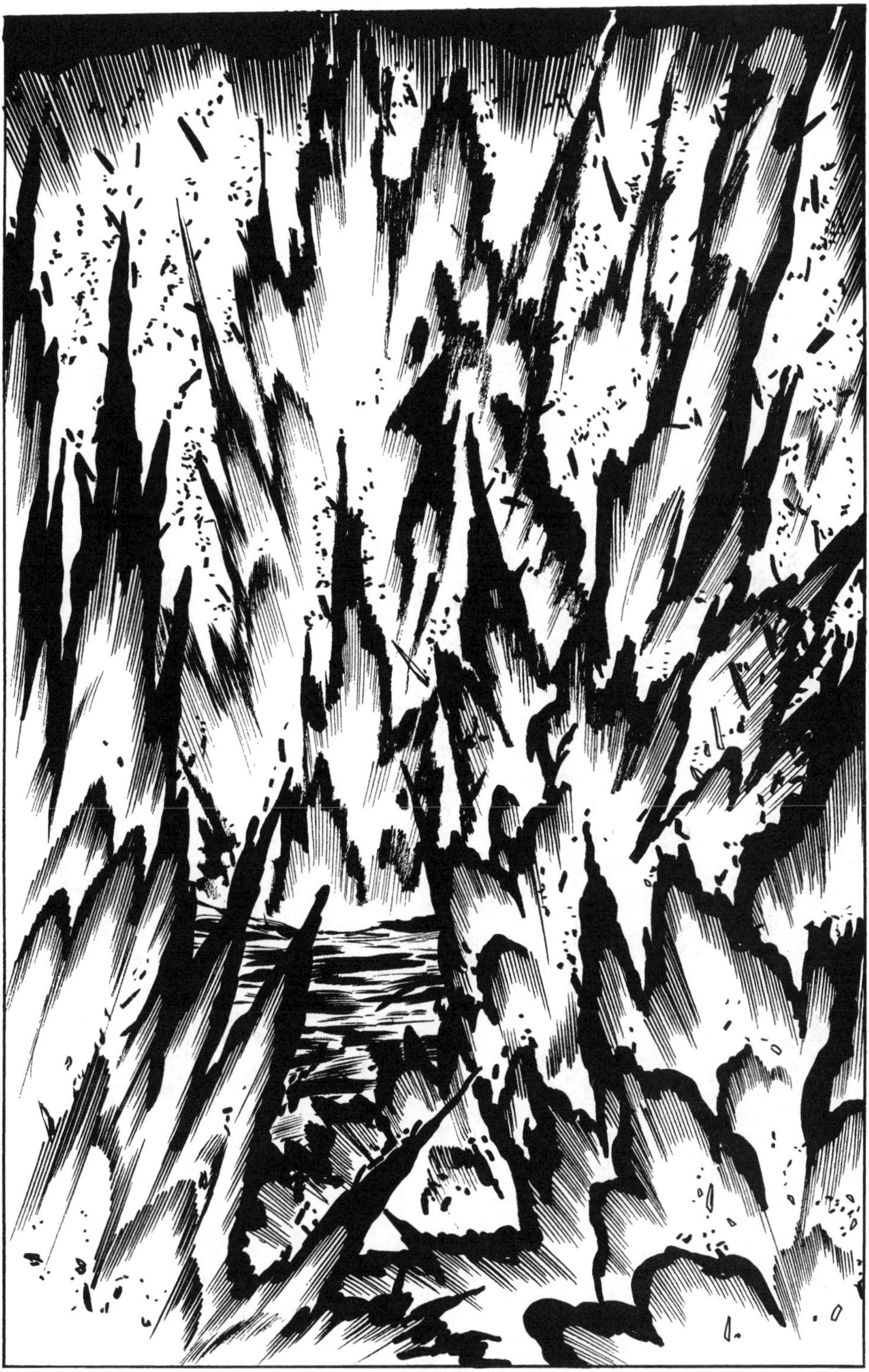

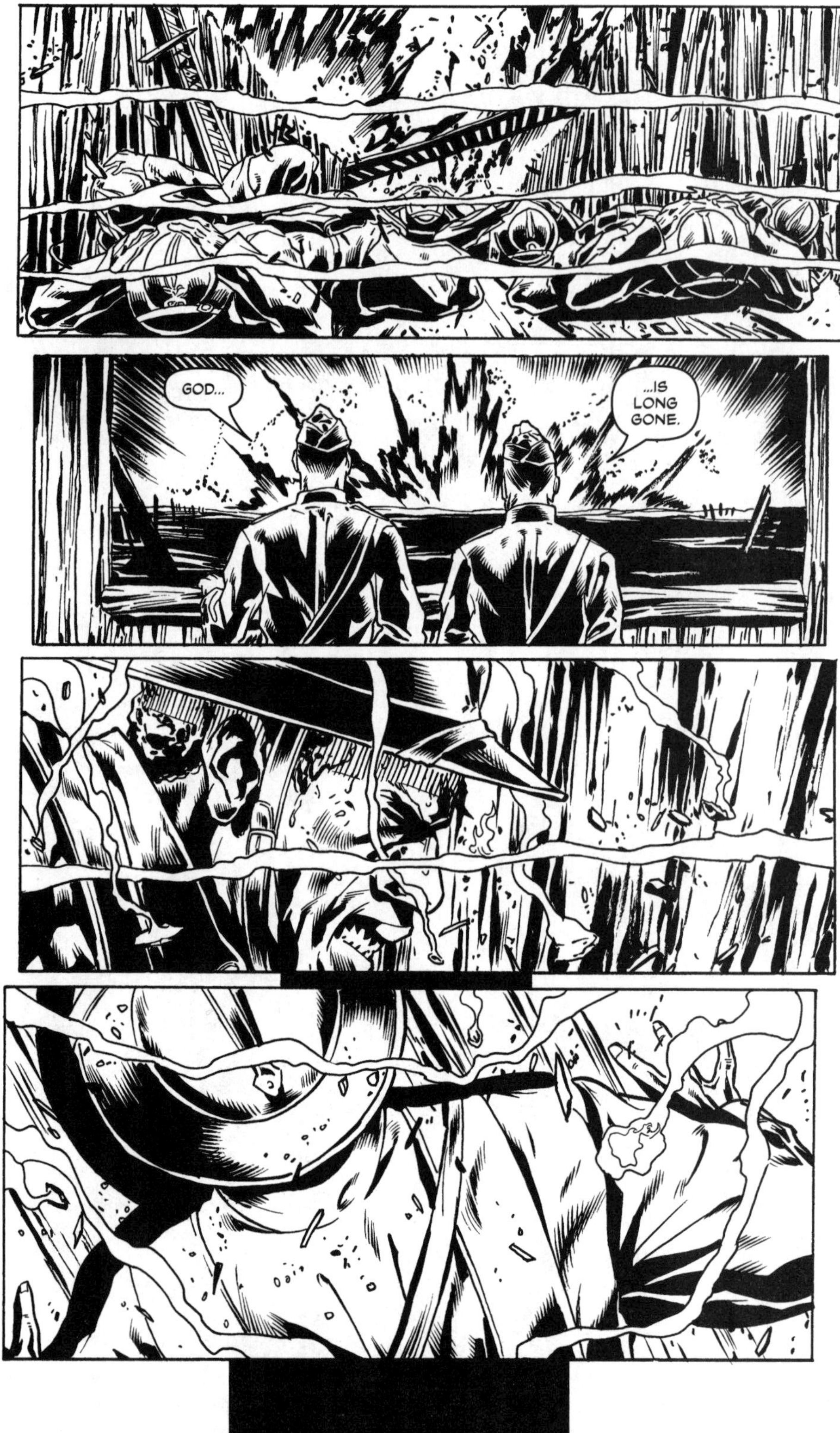
GOD...
...IS LONG GONE.

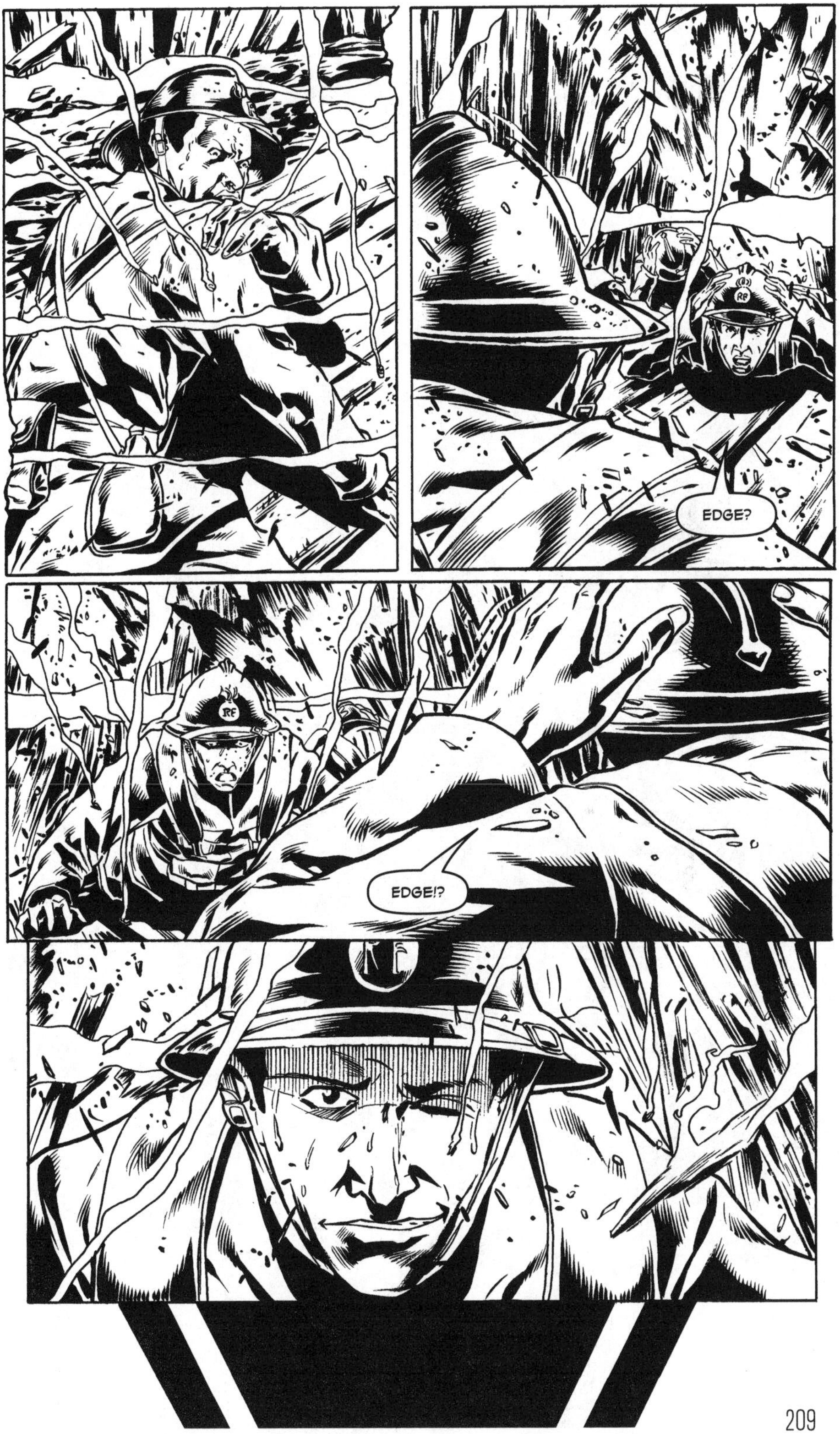
EDGE?
EDGE!?

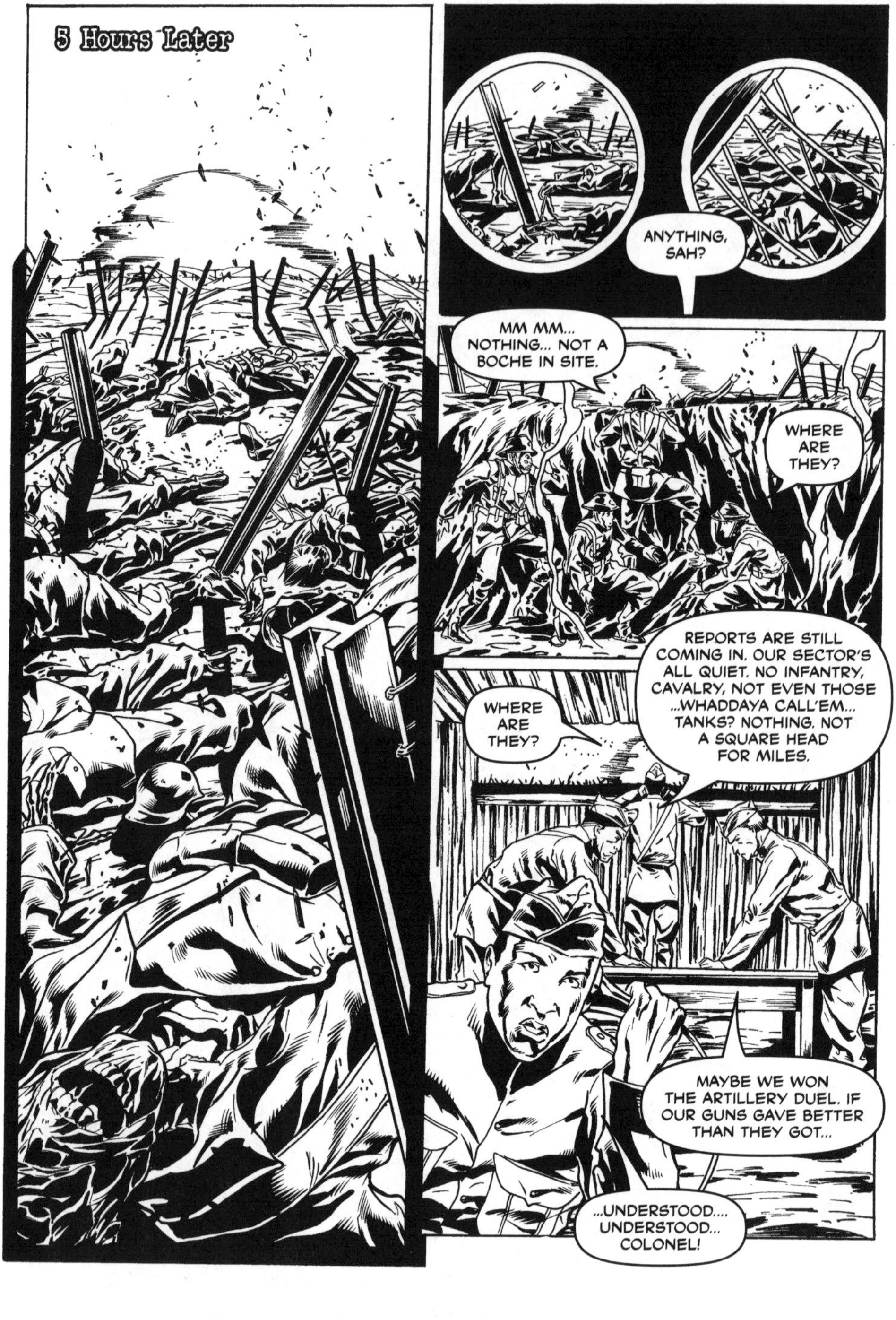
5 Hours Later
ANYTHING, SAH?
MM MM... NOTHING... NOT A BOCHE IN SITE.
WHERE ARE THEY?
WHERE ARE THEY?
REPORTS ARE STILL COMING IN. OUR SECTOR'S ALL QUIET. NO INFANTRY, CAVALRY, NOT EVEN THOSE ...WHADDAYA CALL'EM... TANKS? NOTHING. NOT A SQUARE HEAD FOR MILES.
MAYBE WE WON THE ARTILLERY DUEL. IF OUR GUNS GAVE BETTER THAN THEY GOT...
...UNDERSTOOD.... UNDERSTOOD... COLONEL!

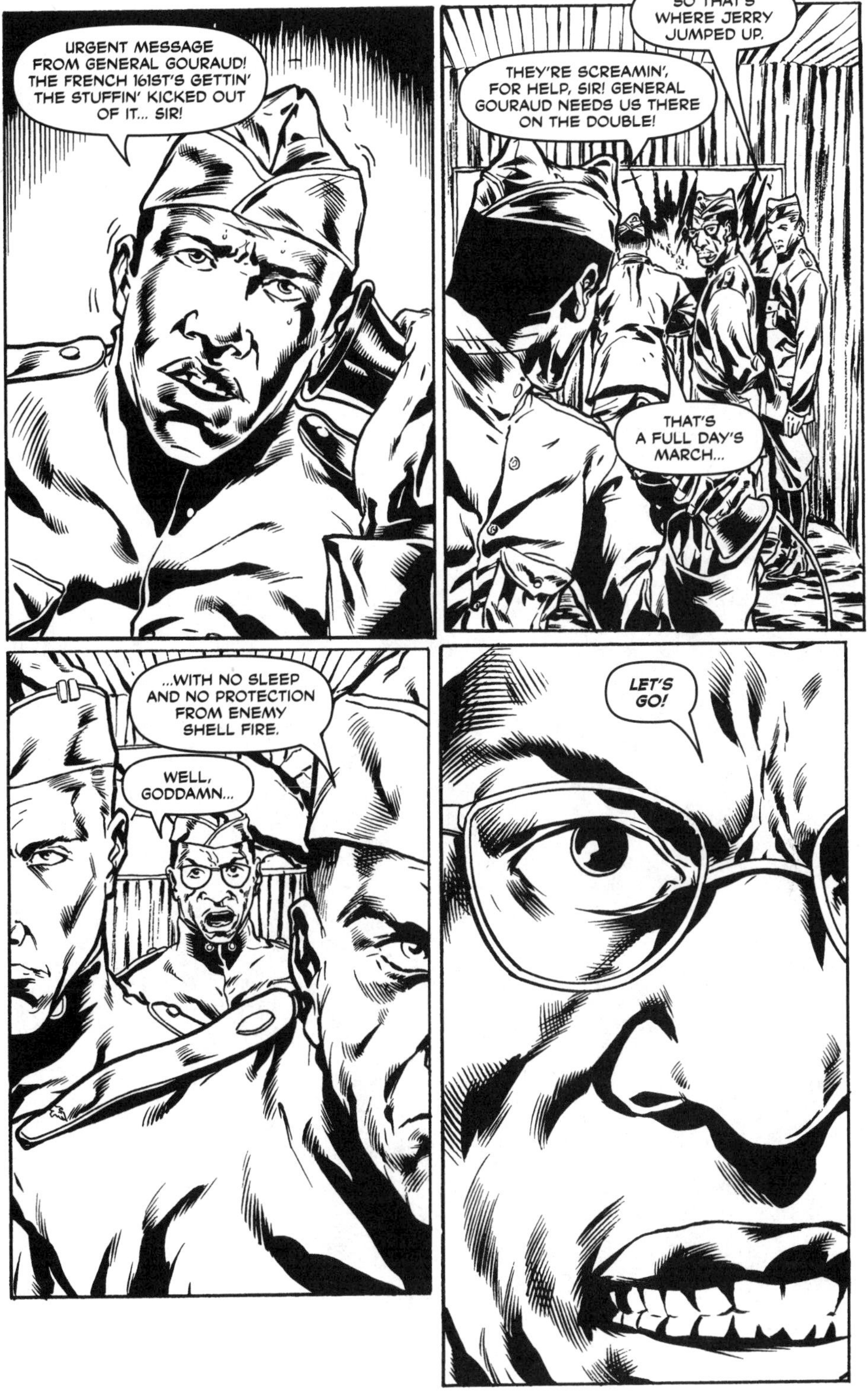
URGENT MESSAGE FROM GENERAL GOURAUD! THE FRENCH 161ST'S GETTIN' THE STUFFIN' KICKED OUT OF IT... SIR!
THEY'RE SCREAMIN', FOR HELP, SIR! GENERAL GOURAUD NEEDS US THERE ON THE DOUBLE!
SO THAT'S WHERE JERRY JUMPED UP.
THAT'S A FULL DAY'S MARCH...
...WITH NO SLEEP AND NO PROTECTION FROM ENEMY SHELL FIRE.
WELL, GODDAMN...
LET'S GO!

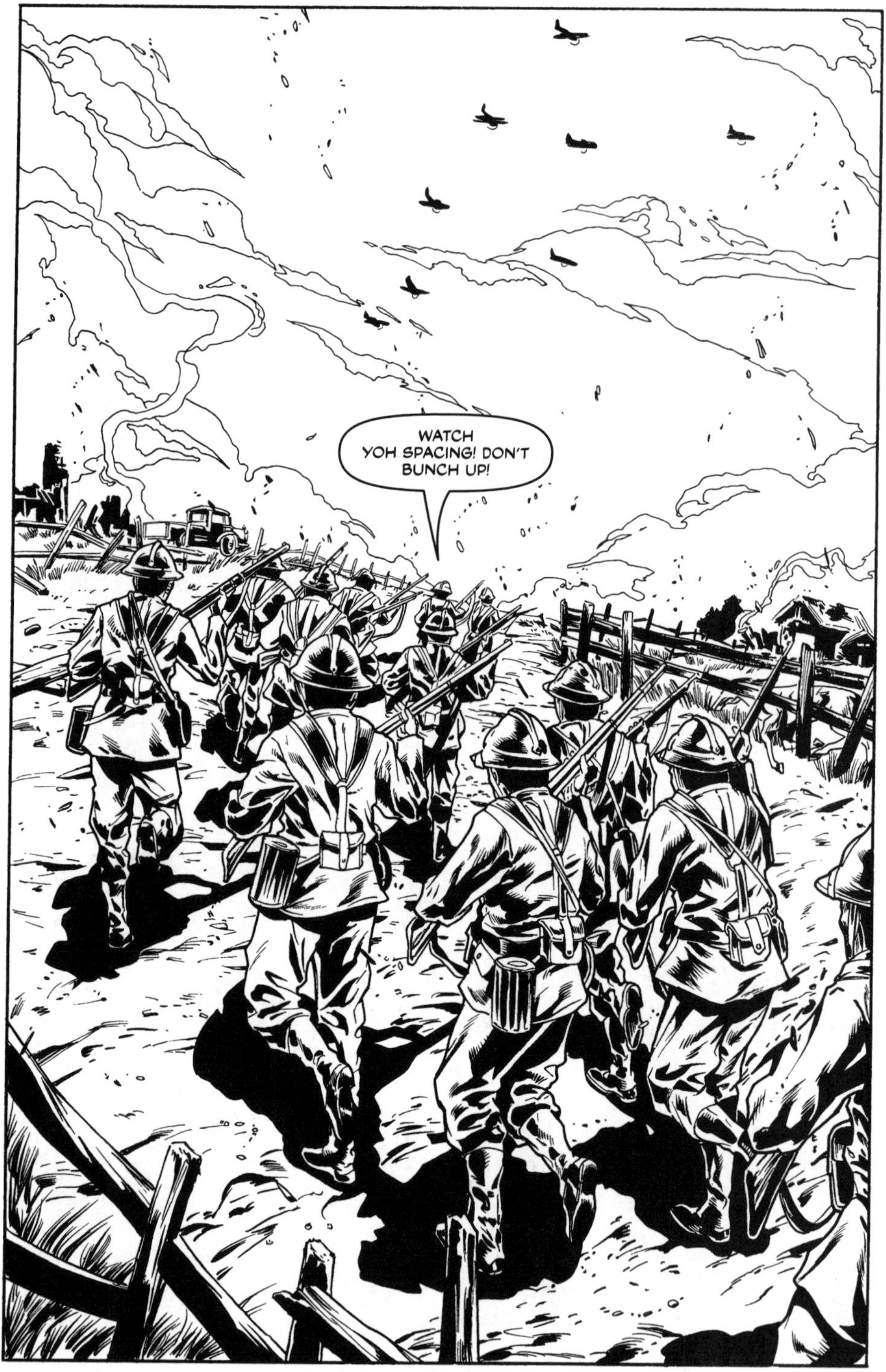
WATCH YOH SPACING! DON'T BUNCH UP!

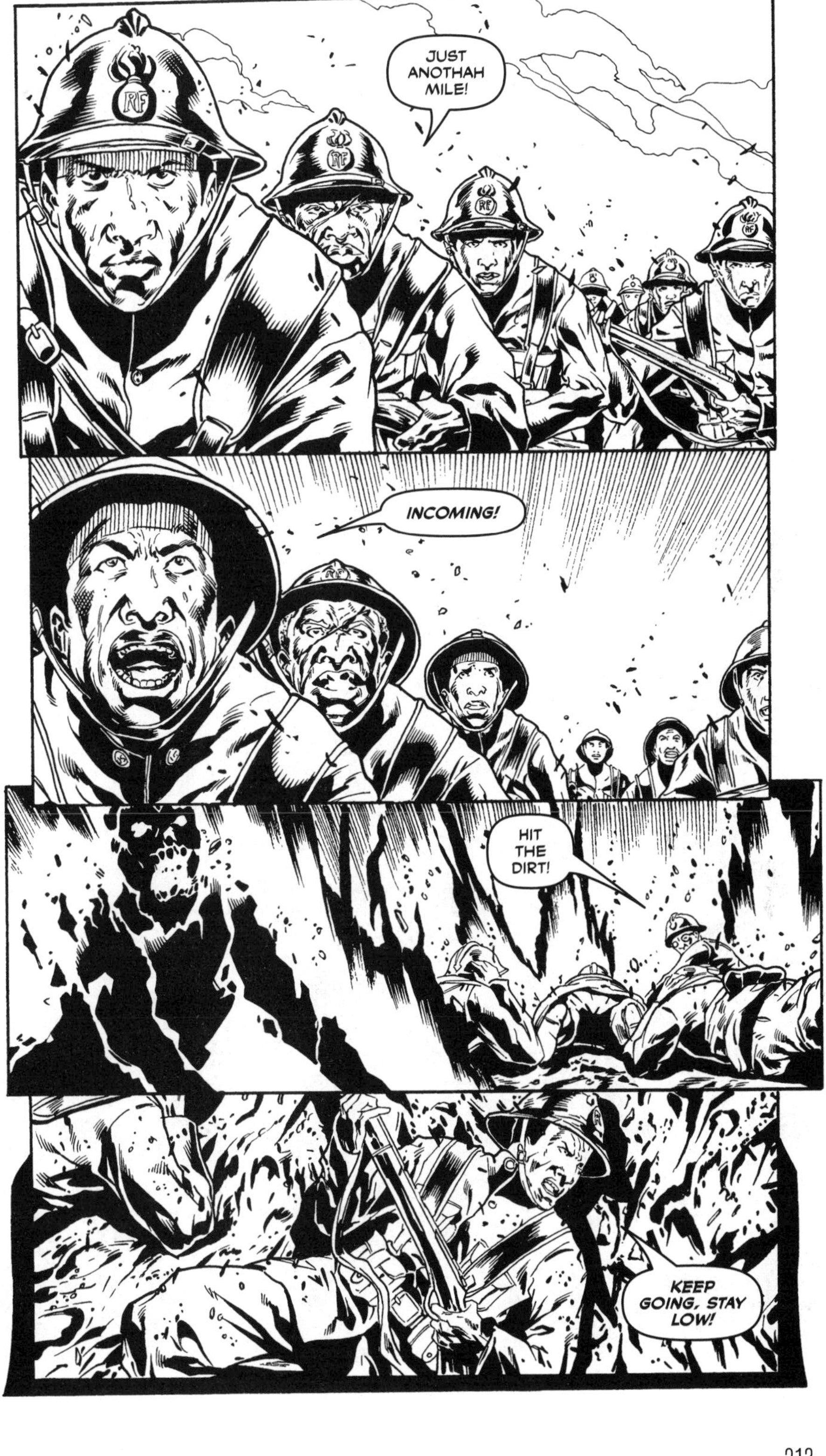
JUST ANOTHAH MILE!
INCOMING!
HIT THE DIRT!
KEEP GOING, STAY LOW!

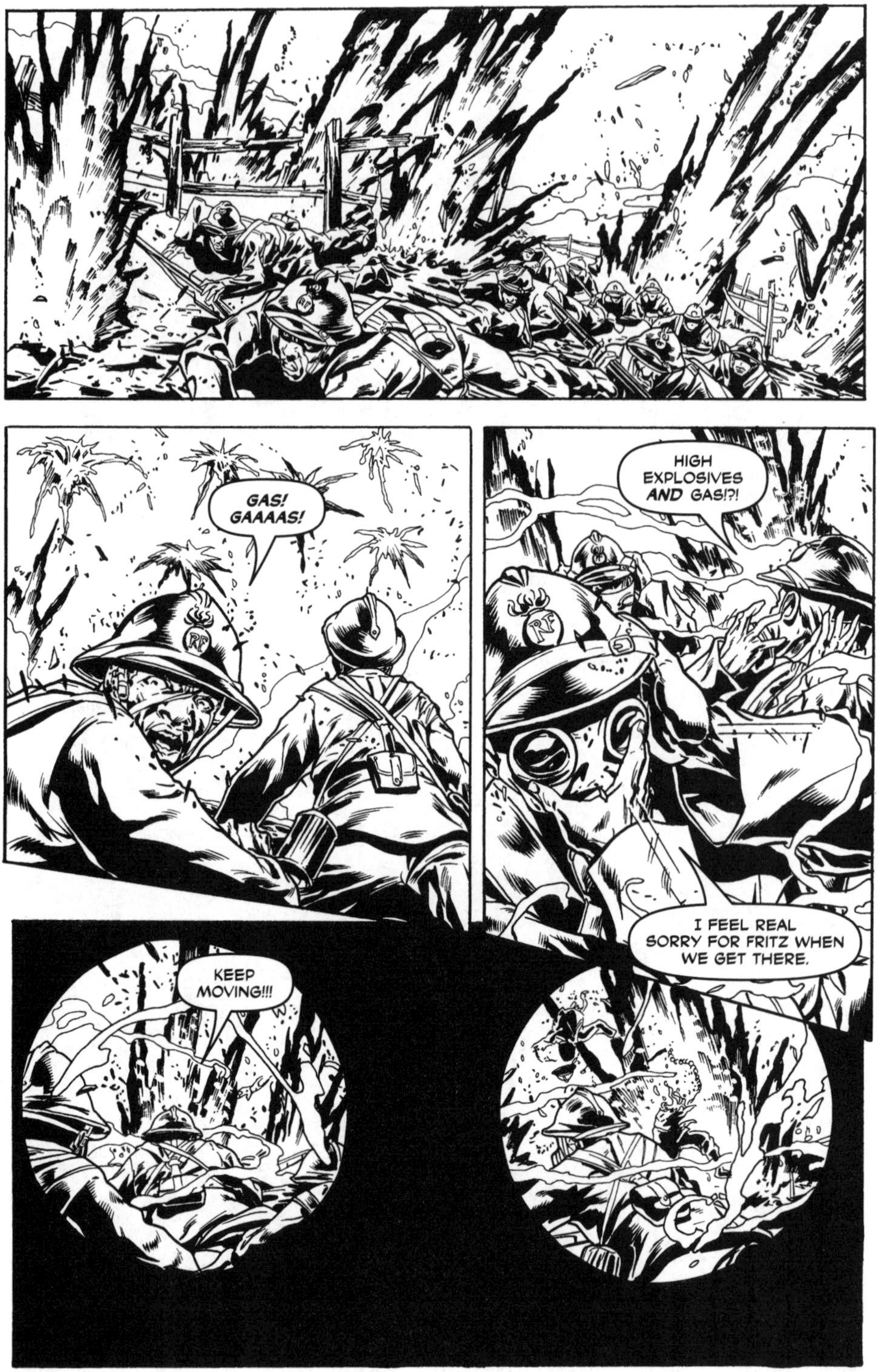
GAS! GAAAAS!
HIGH EXPLOSIVES AND GAS!?!
I FEEL REAL SORRY FOR FRITZ WHEN WE GET THERE.
KEEP MOVING!!!

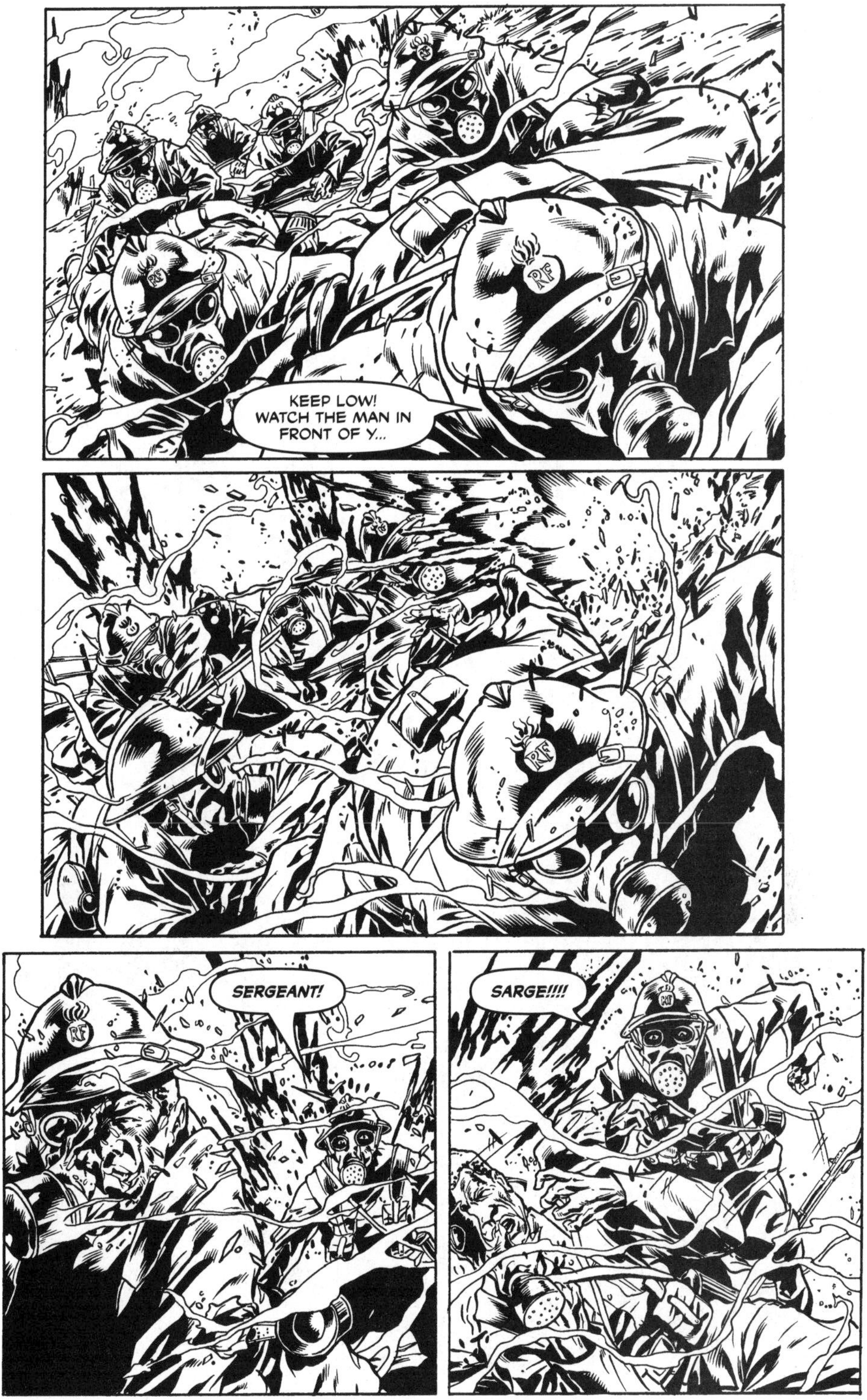
KEEP LOW! WATCH THE MAN IN FRONT OF Y...
SERGEANT!
SARGE!!!!

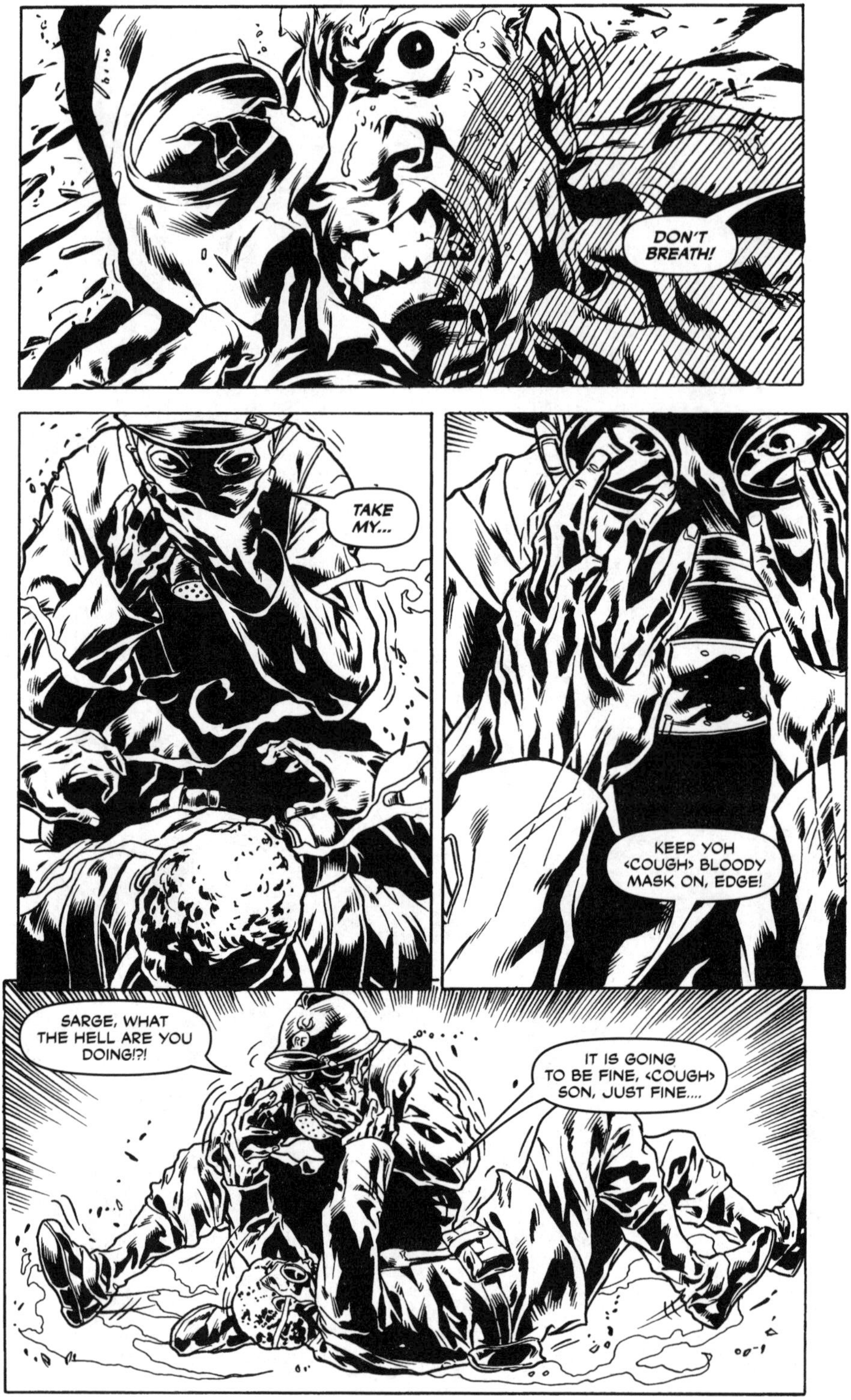
DON'T BREATH!
TAKE MY...
KEEP YOH <COUGH> BLOODY MASK ON, EDGE!
SARGE, WHAT THE HELL ARE YOU DOING!?!
IT IS GOING TO BE FINE, <COUGH> SON, JUST FINE....

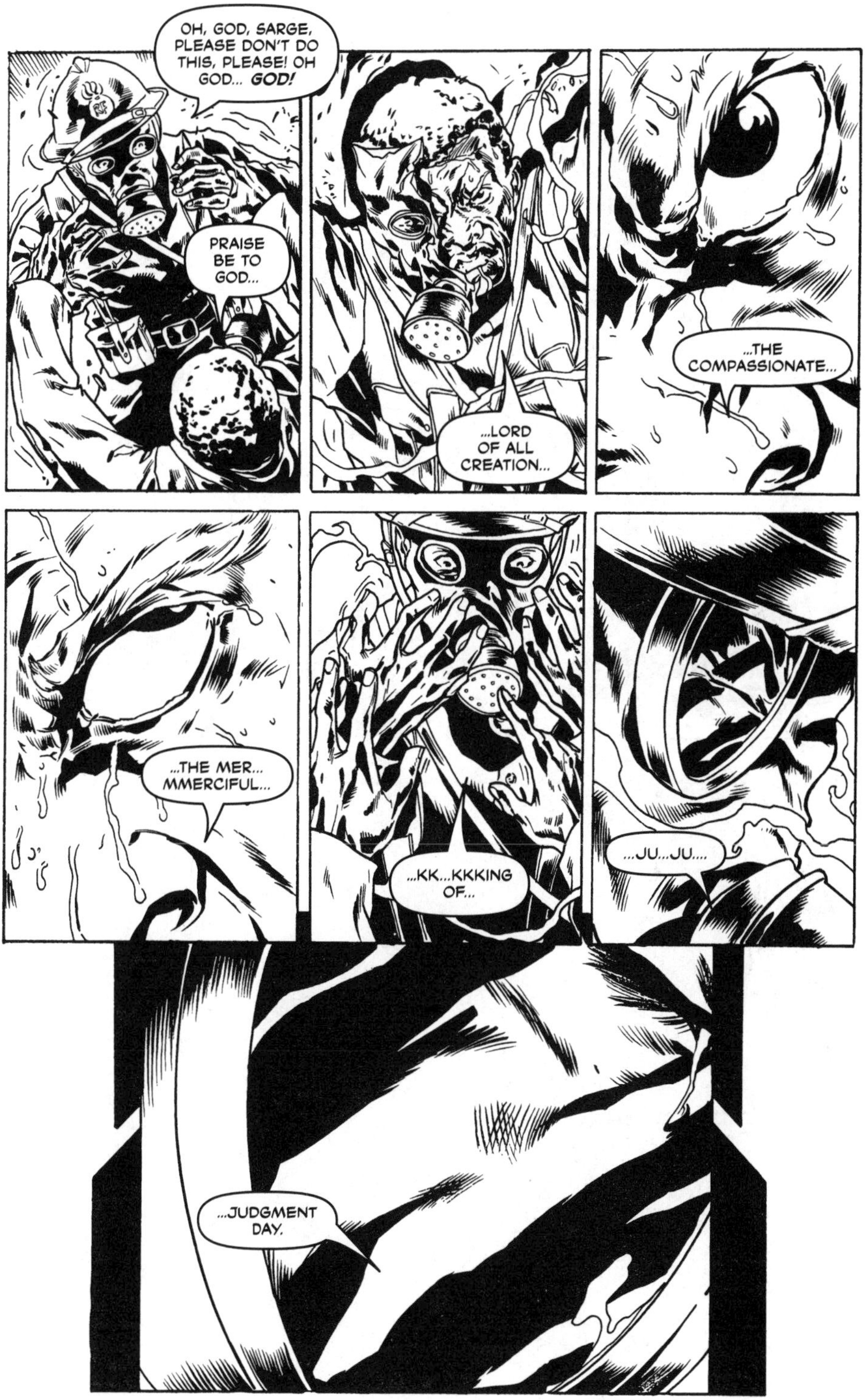
OH, GOD, SARGE, PLEASE DON'T DO THIS, PLEASE! OH GOD... **GOD!**
PRAISE BE TO GOD...
...LORD OF ALL CREATION...
...THE COMPASSIONATE...
...THE MER... MMERCIFUL...
...KK...KKKING OF...
...JU...JU....
...JUDGMENT DAY.

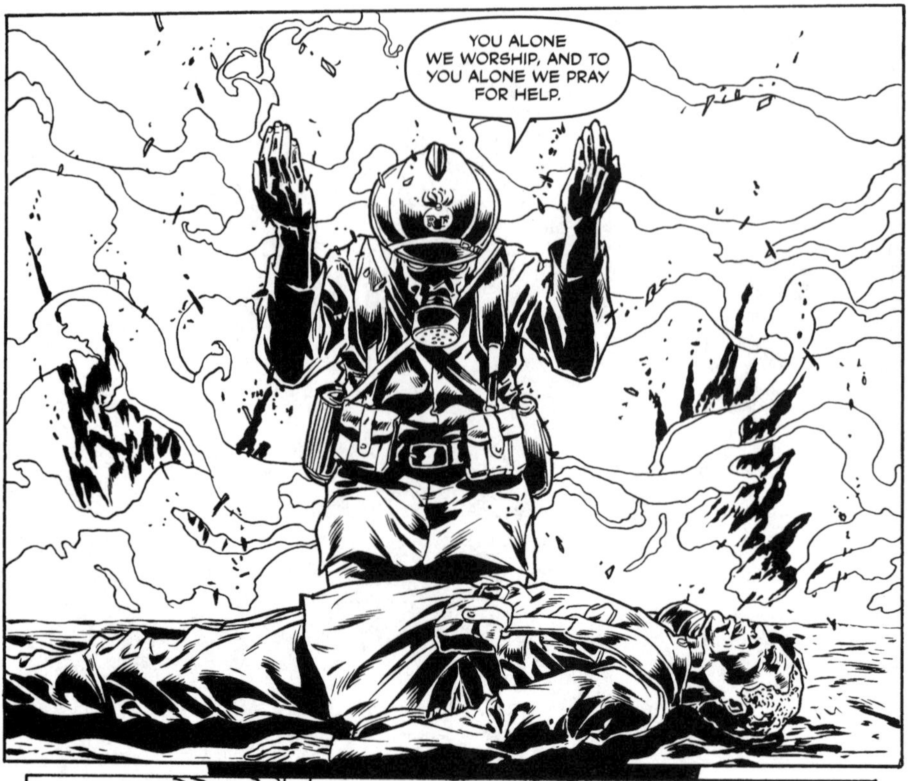
YOU ALONE WE WORSHIP, AND TO YOU ALONE WE PRAY FOR HELP.

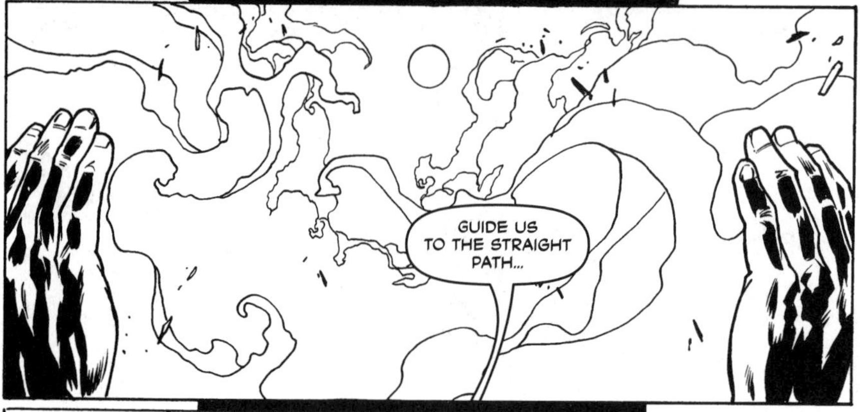
GUIDE US TO THE STRAIGHT PATH...

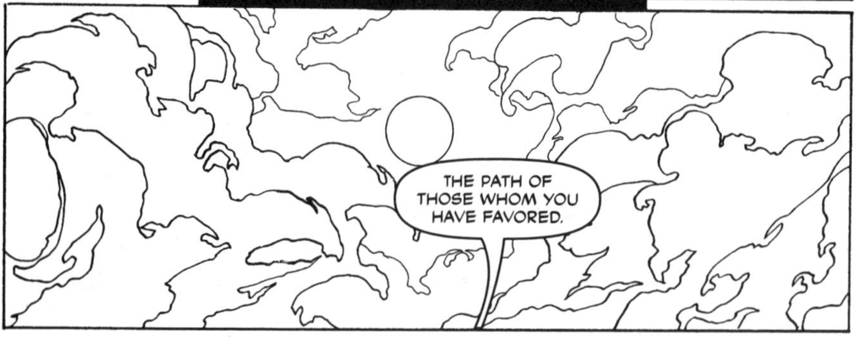
THE PATH OF THOSE WHOM YOU HAVE FAVORED.

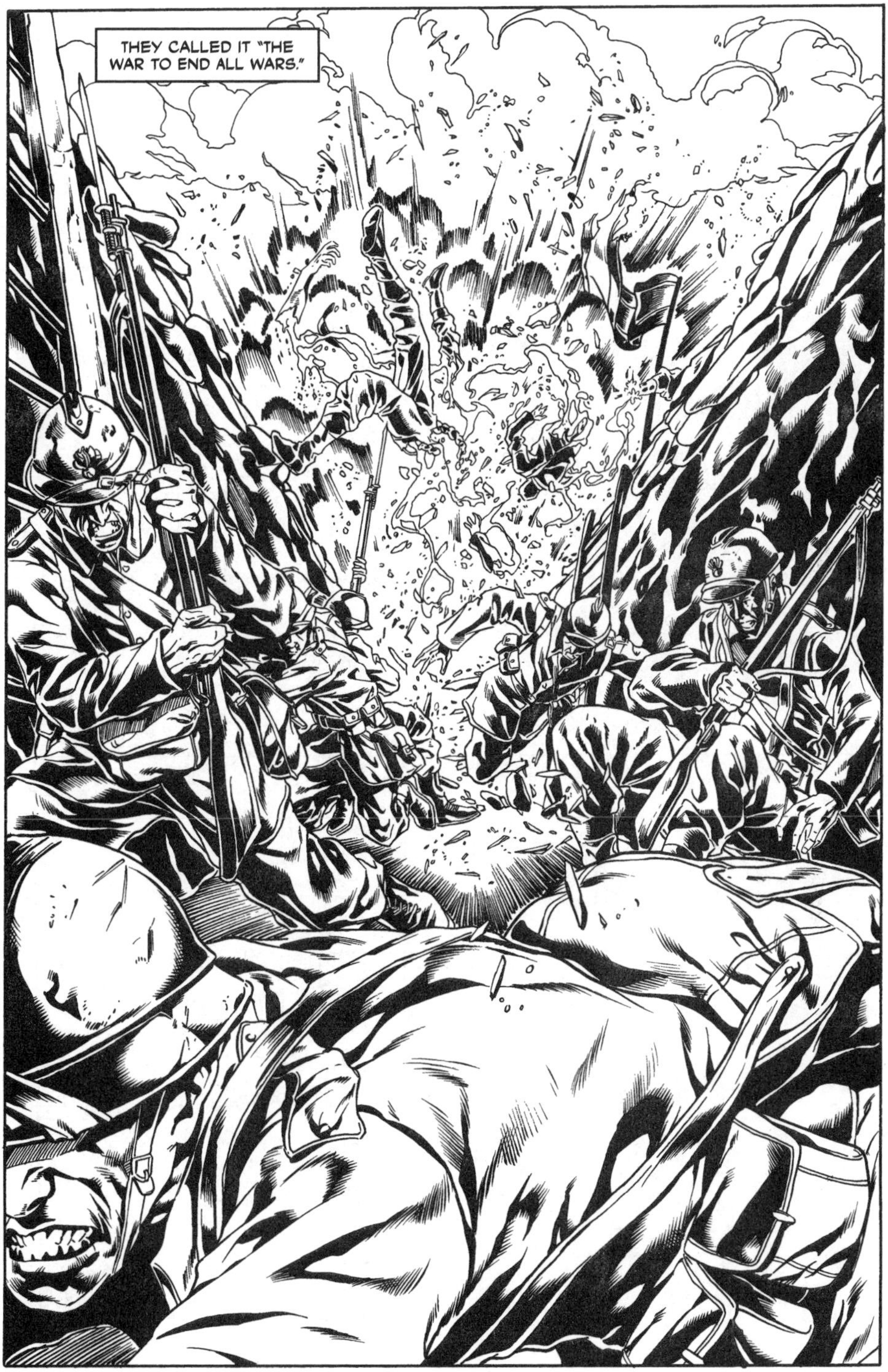
THEY CALLED IT "THE WAR TO END ALL WARS."

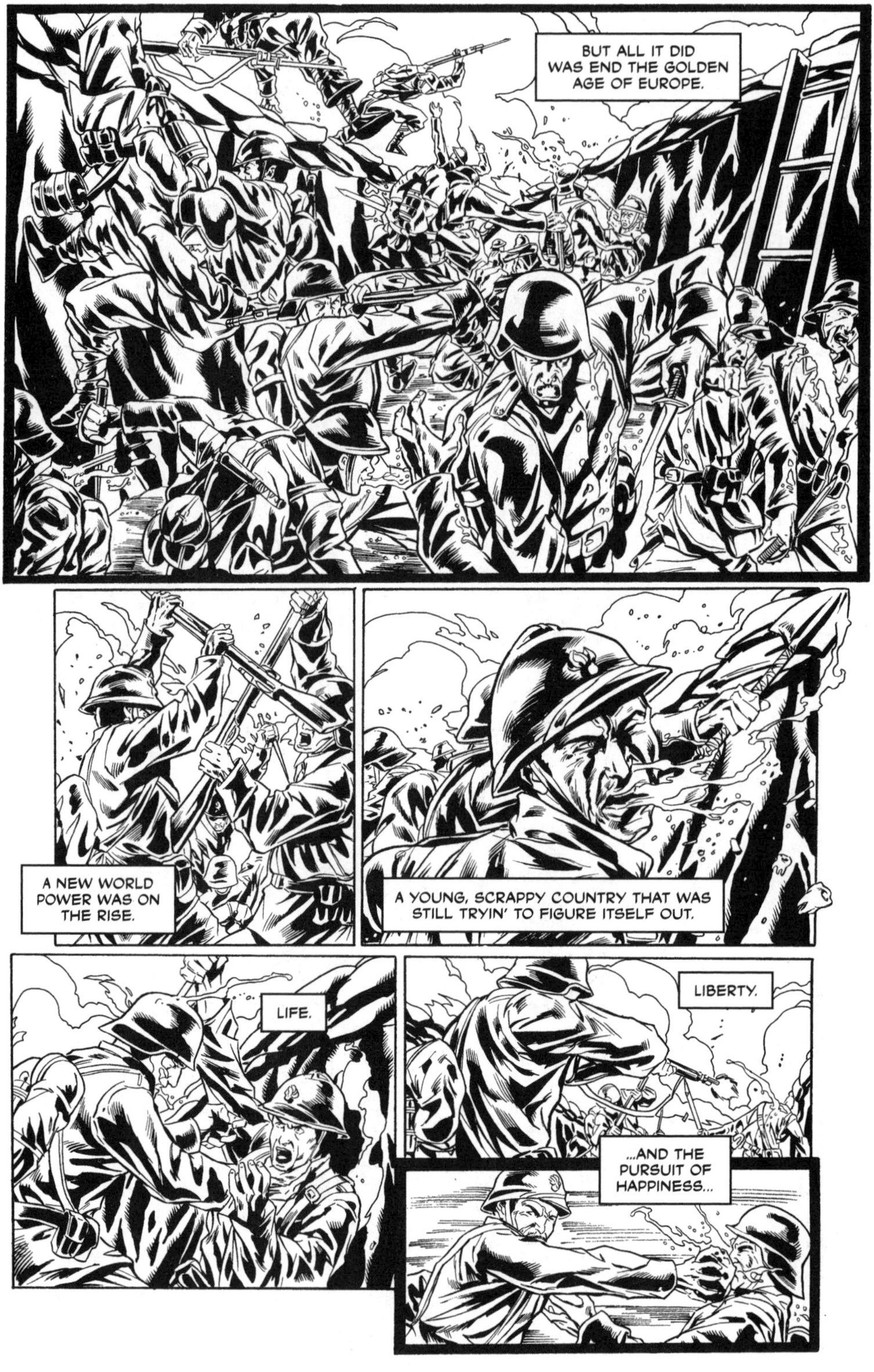
BUT ALL IT DID WAS END THE GOLDEN AGE OF EUROPE.
A NEW WORLD POWER WAS ON THE RISE.
A YOUNG, SCRAPPY COUNTRY THAT WAS STILL TRYIN' TO FIGURE ITSELF OUT.
LIFE.
LIBERTY.
...AND THE PURSUIT OF HAPPINESS...

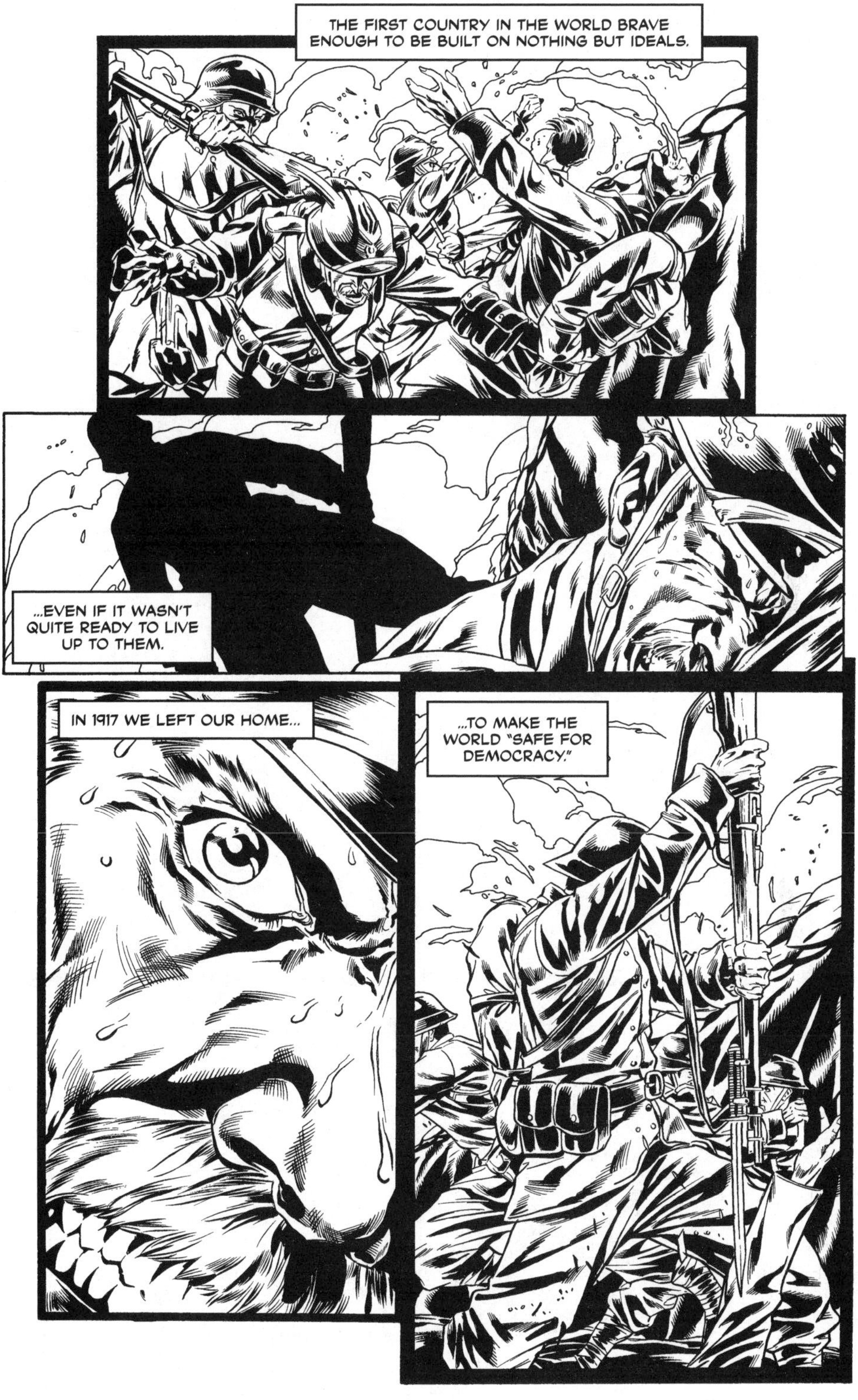
THE FIRST COUNTRY IN THE WORLD BRAVE ENOUGH TO BE BUILT ON NOTHING BUT IDEALS.
...EVEN IF IT WASN'T QUITE READY TO LIVE UP TO THEM.
IN 1917 WE LEFT OUR HOME...
...TO MAKE THE WORLD "SAFE FOR DEMOCRACY."

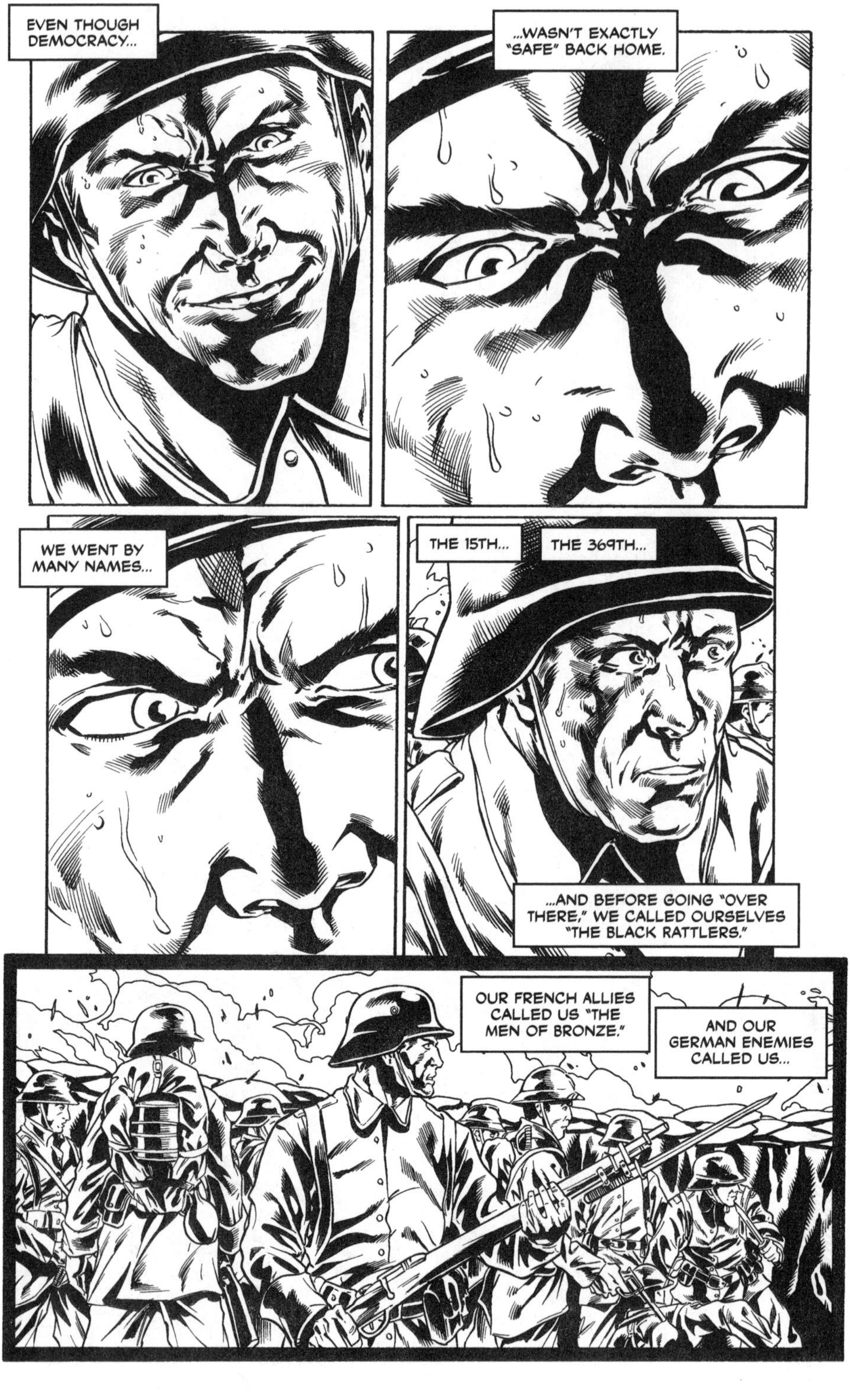
EVEN THOUGH DEMOCRACY...
...WASN'T EXACTLY "SAFE" BACK HOME.
WE WENT BY MANY NAMES...
THE 15TH...
THE 369TH...
...AND BEFORE GOING "OVER THERE," WE CALLED OURSELVES "THE BLACK RATTLERS."
OUR FRENCH ALLIES CALLED US "THE MEN OF BRONZE."
AND OUR GERMAN ENEMIES CALLED US...

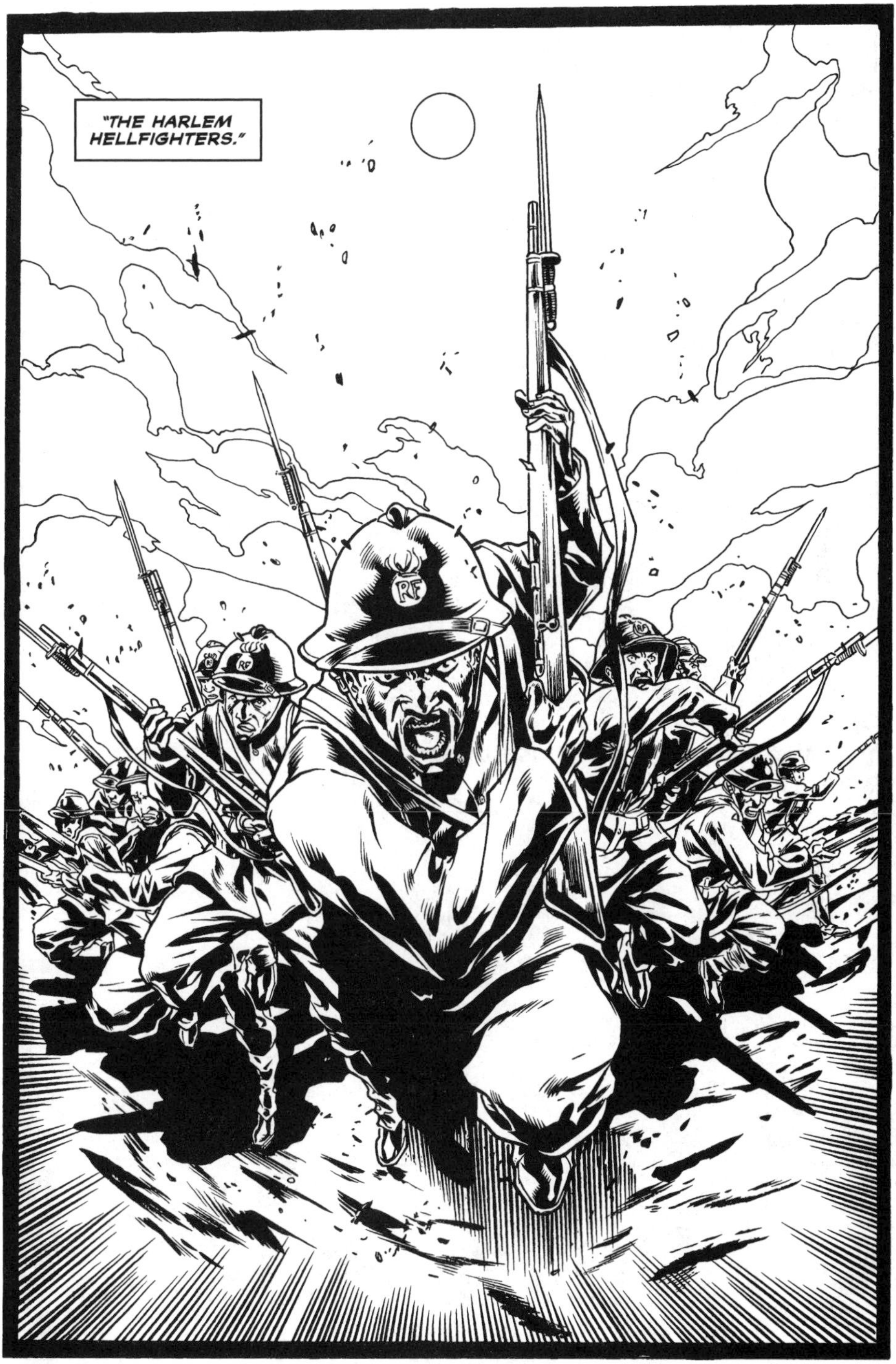
"THE HARLEM HELLFIGHTERS."

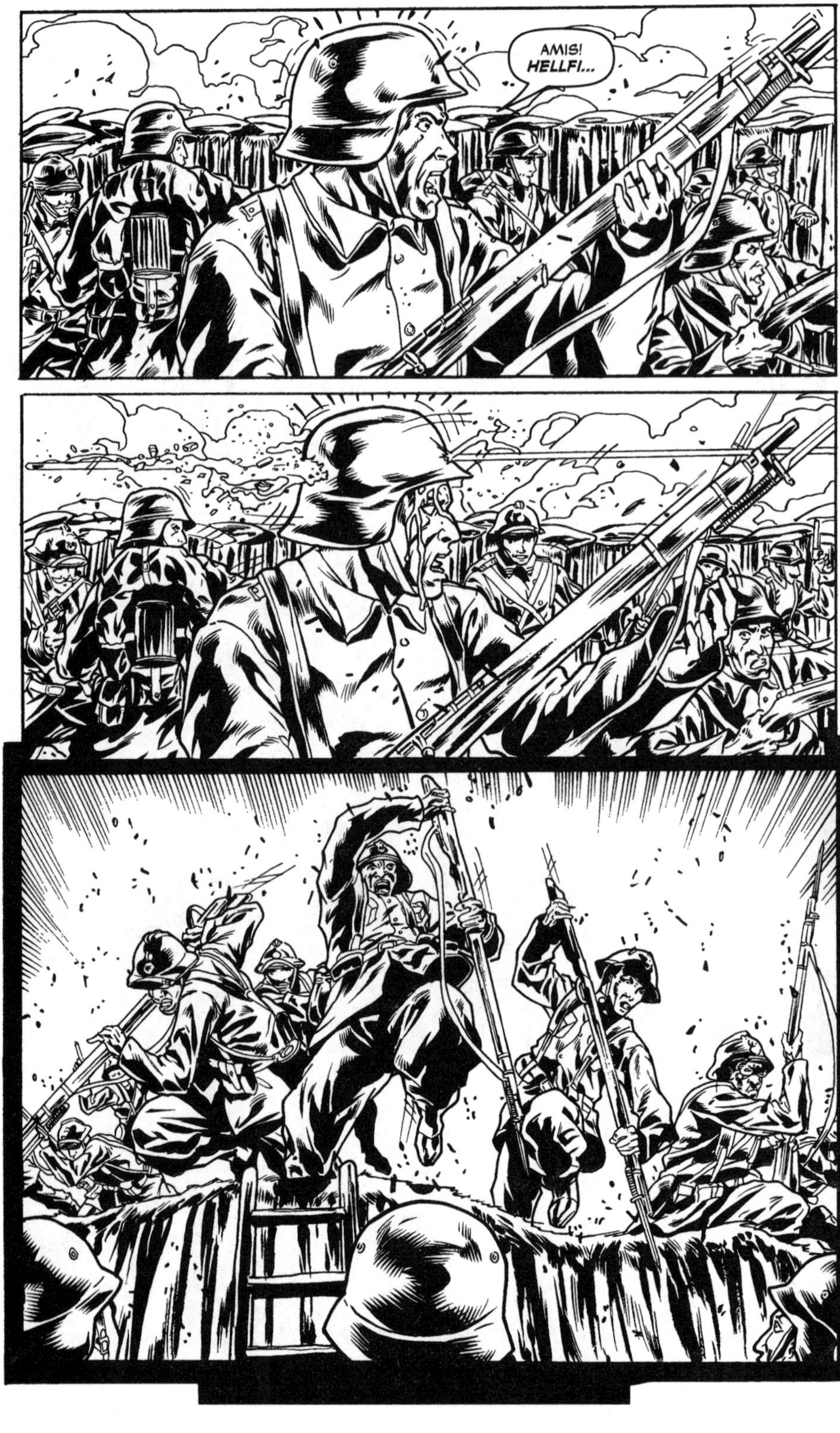
AMIS!
HELLFI...

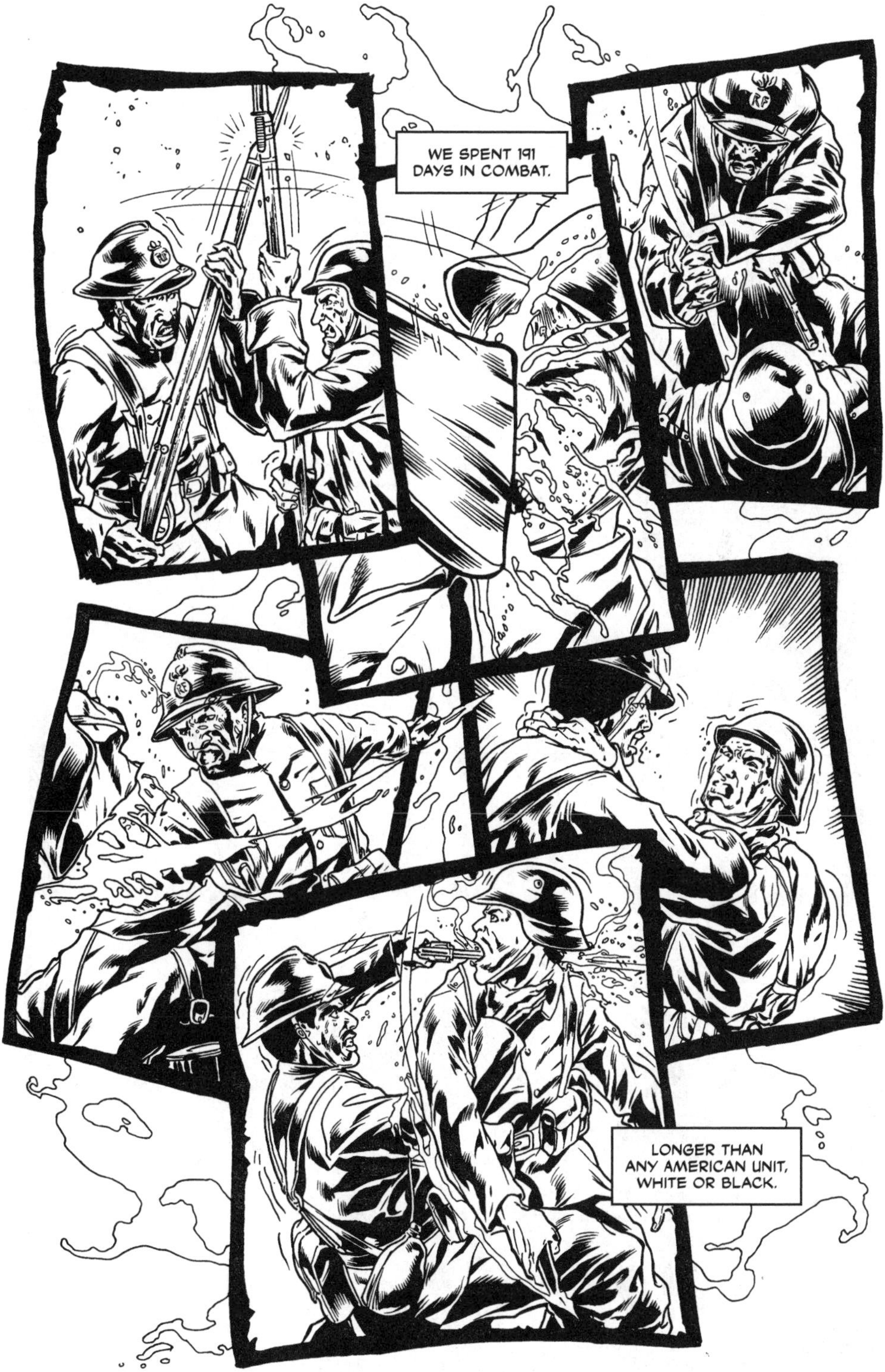
WE SPENT 191 DAYS IN COMBAT.
LONGER THAN ANY AMERICAN UNIT, WHITE OR BLACK.

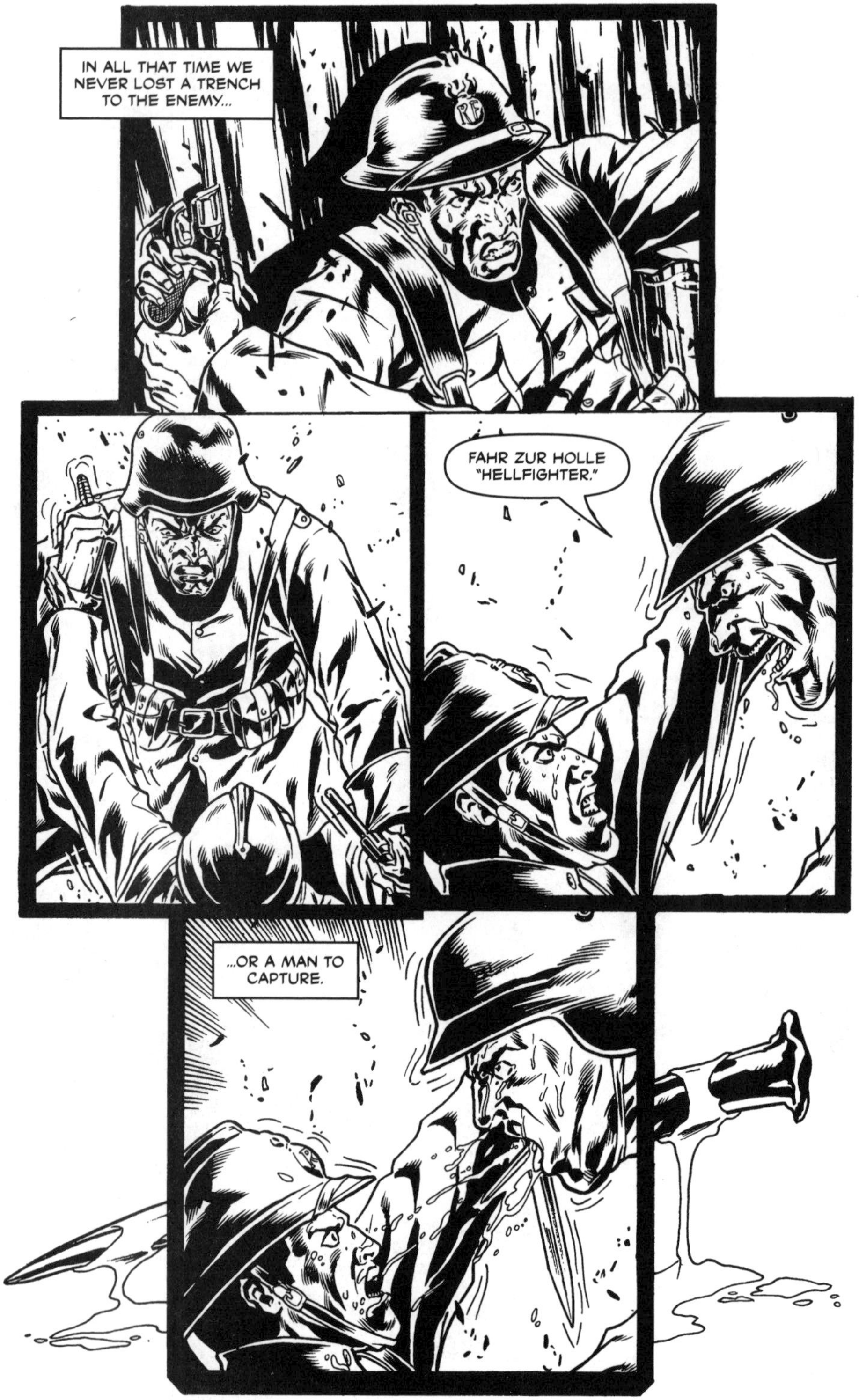
IN ALL THAT TIME WE NEVER LOST A TRENCH TO THE ENEMY...
FAHR ZUR HOLLE "HELLFIGHTER."
...OR A MAN TO CAPTURE.

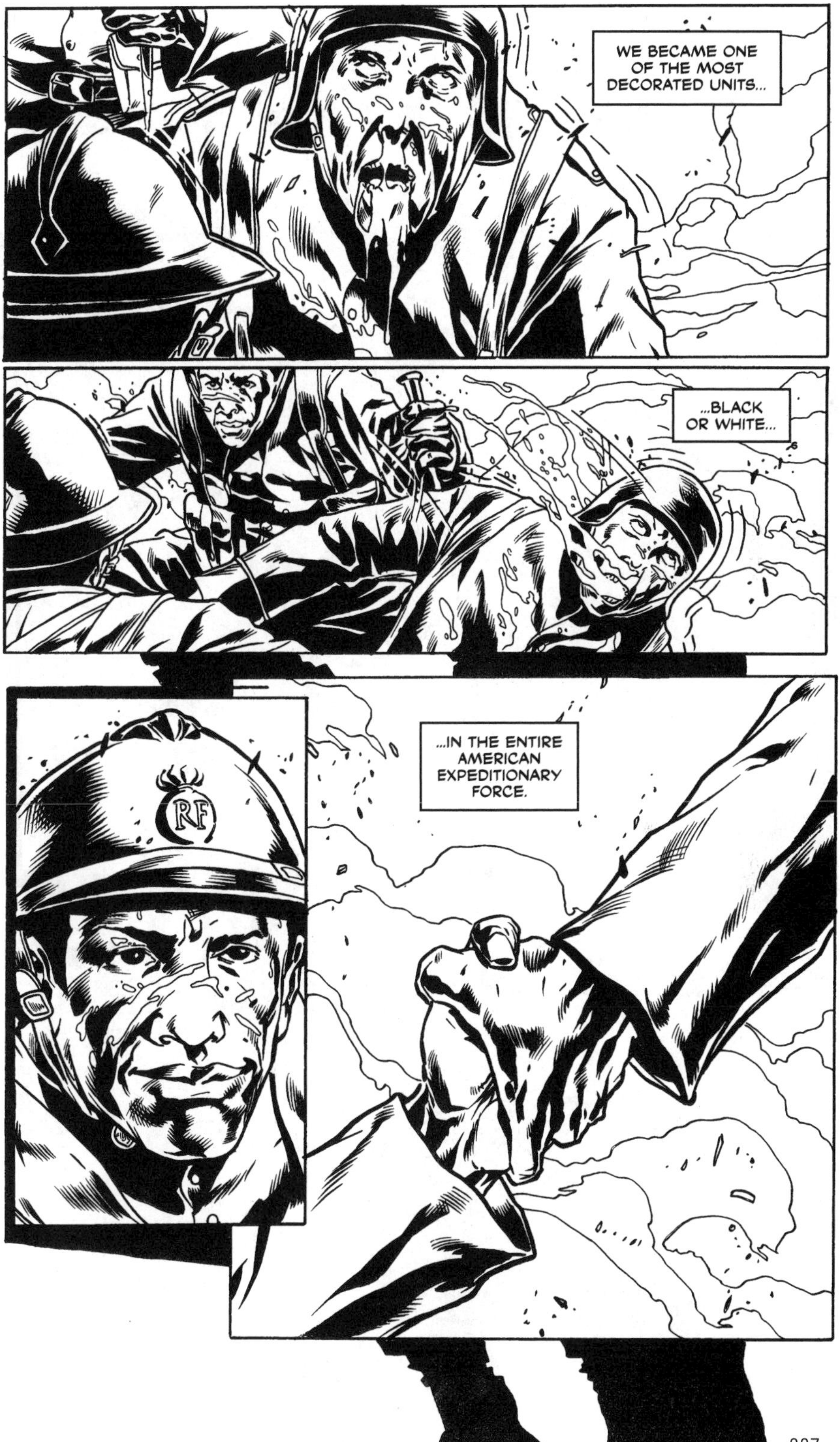
WE BECAME ONE OF THE MOST DECORATED UNITS...
...BLACK OR WHITE...
...IN THE ENTIRE AMERICAN EXPEDITIONARY FORCE.

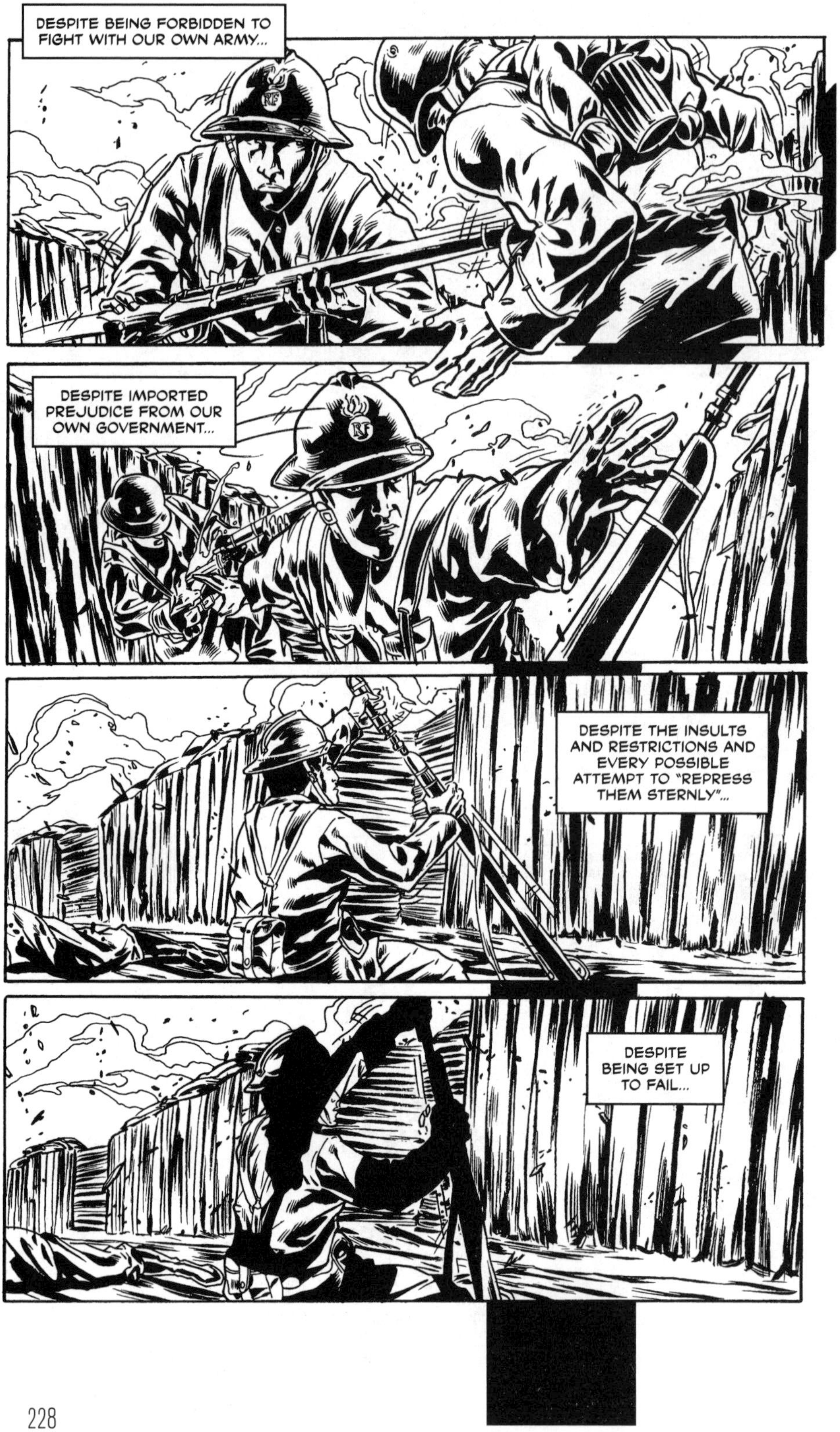
DESPITE BEING FORBIDDEN TO FIGHT WITH OUR OWN ARMY...
DESPITE IMPORTED PREJUDICE FROM OUR OWN GOVERNMENT...
DESPITE THE INSULTS AND RESTRICTIONS AND EVERY POSSIBLE ATTEMPT TO "REPRESS THEM STERNLY"...
DESPITE BEING SET UP TO FAIL...

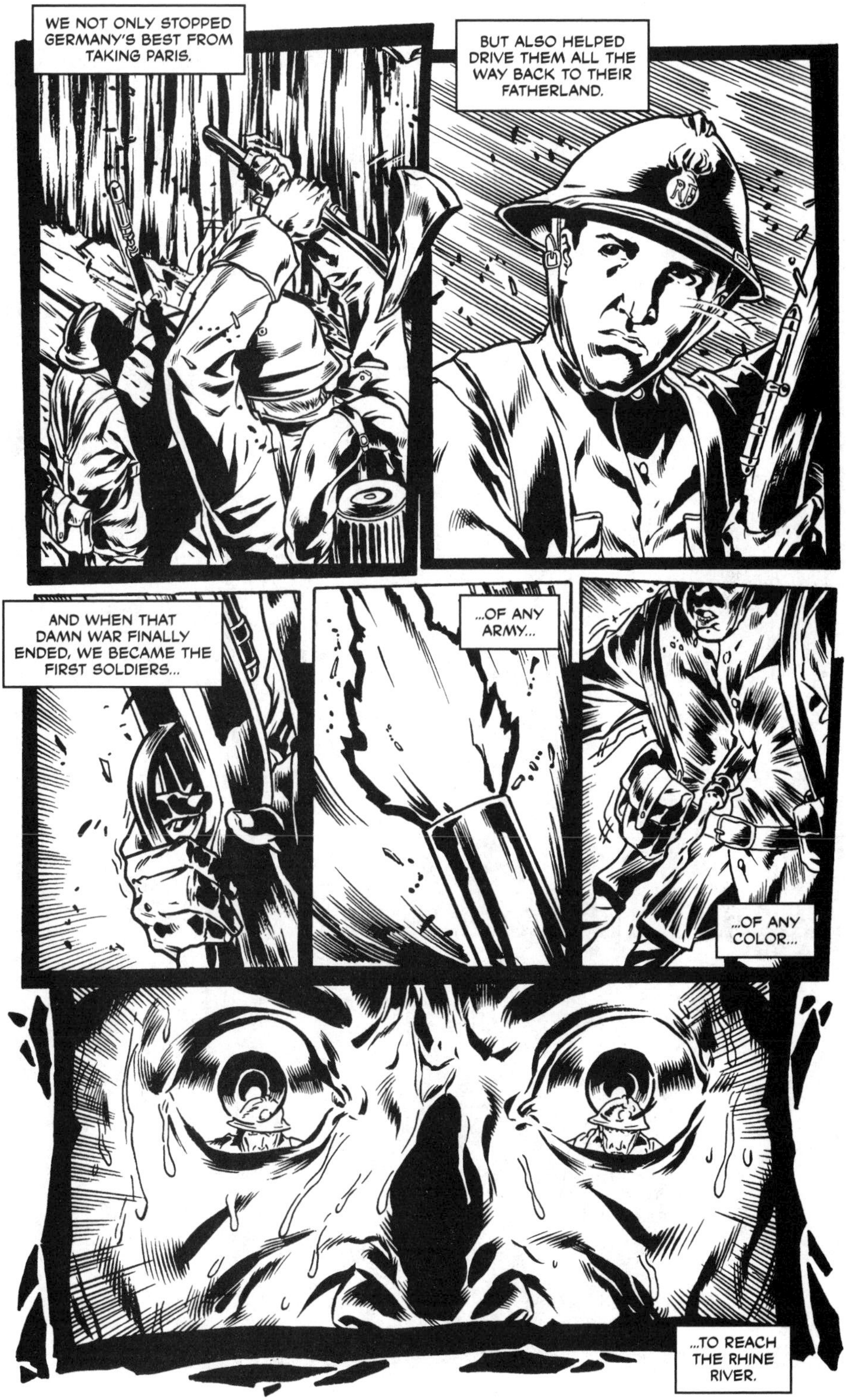
WE NOT ONLY STOPPED GERMANY'S BEST FROM TAKING PARIS.
BUT ALSO HELPED DRIVE THEM ALL THE WAY BACK TO THEIR FATHERLAND.
AND WHEN THAT DAMN WAR FINALLY ENDED, WE BECAME THE FIRST SOLDIERS...
...OF ANY ARMY...
...OF ANY COLOR...
...TO REACH THE RHINE RIVER.

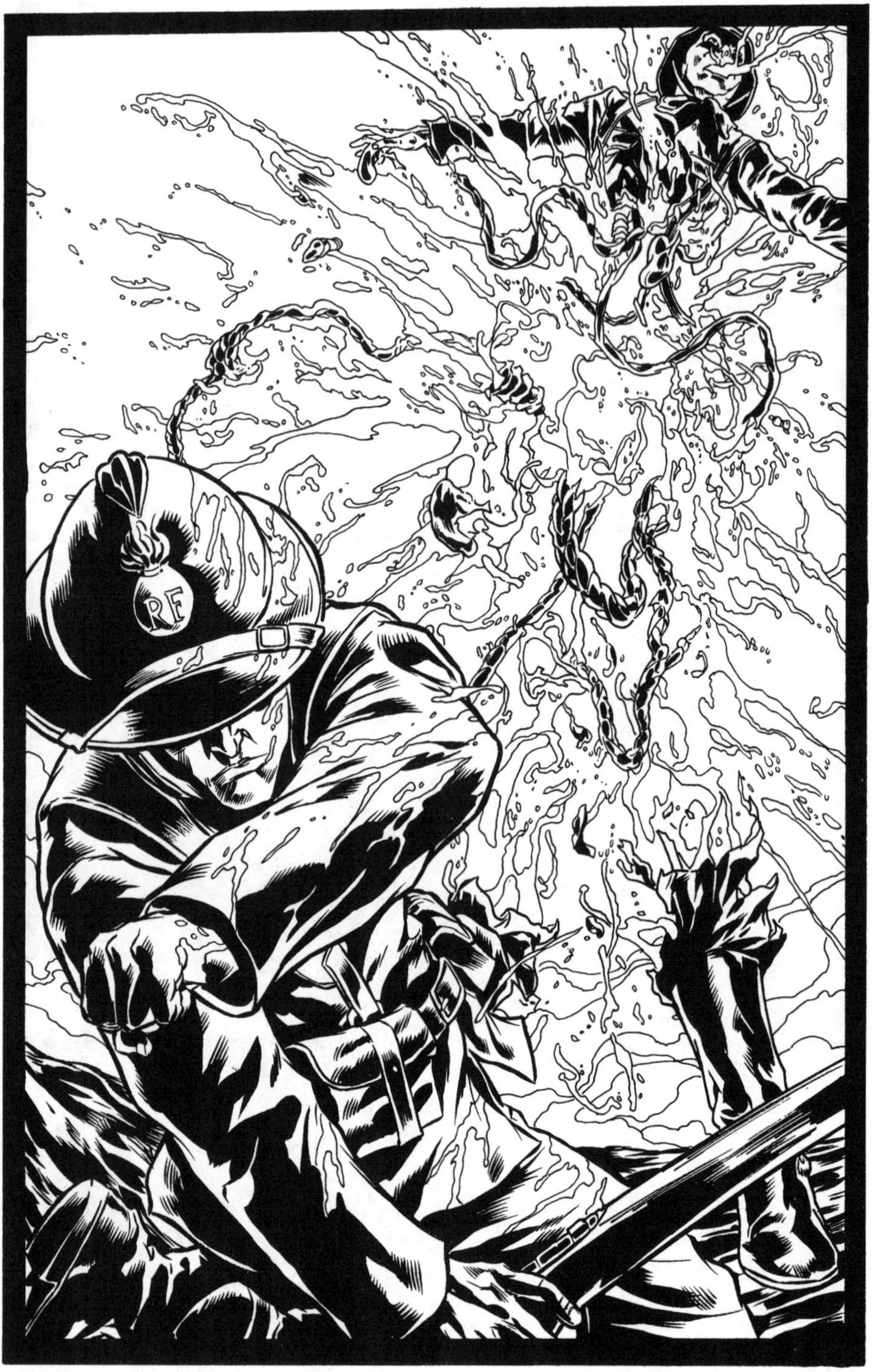
RF

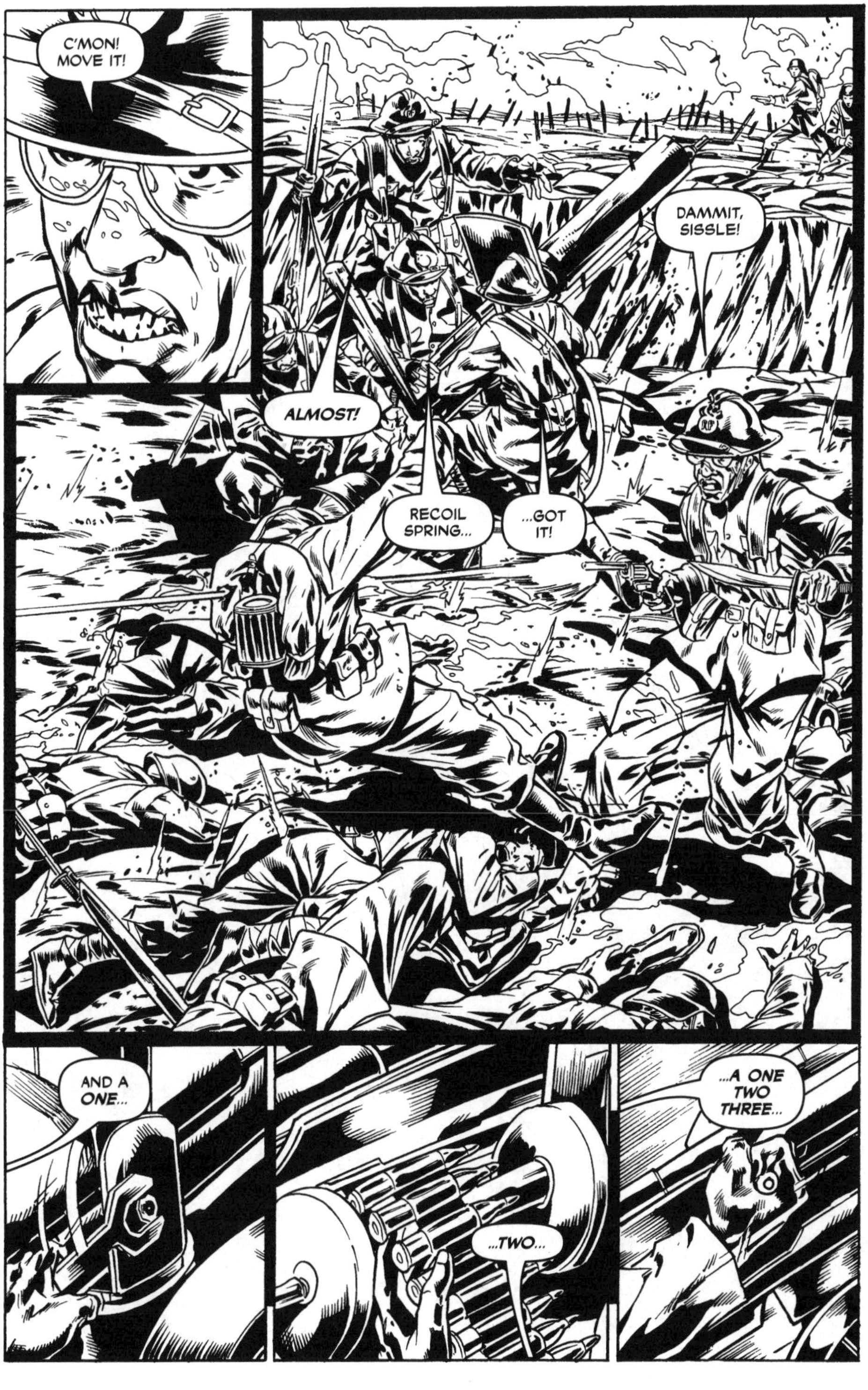
C'MON! MOVE IT!
DAMMIT, SISSLE!
ALMOST!
RECOIL SPRING...
...GOT IT!
AND A ONE...
...TWO...
...A ONE TWO THREE...

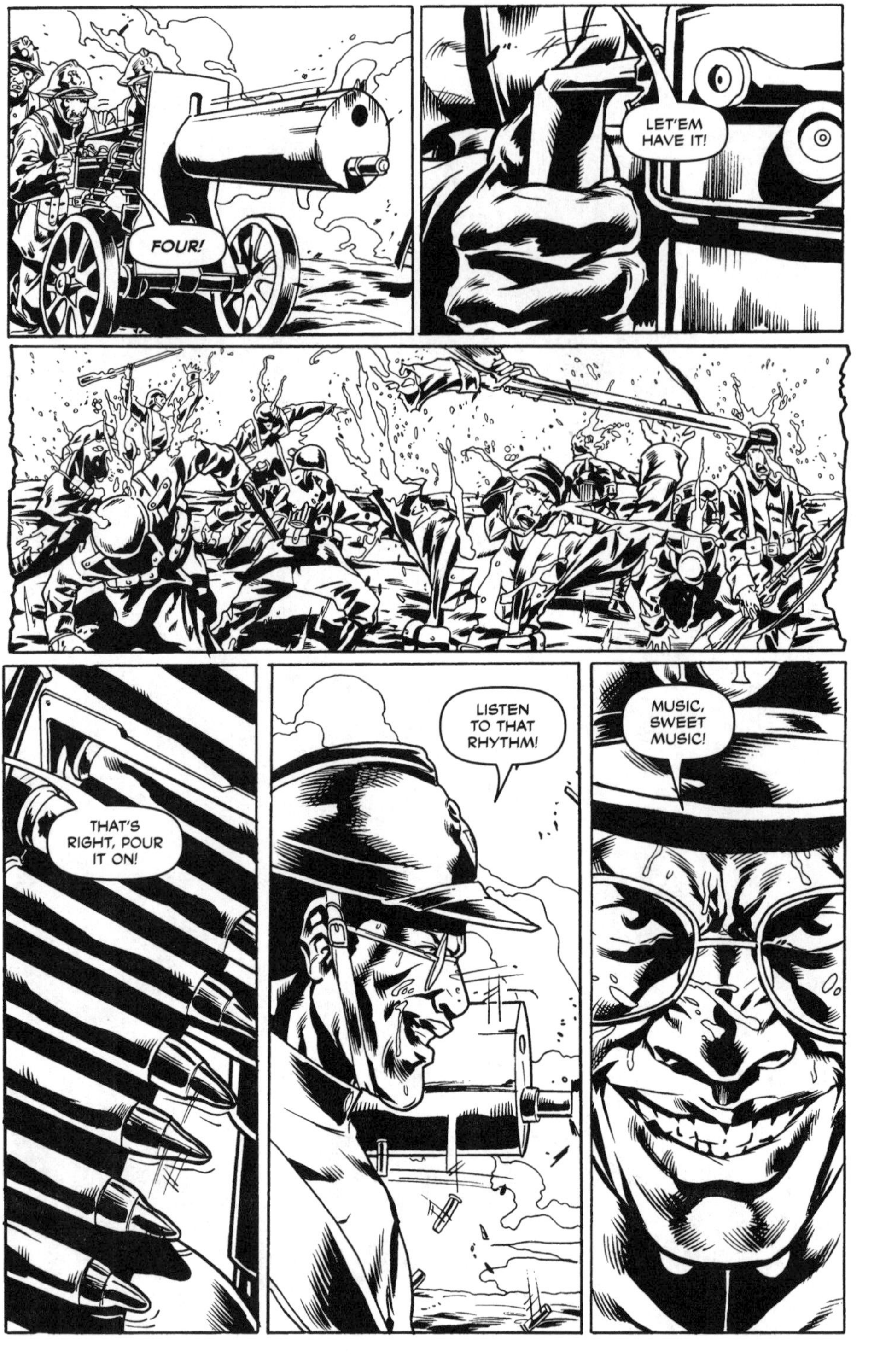
FOUR!
LET'EM HAVE IT!
THAT'S RIGHT, POUR IT ON!
LISTEN TO THAT RHYTHM!
MUSIC, SWEET MUSIC!

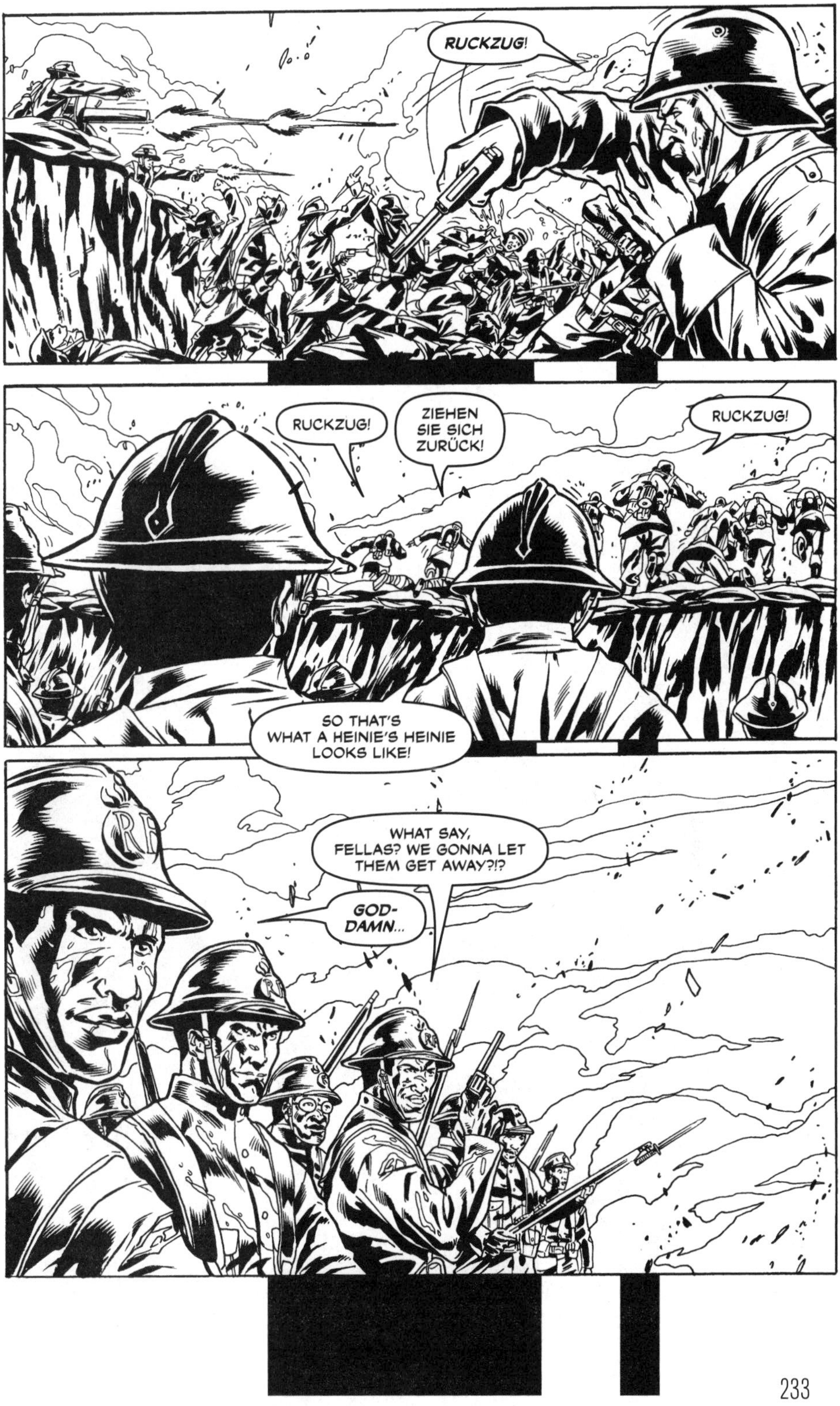
RUCKZUG!
RUCKZUG!
ZIEHEN SIE SICH ZURÜCK!
RUCKZUG!
SO THAT'S WHAT A HEINIE'S HEINIE LOOKS LIKE!
WHAT SAY, FELLAS? WE GONNA LET THEM GET AWAY?!?
GOD-DAMN...

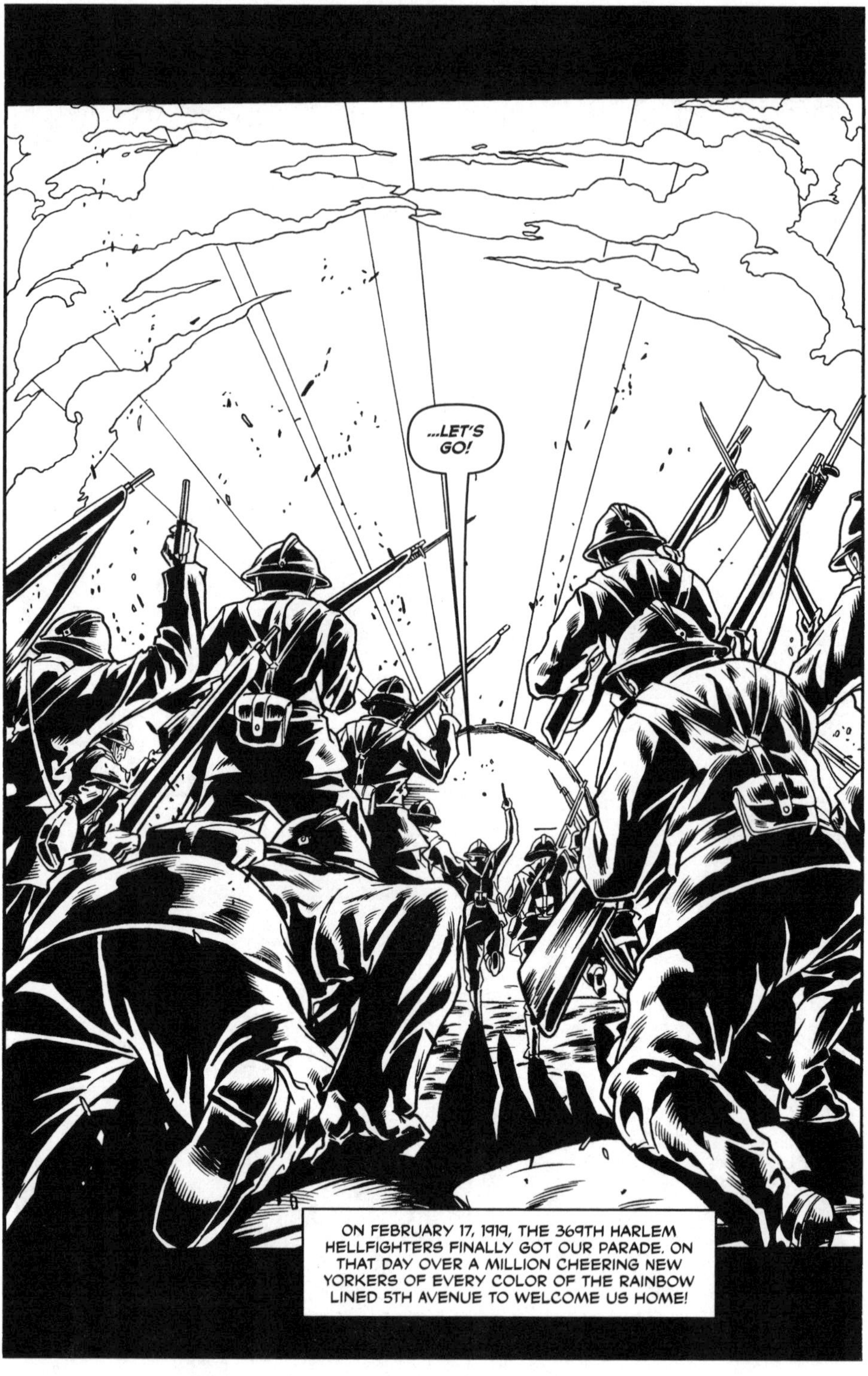
...LET'S GO!
ON FEBRUARY 17, 1919, THE 369TH HARLEM HELLFIGHTERS FINALLY GOT OUR PARADE. ON THAT DAY OVER A MILLION CHEERING NEW YORKERS OF EVERY COLOR OF THE RAINBOW LINED 5TH AVENUE TO WELCOME US HOME!

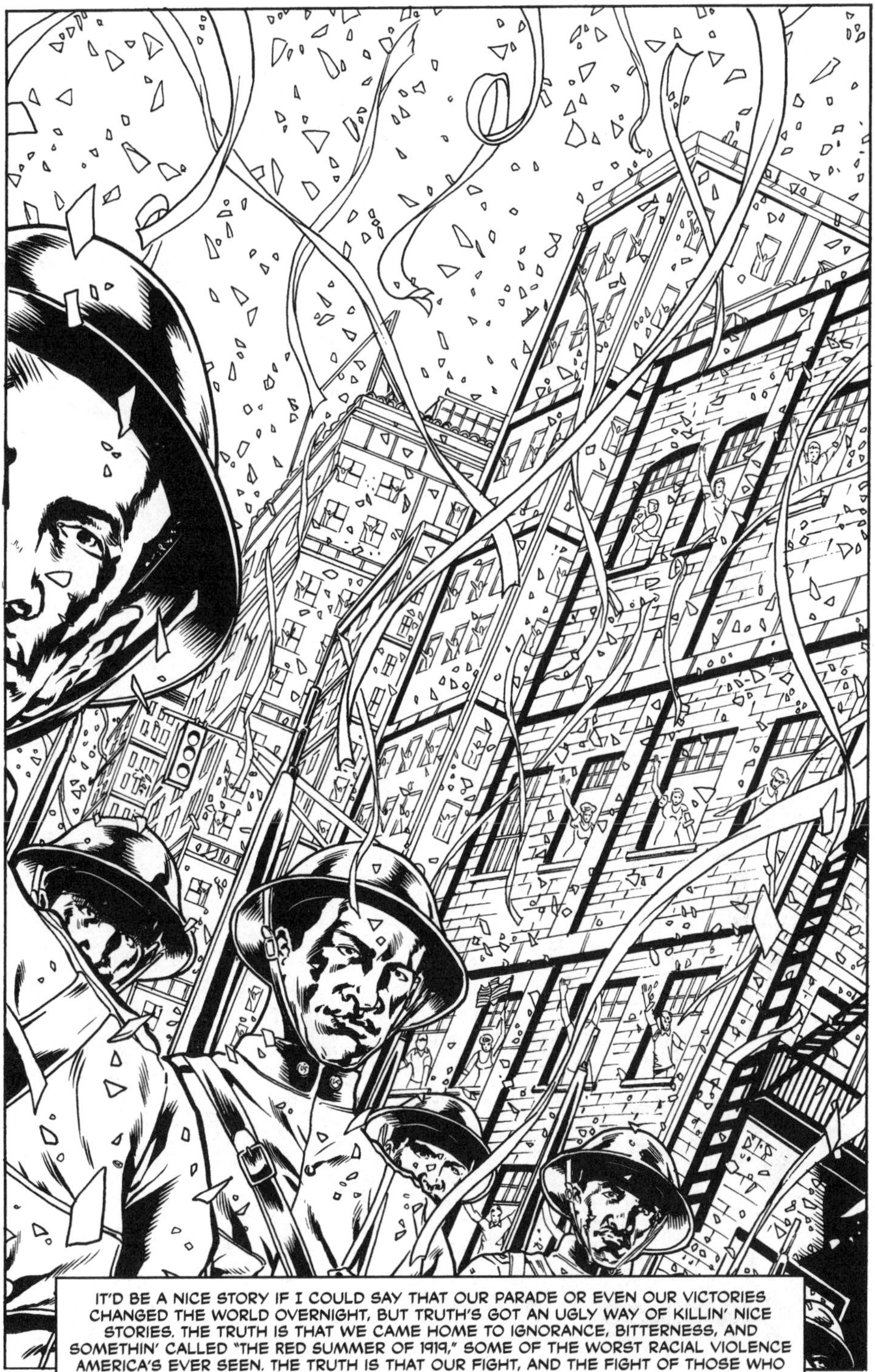
IT'D BE A NICE STORY IF I COULD SAY THAT OUR PARADE OR EVEN OUR VICTORIES CHANGED THE WORLD OVERNIGHT, BUT TRUTH'S GOT AN UGLY WAY OF KILLIN' NICE STORIES. THE TRUTH IS THAT WE CAME HOME TO IGNORANCE, BITTERNESS, AND SOMETHIN' CALLED "THE RED SUMMER OF 1919," SOME OF THE WORST RACIAL VIOLENCE AMERICA'S EVER SEEN. THE TRUTH IS THAT OUR FIGHT, AND THE FIGHT OF THOSE WHO LOOKED UP TO US AS HEROES, DIDN'T END WITH THE "THE WAR TO END ALL WARS."

WAS IT ALL
FOR NOTHING?

ONLY IF WE'RE
FORGOTTEN.

"We return. We return from fighting. We return fighting! Make way for Democracy! We saved it in France, and by the Great Jehovah, we will save it in the United States of America, or know the reason why."
—W. E. B. Du BOIS

My interest in the Harlem Hellfighters has spanned three quarters of my life. I first learned of them from an Anglo-Rhodesian named Michael Furmanovsky when I was eleven. Michael was working for my parents while getting his MFA in history from UCLA. To me, he already was a full-fledged professor. He taught me about the British Empire, the Falklands War, Hiroshima, the Holocaust, and a host of other topics not covered in my fifth-grade western civilization class. Of all his after-school lessons, the one that left the deepest impression was the story of a unit of American soldiers who weren't allowed to fight for their country because of the color of their skin. To a white, privileged kid growing up on the west side of L.A. in the 1980s, that kind of prejudice was inconceivable. When I confessed that I didn't know about them, he assured me that I wasn't alone.

Ten years later I was an exchange student at the University of the Virgin Islands. Officially I was majoring in history with a side of political science. Unofficially, I was majoring in race relations with a side of social isolation. The experience also brought me back into the orbit of the Hellfighters when, while walking through an old cemetery, I noticed some graves from 1918. I wondered if they might be casualties of the Great War, maybe even members of the 369th.

I decided to ask my professor of Virgin Islands history. He was an African American from the mainland, and his intellect, eloquence, and passion set him above all of my other educators. With his beard and spectacles and flaring dashiki, he would rail against the historical crimes committed by white men from Europe and North America. Most heinous was the erasure of black accomplishments by white historians. Colonization, he told us, begins with the mind, and the best (or worst) way to colonize a people is to bury their past.

"There were no black soldiers in World War I." That was his dismissive answer to my question about the graves from 1918. When I started to argue, even bringing up the name "Harlem Hellfighters," he assured me that I must have been confused with the Tuskegee Airmen of World War II. I was shocked. Here was a scholar, a crusader, a thoughtful, driven man who'd made it his life's mission to trumpet the glory of Africa and her diaspora, and *he* didn't know about the Harlem Hellfighters. I wish I could say that I decided then and there to write their story, but that would have to wait for nearly another decade.

In the late 1990s, I was living back in L.A., just out of graduate school and trying to make a living as a writer. My decision to tackle the story of the Hellfighters came after watching two TNT made-for-TV movies about the Tuskegee Airmen and the Buffalo Soldiers. I thought TNT might be interested in a story about World War I's black heroes, especially after A&E's successful *Lost Battalion* movie. I started collecting books about the subject (the most influential was and still is *From Harlem to the Rhine* by Arthur Little), and a year and several dozen drafts later, I pitched my screenplay to the TNT network. They passed. So did everyone else.

I was told that the "marketplace" wasn't friendly to stories about a war that most Americans knew little or nothing about and to focus specifically on African Americans would certainly doom my chances.

All that changed when I sent my script to an actor/director named LeVar Burton. "There are actually more than a couple Harlem Hellfighters scripts floating around Hollywood," he told me during our meeting, "but yours comes closest to the truth." He agreed that the subject matter would be difficult to sell to studios, but that by no means should that deter me. "I don't have the power right now to make this movie," he said, "but I'm not going to give up, and you shouldn't either." Thank you, Mr. Burton.

A year later the Hellfighters had another advocate, my new friend and fellow SNL office-mate Dean Edwards. "I've always wanted to do a death scene," he told me during one of our all-night writing sessions. "You know, one of those 'lookin' around the corner' or 'over a wall' and BAM!" He pantomimed getting shot in the head. "Just something tragic and sudden like that." That was my opening to describe for him the scene in my script in which Dave Scott is suddenly slayed by a sniper. "I made up the scene and the character," I confessed, "but the actual story of the 369th is totally real."

As a black man, actor, New Yorker, and army veteran, Dean could not have been more fascinated. Every few months he would lean over from his desk and ask, "Hey, what's going on with your World War I movie?" And those inquiries were enough to keep my now worn script always close at hand.

Five years and what seemed like a lifetime later, an unexpected opportunity opened up in the world of comic books. In 2006, I began collaborating with Avatar Press on a graphic companion to my first book, *The Zombie Survival Guide*. I learned very quickly how different comic book writing was from prose, but how similar it could be to movie scripts. I also realized that comics presented a forum for telling very visual stories without the cumbersome budget of movies or television. It seemed the ideal medium for telling the story of the Harlem Hellfighters. It's now been close to six years since I began working with William Christensen of Avatar Press and the amazingly talented artist Caanan White. In that time, America, and the world, has gone through some stunning changes. I'm not sure if those changes make the story of the Hellfighters more or less relevant. I'll leave that for you, the reader, to decide.

HISTORICAL NOTES

While researching and writing *The Harlem Hellfighters*, I have tried to balance historical accuracy with vivid storytelling. For this reason, almost all the events portrayed here were either direct historical accounts or fictionalized versions of them.

While some of the characters here are entirely fictional, such as Mark, Dave, and Edge (though he takes his name from someone real from my past), others were inspired by actual historical figures. Desmond Scatliffe's character, for example, was inspired by several Caribbean-born Hellfighters. Sergeant Mandla's character is loosely based on the story of an actual full-blooded Zulu who briefly served with the 15th New York.

Corporal Fabius can be traced to a passage in *From Harlem to the Rhine*, in which Arthur Little describes a one-eyed Frenchman who served alongside the American "orphans."

Lieutenant Adams is an amalgam of many young black men who commanded troops in 1917–18. While black officers were not new to the U.S. military, World War I saw a monumental increase in both their numbers and public visibility.

Many of the characters in this story are real. They include Colonel William Hayward, Captain Arthur W. Little, Captain Hamilton Fish, Sergeant Noble Sissle, and General Henri Gouraud. They also include:

James Reese Europe (above), known on both sides of the Atlantic as "The King of Jazz," did not live long enough to witness jazz's golden age. On May 9, 1919, shortly after returning to the United States, he was stabbed in the throat by a fellow bandmate and died later that night.

Eugene Jaques Bullard (above), who was a boxer, a nightclub owner, an activist, a pilot, and a veteran of both World Wars (for which he was highly decorated), eventually died in 1961 as an elevator operator in New York's Rockefeller Center.

Henry Johnson (left) was the first American (black or white) to receive the French Cross of War. His heroism was not officially recognized by his own government until seventy-four years after his death. In 2003, the U.S. Army awarded him the Distinguished Service Cross, the U.S. Army's second-highest honor. Members of his family and supporters are still waiting for the Medal of Honor.

BIBLIOGRAPHY

ON THE HARLEM HELLFIGHTERS:

Badger, Reid. *A Life in Ragtime: A Biography of James Reese Europe.* New York: Oxford University Press, 1995.

Cooper, Michael L. *Hell Fighters.* New York: Dutton Juvenile, 1997.

Fish, Hamilton. *Memoir of an American Patriot.* Washington, D.C.: Regnery Publishing, 1991.

Harris, Bill. *The Hellfighters of Harlem.* New York: Basic Books, 2002.

Harris, Stephen L. *Harlem's Hellfighters.* Dulles, Va.: Potomac Books Inc, 2003.

Little, Arthur W. *From Harlem to the Rhine.* New York: Haskell House Pub Ltd, 1936. Reprint 1974.

Myers, Walter Dean, and Bill Miles. *The Harlem Hellfighters: When Pride Met Courage.* New York: Amistad, 2006.

Nelson, Peter. *A More Unbending Battle.* New York: Basic Civitas Books, 2009.

R2C2H2. *James Reese Europe: Jazz Lieutenant.* Charleston, S.C.: BookSurge Publishing, 2005.

Stein, Judith E. *I Tell My Heart: The Art of Horace Pippin.* New York: Universe Pub, 1993.

ON AFRICAN AMERICANS IN WAR:

Astor, Gerald. *The Right to Fight: A History of African Americans in the Military.* New York: Presidio Press, 1998.

Barbeau, Arthur E., and Florette Henri. *The Unknown Soldiers: African-American Troops in World War I.* Cambridge, Mass.: Da Capo Press, 1996.

Edgerton, Robert B. *Hidden Heroism: Black Soldiers in America's Wars.* New York: Basic Books, 2001.

Fuller, Charles. *A Soldier's Play.* New York: Hill and Wang, 1981.

Henri, Florette, with Richard Stillman. *Bitter Victory: A History of Black Soldiers in World War I.* New York: Doubleday, 1970.

Lentz-Smith, Adriane. *Freedom Struggle: African Americans and World War I.* Cambridge, Mass.: Harvard University Press, 2009.

Lloyd, Craig. *Eugene Bullard: Black Expatriate in Jazz-Age Paris.* Athens, Ga.: University of Georgia Press, 2000.

Nalty, Bernard C. *Strength for the Fight: A History of Black Americans in the Military.* New York: Free Press, 1986.

Roberts, Frank E. *The American Foreign Legion: Black Soldiers of the 93rd in World War I.* Annapolis, Md.: US Naval Institute Press, 2004.

Rodgers, Lawrence R. *Canaan Bound: The African-American Great Migration Novel.* Champaign, Ill.: University of Illinois Press, 1997.

Scott, Emmet J. *Scott's Official History of the American Negro in the World War.* Charleston, S.C.: Nabu Press, 1919.

Sutherland, Jonathan D. *African Americans at War: An Encyclopedia.* 2 vols. Santa Barbara, Calif.: ABC-CLIO, 2004.

Weir, William. *Encyclopedia of African American Military History.* Amherst, N.Y.: Prometheus Books, 2004.

Williams, Charles H. *Negro Soldiers in World War I: The Human Side.* New York: Ams Pr Inc, 1923.

Wright, Kai. *Soldiers of Freedom: An Illustrated History of African Americans in the Armed Forces.* New York: Black Dog & Leventhal Publishers, 2002.

ON WORLD WAR I, AFRICAN AMERICAN HISTORY, AND GENERAL RESEARCH:

Bull, Stephen, M.D., *World War I Trench Warfare, 1916–18*. Illustrated by Adam Hook. Oxford, England: Osprey Publishing, 2002.

Byrne, Ciaran. *The Harp and Crown: The History of the 5th (Royal Irish) Lancers, 1902–1922*. Lulu.com, 2007.

Dent, G. R., and C. L. S. Nyembezi. *Scholar's Zulu Dictionary*. New York: Hippocrene, 1969.

Dickinson, Paul. *War Slang: American Fighting Words and Phrases from the Civil War to the Gulf War*. New York: Atria, 1994.

Donnell, Clayton. *The Forts of the Meuse in World War I*. Illustrated by H. Johnson, L. Ray, and B. Delf. Oxford, England: Osprey Publishing, 2007.

Farwell, Byron. *Over There: The United States in the Great War, 1917–1918*. New York: W. W. Norton & Company, 1999.

Fitzsimons, Bernard, ed. *Tanks and Weapons of World War I*. New York: Beekman House, 1973.

Griffith, Paddy. *Fortifications of the Western Front, 1914–18*. Illustrated by Peter Dennis. Oxford, England: Osprey Publishing, 2004.

Hochschild, Adam. *To End All Wars*. New York: Mariner Books, 2011.

Hoff, Thomas A. *The US Doughboy, 1916–19*. Illustrated by Adam Hook. Oxford, England: Osprey Publishing, 2005.

Jager, Herbert. *German Artillery of World War I*. Ramsbury, England: Crowood Press, 2001.

Jones, Simon. *World War I Gas Warfare Tactics and Equipment*. Illustrated by Richard Hook. Oxford, England: Osprey Publishing, 2007.

Knight, Ian. *The Boer Wars I, 1836–98*. Illustrated by Gerry Embleton. Oxford, England: Osprey Publishing, 1996.

Knight, Ian. *The Boer Wars 2, 1898–1902*. Illustrated by Gerry Embleton. Oxford, England: Osprey Publishing, 1996.

lukaSonkomose, Ukhamba. *English and Zulu Dictionary*. Johannesburg, South Africa: Witwatersrand Press, 1977.

Matthews, Rupert. *1000 Facts on World War I*. Consultant Brian Williams. Thaxted, England: Miles Kelly Publishing Ltd, 2006.

BIBLIOGRAPHY

Mirouze, Laurant. *World War I Infantry in Colour Photographs*. Wiltshire, England: Crowood Press, 1990.

Remarque, Erich Maria. *All Quiet on the Western Front*. New York: Ballantine Books, 1982.

Retief, Glen. *The Jack Bank: A Memoir of a South African Childhood*. New York: St. Martin's Press, 2011.

Sheen, John. *Images of War: 1918, the German Offensives, Rare Photographs from Wartime Archives*. Barnsley, England: Pen and Sword, 2007.

Strong, Paul, and Sanders Marble. *Artillery in the Great War*. Barnsley, England: Pen and Sword, 2011.

Sumner, Ian. *The French Army, 1914–1918*. Illustrated by Gerry Embleton. Oxford, England: Osprey Publishing, 1995.

Tardi, Jaques. *It Was the War of the Trenches*. Seattle: Fantagraphics Books, 2010.

Thomas, Nigel. *The German Army in World War I, 1917–1918*. Illustrated by Ramiro Bujeiro. Oxford, England: Osprey Publishing, 2004.

Turner, Alexander. *Vimy Ridge, 1917*. Illustrated by Peter Dennis. Oxford, England: Osprey Publishing, 2005.

Westwell, Ian. *An Illustrated History of the Weapons of World War One*. Wigston, England: Anness Publishing Ltd, 2011.

Winter, Denis. *Death's Men: Soldiers of the Great War*. New York: Penguin Books, 1985.

FILMOGRAPHY

A Fighting Force, African-Americans in the Military. The History Channel. A&E Home Video, 2008.

Men of Bronze: The Black Heroes of World War I. Directed by William Miles. Direct Cinema Limited, 1977.

Ragtime. Directed by Milos Foreman. Paramount, 1981.

World War I American Legacy. Directed by Mark Bussler. Inecom Entertainment Company, 2006.

DISCOGRAPHY

The First World War Remembered. London: Imperial War Museum. Audiocassette.

James Reese Europe Featuring Noble Sissle. IAJRC Records, 1996. Compact disc.

ACKNOWLEDGMENTS

As always, a special thank you to my wife, Michelle, who has believed in this project (and *me*) for fifteen years!

To William Christensen who owns, operates, and *is* Avatar Press.

To Caanan White for his phenomenal artwork.

To Meagan Stacey, Sean Desmond, Ellen Folan, and the rest of the Random House publisher's team.

To Luke Dempsey, back from the past to watch my back again.

To those who've helped me with my research throughout the years: Major General Nathaniel James and the 369th Historical Society; Sharon Howard and the amazing staff of the Schomburg Center for Research in Black Culture; Bernadette of the Imperial War Museum in London; Professors Stuart McConnell, Laura Harris, Tracy Walters, and Malik Sekou; and Richard "Mack" Machowicz for his encyclopedic knowledge of weaponry.

To those who have inspired and encouraged me along the way: Michael Furmanovsky, Professor Wayne Edge, Dean Edwards, Randy Aurbach, Dr. Cornel West, and LeVar Burton.

ACKNOWLEDGMENTS

And last but not least, to a man I've never met but spent count-less hours with. Melville T. Miller, my "primary dialog coach" who reached out beyond the grave, through the documentary *Men of Bronze*. For me, Mr. Miller encapsulates the story of the Harlem Hellfighters when he stated to the camera: "We were proud to be Americans, proud to be black, and proud to be the 15th New York Infantry! What's your next question?"

PHOTO CREDITS

Page 236: Courtesy of National Archives and Records Administration, Records of the War Department General and Special Staffs; page 244: Photographs and Prints Division, Schomburg Center for Research in Black Culture, The New York Public Library, Astor, Lenox and Tilden Foundations; page 245, bottom: General Research & Reference Division, Schomburg Center for Research in Black Culture, The New York Public Library, Astor, Lenox and Tilden Foundations

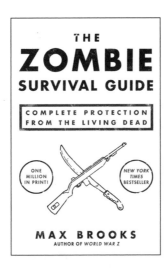
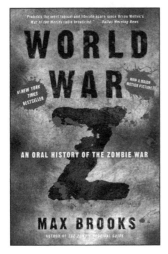
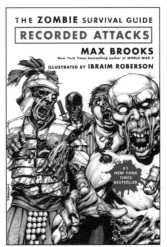